MIRACLES AND THE MEDIEVAL MIND

THE MIDDLE AGES
a series edited by
Edward Peters
Henry Charles Lea Professor
of Medieval History
University of Pennsylvania

MIRACLES

AND THE

MEDIEVAL

MIND

THEORY, RECORD AND EVENT

1000–1215

BENEDICTA WARD

UNIVERSITY OF PENNSYLVANIA PRESS

PHILADELPHIA

First published in the United States
by the University of Pennsylvania Press, 1982

First published in the United Kingdom
by Scolar Press, 1982 ·

Library of Congress Cataloging in Publication Data

Ward, Benedicta, 1933–
    Miracles and the medieval mind.
    Revision of thesis—Oxford.
    Bibliography: p.
    1. Miracles—History.   I. Title.
BT97.2.W36 1982   231.7'3'0902   81–23106
ISBN 0–8122–7836–4   AACR2

Printed in the United States of America

TO SIR RICHARD AND LADY SOUTHERN

WITH AFFECTION AND GRATITUDE

Contents

	List of Illustrations	viii
	Acknowledgements	ix
	Introduction	1
I	The Theory of Miracles	3
II	The Discussion of Miracles in Practical Contexts	20
III	Miracles at Traditional Shrines: St Faith, St Benedict and St Cuthbert	33
IV	Miracles at Three Twelfth-Century Shrines: St William, St Godric and St Frideswide	67
V	The Miracles of St Thomas of Canterbury	89
VI	Miracles and Pilgrimage	110
VII	The Shrines that Failed	127
VIII	The Miracles of the Virgin	132
IX	Miracles and Sanctity	166
X	Monastic Miracles	192
XI	Miracles and Events	201
	Epilogue	214
	Abbreviations	219
	Notes	221
	Bibliography	288
	Index	311

List of Illustrations

1	St Benedict tempted by the devil in the form of a woman	52
2	St Benedict and Totilla the Hun	53
3	St Benedict delivers a captive	54
4	Hugh of St Mary and his family	55
5	A paralytic healed by St Cuthbert	59
6	A pagan punished by St Cuthbert	60
7	St Thomas appears to a sleeping monk	91
8	St Thomas appears to the leper Gimp	92

Acknowledgements

I WISH TO ACKNOWLEDGE with gratitude the help, advice, and encouragement given me by many friends both in the preliminary work for the thesis out of which this book has grown and in the rewriting of it in its present form. My first debt of gratitude is to my Community for their generosity in giving me time to do this work. Coextensive with this is my gratitude to Sir Richard and Lady Southern for their continual assistance, penetrating criticism, and unfailing kindness at all stages of its composition. I also wish to acknowledge the interest and encouragement of the three academic institutions in Oxford with which I have had the privilege of being associated: St Anne's College, Wolfson College, and the Centre for Medieval and Renaissance Studies.

My thanks are also due to those who have given me the stimulus of discussion on particular points: M. André Bredero, Professor Christopher Brooke, the Most Reverend Metropolitan Anthony of Sourzh, Mr Peter Brown, Dr Giles Constable, Dr Margaret Gibson, the late Dr Richard Hunt, Fr Jean Leclercq OSB, Mr Henry Mayr-Harting, Mr Malcolm Parkes, the late Dr William Urry, and Dr Rowan Williams. For immediate and practical help in preparing the text I must thank Mrs Sandra Feneley, Mr Oliver Nicholson, Miss Hélène La Rue, Lady Southern, my typists Dom Mark Gibson OSB and Mrs F. J. Templeton, and especially Mr Rex Tomlinson for help in preparing the index.

The illustrations are supplied by courtesy of the Abbey of Saint Benoît at Fleury (nos. 1–4), the Master and Fellows of University College, Oxford (nos. 5 and 6: photographs from Bodleian Library Roll 131 B (3)), and the Dean and Chapter of Canterbury (nos. 7 and 8: photographs from Woodmansterne Publications Ltd.).

All biblical references are given according to common usage. The Latin text is the *Biblia Vulgata,* the English text the *Authorised Version.* Where no reference is given to a translation from Latin, the translation is my own.

Convent of the Incarnation   *Benedicta Ward S.L.G.*
Fairacres, Oxford
January 1982

Introduction

IT IS WELL KNOWN that miracles occupied a large place in medieval life. This situation was viewed with complacency by churchmen from Augustine to Newman, as presenting evidence of the continuing intervention of God in the world,[1] or with contempt by philosophers such as Hume:

When we peruse the first histories of all nations, we are apt to imagine ourselves transported into some new world, where the whole frame of nature is disjointed, and every element performs its operations in a different manner from what it does at present. . . ;[2]

or with guarded interest by some, such as Bishop Stubbs, who, after a close acquaintance with such material in his editions of medieval texts, was moved to ask how far this belief 'in the constant infraction, by Divine authority, of the ordinary processes of the course of this world'[3] diminished the credibility of writers. Whichever way miracles were regarded, it is certain that there are a great many accounts of them in the literature of the Middle Ages. They provide a major medieval source that only recently has begun to attract the attention it deserves.

The largest number of miracle stories are those connected with the shrines of the saints, and it is with these that I will chiefly be concerned. As a preliminary to this analysis, however, I have tried to discover what, in theory, men thought about miracles. This is not a straightforward task, since very little direct discussion of miracles took place from the time of Augustine to that of Thomas Aquinas. No treatise *De miraculis* survives in which the concept of the miraculous is discussed and related to other kinds of reality. Events called *miracula* permeated life at every level,[4] but they were so closely woven into the texture of Christian experience that there was no incentive to examine or explain the presuppositions that lay behind them. In the twelfth century, however, an interest in the relationship of miracle to doctrine arose, which was occasioned by changes in thought about the concept of *natura* to which *miracula* was increasingly opposed. Thought about miracles, however, remained fixed throughout the Middle Ages, following the lines laid down by Augustine in the fourth century, with some twelfth-century innovations. It was from this complex of ideas that Thomas Aquinas drew out his definitions that have formed later thought about the matter.[5]

Accounts of miracles were found not only at shrines; there are also miracles in the lives of the saints, and there are collections of miracles not associated with a place at all. The largest and most influential of these is the Miracles of the Virgin, which I have examined for the period immediately before they attained a predominant place in the literature of Europe. I have, finally, given some attention to the use made of miracle stories as propaganda, though this field is so wide that I have had to restrict myself to one or two types.

Throughout the Middle Ages miracles were unanimously seen as part of the City of God on earth, and whatever reflections men might have on their cause and their aim, they formed an integral part of ordinary life. The exploration of miracle stories leaves two principle impressions: the number and diversity of events regarded as in some way miraculous, not out of naïvety but from a more complex and subtle view of reality than we possess; and the unity of opinion about miracles in both thought and record, a unity expressed by Augustine:

God himself has created all that is wonderful in this world, the great miracles as well as the minor marvels I have mentioned, and he has included them all in that unique wonder, that miracle of miracles, the world itself.[6]

I

The Theory of Miracles

THE PRESUPPOSITIONS behind any thinking about miracles in the Middle Ages are to be found mainly in four works by Augustine of Hippo: *De Genesi ad Litteram, De Trinitate, De Utilitate Credendi,* and *De Civitate Dei.* Augustine argues that there is only one miracle, that of creation, with its corollary of re-creation by the resurrection of Christ. God, he held, created the world out of nothing in six days, and within that initial creation he planted all the possibilities for the future. All creation was, therefore, both 'natural' and 'miraculous': 'all natural things are filled with the miraculous'.[1] 'The events of every day, the birth of men, the growth of plants, rainfall', are all 'daily miracles', signs of the mysterious creative power of God at work in the universe. But Augustine also held that men were so accustomed to these 'daily miracles' that they were no longer moved to awe by them and needed to be provoked to reverence by unusual manifestations of God's power. These, Augustine taught, were events also within the original creation; God had then created *seminum semina,*[2] *seminales rationes*[3] hidden within the nature and appearance of things, which at times caused 'miracles' that seemed to be contrary to nature but were in fact inherent in it. The most usual channel for these 'hidden causes' to be made manifest was the prayers of the saints, and Augustine himself illustrated this in his account of the miracles connected with the relics of St Stephen in his diocese after 416.[4]

For Augustine, the mechanics of miracles were clear. They were wonderful acts of God shown as events in this world, not in opposition to nature but as a drawing out of the hidden workings of God within a nature that was all potentially miraculous.[5] There were three levels of wonder: wonder provoked by the acts of God visible daily and discerned by wise men as signs of God's goodness; wonder provoked in the ignorant, who did not understand the workings of nature and therefore could be amazed by what to the wise man was not unusual; and wonder provoked by genuine miracles, unusual manifestations of the power of God, not *contra naturam* but *praeter* or *supra naturam:* 'I call that miraculous which appears wonderful because it is either hard or impossible, beyond hope or ability'.[6] Events happened in nature or miraculously, but both were equally the work of God: 'Some things happen naturally, others miraculously; God works in whatever is natural and he is not apart from the wonders of nature'.[7] The emphasis on the wonder caused in men, the psychological understanding of miracle, gave a wide scope for 'miracle', including *monstra* and *prodigia*[8] in its definition, as well as *miracula* and *signa;* and the content of miracle collections, as will be seen, continued to illustrate this.

Throughout the period under discussion, people asked how miracles related man to God, not how they could be defined in their constituent parts. Yet a shift of emphasis can be seen even at the beginning of this period. Discussion about miracles usually arose in connection with either the creation or the incarnation, and it is in discussing the former that the earliest instance of this change of emphasis can be seen. Anselm of Canterbury's discussion *De Conceptu Virginali* is in many ways an unexpected source for this change, since his interests were not directed toward physics, and the main thrust of his thought was toward the Augustinian unities. However, Anselm in this treatise proposed a relationship between events that, while based on the three categories of Augustine, distinguished miracles from natural events and those events caused by the will of men:

> So if we consider carefully everything that is done, we see that they happen either by the will of God alone, or by nature according to the power God has given it, or by the will of a creature. Now, those things which are done neither by created nature nor by the will of the creature but by God alone, are miracles *(semper miranda sint):* so it seems that there are three ways in which things happen, that is, the miraculous, the natural and the voluntary *(mirabilis, naturalis, voluntarius)*.[9]

Events that happen by nature, or by the will of men, have here been distinguished from *mirabilia,* which are caused by the direct intervention of God in affairs, rather than being events that cause wonder in

4

man. Anselm gives as examples of miracles the crossing of the Red Sea by the Israelites, the turning of water into wine, and the interior miracles of conversion.[10] As will be seen later, Anselm's interest in contemporary miracles was confined to precisely this kind of event, in which the action can be ascribed to God alone, especially in the salvation of souls. The ultimate cause of miracles has not changed in this concept, but the secondary causes have been differentiated. Miracles are seen as a particular kind of act by which God works directly in affairs. The actions of men and the workings of nature, though still ultimately actions of God by their mediation, are set free for examination in a new way. Their mode of action can be examined without impiety and *quomodo* can be applied to them more closely. Miracles are acts of God, not subject to the laws of nature or the usual way in which man acts within nature, while nature and mankind are themselves subject to the 'miraculous' power of God: 'The miraculous is not subject to the other two or to their laws, but freely rules them'.[11]

Anselm's distinction between nature, will, and miracle in events was used later, and it was usually applied to the matter out of which it arose, the miracle of creation.[12] Peter Abelard, for instance, used this distinction in his commentary on the Creation narrative in Genesis, where he says the events he calls miracles are those 'against nature' or 'above nature' (*contra vel supra natura*) in which God is acting directly, as he did in the first six days of Creation. Like Anselm, Abelard sees the creation of Adam from the earth and Eve from Adam as *praeter naturam*, and therefore miracles;[13] the Virgin birth and the giving of sight to the blind he cites as other instances of genuine miracles.[14] Like Anselm, Abelard was not here primarily concerned with the nature of things, but his reflections on nature and miracle tended, like those of Anselm, to set miracles in a specific category of events in which God acts directly in this world.

The primary text in the twelfth century for discussing creation was the first chapters of Genesis, but the Platonists of the twelfth century who drew this kind of distinction among events were influenced also by the account of creation given in the *Timaeus* that they read with the commentary of Chalcidius.[15] Thierry of Chartres wrote an account of the book of Genesis 'secundum physicam et ad litteram', the *littera* being the words of Scripture about creation, the *physica* being Chalcidius on Plato's *Timaeus*.[16] The three-fold distinction of Augustine is

5

found also in Chalcidius: 'All things that exist are the works of God, or the work of nature, or the work of a human artisan imitating nature',[17] and was echoed in a Christian context by Thierry of Chartres, William of Conches, and, in a more formal and technical way, by Gilbert de la Porrée:

All things have been made by God as their author; but certain things are called God's works just as they are, namely those which he makes by himself and neither after some resemblance in nature nor through the intermediary service of someone else, as he makes heaven and earth . . . God therefore is the sole author of all things.[18]

In this view, some matters such as miracles belong to Divine omnipotence; other matters, which were created by God but follow their own laws, belong to the natural and created order. This shift from the sacramental view of the whole order of creation as miraculous, in which the power of God could be seen as a sign to men in all events, emphasized, from another point of view, the new freedom to examine the natural events; it also tended to limit the events that could properly be called miracles.

The interest of Platonists in the causes of things received a new impetus with the appearance of Aristotle's work on physics. Those who read Aristotle and his Arab commentators were diverted from the older concern with the unity and symbolism of events in God and began to concentrate on the mechanics of their secondary causes. This change affected the definition of miracle by limiting still further those events that could be called miraculous. This state of mind, which determined which texts would be used and translated, was already established, not an unexpected influence changing the direction of thought. Adelard of Bath's *Quaestiones Naturales* went far toward explaining away, as well as simply explaining, wonders. For instance, he was asked to account for thunder, a phenomenon almost universally seen hitherto as a sign from God, fraught with miraculous significance, and he makes his interlocutor phrase the request in tones of incredulity:

. . . One thing which clearly takes place in the air is an object of wonder to all nations: the death-dealing disturbance called thunder. By it not only are all nations terrified but fear weighs heavily also upon irrational creatures . . . is then your science bold enough to give the cause and origin of thunder, or is it unable to solve this most difficult problem, for in the face of thunder the philosophers are no braver than the rest.[19]

6

Adelard replied that the proper way to discover the 'cause and origin' of thunder was to examine its immediate causes in the currents of air. A storm had become merely a storm instead of a message from God. Adelard was convinced that recourse to miracle as an explanation was a last resort; only when all other causes had been tested and found wanting should the explanation of the direct intervention of God be propounded:

I will detract nothing from God; for whatever is, is from Him, and by Him; and yet not even this is to be said vaguely and without due care, for we must listen to the very limits of human knowledge; only where this utterly breaks down should we refer things to God.[20]

This kind of reasoning when applied to the doctrine of creation brought criticism on William of Conches, in a letter from William of St Thierry to St Bernard of Clairvaux:

. . . describing the creation of the first man by philosophy or rather by physics, he says that his body was not at first made by God but by nature and a soul then given him by God, after the body had been made by spirits which he calls demons and by the stars. . . . As far as the creation of woman is concerned which is clear to all readers, with what stupidity and arrogance he holds the authority of sacred scripture in contempt. By interpreting that account according to physics, he arrogantly prefers the ideas he invents to the truth it contains and so makes light of a great mystery.[21]

Only 'the nature of things', it seems, should be learned from observation and philosophy; here also, the realm of the miraculous was being relegated to a department of the supernatural.

How far did the arguments of the masters of the schools affect their pupils? Gerald of Wales can be seen as typical of the clerk who absorbed a certain amount of new teaching, along with a basic traditionalism.[22] His works are filled with miracles and marvels, mostly of a ferocious nature, in the manner of Gregory of Tours.[23] In the *Topographia Hibernica* he comments on the relationship between miracle and 'nature'. He says he will speak in the second part of wonders that are not contrary to nature, but to the usual course of nature. Augustine also finds miracles and wonders inherent within nature as created by God; the strange and exotic are not *contra naturam,* they are *contra natura cursum,* and are all works of God. This enabled Gerald to exercise his curiosity to the full in observing and recording the strange

7

flora and fauna in Ireland, an interest challenged by other churchmen as too secular and too trivial for serious record, but which Gerald defended as a survey of the wonderful works of God in nature.[24] In this, he is at one with the masters of the schools in their basic Augustinianism. He was, however, in practice also one with their more recent distinctions over miracles: the marvels of nature and of the works of man form two clear sections in the *Topographia Hibernica*, and the miracles of the saints, the true works of God, are grouped separately from both: 'Now let us pass on to miracles'.[25] The miracle by which St Kevin caused a willow tree to bear apples is distinguished as a miracle because it was caused by the prayers of St Kevin to God. But Gerald refuses to call the salmon-leap a miracle, since it is within the course of nature, however marvellous it may seem:

Salmon are moved by wonderful leaps which would be miraculous if this were not the nature of the fish. But this kind of fish makes such leaps because it is its nature to do so.

Thus, Gerald makes events that happen by the will of man the main part of his work, followed by a separate section about events that happen *naturaliter*, in the course of nature, whether marvellously or not, and a smaller section about events that are *miraculosa*, the result of the direct action of God in response to the prayers of the saints.

The distinction between the marvellous in nature and the miracles of the saints was not in this period very clearly expounded or applied. Nevertheless it is possible to see here a narrowing of their secondary causes. There was less and less chance of these being called miracles except by the ignorant. This narrowing was one further step in a pattern known to Augustine, who was himself interested in the causes of things and had explored natural marvels, with a *curiositas* as keen as that of Adelard of Bath,[26] to discover the 'natural properties' of things. But for Augustine this exploration expanded the realm of true miracle, where for the twelfth-century writers it restricted it. The 'how' of events was of interest to Augustine, as to any ancient philosopher, but he says that whereas for the pagans the marvels of nature are simply *mira*, for the Christians they are *signa* leading men to accept those wonders of faith that are beyond their comprehension. The Christians have, he says, a *ratio rerum* for the whole of creation, so that there is no need for them to supply a *ratio* for each of the *divina miracula*.[27] Mira-

8

cles and nature were thus for centuries put on an equal footing as signs from God to man. The twelfth century found a further distinction possible in the relationship between miracles and events of other kinds, and applied this distinction to their thinking here, as well as to practice in other spheres, though in a fragmentary fashion.

While miracles were an accepted way in which Christians were in touch with the supernatural, other modes of supernatural contact to some extent were distinguished from miracles. At first sight, the most obvious and final distinction made was that between miracle and magic. The 'arts of magic' had been consistently forbidden in the Christian church and the 'miracles of the saints' proposed as their antithesis. Edicts of church councils and disciplinary directions in penitentials alike had forbidden magical practices to Christians, and this prohibition continued throughout the Middle Ages. The teaching of the church did not change, nor did the disregard for it at a popular level decrease. In fact, in the twelfth century the revival of learning and the interest in science led to an increase in the amount of magic practised and discussed. It was necessary to make further definitions of what was licit and what was forbidden.

Discussion about magic was older than Christianity. The power of God exercised through Moses was contrasted in the Old Testament with the impotent magic of Pharaoh's magicians (Exodus 7:12ff.).[28] Saul conjured the spirit of Elijah through the witch of Endor (1 Samuel 28:7–20).[29] The ancient classical world argued endlessly about the powers of demons and the wonders of great men.[30] The debate was summarized and fixed for Christians up to the twelfth century and beyond by Augustine. Magic, for him, was *theurgy* and concerned wonders wrought by demons; it was wholly reprehensible because of the contact with demonic forces. The miracles of both Old and New Testaments, he says, were quite different from pagan magic:

Those miracles and many others of the same kind . . . were intended to support the worship of the one true God . . . they were achieved by simple faith and devout confidences, not by spells and charms composed according to the rules of criminal superstition, the craft which is called magic, a name of detestation, or by the more honourable title of 'theurgy'.[31]

The powers of the demons, he says, were essentially cheats, deceptions, and lies, in no way powers equal to that of God, as their practitioners

9

supposed: 'The whole thing is in fact an imposture of malignant spirits
. . . it is from the devil that these phantoms come'.[32] The only way for
demons to exercise power over people after the devil's defeat by the
resurrection of Christ was by deception; the gods of the ancient world
found no place as a separate source of power in the new theology.[33]

The practice of magic, however, was not as dead, either in debate or
in popular practice, as the injunctions of Augustine might have led one
to suppose. Penitentials continued to prescribe penances for the use of
magical arts well into the twelfth century and beyond. Two things
were especially condemned: the invocation of demons and the continued observance of pagan festivals, such as the New Year. The idea of
a witches' sabbath was held to be a delusion, but it suggested enough of
Satan worship and the old cult of Diana to merit penances lasting two
years.[34] Actions connected with medicine, such as collecting herbs,
were thought to be more efficacious if incantations were used, but the
words had to be those of the Creed and the Our Father to avoid blame:
'If you have done otherwise, the penance is ten days on bread and
water'.[35] 'Egyptian days' had survived in church calendars, and their
overtones of 'luck' were easily confused in the popular mind with 'providence'.[36] Both St Martin and St Benedict were said to have over-
thrown demons inhabiting pagan sanctuaries.[37]

The use of magic for contact with the supernatural was as usual in
the northern pagan lands as in the Mediterranean world. Missionaries
in both areas tended to stress similarities between magic and miracle
rather than their differences. The Christian saint was frequently presented to the unconverted as having greater powers through his miracles
than the demons offered by magical deceits; the effectiveness of the
demons' powers was challenged, not their possibility. In the *Life of St
Cuthbert,* it was said that Cuthbert went through the pagan villages of
Northumbria preaching and demonstrating the benefits of the miracles
of the saints in opposition to popular magic.[38] When the country
people were in distress, the same *Life* shows them resorting at once to
familiar amulets and charms, and accusing St Cuthbert of taking away
their best defence.[39] In the conversion of pagans in Europe, magic
remained one of the options for supernatural help long after baptism
had in theory replaced it with the assurance of the prayers of the saints.
Often, the invocation of Christian saints was merely added to older
incantations and their relics to amulets.[40] Though the church stressed a
difference, asserting that prayers to the saints were intercessory requests

for their prayers to God, the peasant using them had firmer expectations and a more resolute attitude, based on his experience of the manipulations of magic.[41] The methods of magic and miracle could appear identical; and they could not always be distinguished by their results. The vengeance of the saints could fall as heavily on men as the results of maleficent magic.[42]

In theory, magic that involved the invocation of demons was condemned by the church and miracles were recommended as the proper method for a Christian to obtain supernatural aid. An intermediate area of practices, however, which later ages would certainly call magic and some would call miracle, in this period was simply an application of current ideas about causation. The theory of Augustine that there were 'hidden virtues' in all parts of creation came very close to the popular idea of 'occult virtues' hidden in all objects, which could be invoked and used.[43] These were used especially in 'natural medicine'.[44] Gems, in particular, were said to have hidden powers that could be exploited for healing and for protection in all kinds of dangers.[45] Such dealings with nature were not forbidden; while the *praestigia inferna* were condemned and the *supera miracula* praised, natural charms and incantations were allowed and were distinguished from both magic and miracle. The power of healing the sick obtained by mixing earth from a holy place or using water connected with a saint was close to the ancient use of the four elements for obtaining power. Hildegard of Bingen illustrates the close connection between miracle and magic in her book of remedies, in which rites and incantations for the use of occult virtues in natural objects are mingled with prayers and the sign of the cross.[46] The wide area of the use of 'natural' properties was in fact neither magic nor miracle, though in retrospect it was to be confused with both.

John of Salisbury's approach to magic, miracle, and 'natural' powers is typical of twelfth-century scholars. He accepted and repeated the list of forbidden magical arts that had been drawn up by Isidore of Seville.[47] He was sceptical about magic that claimed to use demonic powers and cited his own experience as a sorcerer's apprentice when he was a boy:

I was judged useless for such purposes and as though I impeded the sacrilegious practices, I was condemned to have nothing to do with such things and as often as they practised their art I was banished as if an obstacle to the whole procedure.[48]

The deceits of the demons, he implied, rested on the mistaken credulity of the practitioners of magic. *Physica,* that which is non-material, was manifested through normal processes of causation: 'in fact, there is no act or object whose origin is not due to some specific cause or purpose'. But beyond that, 'only those things should be accepted which are the product of faith and are attributed to the glory of an omnipotent God'.[49] Thus, he can cite Julius Caesar and his wife as being the recipients of omens conveyed through nature, which were in fact true and from God, and he goes even further with Vespasian and attributes true cures at his hands to the power of God. Nevertheless, he asserts that what should be most closely considered by Christians are the miracles of the saints. Of the examples he gives of miracles, some are miracles of the saints—Stephen,[50] Benedict,[51] and Cuthbert[52]—but the others belong to the intermediate world of natural medicine. A demoniac was cured by carrying a paper on which the Lord's prayer was written; herbs gathered by moonlight while the gatherer recited the Lord's prayer effected cures; parts of the New Testament written out and carried on the body provided protection.[53] He also held that while most ways of foretelling the future were both erroneous and forbidden, certain means of prophecy were allowed:

Yet it is permissible that one should be consulted about the future on condition that he possesses the spirit of prophecy or that as a result of his knowledge of medicine he recognizes what is taking place from natural signs in the bodies of living creatures.[54]

Certain dreams could also be prophetic.[55] Thus, while in theory the distinction between miracle and magic was clear, the intermediate field of natural causes could confuse the issue if later categories were placed upon this very different area.

The exploration of natural causes in 'science' often brought condemnation on itself as trafficking with demons: Gerard, archbishop of York, was condemned as a dealer in magic when a copy of Julius Firmicius was found under his pillow at his death;[56] St Dunstan's reputation for learning and inventiveness caused him to be called a sorcerer;[57] William of Malmesbury gave Gerbert a lasting reputation as a magician.[58] 'Magic' was also the accusation passed on miracles not acceptable to another party. The miracles of heretics were condemned as magic;[59] the miracles of Becket were called magic by his opponents:

'They spread it around everywhere that the monks of Canterbury did these things by magical incantations and by such devilish arts that they seemed rather than were miracles'.[60] 'Magic' for the period in question meant supernatural dealing with demons. It was condemned and set against miracles. It is an anachronism to call the intermediate sphere of natural causes 'white magic' or to extend this description on the miracles of the saints.[61] Miracles and magic were two extremes, at least in theory, of dealing with the supernatural; the intermediate sphere was a commerce with natural elements, however mistakenly described.

The process of distinction among events called *mira* in this period is seen particularly clearly in relation to the supernatural events called sacraments. In one sense the sacraments always had been 'miracles' *par excellence,* insofar as they were the supreme instances of the regular but mysterious intervention of God in the created order: *quotidiana miracula.* In this period the sacrament of the eucharist in particular began to be regarded as a miracle in a different sense. The other sacraments at times did have miracle stories attached to them, and popular belief made them a means of protection and assistance in temporal needs,[62] but such instances were few, partly because these sacraments were administered only once in a lifetime. Also, extreme unction provided little material for miracles since it involved no outward or psychological change in the people concerned, but effected a change in their status. In certain monastic circles the sacrament of penance, which was increasingly used in personal confession in this period,[63] was concerned more closely with the psychological state of the penitent than with his restoration to his place in the church.[64] Particularly among the monks, miracle stories began to appear concerning the miraculous effects of the sacrament of penance either in its application or its omission. The real emphasis on a sacrament as miraculous, however, was to be found in connection with the eucharist. Unlike the other sacraments, the eucharist involved the use of bread and wine, natural objects that could be observed and discussed in terms other than those of psychology.

Three kinds of miracles were connected with the eucharist: what was later called 'the miracle of the mass' itself (the discussion of the content of the sacrament in theological terms); visions and miracles that illustrated this; and, as there were to a much lesser degree for other sacraments, miracles tangential to the sacrament that demonstrated its

13

power in practical situations. Though the first of these, the change in substance effected by the mass, was invisible and therefore beyond analysis, the nature of the change was discussed. The discussion shows a change from the traditional perception of the eucharist as marvellous to a particular understanding of it as miraculous. There is no complete change from one view to the other in this period, and, as with other aspects of the miraculous already discussed, both the traditional view and the changes were present at once.

The traditional understanding of the eucharist as 'the mystery [not the miracle] of the body of Christ which is the church' (Col. 1:4) was a central theme of patristic teaching.[65] It had been vividly presented by Augustine[66] and was incorporated in the words of the canon of the mass.[67] In this period Anselm of Canterbury had continued this tradition in a personal prayer *Before Receiving the Body and Blood of Christ:*

Make me, O Lord, so to perceive with lips and heart and know by faith and by love, that by virtue of this sacrament I may deserve to be planted in the likeness of your death and resurrection by mortifying the old man and renewal of the life of righteousness. May I be worthy to be incorporated into your body 'which is the church'.[68]

This understanding of the *quomodo* of the eucharist as symbol and mystery received still greater emphasis in the next century, partly as a reaction to a different kind of inquiry. Thus Hugh of St Victor asserted the traditional approach, but in reaction to the recent application of dialectic to the mass:

Here is marvel indeed. The flesh that is eaten below remains whole in the heavens. Why do you start up with your logic, dialectician? What do you think of this, sophist? Why are you seeking arguments? That would be to sprinkle dust on the stars. Your logic does not reach so high.[69]

The understanding of the sacrament in personal and spiritual terms as *mira* and mystery continued and was in fact made more personal in this period; but at the same time Hugh of St Victor's *dialecticus* and *sophista* examined how the bread and wine became the body and blood of Christ in a desire to show that the change was 'real'. Interest in the manner of this change was not unknown in the early church,[70] but the focus of the questions now asked was very different. The discussion that

14

revolved around Paschasius Radbertus and Ratramnus in the ninth century had effectively concentrated attention not on the results of the sacrament for the believer but on the method of the change of substance in the elements themselves. Paschasius had held that the bread and wine of the eucharist changed at the words of consecration into the same body that Christ received from the Virgin at Bethlehem;[71] it was a view taken up in the eleventh and twelfth centuries and illustrated, as will be seen, by miracle stories, several of which were included in Paschasius's work.[72] The host was seen as Christ the Child in visions. The protests of some theologians that the sacramental change was effected spiritually, not visibly, came to a head with the teaching of Berengar of Tours. Eventually he agreed to resign his views in favour of a statement that carried to its extreme the theory that the flesh of Christ was received in a more than spiritual manner:

The bread and wine which are placed on the altar are after consecration not only a sacrament but also the real body and blood of our Lord Jesus Christ . . . with the senses not only as a sacrament but in reality these are taken and broken by the hands of the priest and are crushed by the teeth of the faithful.[73]

The carnal, naturalistic approach apparent here, in which the changed bread and wine is the body of Christ that can be held, broken, and chewed, presents a new focus on the sacrament. It is not so much the 'body of Christ which is the church' as 'the body of Christ which is the host', and the host itself had been changed by a miracle. Hugh of St Victor called the sacrament *miraculum*, Stephen of Autun said the change was *miraculosa* and Simon of Tournai compared it with the miracle of the raising of Lazarus. Both miracles were done 'not naturally . . . but against the course and order of nature'.[74]

The idea that transubstantiation was a miracle *contra naturam*, a marvel, coupled with the over-vivid images of the reality it produced, is connected with a flood of miracle stories that illustrated the 'reality' of the change. Such stories could even be called 'counter-miracles', since they break through the miraculous surface of illusion to a representation of the substance that lies behind the unchanged appearance. These are a second type of eucharistic miracle. The host was seen to change into the Christ child, either as a beautiful boy, or as a child pierced and wounded. Or, in the place of bread and wine, there appeared flesh and blood. Sometimes the figure of Christ crucified appeared at the consecration, with blood flowing from his wounds into the chalice. At other times, the Virgin Mary was seen offering the child to the communicants. The most common miracles were the replacing of bread and wine at the consecration by a child or by flesh and blood. One instance of each stands for many:

One day when . . . Adolph was celebrating mass and before the 'O Lamb of God', he lifted up the host to break it, and saw the Virgin in the host itself sitting upon a throne and holding the infant to her breast . . . he saw also a lamb in the host . . . and when he looked again, Christ on the cross with bent head.[75] Less than two years ago a priest who was in doubt about the sacrament of the body of Christ celebrated mass . . . and the Lord showed him raw flesh in the host.[76]

In the second instance, a bystander, a nobleman called Widekin, claimed to have seen the raw flesh also, which is asserted to show that this was not the imagination of an individual but a reality that could be seen by others. The appearance of these 'realities' in place of the host are said to be either for the conviction of unbelievers or for the reward of special devotion. In either case, miracles of this kind are an inversion of the central miracle of transubstantiation, though they claimed to affirm it.

A third class of miracles is connected with the eucharist, and in these the consecrated elements themselves were regarded as a permanent focus of power, just as a relic was held to be. In stories of punishments that befell those who celebrated mass unworthily, the host turned black or vanished from the hands of the priest.[77] In some stories animals or insects venerated the host or protected it.[78] In other tales communion afforded special protection, as, for instance, in the story of a knight who conquered in an ordeal by battle by receiving communion first.[79] The host was placed along with the relics of saints in altars at their consecration.[80] The pious had a strong inclination to treat the consecrated bread and wine, if they had been subject to a vision of their 'real' nature, as relics to be preserved and venerated.

An instance of the veneration of such consecrated elements was known to Lanfranc of Bec; a century later, a similar instance was known to Hugh of Lincoln. The contrast between the two stories expresses the contrast between the two approaches to the eucharist as *signum* and as

mirum in this period. In the first instance, Guitmund, bishop of Avranches, says Lanfranc, *magister meus* told him that when he was a boy in
Italy he heard of a priest who found the elements turned to flesh and
blood at the mass. The priest asked the bishop's advice; the bishop
summoned a council and ordered the elements to be enclosed in the
centre of the altar 'so that all that remained might be perpetually preserved'.[81]

When Hugh of Lincoln visited Normandy, however, and was in-
vited to venerate a similar shrine, he refused to do so, saying that the
true miracle was the host daily consecrated and received:

Why should we gape at a sensory image of this divine gift when every day we
behold by faith this heavenly sacrifice whole and entire? Let that man look
with his bodily eyes on the minute fragment who cannot by faith internally
behold the whole.[82]

This episode showed no lack of appreciation of the eucharist as a miracle in Hugh; his biographer related that he often saw a beautiful child
between his hands when he said mass and was moved to tears at the
sight.[83] It shows rather the concern of the monk, significantly a Carthusian, a member of a new order, for what is personal and spiritual in
the *miraculum* of the sacrament, while the factual record by Lanfranc
shows a situation in a parish setting, where the host that the parish
priest had seen turn into real flesh at the consecration was treated as a
relic for external veneration. The approach of Hugh is traditional, but
with a more personal and emotional aspect; the approach reflected in
the story told by Lanfranc indicates the other view, in which the host
was a relic among relics, dignified only because it was the relic of
Christ.

The great increase within this period in devotion to the eucharist led
official theology to the position taken by Hugh of Lincoln, but the
other kind of veneration of the host did not disappear in popular devotion. In fact, eucharistic hosts more frequently were held to work miracles once attributed to the saints; the *quomodo* questions of the natural
scientists reinforced this belief. They focussed attention on the nature
of the elements, and therefore on what was visible and immediate. This
attention gave a miraculous aspect to the host and caused it to be regarded as a relic. It therefore could be misused for magical purposes,
and miracle stories relate this.[84] The Fourth Lateran Council forbade

17

the reception of the host in such a way that it could be carried out of the church—an indication of the extent to which the host was regarded as an object of power to be coveted and used.[85]

It is in this third category of miracles connected with the host that the eucharist is most clearly linked with the miraculous. The first category of the theological content of transubstantiation made the mass a miracle *spiritualiter,* and the second category was meant to demonstrate this; the third can only be called miraculous *corporaliter* in that the host was separated from its context to become a focus of power like the relic of a saint.

Thus the sacrament of the eucharist was seen to be in some sense a miracle. However, it differed from other miraculous events in that it was predictable. It was a regular and covenanted act of God through a prescribed ritual that precipitated the intervention of the divine in an expected way. The mass was, in itself, a predictable act of God *'supra naturam'* and additional miracles illustrated this. It is possible to see another ceremony, that of the ordeal, in the same category, as in some sense a miracle in itself, with other miracles to illustrate it. During this period, however, the ordeal ceased, at least in theory, to be used in judicial inquiry, and one can see here a further limitation on the supernatural in affairs similar to those already discussed.

The ordeal was an appeal to the judgement of God; it took place either by hot iron, water, or a duel; it could also use the host. The elements to be used were blessed by a priest, the participants solemnly set apart from society, and the affair conducted as a ritual, with prescribed prayers and actions.[86] If a man were innocent, his burns would show signs of healing within three days; if he had been tried by water, he would float if guilty, since the natural element of water would reject him; the winner in an ordeal by battle was assumed to have won by the power of God 'who judges justly'. It was a clear, public, and final demonstration of the decision of God in legal matters. It was believed to be unprejudiced by men and in correspondence with the facts. The elements of water and fire were created by God and specially open to his direct influence after the blessing given them; they would then reveal the guilt or innocence of a man, who was also created by God. It was a miracle in the sense of *signum,* and, since water and fire did not normally behave in this way, it was also *mirum.*

18

The ordeal as ritualized miracle was accepted by its critics in the twelfth century; it was simply held to be out of place. The arguments presented by Peter the Chanter were perhaps decisive in this matter and can be cited as typical of the new approach.[87] In his view the ordeal was a miracle, but it was demanded, and to do this was to tempt God[88] by assuming that he will intervene in the work of the law. Miracles, according to Peter the Chanter, were unusual and uncovenanted events, coming straight from the act of God, usually in connection with sanctity. In the division of events into those caused by God through the will of men, the course of nature, or directly, Peter transferred the ordeal from the last to the first. Ordeals, moreover, seemed to him to be contrary to the authority of the scriptures. He also showed them to be frequently wrong in their results in practical situations.

This practical discussion of whether ordeals were correct in their results cut at the heart of the appeal *ad judicium Dei*. Miracle stories had not always shown previously that their results were correct; there are earlier instances of ordeals whose results were wrong; but Peter the Chanter compiled a list of instances in which their results were shown always to be wrong. He told anecdotes of failures and of false judgements. He also demonstrated that the ordeal in fact favoured certain participants.[89] It was a practical discussion of the mechanics of the 'miracle' and a reassessment of its results that destroyed both its hold on theory and its reliability in practice. A decree of the Fourth Lateran Council[90] forbade clergy to be involved in ordeals, and the essential connection by which the process claimed to be supernatural was broken. A miracle was no longer a central procedure in law-courts; miracles were relegated to a more theological atmosphere.

19

2

The Discussion of Miracles
in Practical Contexts

THE SPARSE INFORMATION to be gained from direct discussion of miracles can be supplemented by an examination of how miracles were considered indirectly by those recounting them or using the accounts of others. One example of this indirect discussion of miracles is found in the works of commentators on the Scriptures. The vocabulary of miracle was a complex matter, but certain episodes in the Scriptures commonly were called miracles or signs, whatever word was used for them in the Vulgate. One of these was the creation of the world and the creation of Adam in particular; another was the Virgin Birth; a third was the resurrection. Besides these, certain actions of Christ as well as certain events in Exodus in connection with Moses, Elijah, and Elisha were called miracles. These included the feeding of the five thousand, the turning of water into wine, the raising of Lazarus, the healing of the sick. Comments made about the miracle of creation have already provided some insight into the concept of miracle in this period; comments on other miracles fill out this picture.

Writers on biblical miracles predominantly followed part of the patristic tradition of exegesis. This tradition saw events in the Bible as moments illustrating the relationship between God and man, to be explored for their significance for contemporary readers.[1] Miracles were no exception to this. The intense interest felt in this type of consideration was expressed earlier, in a way that continued to be recognized throughout this period, by Rabanus Maurus. In his commentary on the most miracle-filled book of the Old Testament, the book of Exodus, the abbot of Fulda exclaimed:

Among the other scriptures which the Pentateuch of law contains, the book of Exodus is pre-eminent in merit, in which nearly all the sacraments by which the present church is constituted, nourished and ordered, are presented figuratively.[2]

He goes on to consider the crossing of the Red Sea exclusively in terms of salvation and symbol: 'There through the crossing of the Red Sea, and Pharaoh and the drowning of the Egyptians, are prefigured the mystery of baptism and the death of spiritual enemies'. This was precisely the kind of comment that appeared in the *Gloss* whenever the text demanded comment on miracles. Anselm of Laon's gloss on St John,[3] which became a standard gloss on the Scriptures, proceeds in this way. The miracle of the raising of Lazarus, for instance, includes texts from Augustine and Jerome in which typology predominates. In the first, Lazarus is the sinful soul loosed from sin:

When the sinner is condemned he lies in the tomb, when he repents he rises, when he confesses he comes forth, as if made manifest from the darkness but still bound, and the ministers say, 'loose him and let him go'.

In the second, Lazarus is a type for the Jews: 'Lazarus dead is a symbol of the Jews who do not believe in Christ'.[4] The programme of Augustine's *De Doctrina Christiana* was still in force: 'We must meditate on what we read until an interpretation be found that tends to establish the reign of charity.'[5]

The 'spiritual' meaning of the text predominates in the instances just quoted. The question of *how* Lazarus was raised was already settled by the assumption that God does what he chooses; the questions that remained were, when was he acting miraculously? and to what purpose for men were his actions? The miracle of the changing of water into wine at Cana provided a fruitful source for reflection on the miraculous acts of God, and writers connected this miracle with the eucharist. Within this period, however, a more typical approach is that of Rupert of Deutz in his commentary on St John. He assumes, with Augustine, that the process by which water is made into wine by nature and the actions of men was simply speeded up without intermediaries in the case of the water changed at Cana; it is the purpose, not the process, of the miracle that excites his interest:

For it is not to be wondered at that God could make wine out of water . . . how greatly we rejoice that he who alone could do this was made man, walked among men for thirty years, entering into the prison of the flesh. So this new miracle proves that which only the faithful believe, that omnipotent God was made man.[6]

This was the kind of comment most frequently made on biblical miracles, as it was the kind of comment most often used about contemporary miracles. When defending the more unlikely of the miracles attributed to St Faith, for instance, Bernard of Angers set out to show that these stories were edifying for the faithful and in accord with the Word of God. But other questions were being raised about biblical miracles in this period, and these questions were not unlike those raised by the 'natural scientists' about contemporary miracles. The question of *how* an event called a miracle took place, an examination of its mechanics rather than its effects, emerges in the *quaestio* and the *sententia,* in which contemporary opinion predominated over the quotations given from the Fathers on a text.[7] In discussing the text of Romans 5:12, Anselm of Laon had recognized the creation of all men from Adam as a miracle, in which the 'hidden causes' were contained in one man and conveyed to all men.[8] Peter Lombard, however, carried his questions a step further. He asked *how* this was so and illustrated the process by referring to another miracle, the feeding of the five thousand. He gives as an explanation for both miracles the 'hidden causes' of Augustine:

The course of all creatures has natural laws; over this natural course the Creator himself has made them able to do otherwise than that which is natural to them.[9]

As instances of this process he cites the flowering of Aaron's rod, the childbearing of Sarah, the ass of Balaam that spoke, and he quotes Augustine on Genesis as his authority. The difference he introduces, however, into the consideration of the miracles is the shift of emphasis from an exclusive concern with the lessons to be drawn from an event, to the question of the event's mechanics: not 'why is that said?' but 'how can that have happened?'

This questioning of miracles in the sixteenth century and under other pressures led to discarding the concept of the miraculous in certain 'scientific' circles; there is no question of that here. But Peter Lombard's interest in secondary causes found echoes even in a critic such as Robert of Melun, who repeats the comments of Lombard in his own commentary on the same text from Romans.[10] Later still, Simon of Tournai asked similar questions about the feeding of the five thousand and the raising of Lazarus. He asks what kind of event it was: 'whether his raising was a natural or a miraculous event';[11] and he concludes that it was both: 'it was accomplished miraculously but once done it was natural'. The restoration of a dead person to life he regarded as a direct intervention of God and therefore a miracle *contra naturam*. But when he considered how Lazarus behaved afterwards, he had to say he lived 'naturally' rather than 'miraculously': he could eat, sleep, marry, behave as any man would. His discussion is still far from attacking the miracle as such, but again it changes the emphasis from seeing an event as *signum,* as a message from God to the hearer, to considering how it came about in itself.

This was not, in fact, an entirely new approach to the miracles of Scripture. It was known to the early church and was revived by Isidore of Seville and by the Irish schools of the seventh century. In particular, one treatise that had the authority of Augustine until the thirteenth century was produced in Ireland and known in this period: the *De Mirabilibus Sacrae Scripturae.* Here the miracles of the Old and New Testaments were discussed, within the Augustinian framework of 'hidden reasons' but with the *quomodo* questions of a Simon of Tournai. How, the writer asked, did Christ and St Peter walk on the water?

But it is possible to ask whether the bodies of the Lord and St Peter grew lighter in their nature so that the water held them up, or if the water solidified so that it could support human bodies.[12]

This *quomodo* questioning was to attain popularity in the thirteenth century, and it is significant that most of the surviving manuscripts of this work were copied and glossed in that period. The Irish work had the authority of Augustine in the twelfth century and may have been known and appreciated then. It is cited here not for its possible influence, but as a parallel for the kind of interest being shown in bibilical miracles in this period. This interest had its counterpart in the explorations of William of Conches and Adelard of Bath, and in their determination not to resort to 'miracle' as an explanation until other causes had been examined for contemporary events. It is one more instance of the narrowing in certain circles of the concept of miracle from that which by its unusual nature instructs the soul, to a special category of acts of God, outside nature's normal course.

In addition to the bibilical commentators, preachers often discussed miracles in their sermons. In the sermon, a didactic exercise, many kinds of illustrations were used to drive home a lesson, among them stories of miraculous happenings. *Exempla* were drawn from nature, classical literature, contemporary events, and from biblical texts, in a tradition of preaching that can be traced back to the Gospels.[13] It was a method of preaching strongly recommended by Gregory the Great: more are usually pierced by examples than by words of reason . . . The hearts of the hearers are generally stirred to the love of God and neighbour by examples rather than by words.'[14] Augustine of Hippo used the occasion of a miracle as an illustration to a sermon, when he spoke about the powers of the saints on Easter morning in the church in Hippo and directed the attention of his audience to the cure of a young man and his sister, Paulus and Palladia. He made the man stand before the congregation as one just then cured by the relics of St Stephen, and beside him he put his sister who was still suffering from the same kind of illness.[15] This example was for the edification of the hearers, a sign of the power of the saints, and not a wonder, of interest for its marvellous qualities. The process of the cure was of no interest for him or for his congregation, except for its strength as a witness to the powers of heaven:

What do these miracles attest but the faith which proclaims that Christ rose in the flesh and ascended into heaven with the flesh?[16]

This was the recognized approach of the preacher to miracles. They were pre-eminently treated as signs. This was also the pattern for the twelfth-century preachers and in particular the monastic preachers, who continued to present miracles as *signa,* subservient to their end—to implant or strengthen faith. The Cistercians, for example, used as their theme the miracle of the Incarnation rather than the theme most popular with the commentators, the Creation. The Cistercian most renowned as a preacher in his day, Bernard of Clairvaux, rarely referred in his sermons to miraculous events, but he insisted on the 'great wonders', the miracles of the Incarnation and the salvation of men:

When the Almighty in his majesty took upon him our flesh he did three works, made three conjunctions, which were so wonderfully singular and singularly wonderful that nothing had been or could be seen to be grater upon earth. He joined together God and man, mother and virgin, faith and the human heart.[17]

In his sermon on St Martin he says that he values the miracles of Martin, but considers the faith of Martin of greater importance for his hearers: 'Rich is this Martin, rich in merits, rich in miracles, rich in virtues, rich in signs'.[18] And he urges his hearers to distinguish between *miracula* and *signa* on the one hand and *merita* and *virtutes* on the other: 'Consider diligently therefore what is appropriate to your condition, that is, which is to be admired and which is to be imitated'.[19] In a sermon on St Victor, he emphasizes the same idea about the miracles of St Victor:

These and other similar deeds of the holy man we should venerate but not emulate; it is safe to emulate that which is more solid rather than that which is more sublime, that which is filled with virtue, even though it is less in glory.[20]

This is not to say that Bernard underrated miracles. On the contrary, he used them frequently to support his own preaching and to illustrate the power of faith, especially when preaching the Crusade. The point he made about miracles on all occasions was, however, that they were a means to bring men to God and of comparatively little interest in themselves.

This approach was used by other Cistercian preachers. Aelred of Rievaulx, himself known for miracles, preached on the book of Isaiah and noted that miracles could be experienced by unbelievers as well as the faithful and were, therefore, no sure guide to virtue. Is it not better, he concludes, to seek the gifts of humility, patience, and charity? Where these are present, he adds, they will be confirmed by miracles: 'What is taught is confirmed by miracles'.[21] In the next generation another Cistercian, Baldwin, abbot of Ford, continued the same theme:

25

'All miracles are either through faith or because of faith . . . what God requires is faith, not the power to do miracles'.[22] Adam of Persiègne wrote in the same vein, indeed echoing the words as well as the sentiments of Bernard:

Among the wonders that the Creator in his wisdom has done, three are singularly wonderful and wonderfully singular . . . that is, mother and virgin, the Word made flesh, God and man. These are new things, unheard of and wonderful, which exceed nature.[23]

The Cistercians had no monopoly on using miracles in preaching. Peter Damian stressed the inner meaning of every text or example he used, from miracles to the details of his bestiary:

We say nothing to provoke astonishment, but those who look at things from a higher point of view will find here a sacrament of the greatest significance for their lives.[24]

He used miracle stories in his sermons briefly and to illustrate a moral or spiritual message; his use of a miracle of St Benedict is typical. A story was told at Monte Cassino of the deliverance of the monastery from fire when, at the prayers of the monks to St Benedict, rain fell and extinguished the flames.[25] In Desiderius's account in the *Miracles of St Benedict,* several details are mentioned that Peter Damian omits or changes in his sermon on St Benedict. Desiderius emphasizes the power of St Benedict in that particular place and concludes that men should pray to St Benedict and visit his grave, since he cares for his own. For Peter Damian, the fire at the monastery is a symbol of sin, the cloud a symbol of grace, and the message is the need for repentance and prayer to God.

Miracle stories in sermons confirmed the message of the preacher. When collected for preachers, they often lost their individuality. This process can be seen in a large collection of Cistercian miracles made at the end of the twelfth century, possibly by the abbot of Eberbach, Conrad. This miracle book, the *Exordium Magnum Cisterciense,* falls into two parts. Five books contain miracles ascribed to various people, most of them Cistercians, who are named; these stories claim to be about events and to be connected with individuals. The sections in the last two books, however, are thematic, and miracles are added as illustrations. For instance, in the first books, the compiler writes about 'The Lord Pons, Fifth Abbot of Clairvaux', 'A senior monk to whom the Lord Jesus appeared on the Vigil of Easter', 'a Brother in whose hand crumbs of bread were turned into most precious pearls', while in the last books he gives long exhortations 'About the dangers of disobedience', 'In praise of patience', etc. These exhortations are in fact sermons, and he uses miracles to illustrate themes. When he describes the dangers of reciting the psalter carelessly, for example, he uses a story from the *Life of St Anno* as illustration and he refers briefly to a Mary miracle. In each case the details are subservient to the preacher's needs, names are replaced by a 'certain nun', 'a certain clerk', and no precise location or time is given.

Such stories were, at the end of the twelfth century, collected into manuals for preachers and separated from the older kind of miracle collection. One such work was the *Dialogus Miraculorum* of Caesarius of Heisterbach, in which wonder stories were grouped under twelve subject headings:

While others are breaking whole loaves to the people, that is, are expounding hard problems of Scripture or writing down the more important occurrences of modern times, I have collected the crumbs that fell and have filled twelve baskets with them for those who are poor not in grace but in learning.

Popular stories were then grouped under headings for sermons of 'conversion', 'contrition', 'confession', and so forth. The stories could be extracted and used according to theme.

By the beginning of the thirteenth century, handbooks for preachers were more common, particularly among the friars who were undertaking popular preaching and needed sources upon which to draw. *Exempla* thought suitable for a preacher's use were fairly clearly defined. Lessons might be drawn from stories told by ancient writers, from natural history, and from the miracles of the saints. Guibert of Nogent, in discussing how a sermon should be put together, insists on the spiritual preparation of the preacher, who is breaking the bread of God in the words he utters for the good of souls:

Prayer precedes preaching, so that the soul, on fire and burning with divine love, speaks of what he has experienced of God, and just as far as he is on fire within, will he inflame the hearts of his hearers.[26]

27

Miracles might be used for illustration, but secular examples were frowned upon, at least for monks. Caesarius of Heisterbach says that in his own monastery, Abbot Gerard once saw that several of the brothers had fallen asleep during his sermon in the chapter house; he at once said, 'There was once a king who was called Arthur . . .'[27] and then rebuked the monks for waking up at the mention of that name.

The sermons of the period fall into two categories: sermons and didactic literature (such as the treatises of Peter Damian, the miracles of the Cistercians, and the writings of Peter the Venerable) for the monastic orders who were expected to show interest in the matter of the sermon, with a few edifying miracles by way of illustration; and sermons for the *illiterati,* those less concerned with theology, whose interest had to be kept by *exempla* to a greater extent. Guibert of Nogent tells preachers to distinguish between the unlettered and the lettered, who would need less in the way of illustration. The *rusticii* and *simplicii,* he says, need *exempla* of an edifying and arresting kind:

Let us endeavour moreover to please the simple folk by including in our sermons stories and deeds of former times and let us present these as part of a many-hued picture.[28]

James of Vitry illustrated his *Sermones Vulgares* liberally with *exempla,* many of them miracle stories, which were later collected into books of *exempla* for other preachers to draw upon.

The aim in sermons, whether for *rusticii* or *monachii,* was to encourage men in the way of salvation. Sometimes this could best be done by stories: 'Many will be stirred by examples who will not be moved by precepts'.[29] Certain stories were particularly favoured by preachers. They used the miracles of the saints in sermons for their festivals and drew upon the miracles of the Virgin to provide interest in sermons for her feasts. They inserted miracles into sermons on the Eucharist. And above all they enlivened sermons with accounts of miraculous visions of heaven and hell. Monastic devotion fed upon stories of the fate of their members in the next world. Popular preaching also introduced the prospect of heaven and hell, described in detail in miraculous visions and set out for the warning and encouragement of the hearers. The close link between the liturgy and the sermon before the coming of the

28

friars gave a certain limitation to the content of sermons, and it is not usual to find miracles used as illustrations at any length. Monastic discourses included stories of miraculous visions of the dead and their discourses on heaven and hell, but the wealth of detail was curtailed by time, even when the sermons were delivered in the chapter house rather than the chapel. An instance of the contrast between how miracles were set out in miracle collections and how they were used in spoken sermons is provided by the story of Theophilus, one of the most famous of the Mary miracles. In collections of Mary miracles, it is set out in great detail, often including imaginary conversations between the protagonists.[30] In a sermon by Fulbert of Chartres,[31] this story is used as the second of two illustrations. The first is a story of the death of Julian the Apostate,[32] also found in Marian collections, and is mentioned to show how Mary hears the prayers of the righteous. The second story, that of Theophilus,[33] is called *notissima,* but is described at no greater length than the first, as an illustration of how Mary helps even the unrighteous:

Even you, O former sinner Theophilus, she snatched by her power from the very jaws of the devil, when you invoked her with repentance.[34]

Neither story is recounted in full, but enough is taken from them to illustrate the point made by the preacher. In this case he presumes that both stories will be known to his hearers and that the mention of them will help his argument.

Commentaries and sermons are not primary sources for miracle stories. A third kind of writing is more closely related to the primary records of miracles and occasionally discusses theory. The men who put together miracle collections had a purpose in doing so, and the prefaces of their collections, though formal and stylized and repeating the same themes, at least show what the miracle collectors supposed their work to be; and at times variations in the prefaces or narrative add to this information.

Augustine of Hippo, in his account of the miracles of St Stephen, sets out the main reasons for presenting posthumous miracles. His account of contemporary miracles at the tombs of saints is in the last book of the *City of God,* which is an account of the *aeterna beatudine* of the *City of God.* God works wonders through prayers offered through his saints in connection with their relics. Augustine says that such wonders should be recorded and publicized to convert unbelievers and strengthen the faith of the Christians:

I have been concerned that such accounts should be published because I saw that signs of divine power like those of older times were now often occurring and I felt that they should not pass into oblivion, unnoticed by the people in general.[35]

He himself caused careful records of local miracles to be kept and publicized, though he adds that these are only a small proportion of the miracles that happened.

These themes occur in later collections. It is usually said that records should be kept for the glory of God:

The goodness and wisdom of our Lord and Saviour is exalted by the prayers of many, and so much more wonderful does he appear when he works wonders through his saints after their death.[36]

They were to be written down and read aloud for conversion and for the increase of faith: 'Unbelievers are excited to believe by miracles, and they also confirm faith, so that wonders animate the faithful and confound unbelievers'. The accounts claimed to be only a fraction of the miracles done by the saints: 'For a new narrator always takes over from the previous one, since there are always new miracles to wonder at'.[37]

Writers often deplore their inability to do justice to such a great theme; and it is usual to say that some great man has commissioned the work, or that it has been undertaken at the prompting, sometimes on the orders of, the writer's community. Reginald of Durham, for instance, wrote at the suggestion of Aelred of Rievaulx; Thomas of Monmouth claimed that Bishop William Turbe and the monks of Norwich, as well as a vision of the founder of the house, Bishop Herbert, urged him to write; Thomas Becket himself appeared to both Benedict and William at Canterbury to reinforce their commission by the monks.

It is clear from these prefaces that the writers were not much concerned with the theory of miracles. The 'how' question was already answered for them. The miracles of a particular saint and a particular

30

shrine existed, and the writers used everything that could be gathered under such a title. The miracles were primarily advertisements for the shrine or the saint, and even the dedications to great men were simply a way of ensuring interest and patronage. The ability of the saint to work miracles was, for a number of reasons, proclaimed by the miracle collection; it would be vain to look there for an interest in the events in relation to probability or doctrine.

There are, however, a few exceptions to this approach. Where there was criticism, writers defended miracles, and sometimes a collector was moved to reflect about a miracle. One particularly striking instance of this is in the account given by William of Canterbury of a knight who lost his horse in the forest of Ponthieu and attributed its recovery to the prayers of St Thomas:

Some would say that the finding of the horse was due to chance and that it had no cause at all. Others would argue that if it had a cause then that cause was directed towards some other end and the recovery of the horse was merely an incidental consequence. There are others who would hold that it was a combination of causes . . . but the truth is that not a leaf falls from a branch without cause, for to admit the power of chance in the physical world is to detract from the power of the Creator. The Creator has so ordered the laws of matter that nothing can happen in his creation except in accordance with his just ordinance, whether good or bad. If we are to seek the cause of things, we must look for the original cause, which is not itself caused by something else. And the original cause, that is, God, is the true cause of the miracle I have just described.[38]

This passage conveys the average expectation about miracles for the period, and it is significant that it comes from the largest collection of miracles, those of St Thomas of Canterbury. In contrast to the new writers who wanted to reserve the explanation of events as miracles until all other causes had been examined, the mainstream of apprehension of events that is found particularly at the great shrines was to see miracle as a normal explanation, and the one to be preferred. Augustine had taught a belief in God under whose hand all nature is potentially miraculous:

How can an event be contrary to nature when it happens by the will of God, since the will of the great Creator assuredly *is* the nature of every created being?[39]

31

This was the basis of the miracle collections of the period. Miraculous explanations of events were preferred to natural ones; God who created and controlled all things was seen as constantly intervening in inexplicable ways, and most obviously in connection with the power of his saints at the places where their relics lay. Abbot Samson expressed the same opinion of causation as William of Canterbury when he described the miracles of St Edmund. After an account of the immediate cure of William Fitzasketil from fever at the shrine, he added that some might think such a cure unnatural from its suddenness:

Someone may marvel at this; but only to those who consider the ordinary laws of matter instead of the nature of the Creator. For if he created the laws of matter in accordance with his will, why should he not alter them whenever he chooses to do so?[40]

This Augustinian approach to miracles expressed in these two shrine collections underlies the accounts of miracles next to be considered. The reflections on miracles and nature that have been observed in the theory of miracles in the period lay mostly outside the actual daily events at shrines where the most unlikely tales were supported with the simple assertion that 'God is glorious in his saints'; the greater the miracle, the more power it demonstrated at that place.[41] Popular expectations of the miraculous in every kind of situation could be focussed on shrines and their saints; they presented a formidable force in evidence of the theory that produced them, and, in a later age, provided material for those with other theories of events and reality to criticize.

3

Miracles at Traditional Shrines:
St Faith, St Benedict and St Cuthbert

THE DISCUSSION OF MIRACLES during the Middle Ages shows above
everything else the acceptance of the miraculous as a basic dimension of
life. The bounds of reality included the unseen in a way alien to modern
thought. Miracles were the rule rather than the exception, and the
concept of the hand of God at work in the whole of life coloured the
perception of miracles and their records. Given this preoccupation with
miracles, it is to be expected that there would be many records of
contemporary miracles. These records provide the main body of material for studying miracles. The largest number of these miracles were
recorded at the shrines of the saints, since virtually every town had its
shrine and frequently someone able to record the miracles.

This large amount of material about miracles reflects the urgent
needs of the living and their trust in the powers of the dead. Needs of
every kind were focussed upon the bones of the saints in their shrines,
the special places on earth where men could be in touch with the saints,
who enjoy the full vision of God and who could therefore be expected to
offer potent and efficacious prayer for those who asked for their intercession. From the evidence produced by the shrines of Europe, I will
present a general outline of this process, before proceeding to a more
detailed examination of certain major shrines where the collections are
both extensive and illuminating.

The relics venerated in the West in this period can be placed in three
groups. First, there were the relics of saints connected with the Bible
and the early church: relics of the true cross, bones of the apostles,
relics of the early Christian martyrs. The hand of St James at Reading
was the chief relic of Reading Abbey in the twelfth century; the tomb

of the Three Kings was central in the cathedral of Cologne; the Holy
Lance formed part of the imperial relic collection; the remains of the
martyrs from the persecutions were venerated in many places. Very
often such relics were connected with the calendar of the church and
were venerated on certain days of liturgical celebration, for instance on
the two feasts of the Holy Cross or the anniversaries of the death of the
martyrs. Such relics would also receive special veneration on the anniversary of their arrival at a shrine or at their translation to a more
important shrine. Though miracles could and did take place at any
time, these days were a focus for the miraculous powers of a saint.
Secondly, a church might also possess the relics of its founder or of a
venerated bishop or abbot in its history. The body of Adalhard, for
instance, was venerated at Corbie; those of the bishops Virgilius,
Hartwic, and Eberhard at their cathedral in Salzburg; while the body of
Edward rested at the centre of his church at Westminster. These relics
also would be venerated, though more locally, on the anniversary of the
person's death and at the relic's translations. Thirdly, the relics of a
modern saint would be venerated on the anniversary of his death in the
place where he was buried, later perhaps also on the anniversary of his
translation. Veneration elsewhere would be rare for some time, and his
acceptance into the calendar of the church perhaps slow, though not
necessarily so; two new saints, Thomas of Canterbury and William of
Norwich, were venerated elsewhere within a few years of their deaths,
William in Reading Abbey and St Thomas as far away as Sicily and
Scandinavia.

The miracles that happened at these shrines were recorded, in many
cases, for at least a brief time after either the death or translation of a
saint; in some cases, the records continued for much longer. They were
written down for the glory of the saint and to advertise his powers to
pilgrims. The end of the records of miracles for a period does not necessarily indicate that the miracles then ceased. The records at some
shrines are continuous, but at others they are more sporadic. The kinds
of miracles will be observed in detail later, but they can be classified in
a general way as acts of power or acts of mercy. In the first class are the
miracles of judgement by which the saint causes pain or loss to someone
who offends him and preserves and favours his devotees. In the second
class are cures of illness. Cures can, in fact, be organized into a pattern
that recurs at shrines everywhere; this pattern was determined partly by

the kinds of illness that were diagnosed, partly by a literary pattern inherited from the Gospels. The pattern of cures was stated in the second century by St Ireneus:

For they are able to give sight to the blind, hearing to the deaf, to put all demons to flight. . . . The infirm, or the lame, or those paralysed, or those disturbed in other parts of the body, are cured; it often happens that those who have contracted some bodily illness or have had some kind of accident, are restored in this way to good health.[1]

This list is repeated universally throughout the Middle Ages.

The miracle-working shrines belonged in a specific sense to the people who lived near them. Those associated with the the monastery and the people of the parish or town had first claim on their saint; beyond that, a local saint could command the veneration of those in the countryside near the shrine. Pilgrims devoted to the saint or attracted by the fame of his local miracles were also devotees at the shrine. All these men, women, and children, from all classes of society, could claim the prayers of the saint. They would come to the shrine at the great festivals of the church, at the festival of the saint in question, or at any time dictated by their own needs; they would pray there, either for a brief time, or through the night, or for days at a time, offering candles, coins, *ex voto* offerings, with prayers for the intercession of the saint. A miracle might have occurred before they came, in which case they would be there to give thanks and make an appropriate offering; it might happen on the way to the church, or inside during their prayers. Sometimes it took place after they had gone home. The miracles would be proclaimed and sometimes recorded by the officials of the shrine, with or without a public thanksgiving. Some miracles, perhaps most, went unrecorded, particularly those that happened to the poor. And for every miracle that took place, there were many more petitioners who went away as they came, with no visible surcease of their needs.

In this period records of miracles at shrines were kept with particular care, without the need that arose later to streamline the collections. The accounts of individual miracles were written down as they were reported to the officials of the shrines, and often rewritten in a literary form by a capable writer. In the formal introductions to collections, it was a convention for the writer to praise the saint, state that his miracles should be made known for the glory of God and the edification of men, suggest that, in spite of his lack of qualifications, he has been urged to undertake the task, and ask the help of the saint in his undertaking. While the influence of individual writers must be taken into account, these collections do reflect the needs and aspirations of the clientele of the shrines. They are, in the 'traditional' period, concerned with the application of the power of the saint to local needs. They emphasize the religious, social, and economic interdependence of the saint and his people. They show how the saint was used to appeal to the supernatural, as the Eucharist was used later. The reverence for the saint and the richness of offerings to him indicate the 'honour' and 'worth' the people attributed to this focus of the supernatural. On the social level, mutual benefits and responsibilities were established between the patron saint and his people, involving not only his intervention in a supernatural fashion in securing good weather and averting natural disaster, but also extending to his intervention in law suits and in the liberation of captives. Economically, the power of the saint through supernatural sanctions helped increase and consolidate the lands held by his shrine as well as providing his church with great wealth through offerings.

The records are more extensive for certain shrines, and I have selected some of those for close analysis. I have divided them into two main groups: The miracle collections at the beginning of this period I call 'traditional'; those later in the period, 'modern'. These categories are by no means mutually exclusive, but a gradual shift of emphasis takes place from one to the other that suggests this period is a watershed between the two.

The shrine of St Faith in Conques in the Rouergue can be considered traditional. St Faith was said to have been born at Agen at the end of the third century and to have suffered martyrdom at the age of twelve in 303 with Bishop Caprais, Prime, and Felician. In the fifth century her remains were transferred to a basilica in Agen by Bishop Dulcidius, and there miracles occurred. Thus, she was a child-martyr of the first centuries of Christian persecution, mentioned in the Roman martyrology and celebrated with a feast on 6 October, long before her remains reached Conques. No record of her miracles at Agen survives, nor is there a record of her life or her cult in any detail until the eleventh century. It is very probable that her miracles as recorded at Conques are the earliest written evidence for her cult anywhere, the other material being part of the cult itself.

There are three main literary records of the cult of St Faith: the *Passion of St Faith*, the *Chanson de Ste Foy*, and the *Miracles*. In the *Passion of St Faith*, several stories have been fused into one from accounts of martyrdom in the fourth century, and this was done no earlier than the eleventh century.[2] The *Passion* is therefore a product of the cult rather than a cause, though the recognition of St Faith as an ancient martyr is itself older. The *Chanson* also is a result of the cult; it is a dramatic account of the *Passion of St Faith* in verse and may have been sung and also used as a dance, particularly on her feast day.[3] The oldest written record of the cult is the *Miracles of St Faith*.

The Cluniac monastery in Conques claimed in the eleventh century that in 883 one of its monks, Aronisde, had stolen the relics of St Faith from Agen. It was said that he was sent from Conques to join the canons at the shrine of St Faith in Agen with the intention of stealing the relics. After ten years he was left in charge of the shrine and at once removed the relics and fled with them to Conques, where they were rehoused in the abbey church of the Saviour.[4] Like similar thefts, this was regarded as a *sanctum sacriligium, fidele furtum* and given the widest possible publicity. The story was meant to prove that the relics were truly those of St Faith, a matter of far greater importance than the question of the theft. This story was current in the eleventh century, and the church that received the relics was soon known as the church of St Faith, rather than by its previous dedication.

The relics of St Faith were enclosed in the head of a statue that was henceforth the focus of her veneration at Conques. This statue appears in the miracles as more than a symbol for the monks of the intercession of their saint. St Faith was imagined as the living, present, and powerful patron of the monks of Conques, located in a specific place by the relics in her statue. The compiler of the miracles says that some people even thought the statue was alive and looking at them. The saint assumed a visible place in the affairs of the monastery. In disputes about land she had her advocate in the civil courts; her statue was brought to the councils of the church to assist the proceedings; in case of disaster, it was carried to bless the affected area; it was even carried at the charge to quell a riot in the cloisters.[5] In an age when the property of monasteries was scattered and difficult to defend and therefore increasingly at the mercy of rapacious neighbours, such supernatural sanctions focussed on the saint as patron were vital to survival, and miracles of vengeance a necessary deterrent. On the other hand, the consequence of a monastery was affirmed through the glory, visible to all, of its saint, and for this assertion to be known, the saint was not only decked in gold and jewels but carried through the streets preceded by her own band.[6] As the saint protected the monks, so the monks owed service to their saint. An ex-soldier, Gimon, slept in his armour near the statue and defended her with ferocious ill-humour against robbers.[7]

But St Faith's power was not limited to the monks; she provided a focus also for the loyalties of the knights of the countryside,[8] insofar as such loyalties did not conflict with the interests of the monastery. In a country of small isolated castles constantly at war, the influence of the saint was frequently sought to redress the balance of power in favour of one or another. For this reason, St Faith was constantly asked to perform miracles in the deliverance of captives, which she did as much by encouraging their natural ingenuity through dreams as by direct supernatural intervention. Such captives would pray to St Faith, receive her advice in a vision, and if they escaped thereafter they would bring their fetters to Conques and tell their story. They do not seem to have lingered at the shrine, from which it seems proper to assume that deliverance by the saint was not held to constitute any greater immunity from recapture than any other form of escape.

This local loyalty to St Faith took another form that is itself proof of the depth of feeling experienced for this ancient and obscure child-martyr. She was sometimes seen in visions in the form of her statue, but more often she appeared to the local knights as a pretty young girl, engagingly feminine and demanding trinkets of various kinds. This picture is at variance both with the forbidding and archaic statue and with the idea of an early Christian martyr; it springs from the needs and imagination of the knights of the Rouergue. This myth that St Faith demanded jewelry was called by the miracle writer *joca;* it is the application of the miraculous to trivia. It was an image forceful enough for a woman pilgrim to leave her jewelry at home before visiting the shrine, though to no effect.[9] This aspect of the cult of St Faith foreshadows some aspects of the cult of the Virgin. Like Mary, St Faith was endowed by her devotees with capricious power, and a greater concern with devotion to herself than with the rules of society. She helped her people 'juste an injuste'[10] and gave her assistance often to the least deserving. In one miracle, which foreshadows the famous Mary miracle Eppo the Thief,[11] St Faith supported for several days on the gallows a man devoted to her, until he was taken down alive and set free.[12]

St Faith was also the intercessor for a wider circle. Pilgrims visited her shrine and prayed for her help. For them she was one of the great saints of heaven who had access to God and could be asked to intercede with him. The majority of such pilgrims came from France, indeed from the district around Conques. They were petty knights, minor land-holders, priests of the district, monks, and clerks. Men, women, and children came to the shrine, though there was a high proportion of men in its clientele. Peasants are mentioned only once when they tried to demand admittance to the shrine,[13] while at the other end of the social scale there is no record of kings, popes, cardinals, or bishops patronising St Faith. It was predominantly a local shrine, even when its devotees were not directly dependent on the monastery.

The cult of St Faith spread to Spain from Conques,[14] because Conques was on one of the direct routes to Compostela.[15] Her cult was also established in England in the twelfth century by Robert Fitzwalter and his wife Sybilla, who visited Conques in 1100. They took home two monks, Bernard and Gerald, to found the monastery of St Faith at Horsham in Norfolk; this was confirmed to the abbot of Conques by Henry I.[16]

At Conques itself the miracles show a great and elaborate cult in process. The statue was above the High Altar, not in the crypt, and pilgrims were allowed at all times to have access to it; there are descriptions of vigils all night when the sick lay before the statue in the church. When the statue was taken out in procession, it was accompanied by the monks and preceded by music; such a procession might last all day, with the monks saying their offices and eating meals by the wayside.[17] Cures might occur for those watching, or even at a place where the statue had rested. Offerings were made to the statue and increased its splendour; miracles were recorded at the shrine, though in a somewhat haphazard fashion.

The miracle collection itself achieved literary form between 1013 and 1020. Bernard of Angers was a student under Fulbert of Chartres early in the eleventh century; from him he heard St Faith praised for her miracles. He visited the chapel dedicated to St Faith near Chartres.[18]

Bernard and his fellow students found the accounts of her miracles barbarous and superstitious, notably lacking in moral content, and indeed, as has already been shown, Bernard was always to think this of some of them. He heard the criticisms of the miracles and decided to visit Conques and sift them for himself, which he did in three visits. As a result, he wrote two books of miracles, drawing his material from the *scedula* of the shrine and from the personal witness of the monks and of those cured. His work was continued by a monk of Conques who added two more books of miracles. Between them they cover nearly fifty years, from 1013 to 1060.

The kind of criticism Bernard records about the shrine is two-fold. First, the statue was said to be an idol, and secondly, the miracles were said to be incredible. The Golden Majesty of St Faith still exists at Conques and dates from the tenth century. Before that period the bones of saints were kept in caskets engraved and ornamented; these could be kept under the altar or carried about in procession; the requirement for relics to consecrate an altar increased this custom.[19] In the eleventh century relics began to be kept in statues and later in busts of the saints to whom they belonged; a further development was to place the relic in a container shaped like itself, the most obvious example being reliquaries which were crosses shaped to hold fragments of the True Cross. The earliest record of a statue for relics is that of the Virgin, which was made of wood and covered with gold for Clermont Cathedral by Bishop Stephan in *c.* 946; later, as abbot of Conques he enshrined the relics of St Faith in a statue in the form of a seated woman, which could be carried about. It was plated with gold and covered with jewels and given a casket to hold. It was so rich in appearance that it caused an onlooker to wish that it would fall in the mud so that he might secure some of its jewels.[20] These seated majesties, images in three dimensions, aroused adverse comment, such as the indignant remark of a companion of Bernard after seeing the statue:

What do you think, brother, of this idol? If it were of Jupiter or of Mars they would not think such a statue worth very much.[21]

The fact that it was compared to a classical statue is significant; the iconoclastic theories of the age of Charlemagne were still current in the West, and statues were regarded as pagan idols. The symbols appropriate for Christians were the cross, the Bible, and the church itself. Bernard says that in his own opinion, the saints should be represented only by paintings or written descriptions. He himself approached the statue of St Faith with a carefully worded prayer: 'St Faith, part of whose body is present here enshrined in this likeness, help me in the day of judgement'. In a chapter devoted to the statue, Bernard says that such statues were a local custom:

It is an old usage and an ancient custom in the whole country of the Auvergne, whether in the Rouergue or Toulouse, and in all the country around, for a statue to be set up either of gold or silver or of some other metal, in which the head of the saint or some other part of the body is preserved with reverence.[22]

He adds, however, that others thought this a superstition and a way of preserving the cult of demons. He mentions the Majesty of St Gerald that was placed over his altar at Aurillac and says that the Majesties of St Maurius and St Amans were brought to attend the Synod of Rodez between 1025 and 1031, as well as that of St Faith. This is the last time that any qualms were expressed about statues as reliquaries in miracle collections, and it marks the cult of St Faith as the last of an older and more reticent era.

The best known miracle of St Faith was the highly-coloured tale of repeated cures of blindness in a local man, Witbert. Bernard's account of this miracle illustrates his approach to the whole collection of miracles at this shrine. When he heard the story, he was sceptical: 'I did not', he says, 'easily believe it',[23] and when allowance has been made for using doubt as a literary device to heighten wonder, this story would strain credulity in any age. Bernard, in fact, undertook writing the collections because he thought such rough material safer if handled by a scholar and by someone from outside the monastery.[24] Written records of all kinds were becoming popular, and his offer to write down the miracles was accepted with enthusiasm. Bernard placed Witbert's story first in his collection and told it at some length. Witbert still lived at Conques and told Bernard his story himself. He said that as a youth his guardian had suspected him of adultery with his wife and had blinded him; he attributed his cure to prayer for many years to St Faith; subsequently, he twice lost his sight and had it restored. The details he added increased the drama of the tale. His eyes, he said, were torn out and two birds flew off with them; later they returned the eyes to his

eyesockets.[25] Bernard recorded other cures by St Faith, though none
with the style and exaggeration of Witbert. St Faith cured people, and
she also cured animals; she was capable of the ultimate 'cure' of raising
the dead. She freed captives; she punished her detractors; her sanction
controlled weather, plague, and warfare; she demanded jewelry and
miraculously obtained what she wanted. Bernard made such stories
acceptable to the theologically informed by allegorizing them, in the
same way that other writers commented on the miracles of Scripture. In
the case of Witbert's story, Bernard explains a discrepancy, in which
Witbert said that the birds that flew off with his eyes were white and
others said black. Bernard offers a parallel with the biblical story of
Elijah and the ravens and asserts that the birds were white to the righteous Witbert and black to his persecutors. Similarly, faced with a story
of St Faith raising a dead mule to life, a story that appeared to some of
his contemporaries as pointless a miracle as it does to us, Bernard gave
it respectability by saying that it prefigured the resurrection of the
flesh. Earlier collectors of miracles, such as St Gregory and Bede, had
dealt with similar tales this way. Incredulity about a miracle was re-
solved not by a reference to facts or evidence but by a closer examination of the tale's significance.

Under the Latinity and theological reflection of Bernard, the miracles of St Faith at Conques retain a crude and primitive air. They are
miracles for the protection of the monks, the extension of their lands,
and the aggrandisement of their church through their saint. They are
set firmly in the countryside that housed the saint and take their colour
from the needs and aspirations of the surrounding population. St Faith
is seen as the protector of her own people, as great a lord as any in the
countryside. The miracles of St Faith assert her consequence as a protector, and also the consequence of those associated with her; the pilgrims
who asked for her protection and aid extended her power of patronage.

The miracles of St Benedict of Nursia were recorded at the two
centres that claimed to possess his relics, Monte Cassino and Fleury.
The local cult of St Benedict's relics was to some extent the same as for
St Faith. The collections of his miracles, however, cover a longer period
of time, and some changes can be observed within them. The miracles
of St Benedict were first recorded by Gregory the Great at the end of

the sixth century; those at Monte Cassino by Abbot Desiderius in the mid-eleventh century; and those at Fleury by several writers from the end of the ninth century until the beginning of the twelfth. This collection of miracles therefore covers more years than any other in Europe. It might be thought that St Benedict would inevitably have a wider and less localized cult than that of St Faith, since he was not only the founder of a particular monastery but the patron of all monks following his Rule. This was not, however, the case. St Anselm might pray to St Benedict as 'advocate of monks'[26] and the devotion of monks might recognize his importance for them as such, but the miracles of St Benedict centred primarily on the places that claimed his relics. His cult, especially at Fleury, was deeply influenced by local social and economic factors. The new influences noticeable in these miracles at the end of this period are not due to a recognition of St Benedict as founder of western monasticism, but to more localized changes.

My discussion of the miracles of St Benedict will focus on the posthumous miracles in the eleventh and twelfth centuries at the local shrines of Monte Cassino and Fleury. I will, however, look briefly first at the tradition of miracles of St Benedict that was established by Gregory in his record of miracles during the saint's life, since the later miracles were influenced by them. In addition, I will examine the cult of St Benedict in relation to the chief monastery following the Rule of St Benedict at the time, Cluny, to see how this cult developed at a monastery that did not have any relics of the saint.

The miracles of St Benedict, as presented by Gregory in the second book of *Dialogues,* claim to be an account given to the pope by four of St Benedict's first disciples ('I will relate a few of the things which I have learned from his disciples').[27] Gregory's own prologue and the letter he wrote to Bishop Maximian of Syracuse[28] indicate that a community, the papal household, urged him to write the *Dialogues.* The work was meant to encourage contemporary Christians by reflecting on the wonders of God in their own time. It takes the form of a dialogue with an interlocutor, Peter the Deacon. The second book is devoted to the life and miracles of St Benedict: 'There was a man of venerable life, Benedict both by name and by grace, who from his youth upwards had the mind of a mature man'.[29] The miracles he records are those familiar in hagiography: 'dreams, visions, insight so acute that it seemed prophetic, and the assistance obtained by prayer for every kind of need'. Finally, he describes the death of Benedict and says he was buried in the same tomb as his sister, Scholastica:[30] 'He is buried in the chapel of St John the Baptist, which he had built when he pulled down the altar of Apollo'.[31] The *Dialogus Miraculorum* of Desiderius, five centuries later, continued this account of miracles, but this time they were the posthumous miracles of the saint. The book is modelled in more than title on the *Dialogues* of Gregory. Desiderius, the abbot of Monte Cassino, says in his preface that he was urged to write by the community around him and that he undertook this for the same reasons as those that made Gregory write: 'I will take care to set out the story for the edification of readers'.[32] Like Gregory, Desiderius cast his work in the form of a dialogue with an interlocutor, 'Theophilus the Deacon'. Desiderius uses other sources for his material, but the *Dialogues* of Gregory are frequently behind his account of miracles. In one instance he explicitly draws a parallel: 'The blessed Benedict by his merits restored our hammer to us, as he once rescued the iron of a certain Goth'.[33]

There is, however, a fundamental difference between the miracles of St Benedict recorded by Gregory and those by Desiderius: Gregory was presenting a certain kind of sanctity, that of the *vir dei,* the *sanctus abbas,* father of monks and writer of a rule for monks. Desiderius, on the other hand, was abbot of the monastery of St Benedict and responsible for many monks and wide possessions; the monks were not only spiritual sons but also tenants of St Benedict, and for this reason his power was invoked more frequently than his holiness. The miracles recorded by Desiderius illustrate the power of St Benedict as patron, like those of St Faith at Conques. In six instances this is particularly clear. St Benedict is said to have saved his monastery from the first attacks of the barbarians by punishing the attackers;[34] he protected his monastery when fire threatened it;[35] Pandulf of Capua was punished with exceptional severity by a sentence of everlasting and irreversible damnation for his devastations of the monastic lands;[36] when a monk ran away from the monastery he was so alarmed by an encounter with the devil outside its walls that he returned to the protection of St Benedict;[37] thieves who broke into the monastery were miraculously caught and punished; a Norman who interfered with a fisherman of the monastery at work was also punished.[38]

The theme of the power of St Benedict is dominant in these miracles; it seems to have extended to cures of illness relatively rarely. Desiderius mentions the tomb of St Benedict 'on the right of the altar' and describes it as a centre for devotion. When describing one cure there he mentions others by St Benedict: 'They heard that many oppressed with diverse diseases were restored to their former health at the threshold',[39] a generality common in miracle collections. He gives only two instances of such cures. In one case the monk John, who was thought to be a demoniac and was confined to the infirmary, went to pray at the tomb of St Benedict and came away cured. More detail is given in the second instance: Desiderius says he heard the story from the monk Smaragdus who claimed to have heard it from his uncle the priest Leo. The monk Antony, 'no mediocre scholar in both secular and sacred learning', was once ill after an accident and seemed in need of surgery:

He went to the tomb of blessed Benedict, to implore his mercy, hoping that he who was his patron would cure him. As soon as he entered the church he prostrated himself before the altar and prayed at length that almighty God would deign to grant him healing by the merits of such a great father.

He also collected dust from the tomb and placed it on the injured part, 'and the next day he was restored to health'.[40] The localization at the tomb of the saint and the use of dust from the tomb, as well as prayer prostrate before it, are typical of the healing shrines and indicate that the tomb of St Benedict at Monte Cassino was used in this way. But the majority of miracles of St Benedict in this collection are not cures; where cures are described, they are generally connected with other saints, such as St Maur, St Leo, and St John of Beneventum.

Monte Cassino was where St Benedict lived and had been buried. It had first claim to be the centre for veneration of the saint and it continued to be so. Peter Damian, for instance, when thinking of a visit there commended himself to the protection of St Benedict for the journey.[41] At the rebuilding of the monastic church by Desiderius, an examination of the graves found beneath it was undertaken and two bodies were said to be those of St Benedict and St Scholastica, despite the claims of Fleury.[42] Peter the Deacon described miracles continuing at this place and asserted that St Benedict remained there, no matter where his bones lay, since after burial his flesh had decayed into the ground at Monte Cassino.[43] The local tradition was for the power of St Benedict in that place; the tradition of veneration for him there survived even the abundance of miracles connected with his relics in another place.

The 'other place' was the monastery of Fleury on the Loire. The miracles of St Benedict recorded by Gregory were those of a living saint, those at Monte Cassino were those of the acknowledged founder and patron of the monastery. There had been no need to prove that St Benedict could work miracles in Italy. At Fleury the need before anything else was to prove that the monastery did indeed hold the relics of St Benedict; it had no other specific claim on his power as a saint.

To establish this claim, as in the case of the relics of St Faith at Conques, Fleury asserted that the relics of St Benedict had been stolen from his acknowledged resting place at Monte Cassino. The oldest account of this transference states that after Monte Cassino had been devastated by the Lombards at the end of the seventh century, a French priest who visited the ruins found the bodies of St Benedict and his sister and took them back to France where there were buried with honour at Fleury.[44] Two centuries later, Adrevald of Fleury composed a more elaborate account, filled with visions and miracles, all intended to show that St Benedict had encouraged the translation and that it had in fact taken place. He says that Mommold, first abbot of Fleury, inspired by a vision, sent the monk Aigulf to Italy to find and recover the body of St Benedict. He was joined by two monks from Le Mans looking for the body of St Scholastica.[45] At Monte Cassino they discovered, by the aid of miracles, the two bodies and took them back to France on a journey accompanied by miracles and cures. In a dream, the abbot of Fleury was directed to bury the body of St Benedict in the church of St Mary.[46] The claim to keep the relics was fiercely disputed by the monks of Monte Cassino. In the reign of Pope Zacharias, the monks of Monte Cassino demanded the return of the relics, and Carloman came to Fleury with letters from the pope ordering the restitution. According to Adrevald, the body remained at Fleury, and the petition failed.[47] In the eleventh century Andrew of Fleury records a vision of Richard, abbot of Monte Cassino, in which he was told by St Benedict that his body rested at Fleury but his favour was equally distributed between the two monasteries, 'so they both remain one in glory, one in foresight; one in care, one in defence'.[48]

The record of the theft of the relics, however elaborated, was not enough in itself to establish Fleury's claims so strongly that they were allowed even by Monte Cassino. What asserted more than anything else that the body of St Benedict was indeed at Fleury was the fact of

46

miracles at that place. The record of such miracles continued to assert the validity of the relics. They were those of a powerful patron, and what they chiefly proclaimed was the power of the saint at his French shrine.

The first book of miracles was written by Adrevald, who also wrote the account of the translation, around 870. He provides a link with the previous tradition as recorded by Gregory. The miracles he describes take their tone from the specific needs of the monastery in the ninth century. He sets them against the disturbed political background of the times, under the last of the Carolingians and through the Norman invasions. This reference to outside events was a feature of each of these books of the miracles of St Benedict at Fleury, and helps to give them their local focus. The miracles Adrevald recounts are predominantly ones of vengeance and power. In seven instances the anger of St Benedict is experienced by local knights who attack the lands of Fleury; in three cases St Benedict shows special favour toward dependents of the monastery. Adrevald compares St Benedict to Jehovah, as the leader and protector of his own people.[49] As with St Faith, his power extends to the actual protection of the shrine and its goods. Christian, a monk of Fleury, guarded the shrine and could be as angry with the saint as Gimon at Conques was with St Faith. Adrevald mentions several cures, all of local people or of monks of Fleury, 'at the threshold of the tomb of the confessor of Christ, Benedict'.[50] After this, it is the power of St Benedict that dominates the miracles until the twelfth century, when cures again are prominent.

Adelarius of Fleury adds two miracles to Adrevald's account, both of which show the protection exercised by St Benedict toward his monastery during the Norman invasions. The account necessarily lapsed during the disturbances of the tenth century and was taken up again in the reign of Abbot Abbo by the monk Aimon, about the year 1000.[51] Aimon continues to emphasize the theme of the harsh judgement of St Benedict toward the enemies of his monastery. He gives nine instances in his first book of local knights and of rural land-owners punished for proceeding against St Benedict. In the second book, he gives five more such examples. St Benedict is presented as favouring his monks and his dependents and as a stern enemy to their opponents. Only two miracles in the first book and four in the second are cures; these are of local people and workmen at the monastery.

Despite the re-emphasis in Aimon's account of the power of St Benedict as lord of Fleury, two new features emerge. The first is the growth of Fleury as a centre for pilgrimage, and the increasing need to centralize the miracles of St Benedict around his relics. The stories show a great concourse of pilgrims around the shrine; a hospice for pilgrims is mentioned; night vigils, offerings of candles and coins are established features of the scene. The relics had been transferred to an altar in the crypt for the convenience of pilgrims.[52] The power of the saint is shown as available for devotees at his shrine as well as for the monks and their dependents. Secondly, Aimon links the miracles of St Benedict with Mary. Presumably out of personal devotion to the Virgin, Aimon includes her name with that of St Benedict as the saint responsible for half the miracles he records. This association continues in the later books of miracles at Fleury, and is symptomatic of the increase of Marian devotion at the time.

Aimon ceased to record the miracles in 1042 and they were continued by Andrew, another monk of Fleury.[53] He wrote four books of sixty-six chapters, though the period of time they cover is only fifteen years. The books by Andrew are much more a chronicle of events at Fleury than a record of shrine miracles for St Benedict. He records matters of local interest, wars and disputes, that involved the monastery; he deals with events at places connected with Fleury, in Aquitaine, Brittany, Die, and Spain. He includes accounts of miracles by other saints, for instance St Posen (whose relics were transferred to Fleury), St Martin, St Peter, and St Paul, as well as those of St Michael at a favourite shrine of the Normans at Monte Gargano.[54] Several miracles are connected with Mary as well as St Benedict. Like other monastic chroniclers, he inserts records of omens and wonders in the heavens, eclipses, shooting stars, cloud formations of unusual shapes, as presages of disasters such as plague, famine, flood, or war. Moreover, Andrew's style is ornate and rhetorical; he makes the miracles occasions for preaching and drawing out lessons.

Yet there is still a nucleus of miracles of St Benedict in this more diffuse collection of material. Six stories are told of cures at the shrine. Three demoniacs, one paralytic, a blind man, and a cripple came there and were cured by prayer to St Benedict. Andrew mentions vigils at the tomb, with offerings of candles. He also says that the relics were still taken out in procession when plague ravaged the neighbourhood, and that many were cured by the presence of St Benedict in his relics among them. Other miracles of St Benedict record the punishments attributed to him; seventeen stories deal with the fate of local landholders who in some way offended the saint by attacks, trespass, mockery, or harm to the saint's dependents. In one case, a serf, Stabilis, ran away from the monastery and established himself for some years elsewhere as a free man; a dream of St Benedict, however, ensured that he should resume his servile status and return to the monastery.[55] Punishments were also recorded of those who worked on the feast days of the saint. It is a catalogue of the dangers of a violent society, in which calamity was usual and in which recourse was had to the local saint.[56] In these four books of miracles by Andrew, the depiction of St Benedict as a great landholder, a fierce protector of his property, received new dimensions. The miracles at the shrine for the pilgrims continue; the sick are healed of various diseases from the minor to the horrific. But the sensationalism is supplied by accounts of pitched battles in which the monks claimed to win by the power of St Benedict, by litigation in which they also triumphed, by defence of the monastery with the battle cry of 'Sancte Benedicte!',[57] and by protection of monastic goods. When thieves tried to steal wine from the abbey cellars, for example, they found it frozen in its barrels.[58] These books record the place of the local saint in the daily affairs of a rough and ready society.

Ralph of Tortaire, the next monk of Fleury to continue this account of the miracles of St Benedict, wrote his account in verse as well as in prose. He continued the book into the first years of the twelfth century, with forty-eight chapters in all.[59] Like Andrew, he recorded events in the countryside as well as miracles at the shrine. However, the shrine was still the centre of local devotion at Fleury and for the people of the valley of the Loire. Ralph records more cures there than any of his predecessors and gives instances of the mad, dumb, and crippled lying in the crypt awaiting cures before the relics. He mentions the use of 'saint vinage', the water in which the relics had been dipped, which was given to the sick to drink and to pour over their maimed parts, or to take away. Miracles of vengeance still predominate. Ralph gives seventeen instances of the punishments that befell those who offended the saint or harmed his possessions. He includes animals, dogs, cows, pigs, and birds such as peacocks who were also 'punished' by the saint. Fleury was still a great monastery ruled by an all-powerful patron.

49

The last miracles in the collection were recorded by the monk Hugh of St Mary,[60] who added eleven miracles in 1118; the collection ends there, perhaps from a break in the manuscript. These stories differ from earlier ones. Apart from the first miracle, an account of the deliverance of a captive, they are all cures. The cures happened at the shrine and are recorded in detail, with names, dates, diseases, and the manner of the cure. Hugh was also responsible for several capitals in the church that show the miracles of St Benedict. One instance from Hugh's record will demonstrate how similar these cures were to those at other healing shrines and how different from the usual miracles of St Benedict (best described thus: 'He deserved his punishment since his pride had led him to oppose the friend of God'[61]):

There was also a woman of that town called Hosanna; on that same night she lay prostrate before the high altar asking for healing for her hand and arm. For it was a very grave sickness, which had taken all the strength from her hand and from her arm, so that . . . she could not clench her fist. When she had prayed for a long time to the Creator for divine help, she was cured and was as if she had never felt ill.[62]

The miracles of St Benedict achieved their primary purpose of focussing devotion to St Benedict on Fleury, where his body was buried. Relations between Cluny and Monte Cassino were, in the eleventh century, cordial: Hugh of Cluny visited Monte Cassino in 1083 and established a confraternity between the two abbeys;[63] Peter Damian visited and admired the life at both monasteries.[64] But the veneration of the Cluniacs for St Benedict's relics was focussed on Fleury. The feast of the translation of the body of St Benedict was celebrated at Cluny in the eleventh century,[65] and Peter the Venerable supplied a new hymn for it in the twelfth. The vital contact between the two monasteries had been made when Odo of Cluny became abbot of Fleury. John of Salerno says that Odo was called, elected, and preordained to be abbot of Fleury by St Benedict himself. He records a miracle story in which St Benedict was seen to leave Fleury in person, because of the disobedience of the monks; the monks 'rode round on their horses to find him and bring him back'. St Benedict, according to this story, had said he would send them an abbot 'from Aquitaine', whom they recognized as Odo. During Odo's abbacy, St Benedict appeared in visions, supporting his reforms, and he appeared also to Odo himself while he was keeping vigil 'before the body of the saint'. It seems from this account that the body of St Benedict had been removed from Fleury during the Norman invasions and was restored, amid miracles, at this time.[66] That the monks of Cluny believed Fleury to be the miracle-working shrine containing St Benedict's body indicates the importance attained by this shrine through the long record of miracles there.

The shrine of St Benedict drew pilgrims from France, but not from much further away. Ralph mentions a boy from Italy brought for a cure, but most visitors were local. The great emphasis on vengeance against local knights remained a distinctive feature of the cult, as with St Faith at Conques. It is possible to see the cult emerging from a localized, power-centred cult, dominated by concern for the social and political place of the monastery, into a shrine for pilgrims who asked not for vengeance but for mercy and for cures of sickness. Royal persons do not seem to have frequented the shrine in this period; it was of interest mostly to the monks of the abbey and people of the locality.

The miracles of St Benedict at Fleury have their main record in the *Historia Miraculorum*. The church at Fleury, however, also contains a record of some of the miracles of St Benedict in the carving on certain capitals, some of which can be assigned to the twelfth century and the last writer of the miracle stories, Hugh of St Mary. Like the stained glass at Canterbury, these carvings are not an independent source for the miracles, but they do provide a further illustration of the importance of the miracles to the monastery; they are also evidence of the continuity between miracles of St Benedict recorded by Gregory and those known at Fleury. Four of the carvings represented here illustrate miracles found in the *Dialogues* of Gregory. Another carving shows the translation of the relics of St Benedict from Monte Cassino to Fleury.

The southwest pillar at the south crossing has three faces carved with scenes from the life of St Benedict (the fourth face forms part of the arch). The left face is broken and indecipherable. The right face contains a carving of St Benedict seated in his cave at Subiaco; outside, the monk Romanus prays to him; the devil is depicted breaking the bell Romanus was accustomed to ring to tell the saint his food supply was ready. The centre shows a building considerably defaced, possibly the cave of St Benedict at Subiaco.

On the lintel over the north door of the nave a carving shows the translation of the relics of St Benedict from Monte Cassino to

51

I   ST BENEDICT TEMPTED BY THE DEVIL IN THE FORM OF A WOMAN.
From the capitals in the abbey of St Benoît sur Loire, Fleury. *Dialogues* of St
Gregory 2. 2.

2   ST BENEDICT AND TOTILLA THE HUN. Fleury capitals. *Dialogues* of St Gregory 2. 15.

3   ST BENEDICT DELIVERS A CAPTIVE. Fleury capitals. *Dialogues* of St Gregory 2. 29.

4   HUGH OF ST MARY AND HIS FAMILY. Fleury capitals. The author of the last book of the *Miracles of St Benedict* also carved the capitals at Fleury that depict the same theme. Here he shows himself as a monk holding a book, with his family, including his parents who are dead, and his brother, the knight Cleopas.

Fleury—a further assertion that Fleury actually has the relics of the saint. It was completed in 1218. Under a carving of Christ in Majesty are four scenes. On the left a monk removes the relics from their grave; in the centre, cures are effected by the bones of both St Benedict and St Scholastica on the journey; on the right, the monks carry the relics of St Benedict toward Fleury.

The third collection of miracles at a 'traditional' shrine is that of St Cuthbert, abbot and bishop of Lindisfarne. The collection supplies further details of shrines typical of the early part of the period under consideration. The records of miracles of the child-martyr St Faith at Conques illustrate the kind of cult that developed around relics of an early Christian martyr when they were transferred to Northern Europe. The records of the miracles of St Benedict, the greatest of all Western monastic founders, provide much information because of the length of time they covered. The miracles of St Cuthbert are those of a seventh-century monk-bishop. While the collection does not have the same continuity as that of St Benedict, it shows how the veneration of a holy man that started in his lifetime gained new emphasis in later records, especially in the eleventh and twelfth centuries. This pattern of a *vir dei*—a great and holy man in an abbey or diocese, whose reputation for sanctity was recognized during his life and fostered by his community after his death, veneration of whom became focussed on his relics and evolved into a new cult through the miracles there—was repeated on a lesser scale all over Western Europe in this period. The records of St Cuthbert's miracles show this development particularly clearly.

The earliest life of St Cuthbert was written about 699, probably by a monk of Lindisfarne; this *Anonymous Life* represents the consensus of opinion about St Cuthbert in his own monastery after his death. Bede wrote his *Vita Sancti Cuthberti* and the *Vita Metrica* in the same tradition; he also gives an account of St Cuthbert in his *Ecclesiastical History*. The *Historia de Sancto Cuthberto,* written by an anonymous monk in the mid-tenth century, tells how the monks of Lindisfarne wandered with the coffin of St Cuthbert for seven years following their expulsion from Lindisfarne by the Danes. In the eleventh century, the account was continued in the *Historia Dunelmensis Ecclesiae,* often ascribed to Symeon of Durham; a twelfth-century account records in detail the examination of the relics of St Cuthbert in 1104. Finally, Reginald of Durham wrote a long account of the miracles of St Cuthbert in the twelfth century. William of Malmesbury also mentions his miracles. While the main part of this record of miracles to be discussed is that by Reginald, we must look first at the earlier accounts that established a pattern in the veneration of St Cuthbert.

The accounts of miracles during the lifetime of St Cuthbert in the *Anonymous Life* are those usual in hagiography. They are related to virtues, particularly the monastic virtue of obedience; they show the control the saint exercised over the elements and over animals and birds; they illustrate his insight and prophetic vision. Biblical parallels are drawn, and because of the miracles accompanying his preaching as bishop, St Cuthbert is compared to the apostles whose preaching was confirmed *in signis et prodigiis* (Acts 2:43). This collection, as well as Bede's account, contains few wonder-tales. But the end of the *Anonymous Life* shows already a difference of approach: the centre of the future cult of St Cuthbert is established as the incorrupt body of the saint: 'His body remained incorrupt, resting as though asleep in his stone coffin, and so they placed him with honour in the church'.[67]

The body of St Cuthbert was the glory first of Lindisfarne, then of Durham, and it became the focus for the posthumous cult of St Cuthbert. Eleven years after his death, the tomb was opened and his body found to be undecayed. Miracles followed at once. A father brought his demoniac son to Lindisfarne, not because of the fame of the shrine, but so that the monks, famous as doctors, might try to cure him. When they failed, the priest Tydi took some soil from the ground where water had been thrown that had washed the body of the saint, mixed it with water and gave it to the boy to drink: 'As soon as the boy had tasted the holy water, he ceased from his ravings that very night'.[68]

A paralysed boy, also brought to the monks as doctors, asked to put on the shoes of the saint, which he did and was cured. Another man, a monk from the household of Bishop Willibald, fell ill while visiting Lindisfarne and asked to pray before the tomb, where he was cured. The miracles were cures at the tomb and they took their pattern from the shrine-cures of the saints rather than from the life of St Cuthbert.

These miraculous cures provide a typical instance of the change from veneration for a living saint to a posthumous cult at his tomb. It is clear from these stories that in sickness other methods of cure would be used: charms, natural medicine, or, as in this case, appeal to doctors who were also monks. The medical reputation of the monks had drawn two of the patients to the monastery. It was the sick themselves, not the monks, who suggested that they try the powers of the saint. That the requests of those in need, where every other remedy has failed, were made without any prompting, was held to provide, whether in fact or as a literary device, special evidence of the saint's sanctity. The dead man is thus shown to be a saint, and at the same time devotion to him is focussed at the place where his body rests. With St Cuthbert, these three posthumous cures initiated his later cult.

Bede continued the hagiographical tradition of Lindisfarne in his work about St Cuthbert. He stressed even more than the anonymous writer the virtues of the saint and showed that his miracles during his life were part of a long tradition of bibilical sanctity. For Bede, the question about a saint's miracles was not how they happened, but why. The 'how' question was already answered: God was acting through all his creation, and what provoked wonder was a particularly interesting message from God that must be examined and deciphered.[69] Therefore in rewriting the miracles of St Cuthbert, Bede stresses the meaning to be found in them for the reader. One instance of a miracle during St Cuthbert's life reflects in a particularly vivid way Bede's attitude to the miracles he records. A girdle belonging to St Cuthbert was used by the abbess Aelfleda to cure herself and one of her nuns. After a few days, the girdle miraculously disappeared from its box. Bede is in no way interested in the disappearance itself; he does not see it as a warning or a punishment for disbelief. He suggests that it was done by the will of God to avoid the situation where any of the many sick applying for a cure might be disappointed and blame the saint for a failure:

If the girdle had always been there, sick people would always have wished to flock to it, and when perhaps one of them did not deserve to be healed of his infirmity, he would disparage its power because it did not heal him, when really he was not worthy of being healed.[70]

The possibility of cures is linked to the merits of the applicant, and the absence of the relic is as edifying to the reader as its presence. This explanation contrasts, to some extent, with the story of another belt used for cures, the belt of St Anselm, which Eadmer advertised as infallible:

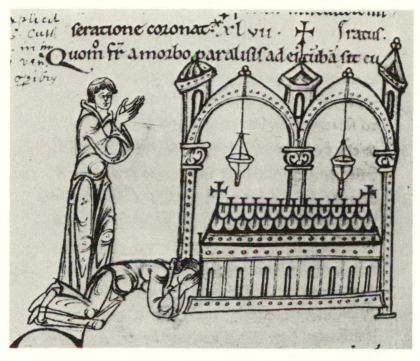

5   A PARALYTIC HEALED BY ST CUTHBERT. A sick monk lies before
the tomb of St Cuthbert and prays for healing. From a manuscript of Bede's
Life of St Cuthbert (University College, Oxford, MS 165), to which have been
added some miracle stories from the anonymous *History of St Cuthbert* (edited
in *Symeonis Dunelmensis Opera et Collectanea,* vol. 1, Surtees Society, 1868). The
story that this picture illustrates is shown there, p. 147.

6   A PAGAN PUNISHED BY ST CUTHBERT. The pagan Onalafbald mocked
St Cuthbert and stated his preference for Thor and Odin; the faithful knelt in
prayer and he attempted to leave the church in Durham where St Cuthbert's
body lay; he was held fast to the threshold and perished miserably. From the
same manuscript as plate 1, edited in *Symeonis,* p. 148.

Nor, of all those to whose care we have seen fit to entrust the belt on their asking for it in firm faith of their recovery, have we to this day heard of one who has hoped in vain.[71]

Here Eadmer stresses the success of the miracles alone; with Bede, the purposes of God are always to the fore. Bede does, however, record several 'external' miracles at the shrine of St Cuthbert[72] and two cures of monks taken from the *Anonymous Life*. Thus the tradition of posthumous cures by the incorrupt body of St Cuthbert was established very soon after his death.[73]

Another tradition about the saint developed soon after the monks left Lindisfarne and carried his body into exile—the tradition of St Cuthbert as a fierce and powerful protector of his own people and goods. The *Historia de Sancto Cuthberto* describes the acquisition of lands and goods by St Cuthbert's guardians, to whom miracles lend force. This tradition was continued in the *Historia Dunelmensis Ecclesiae,* where miracles are directed not only against the Danes but against the threat of local violence. In both these documents, supernatural sanctions are invoked to protect monastic lands. In the former, grants of land from the time of Bede are connected with miracles,[74] and vengeance falls upon those who, like Osbert and Ella, Halfdune and Onalafbald, tried to deprive St Cuthbert of lands or goods:[75] 'So let kings and princes beware lest they be punished, and neither take that which belongs to St Cuthbert nor consent in allowing others to do so'.[76] In the latter account, the theme continues. Someone who tries to plunder the shrine goes mad;[77] the tax-collector sent by William the Conqueror falls ill;[78] those who threaten the saint's property are chastised. The ideals of a later age were imposed upon the past, and the anger of St Cuthbert was said to be directed against those who infringed more recent rules. An outstanding instance of this is found in the disasters that were said to have overtaken women who approached the shrine, a prohibition at variance with the life of St Cuthbert and part of more recent propaganda for the monastic rule at Durham, restored under William of St Carilef.[79]

The records of miracles connected with St Cuthbert in the twelfth century contain both these themes. The focus is still the incorrupt body of St Cuthbert, enshrined at Durham in the cathedral. An account was written of the translation of the body of St Cuthbert in 1104, with details of the inspection to which it was subjected. Doubts had been expressed about the incorruption of the body, and the proceedings to discover if it was still in the incorrupt state recorded eleven years after the death of the saint were distinguished by their caution and their publicity. The monk Symeon was present to make a full record of the examination, precautions were taken against theft, and a second examination was allowed by a less local selection of observers.[80] Finally the cure of a well-known person, Richard, abbot of St Albans, was seen and witnessed by crowds.[81] The testing of ancient relics, particularly those of Anglo-Saxon saints, was undertaken on more than one occasion in Norman England. They might be tested by fire, like the relics at Evesham that were put to the ordeal by Abbot Walter at the suggestion of Archbishop Lanfranc;[82] they might be tested to see if they worked miracles, and William of Malmesbury records an instance of this.[83] But the proof most impressive to the English was, according to William of Malmesbury,[84] the incorrupt preservation of the body. It was the great triumph of Durham that it could display the incorrupt body of a saint that had also a continuous reputation for working miracles; it gave St Cuthbert the right to be regarded as one of the major English saints, in spite of the Conquest.[85]

The translation of St Cuthbert forms the centre of the record of St Cuthbert's miracles written by Reginald of Durham after 1104. This large and unwieldy collection contains a long account of this event, with about forty miracles preceding it and over a hundred afterwards. In it, the themes of power and vengeance combine with the themes of mercy and cures. On the one hand, the interests of the monks of Durham are well represented in instances of the anger of St Cuthbert against their enemies and his; on the other hand, the interests of the pilgrims are equally maintained in accounts of cures both at the shrine and at a distance from it. The pattern observed at other shrines is particularly noticeable here. Miracles, including cures, are recorded during the life of a saint, and his posthumous cult begins with cures at his tomb. A period follows when the needs of the guardians of his shrine are paramount and are formulated in records of judgements and acts of power by the saint as patron of his own people. Cures and acts of mercy toward pilgrims to the shrine continue alongside the miracles of power, to flourish and gradually balance the more ferocious miracles as the shrine becomes established and has less need of asserting its position.

Reginald, in his account of the miracles of St Cuthbert, makes the incorrupt body central, and stresses the importance of the shrine with its formidable patron. Those who mock the saint or doubt his powers are punished by St Cuthbert. The severity of the punishment is proportionate to the honour of the saint rather than the gravity of the crime; for instance, a boy who robbed a nest of birds in St Cuthbert's church found his hands contracted and useless until, repentant, he appealed to the saint.[86] Like St Faith and St Benedict, St Cuthbert had guardians for his shrine, one of whom was Elfred Weston, the sacrist, grandfather of Aelred of Rievaulx, to whom Reginald dedicates the book. St Cuthbert warned him in a dream when the shrine was in danger from fire.[87] The protection of St Cuthbert extended to captives, who brought their chains to Durham in thanksgiving. He was also careful of the fate of books associated with him, Gospel books, psalters, or copies of his *Life,* which he preserved from both fire and water. The copy of his Gospel book that was kept at his tomb was venerated as a relic itself, and Reginald describes how it was hung round the neck of a visiting bishop and all members of his party, as a gesture of respect.[88] Reginald describes with particular pride the wealth of the church at Durham and indicates the amount of riches offered at the shrine. On two occasions some relics of St Cuthbert were taken outside Durham on a tour to collect money to rebuild the shrine.[89]

The honour of St Cuthbert dominates Reginald's collection of miracles and is reflected in the competitive tone of seventeen stories. Cuthbert is described in three stories as a better patron for sailors than St Nicholas and in one as more useful at sea than St Brendan. Twice his miracles are compared to those of St Martin, and once, following the comparisons made by Bede between St Benedict and St Cuthbert, to a miracle of St Benedict. He is favourably compared to St Peter as a miracle worker, and he shares the credit for a cure with St Lawrence. Four sick people who ask for help at the new shrine of St Godric at Finchale are sent by the saint to St Cuthbert. It is notable that these people were all men. The prohibition of women from the shrine of St Cuthbert, however recent its date, meant in the twelfth century that his miracles excluded women, and may account for the large proportion of women at the other northern shrines at Finchale. St Cuthbert is seen in a vision saying mass with SS Aidan, Eadbert, and Ethelwold. When a pilgrim to England wished to decide which was the greatest saint, he lit candles to St Cuthbert, St Edmund, and St Etheldreda, accepting the one whose candle burned out first as the greatest. St Cuthbert triumphed.[90] At the end of Reginald's collection, the great rival of St Cuthbert was the new martyr, Thomas of Canterbury. Several miracles illustrate the need felt in Durham to assert the power of St Cuthbert against St Thomas.

These miracles asserting the power of St Cuthbert stemmed from the ambitions of those in charge of his body and its shrine. But St Cuthbert belonged also to the pilgrims, and there are many instances in Reginald's collection of cures of illness for pilgrims and for those who prayed to St Cuthbert elsewhere and then came or wrote to the shrine later. Reginald describes with pride the beauties of the shrine of St Cuthbert: the marble paving brought from Italy by Harpin of Thornley; the treasures of an ivory casket, a silver cross, as well as the jewels offered there; a bell believed to have belonged to St Cuthbert and ornamented by Prior Turgot with gold; the 'book of St Cuthbert'[91] and the great bells of Durham.[92] A lengthy description of the feast of Pentecost at Durham dwells on the glory of the church and its ceremonies and describes the crowds of pilgrims and their motives for coming. These pilgrims were men, sometimes with their sons, from all ranks of society. Most came from the north of England, but some from Scotland and from the south; one pilgrim came from Norway.[93] Women might pray to St Cuthbert and be cured by him, but not at the shrine; they sent gifts by their sons or husbands and offered their thanks for their cures. This prohibition of women extended to the Countess Ada, wife of Henry, Earl of Huntingdon and mother of Malcolm IV, on whose illness Reginald dwells in some detail. She was cured not at Durham, but by having some clothing worn by St Cuthbert placed upon her.[94] At the shrine, pilgrims might pray before the tomb, even all night; they offered candles, sometimes of great size.[95] The liturgy was continued by the monks, and cures could be proclaimed at any time, with corporate celebrations of joy. St Cuthbert also answered prayer at a distance, sometimes by relics such as hair and nail parings from his incorrupt body,[96] fragments of his clothing, or dust scraped from the tomb and mixed with water, or water in which the body of the saint had been washed.[97] Cures were recorded in the church of St Cuthbert in Lixtune in Cumberland. At other times prayer to the saint was sufficient. For instance, a monk of Durham cured a sick child in Lincoln by making the sign of the cross over him and saying: 'Come to our aid, O Lord, by the intercession of venerable Cuthbert and free us from all the chains of sin to rejoice in your peace'.[98]

The shrine with the body of St Cuthbert at Durham was the main focus of his cult; nevertheless, the place where he had lived as a hermit, Farne, also claimed miracles. Reginald of Durham devoted seventeen chapters of his book to the miracles of St Cuthbert on Farne after his death, and gave as his source Bartholomew, a hermit on Farne, and other monks who had lived there.[99] The life of this Bartholomew was written at this time by Geoffrey of Durham. Another monk who had known Bartholomew before his death in 1193 also recorded miracles on Farne. This brief record of the miracles of St Cuthbert on Farne comprises thirteen stories, some of which overlap with Reginald's account. They agree with the Durham tradition by making the translation of the saint's incorrupt body the starting place of the account. Having established the central miracle of St Cuthbert, the writer proceeds to show that the presence of the saint on Farne had rendered it holy and available for prayer by male visitors. Of these stories, two record the vengeance of the saint against those who disturb the eider ducks on the island;[100] there is one instance of St Cuthbert's protection against fire and a similar incident in his *Life* is quoted;[101] the rest of the miracles are cures of dysentery, paralysis, and madness, by prayer to the saint on the island. The sixth story is a piece of folklore and will be discussed as such later. The collection echoes the tradition about the saint at Durham, but shows that his shrine there was not the only place where the saint performed miracles after his death. The combination of miracles of vengeance with miracles of cures further confirms the pattern of miracles observed in his cult at Durham. Probably the writer describes miracles of St Cuthbert in Farne to assert the monastic claims of Durham to the island that became an important grange for Durham, with a continuing tradition of hermits.[102]

The miracles of St Cuthbert present him either as a fierce northern patron, protecting his shrine and his men, or as the great saint of the North who was available there for any pilgrim in spiritual or temporal need. By the twelfth century, as elsewhere, the theme of healing dominates accounts of his miracles. As with St Benedict, the miracles were to some extent influenced by the miracles recorded in his *Life,* but

65

gradually assumed a different tone in response to changing needs in the recipients. But the harsher tradition continued into the twelfth century and is reflected in William of Malmesbury's account of St Cuthbert as 'one who is said above all to be a severe corrector of sinners'. He ends his account in a way typical of any writer concerned with a saint of this forbidding and 'traditional' kind:

Rightly ought you to be feared by your monks; I beseech you therefore to remember me for good.[103]

66

4

Three Twelfth-Century Shrines:
St William, St Godric
and St Frideswide

SO FAR, we have observed two kinds of miracles: miracles in which the saint protects or avenges (connected, in the 'traditional' collections, with the territorial claims of the shrines' guardians) and miracles in which the saint heals (first experienced, at the 'traditional' shrines, by the guardians themselves and then gradually by a widening circle of pilgrims who put themselves under the protection of the saint). Later, as the need for the saint as patron and protector of the monastery lands, goods, and personnel decreased, the number of cures of pilgrims increased, until cures dominated the miracle stories. Another change in later miracle collections was the growing influence of the men who made the miracle stories into books. The early anonymous records kept at shrines remained the basis of the record, but in the twelfth century, reshaping by writers with some literary pretensions influenced the material itself.

Three twelfth-century shrines display these trends clearly. The main difference between the saints buried at these shrines and those already discussed is that these saints were recently dead or newly translated from obscurity. There was, therefore, no place in the liturgical life of the church for them, nor were there previous written accounts of their miracles. Of the three accounts studied here, two record miracles soon after the deaths of the saints, one at the twelfth-century translation of her relics, and not at stages throughout a long tradition. The three saints are in some ways like those already considered, though each has distinctive traits. William of Norwich was, like St Faith, a child-martyr. But while she belonged to the first centuries of Christian persecution, William was a child of the mid-twelfth century, and his cult marks the beginning of a very different kind of persecution, that supposedly by the Jews. Godric of Finchale was, like St Benedict and St Cuthbert, a hermit, but he had been one of the new merchants of the twelfth century and became a hermit in a style new to the West. St Frideswide was a female saint like St Faith, and an Anglo-Saxon like St Cuthbert, but she aroused no interest until her relics were exhumed.

The child-martyr William of Norwich died in March 1144. A few years later, Thomas of Monmouth, a Welsh monk of Norwich Priory, made a record of miracles at William's tomb. His is a curious work in many ways, not least because of Thomas's personality. The account contains miracles from the year of St William's death until 1172. Most are cures; several, however, are miracles that show the anger of the saint. I will examine these first to see how far they continue the tradition observed at older shrines.

None of the miracles of vengeance recorded by Thomas involve the rights or lands of Norwich Priory; nor are they directed against those who oppose the saint's protectors in lawsuits. The protection of the saint is not connected with a statue that can be carried about to give help over plague, famine, or other disaster; there is no suggestion that St William led armed bands in the manner of St Benedict. The instances Thomas gives of the saint's vengeance are directed against those who withheld reverence from the saint himself. In the second book, he sees divine vengeance as falling first upon the Jews, whom he alleges were responsible for the death of St William:

Since then it is certain . . . that the most blessed boy and martyr William was slain by the Jews, we believe that it was brought about by the righteous judgement of God that these same men, being guilty of so horrible a crime, suffered so prompt a retribution for such deliberate wickedness, and that the rod of heaven in a brief space of time exterminated or scattered them all.[1]

Thomas describes the death of Eleazar the Jew, killed in ambush by Christians, and the death of Sheriff John, who had defended the Jews and later died from internal bleeding, as instances of divine vengeance.[2] He records the anger of St William in matters of veneration of the saint's tomb. The monk Richard continued in his sickness and finally died as a result, Thomas says, of not offering candles that St William had demanded of him in a vision;[3] he suggests that the prior Elias came under the same judgement for not allowing Thomas to place a carpet over the tomb and burn candles there. After a long series of arguments with Thomas about the tomb and its accoutrements, Prior Elias died in October 1149. While Thomas recorded grief at his death, he added:

I cannot be surprised that the thoughts of some are disturbed . . . for perhaps they may say in their hearts that the martyr William punished—and justly punished—by the vengeance of his wrath the insult offered to him by the hardened Prior. For it is said by many that the martyr threatened him and that his death followed thereupon.[4]

In each case, it is Thomas who connects a calamitous event with the saint's vengeance, and the point he makes is always the same: it is dangerous to neglect the young St William or to be remiss in paying him honour.[5]

Thus, the power and vengeance of the saint had been turned to different uses from those apparent in earlier collections. The saint is invoked to increase the glory of his own shrine and to defend his veneration, not to terrify temporal enemies of the shrine or reinforce the claims of his guardians. The chief keeper of the shrine, Thomas himself, does not appear armed (like Christian at Fleury and Gimon at Conques) with threats of physical damage and immediate practical retributions against attackers. Rather, he is a sly and secret manipulator of events, all of which are concerned with due honour paid to the shrine itself.

This impression of a saint who is in some sense the focus of manipulation is amply borne out by a consideration of the relationship of Thomas of Monmouth himself to the cult. It is clear that he was the moving spirit in the cult from the time of his own vision, six years after the death of the martyr, in which Herbert of Losinga, the founder of his priory, appeared to him and told him to remove the body of St William to a place for worthier veneration. Behind this vision it is possible to see the mechanics of the creation of a cult by a writer. Thomas began his campaign for the cult of St William in 1150, six years after the death of the boy saint, and after the deaths of John de Cheyney, the sheriff, Eleazar the Jew, the bishop Eborard, and the chief witness to the boy's death, Aelward Ded.[6] The people who knew what had really happened were dead, and there was a clear field for pious invention. From Thomas's partial and partisan account a few facts emerge. The body of a boy was found in Thorpe Wood on 24 March, before Easter 1144; he had been cruelly treated and violently slain. The boy was identified as an apprentice skinner, William, well known in Norwich, though of no special interest to his fellows. His family raised an outcry at his death, and a rumour began that it had been the work of the Jewish community in Norwich. The body was buried in the cemetery of the priory with some solemnity, and at a clergy-meeting the uncle of the boy asked for an investigation of the matter. A visitor to Norwich, Aimar, prior of St Pancras, Lewes, saw the possibilities in the situation and tried to buy the body for his own priory.[7]

No more was heard of the boy and his cult for six years. When Thomas turned his attention to the matter he could write: 'Assuredly by this miracle the memory of the blessed martyr William revived, for it had gradually been waning, yea, in the hearts of nearly all it had almost entirely died out.'[8] Apparently the cult was neither spontaneous nor universally acceptable. Thomas devotes much of his work to a fierce denunciation of those who scorn the miracles of the boy and deny his sanctity:

There were many, ungrateful for the divine benefits or for the signs shown, who mocked at the miracles when they were made public and said that they were fictitious. These suggested that the blessed boy William was likely to be of no special merit after his death, whom they had heard was a poor neglected little fellow when alive.[9]

These mockers were within the monastery as well as outside its walls. It is also clear that Thomas was the centre of a party devoted to the cause of the martyr. He had the interest and backing of the new bishop, William Turbe; he mentions six of the monks as partisans: Peter Peverall, Richard de Ferrariis, Edmund, Richard, Giulfus, and William the Sacrist. He cultivated the mother of the dead boy and extracted from her a suspect account of William's childhood. Her story of William was couched in terms familiar to hagiography and highly flattering to his mother. Her relationship with the priory became close, and she was buried in the monks' cemetery. Yet there was no disguising the fact that this devoted mother of a saint had allowed her son to go off with a stranger and even received silver for allowing him to do so.[10] Her husband figures not at all in the narrative, but her sister's husband, the priest Godwin, tried to make all the capital he could out of the death of his nephew, including charging for cures by a teazle that he dipped in water and used to cure the sick, saying that the teazle had been used to torture the boy William. His wife Leviva confided to Thomas a vision she had of the boy's death several years after the event, when it seemed profitable to claim a martyr in the family.[11]

Thomas advanced the cult by other and more devious means. He was constant in his demands that the body should be translated first to the priory church and then to a chapel of its own. At each translation, except the first,[12] he was present and secured certain relics for his private use. Two teeth of the saint were among them, and a shoe that he kept; he later persuaded another devotee of the saint, the Lady Mabel of Bec, to pay for a shrine for them.[13] She herself secured through Thomas a stone from the tomb. She would scrape the stone into dust that she mixed with water and used as medicine for herself and her family.[14] Thomas also had a covering that he tried to lay over the tomb in its honour[15] and a secret stock of candles that he stored against the day when the cult should be recognized.[16] Indeed Thomas seems to have been obsessed by the idea of offering candles to St William, demanding them from pilgrims and suggesting that St William had a special liking for candles 'since he was born at Candlemas'.[17] He secured his own position at the shrine by recording a vision seen by Richard of Lynn, in which St William called Thomas 'my private secretary'[18] and urged that he be made responsible for the cult.

Thomas did everything possible to promote the cult of St William. The memory of a boy *pauperculus et neglectus*, killed in distressing circumstances, became in his hands a martyr-cult at the centre of one of the major towns of England. For four years, from 1150 to 1154, Thomas devoted all his energies to the cult. In 1154, however, his interest seems to have waned; he was surprised to find that the cult continued of itself and that miracles continued until 1172 and perhaps longer. It is an instance in which the end of a record of miracles did not in fact mean the end of the miracles. Thomas had to resume his work:

Quite suddenly when we were least expecting it, in the year of our Lord's incarnation 1155, the power of the holy martyr seemed to renew itself and shone forth with a greater multitude of signs than before. I therefore take up my pen once more.[19]

71

He says in the preface to book seven that he had other very pressing duties to undertake, and it seems possible that these finally absorbed all his energies, since he concluded the work in 1173 and sent it with a prefatory letter to Bishop William Turbe. The receipts from the altar of St William continued, however, reaching a peak in the 1330s and declining drastically eleven years later. In the fifteenth century the shrine was still kept in good repair at some expense; perhaps people still expected miracles.[20]

Thomas created the cult, but it was independent of him and can therefore be considered in itself. The needs and concerns of the guardians of the new saint were different from those of earlier centres of veneration for relics. The other side of the cult, the demands of the pilgrims coming to the shrine, had changed also. The miracles recorded by Thomas, where they are not concerned with the glory of the saint himself, fall into two groups: cures and visions, both the most personal of all kinds of miracles.

The cures of St William account for most of the miracles recorded by Thomas. They began in the priory, with the need to establish that the relics were indeed those of a saint. The monks found the body of St William to be 'incorrupt',[21] they saw a rose blossoming in winter on a tree on St William's grave,[22] they saw the coffin rise miraculously above ground level at his first translation.[23] The inhabitants of the monastery were also the subjects of the first cures. Botilda, the wife of the monks' cook, was miraculously delivered in childbirth by drinking water in which she steeped a piece of fern she had taken from the bier of the saint.[24] Among those cured by prayer to the saint were Edmund the Younger,[25] the infant son of Prior Elias's nephew, the wife of a friend of Thomas, Alan de Setchy,[26] Thomas, Richard, William, Robert, and a second William (all monks of Norwich), Hildebrand (kinsman of the monk Paul),[27] the oxen of Denis the Chamberlain, and, at one remove from the monks, the family of Mabel of Bec.[28] In addition, there are three miracles connected with women under some kind of religious vow in Norwich and, therefore, possibly under the care of the monks.[29]

Twenty-three of the miracles concerned people living in Norwich itself. These were the middle-class tradesmen of Norwich, with their wives and children: Aditha, wife of Toke the chandler; Ida, wife of Eustace the moneyer; the son of Colbern and Ansfrid; Godric the money-changer and Ralph, another moneyer; Agnes, wife of Reginald the cowherd; Ada, wife of Siwate; Adam, son of John the bishop's chaplain; Robert, son of Hermeus the baker; the daughter of Martin the fisherman; Ebrand, a fisherman; Goda, wife of Copman of Norwich; Walter, servant of Dean William; Agnes, daughter of Bondo Bloc and Gunhilda; Humphrey of Norwich. Sailors off the coast called on St William and were preserved from danger. The circle of miracles centred on the monastery, then expanded, as at all older shrines, to those nearest to it. Pilgrims came from Norfolk and Suffolk. Very few came from further away: Philip, a knight of Lorraine, was freed from his fetters in Norwich, but he had by then visited most of the shrines of Christendom and came to Norwich more by accident than design.[30] Thomas, a cripple, came from York to be cured,[31] and Reimbert, formerly seneschal of Battle Abbey,[32] was cured of blindness and dumbness in Norwich. The experiences of a girl in Worcestershire were recounted to Thomas by a monk of Pershore, a convent connected with Norwich.[33] Two cures were connected with Canterbury.[34] It is perhaps significant that these foreign, upper-class miracles occur in the last book of miracles, when the shrine was established and known.

These cures were of the usual complaints recorded at shrines. Seventeen pilgrims were crippled, three were blind, two deaf and dumb, one only dumb, one partially deaf. Internal diseases, such as bleeding, cancer, dropsy, and dysentery were cured, as were minor ailments such as headache, toothache, and insomnia. A few people were diagnosed as mad or possessed; one boy was epileptic. A man was said to have swallowed a viper and kept its young inside him until delivered at the shrine. Twenty of the cures are of people described as 'ill'. The ultimate miracle of raising the dead is not recorded.

These cures were usually effected at the tomb of the saint, at first in the chapter house of the monks, then in the church, and finally in the chapel to which the saint was translated for the convenience of growing crowds in 1154.[35] The sick entered the church, prayed at the shrine, often with groans and tears; then they usually touched the tomb, either kneeling on it, or touching the slab with the affected part of their bodies. Very often they stayed all night; usually they offered gifts, most of all candles. The cures were often dramatic and noisy, with shouts from both cured and onlookers. People would roll about in agony during their cure, and leap up in joy at its completion. Others

73

would go home and be cured more gradually there. The cures of the mad were particularly dramatic, as may be seen from Thomas's description of the cure of Sieldeware of Belaugh. She was dragged into the church by four strong men, thrown down, and bound. She was laid by the tomb, *'clamans et eiulans'*; she drummed with her heels and tore at her bonds with her teeth, disturbing other pilgrims so much that she had to be removed for a time. After she had been laid on the tomb, by orders of Thomas himself, she recovered and slept for several days, to awake cured.[36]

Souvenirs of the tomb were few. Dust scraped from the tomb was taken to be mixed with water for the sick to drink, as at the tomb of St Martin in Tours;[37] there was the stone, mentioned above, possessed by Lady Mabel of Bec; a fern gave help to the woman Botilda and she was later told in a dream of a stream connected with St William that healed her and her son, but seems otherwise to have attracted no interest.[38] At Pershore, a girl was told in a dream to wash the feet of a crucifix with holy water and soak crumbs in it that would cure her and others, but there is no account of this process being used.[39] Thomas himself kept the relics of teeth and the shoe; Godwin Sturt used the teazle. But the real focus of the cures was the shrine itself, requiring visits and prayer and offerings at that place.

The second type of miracle recorded by Thomas were visions, and in these the power of the martyr was available away from the tomb. In some apparitions, St William promised a cure, and the patient awoke to find himself well. The setting of such visions was elaborated, either by the visionaries or by Thomas, with the desire to glorify St William and encourage devotion to him. The story of the first cure, that of the boy Lewin, who lived outside Norwich, is a fair example of this. In his illness he dreamed that he was conducted through hell and heaven, where he saw the boy William sitting at the feet of the Virgin Mary; the angel who conducted him told him that St William would cure him and that he should visit his tomb in Norwich; with considerable difficulty, the father of Lewin discovered this shrine and brought his son to pray there, where he was cured.[40] In other visions, St William appeared making demands and suggestions about his own cult. He appeared in visions before each of his translations and gave instructions about the care of his shrine; he praised Thomas for his devotion and care of the shrine and blamed those less devoted. Like the other child-martyr, St Faith, he demanded gifts, but whereas St Faith asked for jewels and trinkets, St William asked for candles. The most extreme example of his glorification in a vision with no reference whatever to his actual life is that of a girl in Worcestershire. She saw St William dressed as a priest, celebrating mass, and giving communion, assisted by 'Robert', in the chapel in the wood where William's body had been found;[41] the girl herself answered the mass in English.[42] In other dreams, St William was seen with Herbert of Losinga, the late bishop of Norwich, a theme which established a strong link between the saint and the diocese.[43] In some visions St William was seen helping sailors in storms off the coast; prisoners escaped from their fetters by his help, as they did with St Faith's help. He was called in a dream 'patron of all Norwich'.[44] He threatened penalties against the man who had stolen a psalter written out by Thomas: 'It was indeed a precious and dear book and not unworthy of being coveted'.[45] Dreams and visions of St William are part of the early account Thomas gives of the shrine, and, as will be seen in the case of the shrine of St Frideswide, such visions were a part of the propaganda for a new shrine; they asserted that the saint himself favoured his own veneration at that place. The flagrant propaganda of these and the other visions recorded by Thomas is best exemplified in his description of a vision in which St William appeared and spoke to Ralph of Norwich: 'I am the boy William, who at God's bidding cured you; thank me and remain devout.' He adds, as is usual, a second remark to the first, and it is possible to see the hand of Thomas in the addition, if not in the original message: 'Visit Thomas my warden and secretary and tell him to be comforted and not to faint—to continue diligent in my service, for I hold the obedience dear which his devotion shows to me'.[46]

The miracles of St William are, as has already been suggested, in some ways similar to the miracles of St Faith. This resemblance was more than fortuitous. Both were martyrs, both were children. Their cults were directly connected. Robert Fitzwalter and his wife Sybilla visited the shrine of St Faith at Conques in 1100, at the height of its splendour, and returned with two of the monks to establish a shrine of St Faith at Horsham St Faith near Norwich.[47] This revival of the cult of St Faith made her known in Norfolk at just the time when the cult of St

William began. One miracle describes a woman preparing candles for both St William and St Faith from the same wax,[48] candles for use at the Norfolk shrine rather than at Conques.

Some similarities can be seen, then, between the miracles of St William and those at older shrines. St William does remain a local patron whose powers can be tapped in the place where he is buried. But his miracles are also different from those at older shrines. First of all, St William's miracles were needed to prove that he was a saint at all, which was not necessary for saints already established in the liturgy, who have records of miracles performed during their lives. St William's *Life* was a product of his cult; he was never an international saint; his liturgical cult remained embryonic.[49] Secondly, though St William was acknowledged as patron of his priory and city, he did not exercise immediate power by threats and sanctions in temporal matters. The miracles of St William were almost all beneficent, and they were personal, performed for those who prayed to him, whether in the local area or as pilgrims. The saint's power was still manifested in miracles and those miracles localized veneration at a particular place, but the kind of miracles needed and thought appropriate had changed.

Two other aspects of this miracle collection distinguish the cult of St William from that of older saints. One is the emotional appeal of St William as a child who had suffered crucifixion; the other is the anti-Jewish sentiment that this image aroused. The two are closely connected. Thomas draws a careful parallel between the sufferings of Christ, one of the dominant themes in contemporary devotion, and the death of the boy at the hands of the Jews. The figure of Mary was woven into this complex theme, and the Jews were the natural scapegoats. This complex of ideas has already been noticed in connection with the eucharistic visions of the child as sacrifice. The 'miracles of the glorious martyr William' were the first to direct attention to the possibilities of the martyrdom of Christian children at the hands of 'Christian-slaying Jews';[50] it was a theme that gathered together many strands of contemporary sentiment and which had successors elsewhere.[51]

The second of the three minor cults that arose at this time is that of a contemporary of Thomas Becket—Godric the hermit of Finchale, who died in May, 1170. The most interesting feature of the posthumous cult of St Godric lies in the cult's relationship to the shrine at Canterbury, and this relationship will be discussed below. The miracles, however, are interesting apart from that connection. Godric, like St Benedict, was a holy man venerated during his life, and like St Cuthbert, whose example, in fact, caused his conversion, he was a hermit. He became, like them, the focus for local expectations of miracles at his tomb after his death, but both his life and his posthumous cult show new elements.

Reginald of Durham wrote the *Life and Miracles of St Godric* at the suggestion of Aelred of Rievaulx.[52] It begins with an account of Godric's early life, which Reginald obtained from the saint himself. He describes the saint's career from the extreme poverty of his Lincolnshire childhood to the comparative affluence obtained by trading with associates between England, Denmark, and Flanders, with some voyages into the Mediterranean.[53] While he was still a trader, he was devout in his attention to the Holy Places, and he visited Rome, Compostela, and Jerusalem, as well as the local shrines at Lindisfarne and St Andrews.[54] While on Farne Island, where St Cuthbert had lived as a hermit, he decided to undertake a more religious and solitary form of life, and began this with a further voyage to Jerusalem as a pilgrim, where he tended the sick for a while in the Hospital of St John.[55] The account then shows his gradual detachment from his family and former life, in varying degrees of solitude, until he finally settled as a hermit on some land at Finchale granted him by the bishop of Durham, Ranulf Flambard,[56] under the protection of the prior of Durham.[57] Thus, from being the paradigm of the twelfth-century self-made man in secular life, he became one of the new, independent religious, a striking phenomenon of the twelfth century, a hermit who had not been a monk and whose life was remarkable, like those of the hermits of Egypt, for personal asceticism rather than for the virtues of communal living.[58] Neither scholar nor clerk, but a layman without education, Godric went to school with the village children in Northumberland[59] and learned to read, until he knew enough for his needs in his hermitage: the Our Father, the Creed, and the Psalter of St Jerome.[60]

The miracles Reginald records of Godric fall into two parts: those performed during his life and those, in a separate section, at his tomb after his death. The miracles during his life follow the pattern of the *vir dei,* though even here he was part of the new hermit-movement, and the atmosphere surrounding his life is closer to the spirituality of the new Orders than to the miracles of the older saints. Godric knew Aelred of Rievaulx[61] and was visited by several other Cistercians.[62] His own links, however, were with the monks of Durham; they provided his land and supported him as far as this was necessary. Seven years before his death, he placed himself under a personal vow of obedience to the prior of Durham, Germanus, who was also his confessor.[63] The monks said mass at the hermitage on major feastdays and visited him more frequently when he became ill. It was no accident that one of his most assiduous visitors was Reginald. Aelred of Rievaulx had suggested to the author of the *Life of St Cuthbert* that he had material for another account of sanctity close to hand in Godric, and thereafter Reginald persuaded the hermit to tell him about his life, in preparation for a biography.[64]

The source for Reginald's *Life* of Godric was mainly the hermit himself. He did, however, also draw upon an account written by Prior Germanus,[65] which does not survive, and also on an account by Geoffrey, a monk of Durham who had known Godric.[66] The fact that three monks of Durham were eager to write about the hermit near them shows an interest in this form of life equalled by their desire to control the saint's body after his death. These interests are found elsewhere in the cases of other twelfth-century hermits, as, for instance, with Wulfric of Haselbury.[67] To the account of Godric's life was added a list of posthumous miracles at his tomb.[68] Though never officially canonized or liturgically celebrated outside Durham, he was venerated locally until the fifteenth century. His coffin has been recently exhumed from its original burial place at Finchale, which suggests that it underwent neither the honour of translation nor the destruction of disinterment.

Reginald's *Life of St Godric* relates the interior miracles of prayer, vision, and prophesy; miraculous cures do not hold a large place. Reginald says that many of the sick who visited the hermit hoped to be cured by his prayers and blessing, or by the blessed bread he gave them,[69] though he rarely gives individual examples of this. In the two most interesting cases the cures were not effected by Godric's deliberate act, but claimed as his cures by the recipients. In the first case, John, archdeacon of Durham, was pronounced incurably ill by the doctors; he went to see Godric and talked with him in his garden, eating some fruit the hermit had grown; he returned to Durham, and pro-

78

nounced himself cured.[70] In the second case, a couple whose daughter had died put her body in a sack and left it in the cell while Godric was out, knowing that the hermit would, out of humility, refuse to help if asked directly. When Godric saw the sack, he prayed for two days and at the end of that time, 'on Easter Day', the girl emerged emaciated but alive. The story was believed by Reginald in its literal form; it seems that Godric himself thought it was true since Reginald gives the story in the hermit's own words and tells how he went to confession about the matter, anxious about his humility and about his solitude.[71]

The picture Reginald presents is not that of a thaumaturge; it follows the pattern of the desert fathers, as understood among the 'new religious' of the twelfth century.[72] Godric's reputation for sanctity rested on his familiarity in visions with the saints, not on practical cures. By far the largest number of miracles recorded of Godric by Reginald are visions. Godric talked with St Cuthbert,[73] who directed him to Finchale; he learned a song from Mary and Mary Magdalene;[74] he frequently saw John the Baptist, whom he considered his special patron.[75] All of them were appropriate saints for his visions: St Cuthbert as the dominant saint of the North; Mary and Mary Magdalene, whose cults were flourishing at this time; and John the Baptist, patron of hermits from the earliest times. Other visions were of demons, who took the forms of black beasts or birds or men, uttering noises and threats—imagery familiar in hermit literature from the days of St Anthony the Great. This familiarity with angels, saints, and demons marked the contact of hermits such as Godric with the other world; they were on the frontiers of the supernatural. On the other hand, their contact with animals, couched in miraculous terms, bridged the frontier between man and the lower creation. In his *Life,* Godric is described as having relationships of friendship and obedience with a wolf, a stag, serpents, a bull, cows, and smaller animals who came to the hermit for warmth and food in the winter. The theme of the restoration of paradise in which the holy man resumes the role of Adam is a *topos* in hagiography; and in this class may be placed the stories of Godric's control over the elements, his prophetic powers, and his insight in spiritual matters. The miracles recorded during his life have more in common with the visions of a Cistercian such as Christian of Aumône than with those of the older saints.

When Godric died, the monks of Durham were careful to preserve the body as their possession. They prepared it for burial at Finchale, appointed monks to look after the church and the grave, and were ready in expectation of miracles. The miracles connected with this posthumous cult have a very different character from the spiritualized events of the hermit's life. About thirty-six dreams or visions in which Godric appeared were recorded, but these were usually in answer to the sick who prayed for help. Only two events were interpreted as instances of the anger of Godric. In one, robbers of the tomb were unable to move;[76] in the other, a Scot who insulted Godric died later.[77] There is no suggestion that Godric was the lord of the lands of Finchale or protector of the monks; indeed, the temporal interests of Godric and his vengeance toward those who infringed his honour were far less in evidence than with St William of Norwich or St Frideswide. It was a local shrine; a shrine evoking spontaneous devotion; and one, in contrast to Godric during his life, which was mainly famous for cures.

The first cure by the dead saint was recorded before the body was buried. The feet of the saint began to bleed while the body was waiting for burial and a sick brother who kissed the feet was cured.[78] The body was then buried under the altar of John the Baptist.[79] A few days later, Godfrey of Kelso, an almsman of Durham priory, secured a ring from the lorica of the saint,[80] dipped it in water, and gave the water to a sick girl to drink; she was cured of dropsy. There the matter rested, though Reginald says that local people flocked to Finchale on feast days, in case their saint had begun to work miracles.[81] Two years later, the posthumous cures began. Two hundred and twenty-two healing miracles were recorded in the following years. The usual procedure was for the sick to enter the church and pray, often all night, at the grave of Godric. Offerings, especially of candles, were made.[82] About half the cures were of the deaf, dumb, blind, lame, or paralysed;[83] others had leprosy, epilepsy, dropsy, fever, throat infections, or tumours; ten were described as mad, six as demoniacs; in one case a sterile woman prayed to Godric for a son, and when she had a child, called him Ralph Godric.[84] Water was given to the sick to drink at the tomb and in this the monks often dipped relics of the saint, such as rings from his lorica, hairs from his beard, or pieces of his girdle.

The devotees of this shrine were most of all local people. Here no monastery's self-interested monks shaped the cult and began the miracles; the monks of Durham were caretakers only. Those who were cured were people, usually from the lower middle classes, from a radius of forty miles of the tomb.[85] Reginald says that many knights came and prayed to Godric, but in fact he gives the name of only one, an Englishman of the Lascelles family who was wounded in Normandy and told in a vision by St Thomas to go to Godric for a cure.[86] This is in contrast to Reginald's account of the visitors to the tomb of St Cuthbert where he stresses the noble and indeed royal visitors and patrons of the cult. Another contrast is made by Reginald between St Cuthbert and Godric, when he records the large proportion of women who frequented Godric's shrine. At least a hundred and sixty women are mentioned in comparison to seventy men; it is possible that the monastic propaganda at Durham against admitting women to the shrine of St Cuthbert had by this time taken effect and caused women to go instead to the shrine of Godric. Women who had either prayed unsuccessfully to St Cuthbert from a distance[87] or been stricken with illness for presuming to enter his territory[88] are said to have been cured at Finchale.

A formula of prayer by which the sick addressed Godric is given by Reginald in connection with the first cure at the tomb in 1172: 'The Lord Jesus Christ by the merits of his servant Godric bestow upon you the cure of your infirmities, and may he show us how great is the grace he has granted to his faithful servant'. This is an elaboration of an earlier form, 'The Lord Jesus Christ heals you by the merits of his servant Godric'.[89] The collection of posthumous miracles begins with this dignified prayer for a sick girl; it also incorporates a biblical reference with the last sentence, 'this beginning of miracles did Saint Godric', with its deliberate reminiscence of 'this beginning of miracles did Jesus' in the Gospel of St John (John 2:11).[90] The rest of the miracles, however, read more like a collection of *scedulae*, bluntly transcribed, than a literary work; for instance, the second cure is described thus, and is entirely typical: 'There was another woman of Bidock, Addoc by name, who had had a withered hand from the fourth year after her birth and she was also blind; she was entirely cured of both infirmities there'.[91] Such *scedulae* were the staple of the new healing shrines. They read like a legal brief, giving the name of the recipient of the cure, the disease, the length of time it had lasted, the place from whence the person came, the occasion of the cure; very often, and in most other instances in this collection, the names of some witnesses are given.

They were used in the formal process of papal canonization and this process certainly shaped the miracles of Godric, though he was never in fact officially canonized.

Godric in his lifetime embodied many of the interests and aspirations of religious men in his time. He was a hermit, one of the great individualists, a man concerned with visions, prophecies, the interior miracles. His visions were centred on matters of contemporary interest, such as the state of the souls of the departed, and took on contemporary images, such as that of the child Jesus, whom Godric saw, frequently during the Eucharist, walking about the church, emerging from the mouth of the Crucified, in the arms of his mother. William of New-burgh saw Godric in his cell when he was an old man and gave this non-miraculous description of him:

I had the good fortune to see him and speak with him as he lay in the church near the holy altar . . . there he died, old and full of days, and his body now lies in the same place where he used to kneel during his life when praying or lie when sick.[92]

This venerable figure was surrounded by miracles appropriate to his way of life; after his death, miracles were associated with him that were altogether different and that can be related to the formation of a healing shrine of local importance at the end of the twelfth century, rather than any recollection of the character of the saint himself. It is a shrine in which the needs of the local people for cures in illness provide the majority of miracles.

The third minor shrine I will discuss is that of St Frideswide, which flourished as a centre for miracles in Oxford ten years after the death of St Thomas of Canterbury. Its relationship to the shrine of Becket was an important factor in its establishment.

St Frideswide, like St Faith, was a female saint belonging to a distant past; virtually nothing is known about her. While St Faith was a martyr of the fourth century, St Frideswide belonged to the Anglo-Saxon past, as a princess and religious founder in the mid-eighth century. The first mention of her legend is in a twelfth-century history, the *Gesta Pontificum* of William of Malmesbury. St Frideswide was, he says, a princess promised in marriage by her father to the king's son; she, however, wished to be consecrated to God and fled; her suitor pursued her, and, in answer to her prayers, was struck blind at the gate of the city of Oxford. After renouncing her, he received his sight and she founded a community in the city.[93] Local tradition gave the prince the name of Algar, and said that a holy well had sprung up at Binsey, where he received his sight.[94] It seems probable that Frideswide was in fact the head of a religious foundation and that she was buried in her monastery: 'She is buried in the Church of St Mary in Oxford near the Thames'.[95] Thus she was part of the royal, monastic, English traditions of Oxford, and her body belonged without dispute to the church she had founded.

The church of St Frideswide was reputed to have been rebuilt by King Ethelred, who introduced canons in place of nuns;[96] under Henry II, Augustinian canons were installed, and the first prior, Guimond, set about restoring the fortunes of the house. Thus at the end of the twelfth century, St Frideswide's was virtually a new monastic house, needing to establish itself in the social and economic setting of Oxford. It was the third prior, Philip, who used the relics of St Frideswide as a central part of the publicity of the community he ruled, and it was he who wrote the *Miracula S Frideswidae,* the main collection of miracles of this saint. Like the cult of St William at Norwich, the miracles of St Frideswide were the main part of the construction of a cult, and, as there, one man was responsible for the record. Prior Philip was in no sense as obsessive or as unscrupulous as Thomas of Monmouth, but, like him, he arranged the miracles to the maximum effect in his account of them. They are miracles that centre upon the one great and public event in the cult of St Frideswide, the translation of her relics from her first grave to a feretory in the church on 12 February, 1180. The translation is central in this account, and it could be said that the miracles are focussed entirely on it. The first section of the *Miracula* describes the ceremony of the translation; the king was not present but gave his approval to the proceedings.[97] Richard, archbishop of Canterbury, presided, with the bishops Richard of Winchester, Geoffrey of Ely, John of Norwich, and Peter of St Davids; Alexius, papal legate in Ireland, and Master John of St Andrews are also mentioned by name.[98] The translation was carried out with much splendour, visions were alleged to have preceded it, the odour of sanctity accompanied it, and miracles followed, beginning on the night of the translation and continuing for at least a year. Prior Philip records 110 miracles in that time. Where they do not immediately precede or follow the translation, the translation is mentioned, usually as attracting the attention of someone chronically sick, who had tried both doctors and other shrines in vain for help,[99] like Winneva of Estrope, 'who had visited many shrines of the saints in order to obtain the restoration of health'.[100] This does not mean that cures took place at the feretory only at the time of the translation; cures could happen, as at any other shrine, at any time of any day or night. They were confined neither to the event of the translation nor to major feast days;[101] but the translation is mentioned throughout the miracles, as the focus and the beginning of the new shrine.

The translation established the shrine of St Frideswide as part of the tour of holy places for a time, at least for the local population. Two other facts may be deduced about the place of Oxford and its shrine in the overall pattern of shrines in Europe. Two men were cured by St Frideswide in order to visit the Holy Sepulchre;[102] a man was punished for stealing money from the shrine of St Frideswide in order to go to Compostela.[103] It seems from these miracles that, first, people came to a local shrine for cures of illnesses, before undertaking a pilgrimage abroad; and secondly, the accessibility of Oxford made it easy to go there in connection with longer voyages.

The twelfth-century miracles of St Frideswide were not primarily those of vengeance. Her first miracle, by which Prince Algar was blinded for pursuing her, in the legend of the saint, is in fact a miracle of retribution, similar to those of St Faith and St Benedict; it belongs to an older age, and its place in the legend indicates this. The new miracles in the twelfth century were almost all visions or cures. As with St William, the instances of the vengeance of St Frideswide are limited to disasters that befell those who, like a visitor from Winchester, delayed their veneration of her shrine.[104] She did not demand gifts or exact vengeance against the enemies of the shrine's guardians; the myth of the saint as a dignified and royal person persisted in her cult, but not as patron in the sense that St Faith or St Benedict were so regarded.

Like the shrine of St William, the shrine of St Frideswide was said to have been established at the express command of the saint, and its veneration was accompanied by visions. Prior Philip gives three instances of visions as the first of his miracles, all indicating that the saint

84

wanted to be reverenced more devoutly and with greater honour. Martin, an Oxford man coming home from business in London, saw a great light over the roof of the monastery;[105] Edith of Oxford said that eight years before the translation she had seen a similar light radiating from the tomb of the saint into the surrounding country;[106] Robert, a relation of the prior and employed by him, dreamed, on his return from London, of a beautiful lady who asked him to hurry on the translation—a dream repeated three times, like that of Thomas of Monmouth.[107] In several instances St Frideswide appeared to the sick who prayed to her for cure; Walter of Wales, for instance, saw her as a great lady of his own time: 'with a beautiful face, richly dressed with solemn demeanour, wearing a white fur like the pelt of a bear'.[108]

The main miracles of St Frideswide, however, were cures. The usual pattern at a healing shrine was followed, with the sick praying before the feretory in the side aisle of the church, while the community continued their liturgical duties in the choir. Offerings were made, of candles and coins, and the practice of being measured for a candle occurs more than once: 'The father measured his daughter with a thread and surrounded the thread with wax and offered it as a candle to the blessed virgin saint'.[109] The same cure mentions other customs in use for the sick at the tomb—giving blessed water to them to drink or wash their ailing limbs with: 'Nor were her faithful prayers in vain, for as soon as the girl drank the blessed water, the tumour began to go down a little . . . and within a short time she was fully restored to health'.[110] This method was perhaps in imitation of the shrine of St Thomas in which the 'water of Thomas' played so large a part. There is only one mention of it being taken away and that, significantly, is done by putting it into a bottle that had once contained water from Canterbury.[111] This water used at the shrine of St Frideswide was simply *aqua benedicta,* water blessed in the usual manner; it is not to be confused with water from the holy well at Binsey, also associated with St Frideswide, which was the scene of crowds seeking cures at a later date: 'The populace used to frequent the well, as much as the statue and the relics in the shrine, and with great faith they came there to obtain cures in pain and advice in perplexity'.[112]

The feretory was placed to the right of the High Altar. In one vision a boy cured of madness told bystanders that 'he had seen two swans of a great size and ineffable whiteness which were over the top of the

85

shrine'.[113] Mad men and women were dragged toward the shrine bound by ropes, and forced to touch the feretory; the sick came and lay near it, touching or kissing it, sometimes sleeping there all night. Cures were recorded by the monks and greeted with public acclaim. The diseases cured were those familiar at healing shrines. Thirteen blind or partially blind people were cured of eye diseases; five people who were deaf were cured, three who were dumb, a dozen or more who were paralysed, the same number crippled and an equal number with fever; fourteen are described more vaguely as 'ill'. Five people cured were afflicted with madness, one with epilepsy. One of those diagnosed as mad was Helen, a woman from Luttershall who had been the mistress of a priest for three months; she was suffering from sleeplessness and nervous exhaustion, presumably brought on by guilt, and was cured by confessing her sins and praying at the shrine.[114] Equally informative was the cure of Emelina of Headington who tried to commit suicide by drowning, was rescued by the local miller, and was brought to the tomb dumb and paralysed; she was cured by sleeping for five days at the shrine.[115] Instances of skin diseases, swellings, tumours, and ulcers are mentioned, and once a woman who had been a leper for eight years prayed there and was cured.[116] Margaret, the granddaughter of Ralph of Stretona, was cured there of scrofula. This story is an interesting example of propaganda, since she was only partly cured by the Norman king and fully cured by the Anglo-Saxon princess. The climax of the collection is the last miracle, which is told as an instance of St Frideswide raising the dead. A child related to one of the canons had stones, which were extracted by a doctor; the child 'died' as a result of the operation but revived after his mother had prayed to St Frideswide; the stones were preserved at the shrine as proof of the miracle.[117]

The pilgrims who came to the shrine were predominantly local people, but not, as they were at Norwich, primarily members of the community. The only monk to be cured was Prior Philip himself, who devotes twice the amount of space to the account of his cure than he gives to any other miracle.[118] The canons had already shown themselves sceptical about the cures of St Thomas of Canterbury and were perhaps equally aloof from those of St Frideswide. The first cure was that of a child of four, of Oxford parents,[119] and eleven other miracles were performed for Oxford inhabitants. Stephen, a clerk of York, was cured of fever while he was in Oxford to study.[120] Adelitha, from outside the city walls, was cured of blindness;[121] Leviva, who was cured of a crippling disease on the threshold of the shrine, was presumably from Oxford, since she had five children buried there.[122] The cures of Walter, Iachelia, Hugelina, and the son of a brother of one of the canons were all local. Thurben was said to be 'of Holywell', also in Oxford.[123] Eleven people cured were from nearby: Abingdon, Eynsham, Banbury, Newbury, Dorchester, Wallingford, and Aylesbury. Where their homes can be identified, the rest came from the midlands or the south of England: Winchester, Warwick, London, Exeter, Gloucester, Buckingham, Hereford, Salisbury, Bristol, Leicester, and Wendover. No pilgrims from abroad are mentioned, except for Walter of Wales, who came there on his way to the Holy Land[124] and an old Breton knight, cured while visiting relatives in Oxford.[125]

Philip the Prior says that the pilgrims included rich and poor, old and young, of both sexes.[126] Of the really rich there were few. He mentions only five cures of the nobility: John, Constable of Chester; a noble matron, Margaret; two noble ladies, Mabilia and Emma; a goldsmith from Leicester; and with these he includes himself.[127] Nothing is said about the very poor coming to the shrine; the middle classes formed the core, as at most other shrines. Many children were cured there, and a larger number of women than men: twenty-eight men and about sixty-eight women. There is little evidence in the miracle collection to show that the shrine was, as Prior Philip claimed, a centre for organized pilgrimages.[128] The instance he gives of pilgrimage is of three men from Winchester, but they were clearly in the city for purposes of trade, and the cure of one of their number was incidental to their visit, not its purpose.[129] Several people are described as being cured away from Oxford by prayer to the saint and coming there to give thanks, but most of the cures happened at the shrine.

The revived cult of St Frideswide was carefully planned and deliberately established. It owed much to the organizing ability of Prior Philip, who was concerned for the economic needs of the community as much as for the glory of its patron saint. Like other healing shrines, it answered the ever-present needs of the sick in the countryside around Oxford, to whom the city was central and easily accessible. It caught contemporary interest in the old English saints, many of whose relics were being translated at this time to splendid shrines. St Frideswide was not a saint mentioned by Bede like St Ithemar, whose cult was revived at this time in Rochester,[130] but veneration for her memory had survived in Oxford and was still present at the place where she was buried. It was a cult that remained local, though in the Sarum rite her feast attained the status of a feast with nine lessons for her feast day, 19 October.[131] Offerings continued to be made at her shrine, with gifts from Henry III at a second translation of the relics in 1264; in 1518 Catherine of Aragon, accompanied by her husband, visited the church where she venerated the relics;[132] at the Dissolution, the value of the shrine was still highly rated.[133]

5

The Miracles of St Thomas of Canterbury

THE LARGEST COLLECTION OF MIRACLES for the Middle Ages concerns another twelfth-century saint, Thomas Becket, the archbishop of Canterbury. Becket's murder in his cathedral on the evening of 29 December 1170 excited the attention of Christendom and raised him at once to the status of martyr. The death of the archbishop was immediately followed by miracles connected with his name. For the first fifteen years after his death, the official accounts number over seven hundred miracles, an unwieldy mass of material containing information about all kinds of matters, social and economic as well as religious. The immense and immediate popularity of St Thomas after his death affected the development of his cult and therefore the development of miraculous cults in general. I first will discuss the 'traditional' aspects of the miracles, which connected the cult of St Thomas with the place where he was killed and where his body was buried. Next I will consider the nature of the devotion to St Thomas, how it was not confined to the local population and how miracles were effected in his name in many places away from Canterbury. Last, I will discuss the shrine of St Thomas as the dominant shrine of the period, comparable with the Holy Sepulchre and Rome. It was an international shrine, attracting pilgrims from long distances, but its impact can be most clearly seen in its relationship to the shrines of England that were close to it geographically; I will therefore examine this relationship as far as it can be seen in the miracles.

The main evidence for the miracles of St Thomas is found in the account kept at Canterbury by two monks, Benedict and William, from 1171 to c. 1184.[1] Immediately after the murder of St Thomas, the monk Benedict was appointed to record any miracles that occurred at the tomb in the crypt. He had been present in the cathedral at the time of the martyrdom and wrote an account of the death of St Thomas, which was used as a fifth authority by the composer of the *Quadrilogus*.[2] It is apparent from references in the *Miracles* that Benedict regarded this account of the *Passion of St Thomas* as the first part of the whole work.[3] Benedict says he was urged to write by the monks of Canterbury ('by the wish and command of the brethren'[4]), and this arrangement was confirmed for him by three visions in which St Thomas himself directed him to undertake the work.[5] For the first four months after the murder, the tomb of St Thomas was not generally open to the public for fear of the archbishop's enemies;[6] Benedict, however, recorded miracles that happened elsewhere, as well as a few that happened privately in the crypt;[7] and accounts of these were read aloud in the chapter house to the monks. After Easter 1171, when crowds of pilgrims were admitted to the tomb, Benedict was given the care of the sick in the crypt and was also required to record miracles that happened there. The two hundred and fifty or so miracles that he recorded happened either at the tomb in the crypt or in places outside Canterbury; they cover the years 1171 to 1177[8] and form a chronological account of the early miracles.

In 1175, Benedict was made prior of Canterbury and given an assistant in recording the miracles, a monk called William. When Benedict was made abbot of Peterborough two years later, the record passed entirely into the hands of William. William had become a monk of Christ Church during the exile of the archbishop; he was ordained deacon by St Thomas when he returned to Canterbury and was, like Benedict, present in the cathedral on the night of the martyrdom. He also wrote an account of the death of St Thomas that is one of the sources for the *Quadrilogus*.[9] Like Benedict, he claimed to have had three visions of St Thomas, urging him to the work of recording the miracles. Like Benedict, William used notes of the miracles performed at the tomb as the basis of his account of the miracles; sometimes, both writers describe the same miracle,[10] but after 1177, the record was made by William alone. He incorporated into his account descriptions of miracles sent in from other places or recounted by pilgrims as happening elsewhere. Unlike Benedict, William ignores chronological order and groups various kinds of miracles together. His style is elabo-

7   ST THOMAS APPEARS TO A SLEEPING MONK. The saint is shown
issuing from the end of his new shrine in the cathedral (c. 1220); he is ad-
monishing a monk to write down his miracles. This story is told of both
Benedict and William. *Becket Materials*, 2:27–28, 1:138. The picture forms
part of the stained glass windows in the Trinity Chapel, Canterbury cathedral.

8   ST THOMAS APPEARS TO THE LEPER GIMP. The saint is shown
appearing to Gimp to urge him to remind Sir Jordan Fitzeisulf of his promise
to St Thomas. *Becket Materials* 2:229, 1:160. This is also part of the stained
glass of the Trinity Chapel, where it is one incident in the whole story of the
Fitzeisulfs and the saint.

rate and sententious; where Benedict uses a biblical quotation, William turns to the classics. Toward the end of his account, he includes trivial material, with few details of events and a great deal of superfluous comment.

The miracles recorded by both writers are posthumous; they begin at the first tomb of the archbishop and end before the 1220 translation of the relics to the shrine in the church. William's book was presented to Henry II by the monks of Christ Church and seems to have been regarded as a more worthy account than that of Benedict. Odo, then abbot of Battle, sent a copy of Benedict's work to the monastery of Igny as a substitute for a 'much better' book, presumably William's,[11] on the same subject, that had been lost. Gervase of Canterbury, however, regarded both books as the official record.[12] For the purpose of assessing the miracles themselves, the evidence of each writer is essential.

Both writers preface the miracles of St Thomas with descriptions of visions concerned with establishing the sanctity of the martyr: 'I come first to visions and revelations of the Lord by which he consoled his grieving servants and made known in a short while the glory and sanctity of his martyr to the world'.[13] Not surprisingly, these included, especially in William's account, visions in which St Thomas administered punishment to his detractors, in the tradition of St Faith, St Benedict, and St Cuthbert. The visions of weeping queens gathered in the crypt of the cathedral,[14] of the archbishop's name written in the book of life,[15] of a popular demand for his antiphon to be sung in English,[16] are followed by visions in which punishment was meted out to William, a monk who denied that St Thomas was a saint; to a clerk, Oliver of Nantes, who blasphemed against the martyr; to Thomas of Etton for a similar offence; and to Ralph of Nottingham, who kept back sheep belonging to a pilgrim to Canterbury.[17] Those who prayed to St Thomas and failed to fulfil promises made to him were punished, and such miracles occur throughout both accounts. The most notable instance of the vengeance of St Thomas was in the case of the family of Sir Jordan Fitzeisulf. Both Benedict and William tell this story at length, and it forms part of the stained glass windows that later surrounded the shrine of the martyr. Jordan, son of Eisulf, a knight of Pontefract, had a son William who was restored, when on the point of death from the plague, by the 'water of St Thomas'. His father promised four pieces of silver to the martyr, but delayed payment; it was held to be a result of this that an older son died of plague and all the household sickened. The family then undertook the promised pilgrimage and made their offerings, but the death of the second boy was irrevocable.[18] In other cases, the punishment was less extreme, being usually a return of some illness that had been cured by the martyr. Work during the feast or vigil of the saint was also visited by punishment. The imaginary punishments of the four knights involved in the murder called forth other flights of fancy, particularly in the case of Tracy who was said to have died miserably calling on St Thomas for mercy.[19]

As with the older saints, the tomb itself was rapidly made into the focus for the miracles of St Thomas. As soon as it was feasible, after Easter 1171, the crypt of the cathedral was opened to pilgrims, and the tomb of the archbishop was venerated as that of a martyr. The method of veneration followed a familiar pattern. The tomb had been surrounded by a stone wall with holes in it, so that pilgrims might reach through and touch the coffin.[20] The sick came into the crypt and prayed at the tomb, touched it, lay around it, sometimes all night, and made offerings of money or candles. A monk sat there to record miracles as well as to receive the offerings.[21] The sick would also be given the 'water of St Thomas' to drink or to wash in. Benedict records the jubilation of the monks when the sick crowded in for healing after 2 April, 1171, for 'very great and marvellous events occurred at the tomb of the martyr daily'.[22] The offerings were profitable and continued to be so; coins were offered as well as jewels.

Later the body of the saint was placed in a shrine in the church—one of the most exotic shrines of Christendom, plated with gold and covered with jewels, among them apparently the 'Regale', a famous ruby offered by the King of France.[23] Candles were offered at the tomb, and the monks made candles for sale, probably manufacturing them in the wax-chamber above the crypt. Offerings were placed on the tomb, or on the altar at the end of it; when the new shrine was consecrated, offerings were placed on an altar at the end of the feretory. A monk sat or stood by the tomb to record miracles and receive offerings, and there was a money box on the tomb for coins, which are also mentioned in many miracles. Sometimes wax was offered in the shape of a limb that had been cured; possibly this was later used for candles.[24] In certain of the miracle windows another type of offering appears, the significance of which is not clear. This is a coil of thread that in many cases is placed beside the candles as an offering. There is frequent reference in the miracles to being 'measured for a candle' for St Thomas. Salerna of Ifield, for instance, an attempted suicide, was preserved from death. After her rescue she offered a candle: 'She wished to have made a candle which measured the length of her body, to offer it to the martyr for her cure'.[25] Juliana, the wife of Robert Puintel, was cured after childbirth when the nurse persuaded her husband to have her 'measured':

The nurse of the sick woman . . . came to him and persuaded him to have recourse to his [St Thomas's] merits, and to make a prayer to him by making in honour of the saint a candle which was the length and width of her body. . . . So taking an unravelled thread, he measured her, and at once she turned over onto her back and slept a little, breathing slowly like someone who has run a mile race.[26]

It seems probable that a candle was usually made to the length of the thread, but in some cases the coils of thread were taken to Canterbury and offered at the tomb, then used either as wicks for candles or to measure the length of candles required.[27] At least once the thread was made of silver wire, perhaps as a special offering.[28] The offerings at the shrine were extremely profitable. By 1275, the accounts of the cathedral show the keeper of the shrine as the centre of financial activity in the monastery, able to make loans to other departments.[29] This affluence continued, as is shown in other records of offerings, and the fifteenth-century Customary of the shrine shows little diminution in its affluence.[30]

As with the 'traditional' shrines already discussed, the tomb of St Thomas was first venerated by local people from Canterbury and from the home counties. After the murder, the monks were unanimous in their veneration of St Thomas, and his tomb was at once made into a centre of devotion. At first, only they and a few friends whom they admitted had access to the crypt, and inevitably the first miracles happened to them. The poor of Canterbury were said to have been the first to invoke St Thomas, but the long record of miracles eventually included all classes of society, from the very poor,[31] who were first to venerate him, to kings of England and France. In the miracles recorded by William, the greater number are of the well-to-do; this may be because the shrine was better known later and had become a fashionable centre to visit. William himself suggests another reason for there being fewer records of miracles for the poor. In recording a miracle in which a noble lady called Mabel claimed that her son had been raised from the dead, he argues (in a tortuous piece of prose, in which he addresses his hand, 'scribe, *manus*') that the evidence given by the nobility is to be preferred, because the poor are always liars, '*mendicos mendaces*', a pun that is hardly a serious statement.[32] Benedict, however, confirms the idea that more miracles were recorded of the rich than of the poor; he says that the poor who were cured left the shrine without mentioning it, since they could not afford a gift to the saint.[33] Only when they were clear of the cathedral could a miracle be of use to them for gaining alms, as subjects of St Thomas's miraculous powers. Throughout the records of miracles at shrines, the poorest members of society are less frequently recorded as benefiting from the powers of the saints; this is perhaps because they were inarticulate and made no mark in the records, rather than being less frequently subject to cures.

The illnesses cured at the shrine of St Thomas covered the whole range of sickness as diagnosed at the time. Blindness, deafness, paralysis, lameness, dumbness, and withered limbs are mentioned. Frequently a skin disease was diagnosed as leprosy and presented for cure at the shrine, perhaps because of the leper hospital at Harbledown, just outside the city. The many cases of madness were treated at the shrine with customary brutality; William observes that the English regarded moodiness as madness and treated it as such. The ultimate miracle of raising the dead is recounted several times, usually of young children. Cures were such a prominent feature of the shrine of St Thomas that a boy in Harbledown protested, when his parents wanted him to visit Canterbury with them, that he was not ill; he needed a mysterious and sudden illness to persuade him to go.[34] The conviction that sin was the basic cause of sickness is portrayed in these miracles, as it will be seen to have been in the miracles at the shrines of the Virgin. It is possible, however, that at Canterbury, as at other shrines, some use was also made of medicine for the sick, and some miracles mention this.[35] William and Benedict, in the tradition of miracle writers, disparage doctors, but it is possible that William, at least, had used the large medical library owned by Christ Church[36] to good effect.[37] The account of the miracles concludes with some stories of cures performed on animals and birds; but these are told in a lighter vein and will be considered below as the '*joca S Thomae*'.

The martyr of Canterbury was in many ways the centre of a 'traditional' cult focussed on the place where his body lay, and he appeared as a vengeful and powerful saint, as well as one powerful to heal those who came to his tomb and prayed in the traditional manner. A closer examination shows that from the first the cult was shot through with other elements. First of all, the vengeance of Becket was not directed toward those who encroached upon monastic lands, nor were his relics used in defence of territorial rights. The lands of Canterbury were already secured and by quite different means than threats of revenge from a saint.[38] The prestige of Canterbury as one of the great metropolitan sees of the West was also already established by a succession of saints and ecclesiastics of note; the only sign in the miracles that this prestige was still in need of support is a miracle directed against the rival of Becket, the archbishop of York, against whom he had repeatedly urged the rights of his see.[39] Usually, however, like St William of Norwich, the anger of St Thomas is more personal. It is directed against those who fail to venerate him properly, those who do not bring offerings or fail to fulfil their promises, those who work on his feast day. His protection extended toward those devoted to him rather than to those who were his men and he their patron. What impressed his chroniclers about St Thomas was not that he worked miracles on behalf of the monastery at Canterbury, but that he worked miracles for his enemies: for Henry II, in the victory over Scotland at the time of his penance;[40] in a cure of both a servant of Gilbert Foliot and of Foliot himself;[41] and in the cure of a member of the De Broc family, one of whom had assisted in his death.[42]

A second element that made the cult of St Thomas less 'traditional' was the international character of devotion to him. Visions of St Thomas, cures by St Thomas were claimed at once all over Europe; pilgrims came to the tomb having already experienced the power of the martyr. Thomas Becket was a great man; his career was well-known not only in England but throughout Europe; the causes for which he fought were more than the local concerns of Canterbury versus York, of criminous clerks or appeals to Rome—they were part of the conflict of papacy and empire. The archbishop became involved in European affairs during the six years of his exile, 1164–1170;[43] Becket and his causes were a part of the affairs of Alexander III, of Louis VII of France, and of Frederick Barbarossa. His death reverberated throughout Europe, with the result that his veneration as a martyr occurred in distant places almost as soon as in those near home. His death was the occasion of visions at Argentan:

At Argentan it happened the night before his martyrdom, that there was the sound of grieving, by which grief the rumour of the death of the martyr was first heard in that town; 'The voice was heard saying, "Behold, blood cries to the Lord from the earth which is greater than the blood of the righteous Abel who was killed from the foundation of the world".'[44]

A clerk in Orleans, a clerk at Coutances, and Dom Oliver of Nantes were all made aware of the martyrdom at once by visions.[45] Much was made of a dream Thomas himself experienced about his death while he was at Pontigny.[46] Peter, a monk of Poitiers, came to Canterbury within three years of the death of Becket to be healed of his leprosy;[47] Matilda of Cologne was brought there to be cured of her madness;[48] Gerard of Liège was also brought there to be cured of madness.[49] The bishop of Evreux related how a Saracen had dreamed of St Thomas at Palermo and been converted as a result;[50] John of Salisbury says that the bishop of Clermont publicly related the miracles of Becket at Bourges;[51] William records as many miracles performed by St Thomas in France as in England. Both Benedict and William stress the fame St Thomas had abroad, and include accounts of miracles performed 'east and west', in the Holy Land and in Norway.[52] Although the main centre of the cult was the tomb, the cult was also a spontaneous movement that sprang up without any urging among those devoted to the cause of the archbishop elsewhere.

This enthusiasm is the more remarkable, since it is clear from the miracles that St Thomas was not regarded as a saint for supreme holiness of life. John of Salisbury thought he dominated society, but as a recent writer has observed, greatness is not synonymous with sanctity.[53] In this period, however, there was increasing demand for virtue and holiness in those acclaimed saints; the monastic, and particularly the Cistercian, concept of virtue rather than miracles as the true sign of sanctity was being made explicit by the papal process of canonization. St Thomas of Canterbury was acclaimed a saint in the old-fashioned manner. He was a martyr, and martyrdom was held to be sufficient cause for calling him 'sanctus';[54] he was called 'saint' by the people, who saw him as a saint at once, without waiting for the official declaration;[55] and he was confirmed as a saint by his posthumous miracles, not by his living virtues. Yet even in this most 'traditional' of all approaches to sanctity, some wanted to see him as a saint with a virtuous life.[56] The various accounts of the life and death of St Thomas included some miracles alleged to have happened in his lifetime, and all writers agreed, perhaps with too much emphasis, on one indisputable mark of sanctity (significantly a mark of monastic sanctity):

Then the monks removed his clothing, and they found underneath a very harsh hair shirt, and his flesh severely lacerated and full of worms.[57] When the monks saw that the most holy man had secretly borne all the marks of sanctity and religion they rejoiced beyond measure and wonderingly said quietly to each other, 'Lo, here is a true monk and ascetic! Lo, here is a martyr indeed, who suffered torments not long in his death but in his life.'[58]

Grim records with disapproval that only a few minutes earlier the monks themselves had been heard to express doubts about the archbishop's sanctity;[59] the discovery of the hair shirt was held to prove heroic asceticism, and later it became the subject of pious speculation in a manner entirely typical of the late twelfth century. The question 'how?' replaced the question 'why?'. If Becket wore a hair shirt in secret, how did he keep it repaired? The answer was that the Virgin Mary mended his drawers for him, and a new cycle of miracle stories was added to the original fact.[60] Other writers tried to find evidence of sanctity during Becket's life: Arnold of Lübeck told how Thomas had changed water into wine at the table of the pope, and his story was repeated by Roger of Hoveden.[61] Grim gives instances of miracles during St Thomas's childhood,[62] drawn from the stock miracles of hagiography, and Becket's own visions and forebodings were exaggerated to the point of prophecy.[63] But none of these stories made Becket a saint, at home or abroad. What caused his acclaim was first of all his heroic and public defence of the church, then the outrage of his murder in his cathedral, and thirdly the rapidly spread report of his miracles. But it is noteworthy that his supporters felt it necessary to add claims for a life of sanctity, however sparse the material, especially when seeking his canonization.

The monks of Canterbury regarded St Thomas as their own martyr, and took immediate steps to preserve his body from further desecration and to ensure that it remained in their possession. They also kept a careful and exact record of the miracles, rejecting evidence that did not convince them, at times to the indignation of their visitors who thought themselves misjudged.[64] They did not, however, escape charges of working miracles by magic,[65] and the debate about the sanctity of their saint was by no means settled by either the manner of his death or the number of his miracles.[66]

In the first days after the murder there was one factor that to some extent made the cult less focussed on the tomb. The desecrated church was closed to pilgrims. The first miracles of St Thomas, even in Canterbury, took place away from the tomb. A tradition was established that St Thomas would hear the prayers of those who prayed to him, wherever they were. On the night of the death of St Thomas, a cure by invocation of the martyr occurred some miles away; Emma, wife of a knight in Sussex, was cured of blindness: 'This beginning of signs Jesus did in Sussex and manifested the glory of his martyr before his disciples' says Benedict, echoing the words of St John's Gospel.[67] Three days later Huelina, the sick daughter of Azaliza of London, was cured at Gloucester by her mother's prayers to St Thomas;[68] the swollen arm of a knight was cured in Berkshire;[69] cures were known in London,[70] Hoyland,[71] Harbledown,[72] Surrey;[73] over twenty cures in Benedict's collection are recorded before the opening of the crypt made it possible for pilgrims to approach the tomb and pray there. After Easter 1171, the situation was different. The church had been restored to use, pilgrims were able to visit the shrine, the pressure of public opinion had turned against the enemies of Becket and ensured that his cult would be unimpeded.[74] John of Salisbury, writing to a friend both of himself and Becket, described the cult thus, early in 1171:

In the place where Thomas suffered, and where he lay the night through, before the high altar awaiting burial, and where he was buried at last, the palsied are cured, the blind see, the deaf hear, the dumb speak, the lepers are cleansed, those possessed of a devil are freed, and the sick are made whole from all manner of disease, blasphemers taken over by the devil are put to confusion. . . . I should not have dreamt of writing such words on any account had not my eyes been witness to the certainty of this.[75]

He mentions three places for veneration of the martyr—the place of his death, the altar, and the first tomb in the crypt. He also says that he had seen the miracles with his own eyes, and in spite of the biblical reminiscence of the cures mentioned, there is no reason to suppose that he lied. Garnier gives a similar account of these early miracles at the tomb:

God is here with us upon earth for love of the martyr. He brings the dead to life, makes the dumb speak, the deaf hear, cripples stand up straight, he cures the gouty and the fevered, restores the dropsied and the leprous to health, makes the blind see and brings lunatics into their right mind. Kings have sought him on pilgrimage, princes, barons, dukes, strangers from foreign countries, speaking many languages, prelates, monks, recluses, crowds of travellers on foot; they take phials home with them as a sign of their journey.[76]

This multitude of miracles, however, at the places in the cathedral most especially connected with the murder, account for only half of the actual cures reported by Benedict and William. Canterbury was a shrine at which cures happened; but even more it was a centre for pilgrims who offered thanksgiving for cures elsewhere in the name of the martyr.[77]

This matter of being cured away from Canterbury is closely connected with another factor that caused the dispersion of the cult: the use of relics of the martyr at a distance from the shrine. The first and most important of these was 'the water of St Thomas', water into which a little of the blood drained from the body of St Thomas had been infused. Until this time, the most common way of asking for the prayers of the saints was by praying and making offerings at the tomb; however, another popular means of contact with the saints, alive as well as dead, was by using water that had in some way touched them. Water in which the tomb of St Benedict had been washed cured thousands at Chateaux-Gordon;[78] water containing dust from the tomb of St William was used at Norwich;[79] water that was blessed was used at the tomb of St Frideswide.[80] All these uses of water continued a long tradition that can be traced back through the miracles of St Martin into a pre-Christian past.[81] Using the 'water of St Thomas' had been foreseen from the moment of the martyrdom. Ernold the Goldsmith and some others had at once been called into the cathedral to clear up the mess of blood and brains from the flagstones, and the results were preserved.[82]

The body was then placed before the High Altar, where the monks kept watch all night to collect any more blood that flowed from his wounds:

They carried the most holy body and laid it before the high altar, and it lay there throughout the night, surrounded by the monks in great sadness and grief. They placed under it a container to catch the blood that flowed from it, being not ignorant of the value of the most precious blood of the martyr which flowed for the love of God and the liberty of the church.[83]

Herbert of Bosham says that some of the poor of Canterbury came and dipped rags in the blood of the martyr,[84] and one later used this relic to cure his paralysed wife.[85]

Writers compared the blood of the martyr to the blood of Christ, 'the lamb of Canterbury' to the 'lamb of Bethlehem', and said that water and blood from the side of Christ on the Cross (John 19:34) was parallel to the water and blood of St Thomas, 'the blood of the Lamb of Bethlehem, and the blood of the lamb of Canterbury'.[86] The cure of William, a priest in London, on the eighth day after the martyrdom, was done by blood mixed with water. William was dumb and paralysed; he had a friend who dreamed that 'if a drop of the holy blood were to be placed upon his tongue, he would regain his speech'.[87] William went to Canterbury, entered the tomb in the crypt secretly by permission of the monks, and drank the water mixed with blood, thereby obtaining his cure. The son of Godfrid the Baker[88] was also cured by the 'blood of St Thomas'. The blood was not always mixed with water, as is clear from the experience of Audrey, a matron of Canterbury, who was horrified at being offered blood to drink and for whom it was mixed with water:

A monk diluted it [the blood], as he used to do for others, lest they should be horrified by the taste and colour of the blood they were drinking.[89]

The blood and water mixture was the monopoly of the monks at the tomb, but from there it could be taken away. At first it was carried off in wooden boxes, but these were found so unreliable that a young man was employed to make tin containers.[90] The phials were often carved with scenes from the martyrdom and became the distinctive sign of the Canterbury pilgrimage, as the scallop shell was that of Compostela and the palm that of Jerusalem. Many miracles are connected with the blood itself. It vanished from unworthy hands,[91] it multiplied for the deserving,[92] it boiled with anger at instances of uncharity.[93] The instinctive use of the blood of the martyr by the poor of Canterbury and by the monks points to part of the reason for the immense interest shown in this cult. The cult was essentially popular, a cult that sprang up spontaneously for deeply-rooted reasons, not one that needed to be cultivated by the keepers of the shrine. Its appeal was widespread and focussed on the person, not of the great churchman, but of the great martyr; the use of his blood is the most intimate strand in this personal devotion, as well as one of the means by which the cult was decentralized.

Other relics of Becket were also venerated away from the shrine. William, a priest of Bishopsbourne near Canterbury, removed from the cathedral the blood-stained cloak in which the martyr was slain, in order to use it for miracles in his own village.[94] The monks were ready to send fragments of Becket's clothing or even more intimate relics on request: William Fitzralph, for instance, was given from the martyr's hair shirt scraps that he placed in Whitchurch, where the relic effected twenty-two cures on behalf of the Welsh.[95] The demand for relics of Becket for veneration away from Canterbury grew. A letter to Prior Eastry, for instance, c. 1285–1291, says that a monastery in France had received some hairs from the head of Becket by the dubious means of the boy Huet, a runaway servant from Canterbury, and they asked for the relics to be guaranteed.[96] When Erasmus and Colet visited Canterbury, they were offered Becket's shoe for veneration, as well as the head of the martyr.[97]

While the diffusion of relics helped diffuse the cult, a tendency to stress the saint's ability to answer sincere prayers of his devotees, even if they used false relics, also helped. Benedict related how an ill young man asked for the water of St Thomas: 'Not having any to hand, someone ran to the well and filled a container with water. "Behold", he said, "here is the water of the saint you asked for".' He drank it and was cured.[98] Caesarius of Heisterbach expressed this 'inward' view of relics in connection with those of St Thomas. He tells how a knight bought a false relic of St Thomas's bridle: 'God . . . willing to reward the faith of the knight deigned to perform many miracles in honour of his martyr by means of this bridle'. The subjective belief of the person using the relic is more important than its provenance, and Caesarius adds: 'It is certain that this is true, since sometimes the Lord works miracles through false relics to honour the saints to whom they are ascribed and for those who do them honour in good faith'.[99] At the close of the period under discussion, the fourth Lateran Council urged a method of verification of relics more careful than ever before.[100] The proliferation of relics in cults such as that of St Thomas led to the desire to verify the relics and to a subjective, personal element in their use. This personal element in devotion marks a new religious sensibility, and it can be found within the cult of the immensely popular St Thomas.

St Thomas of Canterbury was canonized three years after his death. Pope Alexander III had proceeded in the matter with what seemed to him all the speed possible, but which looked to the English like irritating slowness. The accounts of St Thomas's miracles had been examined by the legates Albert and Theodwin, and on 10 March 1173, the pope wrote to them, accepting their report and announcing that St Thomas was officially acclaimed as a saint.[101] Two days later he wrote to the community at Canterbury with the bull *Gaudendum est* and ordered them to translate the body to a shrine and observe the anniversary of the martyrdom yearly.[102] The mass and Office of St Thomas, both for the day of his death and his translation, formed part of the liturgy of the universal church, completing the picture of St Thomas as an international saint.[103] In England, his canonization had been eagerly awaited. One incident in the miracles recorded by William shows that the church had waited for papal approval before according him full liturgical honour. Reginald, a priest of Wretham, dreamed that at Divine Office a monk asked for the antiphon of St Thomas to be sung. It was not sung in Latin, since St Thomas had not yet been officially canonized ('the martyr was not yet enrolled by apostolic authority in the list of martyrs'), but the writer says that it was permissible to sing the antiphon in English, the language in which he wrote it down.[104] In the cult of St William of Norwich a similar contrast has been observed between enthusiastic devotion and official recognition; the steadying power of authority was recognized in the case of the cult of St Thomas, which like other cults of the period was liable to be submerged in enthusiasm and emotion.

The influence of St Thomas upon the devotion of Europe was considerable. His festivals were introduced, churches were dedicated to him,

104

and he was included in representation of the saints, for instance in Monreale.[105] It was in England, however, that it is possible to see in detail how this supremely popular shrine affected other cults. The first cult to which it can be compared is that of St William of Norwich, established nearly twenty-five years before the death of St Thomas. The cult had been known in Canterbury as early as 1155, when the sacristan of Holy Trinity Church in Canterbury visited Norwich on family business and was cured of an illness there by prayer to St William.[106] Christ Church itself had an interest in Norwich, since it drew annual rents from lands there.[107] The cult of St William anticipated the cult of St Thomas in its central attraction. Both saints were martyrs, and the biographers of both drew the parallel between their sufferings and those of Christ. In the last story about St William recorded by Thomas of Monmouth, the rivalry with the cult of St Thomas is made explicit. In 1172, when the Canterbury cult was well established, Gaudfrid, a citizen of Canterbury, ate a good supper of 'white peas and a fat goose' after the extraction of three teeth. His head swelled as a result, and he spent all night praying for a cure at the tomb of St Thomas in Canterbury. He had a vision of the saint, who advised him to apply hot wax to his swollen face and then go to Norwich to give thanks for his cure. Gaudfrid's journey was miraculously accomplished in one day, and he claimed to have had as his companions St Thomas himself and St Edmund from the nearby shrine at Bury.[108] Thomas of Monmouth assures the reader with suspicious fervour of the credibility of this. With this piece of propaganda, Thomas of Monmouth attempts to make the cult of St William share the popularity of the new saint at Canterbury and asserts the equality of St William with the archbishop whose cult was so rapidly turning devotion toward itself.

The cult of St Thomas also rivaled the cults of two northern saints. Reginald of Durham was a less emotional writer than Thomas of Monmouth, and, in his accounts of the shrines of both St Cuthbert and St Godric, he had more certain grounds for his support of them against St Thomas. He frequently compared St Cuthbert with other saints to their detriment, but even the dominant saint of the North had to meet the challenge of the new martyr. Twice in the *Miracles* Reginald gives the names of the three greatest saints in England, always with St Cuthbert as the greatest of the three and St Edmund as the second; it is the third place that changes. In the first story of a choice between saints, probably before 1083, a pilgrim drew lots between St Cuthbert, St Edmund, and St Etheldreda;[109] by 1172, when a pilgrim came from Norway seeking a cure in England and drew lots again between three saints, he chooses between St Cuthbert, St Edmund, and St Thomas of Canterbury.[110] Within a year of his death, therefore, St Thomas was, for a foreigner, one of the three greatest saints in England; but Reginald makes it clear also that locally St Cuthbert maintained his preeminence. He asserted the position of St Cuthbert against St Thomas in three other stories. In two cases, North country people who would properly come under the jurisdiction of St Cuthbert prayed at Canterbury for a cure and were directed by the saint to go to Durham. A boy from Berwick with dysentery walked all the way to Canterbury, only to be ordered back to Durham in a vision.[111] A man from Rudby in Cleveland became ill with grief at the death of his brother and prayed to St Thomas and St Godric; both saints appeared to him, one at Canterbury, the other at Finchale, with directions to return and pray at Durham.[112] The other man to be sent to Durham after prayer at Canterbury was a former clerk in the service of Becket, who had prayed at the tomb of his master, yet was sent to be cured by *potissimus*' St Cuthbert.[113]

The power of St Cuthbert in the North was not seriously challenged by the new devotion to St Thomas. But it was a different matter for a new shrine to be established in the shadow of the cult of Canterbury. Two cults that emerged after the death of St Thomas bear marks of a struggle with his popularity. In the case of the first, that of St Godric, whose life was also written by Reginald, the miracles of St Thomas are used skilfully to support those of St Godric. Thomas and Godric died in the same year, and Reginald devotes three chapters of his work on the miracles of St Godric to the relationship between Thomas and Godric while they were alive.[114] He says that in 1162 Thomas heard of Godric from a monk of Westminster who had visited Durham; Thomas claimed that he already knew Godric and asked the monk to take a private message to the hermit from him. On receiving the message, Godric replied by prophesying the archbishop's exile and return and asking for his absolution; Thomas refused the absolution saying that Godric was not under his jurisdiction. Although Reginald interpreted this exchange with the knowledge that both are acclaimed as saints, the communication between Thomas and Godric is not inherently unlikely. It has its counterpart in the relationship of other great men with hermits, for instance, St Bernard and Wulfric of Haselbury.[115]

Throughout the two hundred and twenty-five posthumous miracles of St Godric, Reginald frequently refers to St Thomas. He gives the gist of a scholastic discussion held in Durham on the comparative merits of Thomas and Godric as saints and says this topic was popular at the time.[116] Reginald claims that Thomas and Godric are equal in the sight of God, and in later miracles Reginald presents Godric and Thomas as friends who share miracles. In one case, St Cuthbert joined them. A woman of Esindene had been poisoned, though not fatally, by her husband's mistress, and after fourteen years of sickness she went to Finchale for a cure. There she claimed to see Godric with St Thomas and St Cuthbert in a tree outside the church, though bystanders only saw three white birds; she said that St Thomas had given his blessing to the crowd, and she herself was promptly cured.[117] A blind woman in a hospital in Durham said she could see St Thomas in the form of a dove, flying toward her; she confessed her sins, was cured, and went to give thanks to both St Thomas and Godric at Finchale.[118] Another woman saw a vision of Godric walking round a church with St Thomas and was cured by them.[119] Raithmildis attributed her cure at Finchale to both St Thomas and Godric.[120] Hathwisa, a blind woman from Durham, Adlusa, who was dumb, and Cecilia of Bothdale, whose daughter was blind in one eye, all went at different times to ask for cures at Canterbury and were directed in visions to Finchale with better results.[121] Agnes of Karelton and a man from Appleby both planned to go to Canterbury to ask for cures, but went instead to Finchale. These miracles assert a friendship between the two saints that enabled the shrine at Finchale to draw support from Canterbury.

The rivalry between the cult of St Thomas and that of St Frideswide was open and obvious. The Oxford shrine was set up ten years after the death of Becket and the miracles seem to rival those of St Thomas, though they are few in number compared with those at Canterbury. In the miracles Benedict records of St Thomas, he gives an account of the cure of Robert of Cricklade, prior of St Frideswide's in Oxford, who had contracted a painful illness in his foot while in Sicily twelve years previously; finding all remedies in vain, he decided after Easter 1171 to pray at the tomb of Becket; this he did and was cured, relating his cure in detail to Benedict, who recounted it verbatim.[122] Later, Robert, a canon of St Frideswide's, was given the water of St Thomas when ill, and he recovered.[123] The prior then asked the brethren who had seen the cure if they still doubted the power of St Thomas, indicating that up to that time they had not been convinced. When Prior Philip succeeded Robert, he began to organize a cult around the relics of their own saint in opposition to Canterbury. The relics of St Frideswide were translated to a shrine in 1180, and the next Easter a knight from Brittany came there after praying in vain for a cure of his many ills at Canterbury. He slept all night at the tomb and was cured.[124] There is no question of the saints sharing the honours of this miracle or gracefully making way for another; St Frideswide had succeeded where St Thomas had notably failed. Isabella of Beckhampton was cured by St Frideswide after an illness following childbirth, and not by St Thomas whom she visited first.[125] Margaret, wife of a man in Burford, was cured by St Thomas only partially, but fully by St Frideswide;[126] Adelicia was sent to Oxford expressly by St Thomas to be cured of her deafness by St Frideswide.[127] William of Shrivenham was cured first by St Thomas, but more completely by St Frideswide.[128] In the final miracle of St Frideswide that concerns St Thomas, a noble matron Margaret had one of the bottles made for the water of St Thomas; it was empty, and she filled it with water blessed at the shrine of St Frideswide; the water turned to milk, and she kept it for veneration of St Frideswide in her private chapel.[129] Several of the Oxford miracles seem parallel to those of St Thomas, but this similarity is perhaps illusory because the number of the miracles of St Thomas makes it easy to find parallels to practically any miracle. But it seems probable that Prior Philip had read or heard at least some of the miracles at Canterbury and was influenced in his selection of those for his own shrine, even if he did not imitate them more directly.

The great cult of St Thomas was securely established in England. It had no rival for many years. It could, in fact, afford one thing that few other shrines could risk: the admission of failure. Among the miracles recorded by Benedict, there are accounts of people praying to Becket and not being cured; in two cases, the men died peacefully instead.[130] Twice, pilgrims were told by visions of the archbishop that they would not be cured.[131] Sometimes, partial cures were recorded, which the chronicler explains as happening because 'the saint willed it'.

The miracles of St Thomas belong to a cult of the oldest and most traditional kind, that of a martyr venerated at the place of his death. Where it differs from the usual pattern is in its immense popularity and the spontaneous devotion offered to St Thomas throughout Europe. This devotion ensured a continuous stream of pilgrims to Canterbury for many years, longer than to any other English shrine, and a large proportion of these pilgrims were people who had already called on the name of St Thomas at home and experienced a miracle there. The use of the water of St Thomas added to the widespread veneration of him. A secondary result of the popularity of the Canterbury pilgrimage was observed even by the monks Benedict and William: beggars and mountebanks exploited the cult and brought the relics of St Thomas into some disrepute. The end of that process was seen in the most famous of all Canterbury pilgrimages, described by Chaucer, of pilgrims who came with past benefits in mind:

> The holy blisful martir for to seke
> that them hath holpen whan that they were sick.

The atmosphere of jollity caused the host of the Tabard Inn to remark that he 'ne saugh this yeer so mery a companye'.

6

Miracles and Pilgrimage

THE SHRINES SO FAR CONSIDERED have been those that drew their
clientele from a relatively local area, but there were other shrines that
were distant goals for the inhabitants of Northern Europe. All shrines
attracted pilgrims, but three of these distant shrines are 'pilgrimage
shrines' in the particular sense that they drew pilgrims from a very wide
area. All three places were connected with biblical persons of the first
importance: St James, St Peter, and Christ himself. The miracles connected with St James can be examined both in Spain, where it was said
that his body was buried at Compostela, and in the shrine made to
contain the relic of his hand in Reading Abbey.

The main record of the miracles of St James is found in the *Liber
Miraculorum S Jacobi,* the oldest version of which is in the *Codex Calixtinus* in the archives of the cathedral at Santiago.[1] The Codex consists of
five books. The first contains materials for the celebration of the three
feasts of St James (25 July, 30 December, and 3 October); the second is
the book of miracles; the third gives an account of the evangelization of
Spain by St James and the arrival of a relic of his head to complete the
body discovered in Spain; the fourth book is an account of the legend of
Roland and Charlemagne; the fifth a guide for pilgrims going to Compostela. The book takes its name from its preface, an apocryphal letter
of Pope Calixtus II. This seems to have been the book found at Compostela in 1173 by Arnold de Monte and described by him when he
sent a transcription of books two, three, and four to the abbot of Notre
Dame de Ripoli: 'I found a book containing five sections of accounts of
the miracles of the apostle by which his glory shines out in diverse parts
of the world like the shining of the stars'.[2] References to miracles of St

James are found in each book except the fourth, but it is the second book that forms the core of the miracle collection for St James. It is not a shrine collection like those hitherto discussed. At the shrine of St James records of miracles may have been inscribed on scedulae as elsewhere, and such cures are mentioned in a sermon attributed to Calixtus II:

From the time it was begun until today that church displays the glory of the miracles of St James, for the sick are restored to health, the blind receive their sight, many tongues that were dumb are loosed, the deaf hear again, the lame are given the strength to walk, demoniacs are set free, and what is even more, the prayers of the faithful are heard, their vows are fulfilled, and the chains of their sins are unloosed.[3]

The notion of continuous cures at a shrine during its rebuilding will be considered in more detail in connection with shrines of the Virgin. The cures are here mentioned in a general way, and the illnesses listed are those stock illnesses of any miracle collection. It is possible that records were also kept of detailed instances of such cures, but if so they do not survive, nor are they among the miracles in the *Liber S Jacobi,* in which only two cures are mentioned, one of which was in Italy.

It seems probable that the miracle stories were meant to form a set of lessons for liturgical reading, in chapel and in refectory, for the feast of the Miracles of St James on 3 October—a feast kept in the twelfth century, whose origin is attributed to Anselm of Canterbury.[4] Each story is related in a stylized form, beginning with a similar introductory phrase giving the date and place of each miracle, and concluding with the biblical and liturgical phrase: 'this is the Lord's doing and it is marvellous in our eyes'.[5] Moreover, the material may have been meant for use in monastic houses rather than at Compostela, since it is suitable for a twelve lesson office of vigil rather than for the nine lesson vigils used at the cathedral in Compostela.[6] If so, the miracles of St James would be within the monastic tradition, possibly that of Cluny.

The miracles of St James in this collection are predominantly instances of protection for his devotees. Those thus helped were all men; there is no mention of women directly experiencing his miracles.[7] Of these men, most were soldiers, and only seven persons pursuing other occupations are mentioned. Of these, three were merchants, two bishops, one a tanner, one a peasant, and the other a child. The first of these miracles describes how Count Ermengotus and twenty other soldiers captured by the Saracens during the invasion of Spain by Almoravides (1086) were delivered by prayer to St James.[8] A French knight, Bernard, was set free by St James from an Italian prison.[9] An Italian knight who had been a pilgrim to Compostela obtained the help of St James when escaping from his enemies in battle in Italy.[10] A knight who was a vassal of Count Fontis Calacres was delivered by St James.[11] A French knight had the help of St James in battles with the infidel in the Holy Land.[12] A knight returning from the Holy Land had the protection of St James when he fell into the sea.[13] Three knights went on pilgrimage to St James together,[14] and thirty knights made a pact to do the same.[15] Of the two cures attributed to St James, one was the cure of a nobleman from Burgundy,[16] the other a knight in Italy.[17] In a miracle connected with the shrine itself, the participants were the Count of St Gilles and his brother.[18] In the miracle of the knight temporarily restored to life, another knight is introduced in the second theme of the story by a message of warning conveyed to him by the one who returned from the dead.[19] The clergy mentioned are bishops rather than plain clerics.[20]

The protection of St James for the fighting class was reinforced by visions of the saint. He was seen as *Santiago Matamoros,* the supernatural defender of Spain against the infidel. Visions were seen of him on a white charger at decisive points in the reconquest of Spain: at Clavijo in the ninth century, at Simancas in the tenth, Coimbra in the eleventh, and in the decisive battles at Las Navas de Tolosa in 1212. When the reconquest was complete, it was at the shrine of St James that Ferdinand and Isabella gave thanks in 1492. On one hand, churchmen were interested in St James as the senior of the apostles and claimed ecclesiastical preference for the see of Santiago on those grounds;[21] but on the other, the pressing need of Spain for a rallying point against the infidel led to emphasis on St James as a soldier.[22] These two themes are shown vividly in a miracle about a Greek bishop who made his home at Compostela. He heard the pilgrims praying to St James as a soldier ('blessed James, good soldier, deliver us from all evils both now and to come') and rebuked them, saying St James was not a soldier but a fisherman and apostle. That night he dreamed that St James appeared to him clad as a crusader ready for battle:

Blessed James appeared, clad in white garments, bearing the arms of a warrior, shining with radiance and arrayed as a soldier, holding in his hand two keys. Then he made this position even clearer in words, 'I am appearing to you so that you will not doubt that God has made me a soldier and a contender and set me to fight for the Christians against the Saracens and to gain the victory for them.'[23]

In confirmation of this, he foretold that Coimbra would fall to the Christians next day.

As patron of the forces fighting the infidel, St James attracted the devotion of all those engaged in this warfare, including many knights from France and especially from Burgundy. Their offerings to Cluny from the spoils of war were notable and forge another link between the miracles of St James and Cluny.[24] The appointment of the Cluniac Dalmace as archbishop of Compostela made the connection tighter.[25] The miracles themselves went under the name of Pope Calixtus II. It is possible that he was directly responsible for the collection. It originated in Vienne when he was archbishop there; he knew Anselm, who, as will be seen, was also concerned with the collection; and he was known to be interested in St James.[26] On the other hand, a less well-known author may have taken the name 'Calixtus' for his work, precisely because of the interest Calixtus II had in the saint and his pilgrimage.

This collection describes miracles of St James that happened away from the shrine; they were miracles either of protection in battle or of protection for pilgrims. At the shrine itself, 'the body of St James is to be venerated under the high altar that was built in his honour, where, it seems, he lies buried in a marble tomb'.[27] One of the miracles shows that the tomb was not normally accessible to pilgrims, but closed off by gates, except at specific times.[28] The collection does not describe crowds lying around the tomb as at Canterbury or Fleury; it does, however, describe pilgrims who came to the tomb to give thanks for benefits from St James conferred elsewhere. Miracles of protection often took place along the pilgrim route, and in these accounts the influence of Cluny is clear. Most of the places mentioned in the miracles lay along the routes between Cluny and Compostela: in Burgundy, the Viennois, the Lyonnais, even within a few miles of Cluny itself. Those who told the stories had close connections with Cluny: a canon of Besançon, the abbot of Vezelay,[29] but especially Abbot Hugh and Archbishop Anselm.

113

The letter prefacing this collection states that the miracles were collected for the benefit of the monks of Cluny.[30] Three of the stories were taken from the *Dicta Anselmi,* the record of conversations between Anselm and Abbot Hugh, when the former was at Cluny during his exile, either in 1099–1100, or 1104–1105. One of these tales later found a place in the Miracles of the Virgin, with any mention of the power of James replaced by that of the Virgin. Anselm and Pope Calixtus are given as sources for the miracles from the *Dicta Anselmi* in the St James collection. The sixteenth miracle has this rubric: 'a miracle of St James, related by St Anselm archbishop of Canterbury'; the seventeenth: 'a great miracle of St James related by St Anselm, archbishop of Canterbury';[31] and the eighteenth: 'a miracle of St James recorded by Pope Calixtus'. Here *conscribere* is used instead of *edere,* which may suggest that the pope was writing the account from his own knowledge while the Anselm miracles were copied from elsewhere, or it may be simply a variation of style.

The first two miracles are of particular interest. They are very much longer than the rest, and instead of the phrase 'this is the Lord's doing', they end with 'who lives and reigns'. They are also found in the *Miracula S Anselmi.*[32] The first of these stories is about three knights on pilgrimage to Compostela; one of them helps a poor woman pilgrim and also a sick man on the route; at the shrine itself he becomes ill and dreams that St James has defended him from the demons because of his good deeds to the poor pilgrims; restored to life, he tells his story and dies later.[33] The story's moral emphasizes the rewards for those who do good to pilgrims; a moral that would undoubtedly appeal to both St Anselm and St Hugh, with its stress on salvation rather than earthly help. The reaction of the companions of the sick knight to his illness at Compostela is also revealing. They say that he must be ill because of a hidden sin, and they urge him to repent. The connection of illness with sin is made clear, as in the miracles of the Virgin; the difficulty of salvation for a knight is also illustrated by the immediate claims of the demons upon the man. It is a typical piece of propaganda for the Cluniac ideal of knighthood saved by pilgrimage and good deeds or by conversion to the cloister.[34]

In the second Anselm miracle, the theme of salvation is again central. It is about a tanner who goes on his yearly pilgrimage to St James and is deluded by the devil into castration and suicide on the way. His soul is carried off for judgement to Rome, 'where before the church of

St Peter the Apostle in the open air there is a wide green space'.[35] There he is defended by St James and the Virgin against the demons who claim him; he is restored to life, proceeds to Compostela, and meets again the companions who had left him for dead. The main interest here is in the man's escape from damnation rather than in his restoration to life.

In these stories, St James appears as a protector, but stories of miraculous punishments meted out by St James are also known. A sermon, *Vigilie noctis sacratissimi,* attributed to Pope Calixtus II, contains five examples of punishment for those who work on the vigil of the feast of St James.[36] In the *Guide for Pilgrims to St James,* the author gives three instances of the punishment of those who refuse hospitality to the pilgrims of St James.[37] These stories are examples of preaching to forward a cause, a use of miracles that has already been discussed; they add little to the miracles connected with St James, except that those instances of vengeance connected with turning away pilgrims happened in Nantua, Villeneuve, and Poitiers, along well-known pilgrimage routes.

The miracles of St James of Compostela were widely known and assiduously copied; they appeared in stained glass all over Europe and are found in later literature of many kinds.[38] The fact that there are relatively few records of miracles of St James of Compostela surviving does not exclude the possibility of a greater number at the shrine itself.[39] It is, however, significant that the miracles I have discussed are the best-known miracles of St James. It may well be that the miracles of St James were predominantly those of pilgrimage and of battle rather than shrine cures, and that the difference noticed in the content of this collection presents a real contrast with the collections of more recently established saints.

The miracles of St James of Compostela contrast in this way with another collection of miracles of St James written in this period—the miracles at the shrine of St James at Reading. The body of St James had been discovered in Spain in the tenth century; the head of St James was solemnly taken from Jerusalem to Compostela in 1116.[40] It was the hand of St James that was in Reading Abbey.

The hand of St James and its political implications in the reigns of Henry I and Henry II have been discussed recently.[41] The relic passed from the treasures of Archbishop Adalbert of Hamburg-Bremen at his death in 1072 into the imperial treasury. At the death of the Emperor

Henry v in 1124, his widow brought it with her on her return to her father's court in England. It then became the chief relic of Henry I's new monastic foundation at Reading, which was particularly patronized by the royal house.[42] The relic was removed by Henry of Blois, but restored in 1155. Between 1190 and 1200 a collection was made of the miracles at the shrine. It was a carefully constructed list, selected from scedulae, but designed to show that the power of the relic had been used by each class of society in turn. The preface uses the stereotyped language of such compositions and calls the relic a 'talent of the Divine Bounty', invested at Reading for the glory of God and of his saint. The proclamation of miracles, the writer says, was therefore a pious duty.

The miracles at Reading could be those at any healing shrine of the period. The relic lay under the high altar, 'enclosed in a case of gold'.[43] Men, women, and children came there from the surrounding countryside to pray before the altar. They offered coins or candles; they were given water in which the hand had been dipped. The reliquary was at times exposed for the sick to kiss. Violent symptoms and loud noises accompanied cures here as elsewhere; the illnesses cured are familiar—dropsy, blindness, deafness, dumbness, fever, tumours, withered limbs, and undifferentiated illnesses. St James at Reading was the *divinus medicus,* not *Santiago Matamoros,* available for all, and particularly of interest to those who knew the abbey and could visit it. A miracle in 1173 shows, like those at other shrines in England, the impact of the cult of St Thomas at Canterbury. Ysembela, daughter of John, a fisherman in Seaford, became paralysed on one side. While she slept at Canterbury before the shrine of St Thomas, she was ordered by St James in a vision to go to Reading; after some hesitation, she went, taking a candle with her, and after much prayer and emotion, graphically described, she was cured by St James, rather than St Thomas.[44] This was a local shrine, which could be affected by a shrine near to it, and such propaganda was necessary, here as elsewhere, against the cult of Becket. The hand of St James was a relic valued by the English nobility as well as the local people. Twice Henry II had it brought to him,[45] and it was visited by the earl of Gloucester and his wife.[46] Gilbert Foliot translated the hand to a new reliquary;[47] later, in less happy circumstances, the gold plating of the reliquary was given to Richard I in settlement of his accounts with Reading.[48]

The miracles at the shrine of the hand of St James present a different picture from those connected with Compostela. In the miracles ascribed to the former, we see a typical, newly-established shrine with a local clientele and a focus on the shrine itself, as the place of miracles that are predominantly cures. In the latter we see a pilgrimage shrine important for the pilgrims who came there as penitents[49] or to give thanks for help already received from the apostle; they came to a saint who needed no extra veneration to establish his claims to sanctity. The miracles of St James took their tone at either place from the needs of the people who used the shrines rather than from the saint himself, whose image was changed radically by his devotees.

The miracles do not seem to be the primary motive for pilgrimage to St James's shrine at Compostela; the same may be said with even more assurance of the shrine of St Peter in Rome. This was the main goal of pilgrimage in Western Europe; the *romipetae* had come to the 'threshold of the Apostles' for centuries, and Rome was organized to meet their needs. Some came for a brief visit, sometimes repeated annually; others settled there, living the life of pilgrims within the city until their death. There were national hostels for pilgrims, such as the Anglo-Saxons, Lombards, Frisians, and Greeks, as well as papal hostels for foreign visitors.[50] Guidebooks were available so that pilgrims need miss nothing of the sights they had come to see.[51] By the eighth century, the tomb of St Peter at the Vatican was the centre of all this activity and the Vatican a city in itself, with its focus on the tomb of the prince of the Apostles, whose body was held to lie where it had been buried in the pagan necropolis on the Vatican Hill.[52] In the eleventh and twelfth centuries the overland route to Rome was widely used, and northern visitors appeared in increasing numbers until the end of the twelfth century.[53]

There is no evidence, however, that these pilgrims came to St Peter for miracles. At Rocamadour, at Canterbury, at any other shrine that was the centre of pilgrimage, the pilgrims came to pray by the tomb or altar and offer requests there for protection or cure. Compostela may have been an exception to this; Rome was certainly an exception. There is no miracle-book of St Peter, no account of his miraculous cures, either at the shrine or elsewhere; he was not *divinus medicus* like other saints. Indeed, one man who was brought to the tomb of the Apostle to be cured was taken away again and cured at the tomb of St Benedict at

Monte Cassino.[54] Admission was granted to the tomb of the Apostle, which was under the altar, enclosed by gates; even in the time of St Gregory I, the tomb itself was 'rarely entered',[55] though pieces of cloth could be lowered onto the tomb from above and were taken away as souvenirs;[56] in the twelfth century, these *brandea* were still collected by visitors. Other souvenirs, such as oil from the lamps burning before the shrines of the martyrs[57] and filings from the chains of St Peter kept at St Peter ad Vincula,[58] were valued and taken away from Rome, often with their use for miracles in mind. One of the knights of the Emperor Otto, for instance, was held to be possessed by the devil; he was cured at St Peter ad Vincula in Rome by touching filings from the chains of St Peter.[59] It was said that such filings healed the sick; they were also a vehicle of divine retribution, as in the case of an Arian Lombard who was struck dead for impiously trying to obtain the gold they contained.[60]

Even at St Peter ad Vincula cures were expected not only in the church but wherever the filings were taken. Other churches in Rome may have been curing-shrines; there is no reason to suppose the Romans less ailing or more stoical than the rest of mankind. There were riots in Rome when Bishop Hatto of Freising proposed to carry off the body of Pope Alexander, since 'the people were accustomed to visit his tomb with solemnity, since they held that he cured the sick'.[61] St Sebastian had been venerated as a thaumaturge since the plague of 680.[62] SS Cosmas and Damian may have continued to attract those in need of cures since their church occupied the site of the former temple of Castor and Pollux, a pagan healing place.[63] But these were not miracles at the tomb of St Peter; nor is there any record of details at these other shrines.

St Peter did at times cure people in visions, but these visions are more concerned with establishing the authority of the saint, or the power of one of his relics, than curing the sick and urging them to visit his shrine. The *Life of St Hugh of Cluny* by Raynald contains the story of how St Hugh cured a paralytic in the church of St Genevieve in Paris. During mass, he took the relic of the cloak of St Peter preserved there and held it over the man, saying, 'Peter the Apostle says to the paralysed man, Robert, get up and walk'. St Hugh attributed this cure to St Peter, since he regarded him as his own patron, but his biographer and later writers regarded it as a miracle of St Hugh and part of the hagiography surrounding him.[64] In a second instance, the monk Baldwin recounted a dream of St Peter on his journey with archbishop Anselm to Rome.[65] They had recently been to the abbey of St Peter at Cluny and were on their way to the tomb of St Peter in Rome. It is in no way surprising that Baldwin, with an infection in his foot, should dream one night of St Peter. The saint did not play the usual role of merciful healer nor did he urge Baldwin to venerate him at Rome; instead, he sat on the edge of the bed and offered, with ferocious good humour, to cure Baldwin by taking off his leg entirely. Baldwin says he prayed to him for a cure only for his own benefit, but also for a sign of the good outcome of the archbishop's cause:

Forgive me my sins, and if my lord the archbiship has a righteous cause for which he was exiled from his country and goes to Rome, or if I can in any way gain your favour in his business, grant that I may be quickly set free from this serious illness which I suffer.[66]

St Peter as the mediator of forgiveness and arbiter of justice is the theme of this miracle—as is the case in the prayer of Anselm himself to St Peter[67]—rather than the simple cure of illness.

The third instance is from the *Life of St Bernard* of Clairvaux. When St Bernard's uncle Galdricus was ill and near death, he dreamed of evil spirits from which he was delivered by St Peter:

He said that at that moment two evil spirits came as if from the bottom of the lake of hell to seize him, but while he was trembling with terror at this, St Peter came and snatched him away and thereafter he felt no wounds.[68]

In this case, St Peter did not appear in order to heal the man, but as one powerful against the demons, presumably because he was 'door-keeper of heaven'.

St Peter rarely appeared as a thaumaturge even in dreams; his tomb was not, so far as the records go, a place for cures. Why then did pilgrims seek the threshold of the Apostle so assiduously? In this period his cult increasingly emphasized the power of St Peter to absolve from sin. Pilgrimage, especially pilgrimage to Rome, was seen as a penance and imposed as such. Some thought pilgrimage to be in itself absolution, an error contested by respectable theologians.[69] The reservation of certain sins to the papacy and the offer of indulgences increased the

119

number of penitents in Rome—an increase that reached a climax with the year of Jubilee in 1300.[70] There were also practical reasons of a legal and political kind that drew men to Rome. St Peter and his heirs occupied the position of 'pastor et princeps'. By their share in the merits of St Peter, Gregory VII had held that all popes were saints in virtue of their office;[71] besides this high view of petrine authority, certain popes were known for their miracles, as saintly individuals. The tomb of Pope Leo IX, for instance, was the scene of miraculous cures;[72] Gregory VII himself had several miracle stories attached to his name.[73] But these were instances of individual holiness, and, in the case of Leo IX, their posthumous miracles conformed to the traditional pattern.

There was no need for the power of St Peter to be asserted by miracles. His miracles were already known throughout Christendom in the Acts of the Apostles and in the apocryphal accounts of the contest between St Peter and Simon Magus in magic arts.[74] The 'miracle' of absolution from sin, sometimes the assurance of a safe conduct into heaven, drew men to Rome. But there was also the tradition of Rome as the centre of the Christian world. The sentiments that made men go there were expressed by Richard, abbot of St Vannes, in a sermon he preached after his visit to Rome in 1026:

The city of Rome, the capital of the world, is rendered more special by the most glorious triumphs of the holy apostles Peter and Paul. Thither flock daily the races and peoples with devotion of heart, to plead with the holy apostles to hear their prayers, either by compunction of faith, or by grief for sins, or in hope of the more abundant life of heaven.[75]

Compostela and Rome attracted many pilgrims, but the greatest of all shrines for Christians is and was the Holy Sepulchre in Jerusalem. It was the centre of the world first for Jews, then for Christians, and finally for Moslems. Here the central miracle of the Christian faith, the resurrection of Christ, happened;[76] it was the focus of pilgrimage throughout the centuries, however difficult the voyage. Here, if anywhere, miracles could be expected; but what part did typical shrine-miracles actually play there?

First of all, one outstanding miracle was connected with the central miracle of the resurrection: the annual miracle of the New Fire. It had been known in Jerusalem for centuries, and in this period it aroused interest and speculation in the West also. On the afternoon of the day before Easter Sunday, when all lamps had been extinguished in and around the Holy Sepulchre, Christians congregated in the church and waited, with prayers and litanies, until a lamp was kindled with fire in the Sepulchre itself and brought out to them, to be hailed as 'Lux Christi'; this lamp was used to rekindle the lamps in the church and was taken by runners to other churches for the celebration of the Easter Vigil ceremonies. It is an event that still occurs in the Holy Sepulchre and that has given rise to the first part of the Easter Vigil ceremonies of the Christian church in the West.[77]

There are at present three positions about this event. Some hold that the fire is kindled by God without human agency; others see it as a liturgical ceremony, in which the light struck from flint in the darkness symbolizes Christ bursting from the tomb at Easter; thirdly, it is held to be a fraud, in which the faithful are deluded by a light humanly kindled and presented as a miracle. In the twelfth century, it was certainly a liturgical ceremony; it was an annual, ritualized event that occurred at a certain moment in a ceremony; opinion was only divided about whether it was produced miraculously or by fraud. In any case, the records leave no doubt about what happened; it was described by the crusaders eagerly and attentively, with all the interest evoked by a novelty.[78]

The sending of the New Fire appeared to Western eyes as a miracle and one of emotive force. Pope Urban referred to it at Clermont in his appeal to the crusaders in 1095:

Then each year God allows this miracle to take place during the days of his passion: when all the lights in the Holy Sepulchre and the church have been put out, he ordains that the extinguished lamps shall be rekindled by divine power. Whose heart is so hard, my brethren, that it will not kindle at so great a miracle?[79]

On two occasions at least it provided a weapon with which to beat an opponent. In 1002 the Greeks and Armenians disputed the date of Easter;[80] the fact that the New Fire was kindled in the Holy Sepulchre on both the Greek Easter night and the following Saturday for the Armenians was held by the Armenians to be due to fraud by the Greeks:

At Easter the inhabitants of Jerusalem lit their lamps by treachery and fraud, and deceiving their countrymen they substituted for the divine light a manufactured flame; but the lamps of the Armenians rekindled of their own accord at Easter, as all the Christians to be found in Jerusalem witness; and the Greeks were covered with shame and confusion because they had celebrated the feast on Palm Sunday.[81]

'Confusion' was a small price to pay for such a clash of opinion: In 455 a similar difference had led to a massacre of pilgrims.[82] For the Western visitors, also, the New Fire could be an ambiguous sign. In 1101 the Latins waited for the expected miracle with devotion and it did not appear. There were murmurs among the Greeks that this was because of the sins of the newcomers: 'Oh how great a cry was raised to the Lord, that it was because of our sins that this had happened, which had never happened in former years'.[83] Baldwin and his court took the reproach to heart and went next day to the Sepulchre barefoot as penitents, begging for the restoration of the miracle.

The New Fire was the centre of the celebration of the main Christian festival at the most sacred of Christian shrines; it drew men from many places and was accepted as the miraculous centre of the liturgical ceremonies. The abbot of Verdun visited Jerusalem in 1026 and saw the New Fire descend onto the lamp.[84] Guibert of Nogent examined the accounts of the miracle and declared that it was a genuine miracle.[85] The Russian Abbot Daniel saw the Holy Fire with awe, and went forward to secure a spark from it for his own lamp.[86] The significance of the miracle was what mattered, the symbolism of the Resurrection and distinctions about its mechanics were only raised in a polemical situation. With the coming of the Latins, however, a new question was heard. They asked 'how' the miracle happened. Suspicions of fraud were levelled at it; religious enthusiasm was replaced by suspicion of profiteering. The contrast in mood is shown by a comparison of the speech of Pope Urban at Clermont already quoted and a letter of Gregory IX to Gerard of Lausanne, Patriarch of Jerusalem, in 1238:

We understand that the canons of the sepulchre in Jerusalem say that fire from heaven descends into the sepulchre on Easter Eve, and that our Lord Jesus Christ our Redeemer was buried there; and not without shame they show the place where he was buried for a price. Indeed because the Lord, as we told them, does not need our lies, we order anyone who has presumed to believe this by our authority never to attend there again.[87]

Besides the 'liturgical miracle' of the New Fire, the Holy Sepulchre was known as the place where the first miracle of non-entry took place. The legend of St Mary of Egypt, a prostitute who found she was unable to enter the church because of her sins, was widely known and included among the Mary miracles,[88] as well as being incorporated in individual miracle collections designed to show the terror of a particular shrine to sinners.[89] This was not a miracle that was frequently repeated at the Holy Sepulchre, nor can it be said to have provided an attraction for pilgrims; with its severity and note of judgement the reverse is perhaps the case.

It does not appear that the Sepulchre was known as a place where the sick came for cures. In one case, a woman who prayed there for her blindness to be cured was told to return home and ask for a cure of Our Lady of Rocamadour.[90] In the miracles of St Frideswide, William of Wales and Thurben of Holywell both came to their local Oxford shrine to be cured before they braved the hazards of the journey to Jerusalem. Godric of Finchale visited Jerusalem, but it was his conversion there, not his cure, that he recorded.[91]

There were other places in the Holy Land that had local healing shrines. Abbot Daniel went to the tomb of St John the Evangelist at Edessa where 'on the anniversary of his death, holy dust arises from his tomb, which believers gather as a remedy against every kind of disease'.[92] In Cyprus he found a cross erected by the Empress Helena that was 'able to drive away evil spirits and heal all sorts of diseases'; moreover, he says he saw it suspended in the air, 'held up only by the Holy Spirit'.[93] In the sepulchre of St Joseph in Nazareth, he saw 'white water which drops like holy oil from the wall . . . people collect it for healing the sick'.[94] In a sermon attributed to Pope Calixtus he said that on the mountain of the Transfiguration white stones were made for pilgrims into crosses, which were dipped in wine to heal the sick.[95] Crusaders found relics to take home that they believed would work cures, such as hairs of the Virgin. But there were no relics that were miracle-working within the Holy Sepulchre.[96] It seems that the Holy Sepulchre, like St Peter's and to some extent that of St James of Compostela, was not a shrine renowned for the ordinary type of miracles.

But if this is so, what was it that drew people to these shrines? How did they differ from those other shrines where miracles were of central importance? At Rome, Compostela, and above all Jerusalem, the sanctity of the saints involved was not in question, nor was the place where they were to be venerated a matter of much dispute. Moreover, in each case their miracles were recorded already in the Bible and were well-known to all Christians, so that accounts of miracles were not needed to establish a claim to sanctity. Secondly, miracles were not necessary to stimulate devotion to such well-known holy persons; the desire to venerate the apostles and Christ himself in some visible place on earth was spontaneous. It is especially clear that the desire to be in the place where Christ had suffered was in the twelfth century the central reason for the pilgrimage to Jerusalem. Richard of St Vannes was overcome with emotion when he reached Jerusalem on Palm Sunday: 'It is not for me to describe', writes his biographer, 'the flow of tears with which he watered the places which were the object of his devotion';[97] Abbot Daniel wrote: 'God . . . granted us . . . the favour of seeing with our own eyes, all the holy places that Christ our God had visited for our salvation'.[98] The increase in devotion to the humanity of Christ, especially in his Passion, caused pilgrims to go to the land and the city of his earthly life.[99] But there were more practical gains to be obtained in Jerusalem, as at Compostela and Rome.

The first of these was absolution. All three shrines were specifically named as places to which penitents might go on pilgrimage and fulfil their penance. The penitential aspect of the pilgrimage to Compostela has already been discussed. At Rome, the pope was 'the high priest of the Roman privilege, the dispenser of benediction, of privilege, and of anathema'. In 1026, Canute had gone to Rome:

I heard from wise men that St Peter the Apostle had received from the Lord a great power of binding and loosing and the keys of the Kingdom of heaven. I therefore deemed it useful in no ordinary way to seek his patronage before God.[100]

Many followed him, secure in the power of the keys for their absolution. Others were sent to Jerusalem as a penance, like the German soldier who killed a companion and was sent to Jerusalem with the dead body strapped to his back.[101]

Others went to these places to die. It was thought that heaven and earth intersected in Rome and Jerusalem. Rome was the city of the martyrs and under the patronage of the prince of the apostles; in Jerusalem, Christ himself had died and ascended to heaven. To die under the patronage of St James in a crusade secured salvation. Pilgrims came there and stayed until they died, not for miracles but for the greater miracle of salvation.

Forgiveness, salvation, and devotion to Christ were more powerful reasons for pilgrimage than an expectation of cures. These ideas were possibly supplemented by practical considerations. It is hinted in certain miracles[102] that stamina was needed for such long journeys, so that people sought cures of illness at their local shrines before venturing to make the longer journeys. In some ways, it is obvious that distant shrines would not attract the sick, who would find travelling particularly hard; it is the railway that has made the concentration of the sick at Lourdes possible. Healing shrines are of necessity local shrines. Compostela, Rome, and Jerusalem had local inhabitants, however, no more healthy than people elsewhere. Yet no record exists of local cures at the shrines of St James, St Peter, and the Holy Sepulchre. Distance cannot, therefore, be the only reason for the lack of miracles at these shrines. There are other possible explanations. For instance, at the Holy Sepulchre the body, the usual focus of thaumaturgy, was by definition not there: 'The Tomb of Christ who is living; the glory of Jesus' resurrection'.[103] The tradition at the Holy Sepulchre is comparable in some ways to the tradition of 'salvation' miracles attached to the cult of the Virgin Mary, in which there was also no body. The desire for practical benefits such as cures was perhaps a particular interest of the Northern races. When they removed the bodies of the martyrs from Rome and the hairs of the Virgin from Jerusalem, they expected them to work miracles in their new homes; when they visited Jerusalem, they insisted that the New Fire was a 'miracle' in their sense of the word; St James was 'miracle-working' mainly for a clientele that consisted very largely of Frankish knights.

With these practical considerations in mind, as well as the more spiritual ones, it is possible to see that personal cures were not appropriate at Rome, Jerusalem, nor to some extent at Compostela. These cults flourished for centuries, and not because of miracles. While the new twelfth-century shrines needed miracles to establish or reassert the power of the saints or affirm that their bodies truly rested there, the major shrines of Christendom were already established beyond question, and no new discovery or translation was needed. The difference between them and the earlier shrines points to the use of miracles at shrines as propaganda for the establishment and continued veneration of a saint in a particular place. These shrines drew on local and immediate needs of people round about for a limited time at best.

7

The Shrines that Failed

MIRACLES HAVE SEEMED to us essential for the continued existence of shrines, and yet the chief shrines of Christendom had no recorded miracles at all. On the other hand, it would appear that miracles in themselves were not enough to set up and maintain a shrine in popular esteem, for some shrines failed to become established cults despite having been popularized by miracles. These shrines had no later record, and their clientele gradually dwindled. Contemporaries said that older saints made way for younger ones, who needed to make a name for themselves by miracles. William of Canterbury, for example, defended the miracles of St Thomas by saying that St Denis had done this for him.[1] He recorded the story of Hugh Brustins, a demoniac, who visited St Denis but was told that he would be cured by St Thomas:

It was fitting that a martyr should pass on this case to a martyr, a contender to a contender, a citizen to another citizen, so that the new martyr might shine out in his deeds, as being new and not yet known.[2]

All shrines 'failed' in the end, but the shrines hitherto examined were established for a notable length of time, and most had recurrences of popularity. Many other cults, however, flickered and died out at once, even where they had miracles to show. Guibert of Nogent protested at the ease with which miracles were proclaimed and incipient cults begun in this period. The evidence of them is necessarily very sparse, but it is worth examining some instances of these cults that died out at once.

Guibert of Nogent supported his protest against transitory cults by describing how one such shrine was almost established at Beauvais. He says that a young armour-bearer died there on Maundy Thursday. The signficance of the day persuaded the local people that he was a saint, and they began to pray to him and offer candles at his grave. Soon a shrine was erected and a neighbouring abbey took the cult under its protection. Cures and other miracles that Guibert calls 'falsa' were reported there. Nevertheless this cult vanished without trace within a few weeks; Guibert attributes this disappearance to the fact that the man venerated was not a saint and urges that virtue and holiness of life should be established before such cults are encouraged.[3] This cult is clearly similar to the highly successful cult of young St William of Norwich. When the facts about St William have been sifted, the picture has almost as little to commend it as that of the armour-bearer of Beauvais, yet one cult grew and the other did not. Both deaths happened at Easter, both men were young, and in both cases miracles were reported.

Three factors distinguish the cult at Beauvais from that at Norwich, and in them the reasons for the survival of the Norwich cult may be sought. First, St William of Norwich had a biographer devoted to his cause and able to assist it in every way; at Beauvais, there was no such 'middleman' to link the miracles with the populace. Secondly, the armour-bearer had no local connections in the place of his cult—no family or relatives to take an interest, whereas St William was a boy of Norwich with a vociferous and interested family there. Thirdly, a factor that can be called 'political' was present at Norwich. The Jewish element in the story gave it a dramatic appeal at that moment and made it acceptable to a wide section of society. The cult at Beauvais, while drawing on the same religious emotion symbolized by a death at Easter, nevertheless failed through lack of this wider reference. It is in these three factors that the difference lay, rather than in the presence or absence of miracles or in the evidence of any superior holiness of life.

This contention is supported by the situation of another 'failed' cult that is in many ways similar to that of St Thomas of Canterbury, the cult of Bishop Albert of Louvain, murdered in his own cathedral by the supporters of the Emperor Henry VI in 1192.[4] He had resisted the designs of the Emperor on the freedom of the church and went into exile for defending freedom of election and his own rights to appeal to Rome. His biographer and friend, Werric of Lobbes, drew a conscious parallel between Albert and Becket; Werric quotes a friend as saying, 'Behold, a greater than Thomas is here'.[5] Yet the cult of Albert died out, while that of Becket exceeded every other saint in the twelfth century.

In both cases, there were miracles. Only two are recorded of Albert, but manuscripts of Werric's *Life of Albert* are incomplete and may have contained more. Besides these two, there was a general claim for other cures:

Some were cured at his grave of serious fever or other illnesses, when for the first days after his burial he prayed for them in response to their recent faith and ardent devotion.[6]

It was a beginning. As at Canterbury, a violent death in a consecrated place produced miracles; but Albert lacked a convinced propagandist to record and publicize his miracles. Albert's biographer was concerned with his life, and lacked the conviction and ardour for his posthumous cult found in biographers of William of Norwich or of Becket. Secondly, like the armour-bearer of Beauvais, Albert was not well-known where he died and so lacked the appeal of familiarity that William of Norwich and Thomas of Canterbury in different ways achieved. Thirdly, the 'political' element—the very similarity between the causes that prompted the death of Albert and Thomas—made it less likely that a second bishop-martyr cult would succeed so soon. Once again, the issue does not lie with the presence of miracles, nor with the relative sanctity of the two; indeed, Albert's biographer makes a slightly better case for Albert's holiness of life than do Becket's biographers for Becket.

Another record of cults that had miracles but failed is provided by the English chronicler William of Newburgh. He was particularly interested in wonders of all kinds, omens, ghosts, freaks, and fairies as well as miracles, and he struggled to discover their causes: 'I call things of this nature wonderful, not merely on account of their rarity but because some latent meaning is attached to them'.[7] He applied his mind to several popular cults that started in his own day, involved miracles, but disappeared. The first was the case of John, a dissolute young man murdered at Northampton for his money; he had been visiting the town to collect enough money to go on pilgrimage and had taken part in a massacre there of the Jews.[8] A report spread of supernatural events at his grave and William says he was regarded by the 'simple people' as a martyr; pilgrims began to come from a distance, 'desiring to witness the miracles and obtain the help of his prayers'. It was a promising cult, but it was ridiculed by *prudentes* as a superstition. The matter was examined by St Hugh of Lincoln and condemned; a ready clientele, avid for miracles, once again was insufficient to establish a saint in the eyes of someone as concerned with virtue and sanctity as St Hugh. It is noteworthy that St Hugh was also responsible for suppressing the incipient cult at Godstow nunnery of Fair Rosamund, mistress of Henry II, where the nuns, at the instigation of the king, had begun to venerate her after death with candles and prayers at her tomb.[9]

William of Newburgh describes two other 'cults', both of which failed almost at once. He describes the life of Eudes d'Etoile, a Breton of Loudeac, who was leader of a considerable band of disciples in William's own day.[10] Eudes believed himself to be God, having confused his name with 'eum' in a phrase he heard in church, *'eum qui venturus est judicare vivos et mortuos et seculem per ignem'*.[11] William describes him as not only *'illiteratus et idiota'* but possessed by demons. His followers claimed that he provided them miraculously with splendid food and performed many other wonders. He was eventually arrested, tried by the archbishop of Rheims for heresy, and condemned to prison where he soon died. Eudes was mocked as deluded and his 'miracles' said to be frauds and diabolic delusions, but the difference between him and a saint did not lie in the miracles; the 'miracles' were called 'frauds' only when his claims to sanctity had been condemned for other reasons.

Equally unsuccessful for somewhat similar reasons was the cult of the rebel William Longbeard, who was executed for treason in London on 6 April 1196.[12] After his death, he was honoured as a martyr. A relative of his who was a priest claimed that a relic of him worked a miracle; soil was taken from the place where his blood had soaked into the ground, and crowds gathered at the spot expecting further miracles. Cures were claimed, and the cult assumed proportions dangerous to the government that had condemned Longbeard for his views on taxation. The priest was arrested on the orders of Archbishop Hubert Walter, and soldiers dispersed the crowds. William, sure of the iniquity of Longbeard, rejoiced that a fraud was exposed:

For truth is solid and waxes strong by time, but the device of falsehood has nothing solid and in a short time fades away. The administrator of the kingdom therefore . . . sent out a troop of armed men.[13]

It would be more correct to say that the opposition to Longbeard's politics was solid, too solid for incipient miracles to make him a saint, however just his cause. There is some evidence that his protest was not without foundation. Roger of Hoveden[14] and Ralph of Diceto[15] both testify to the weight of taxation at this date, and the cause for which Longbeard conspired appears to have been to some extent justified. It is significant to compare the suppression of this cult with that of Eudes. Both of them were seen as dangerous to the established order and put down by force, with that of the cult of Earl Waltheof, which undoubtedly owed its survival to the discretion of the monks of Crowland in regard to it.[16]

In all these instances, miracles were claimed for a new 'saint' who was venerated by many or few. Those who suppressed the cults claimed that these men had shown no sign of sanctity in their lives and the miracles were the deceitful works of demons. William of Malmesbury, comparing the death of Gregory VII with that of the witch of Berkeley,[17] says the events at the death of one were miracles, at the death of the other the work of demons: 'Not miracles of heaven but wonders of hell'. The problem, as always, was how to decide between them in practice. One line of reasoning especially appealed to the ordinary man: miracles were God's proclamation of sanctity; if miracles happened, the man was a saint. Roger of Hoveden records the case of Bishop William of Poitiers, of whom he says: 'Although in his life-time his life seemed to men most reprehensible, yet after his death God glorified him by miracles'.[18]

The idea of the inexplicable favour of God toward individuals, made known through miracles, was by no means dead in this period. It is clear, however, from the comments of those recounting the failure of these cults, as well as from the arguments of theologians, that a stress on virtues as authenticating miracles and not vice versa was gaining ground. It was reaffirmed in this period by the demands of the process of papal canonization, which will be more fully discussed later. What is also clear from the evidence of the failed shrines is that miracles were not at any time the decisive factor in the survival of a cult. They were a vital ingredient in most cases and were seen as the primary power for spreading the fame of a shrine, especially at its beginning. But the survival or immediate failure of a shrine owed its chances to influences other than the presence or absence of miracles.

8

The Miracles of the Virgin

THE COLLECTIONS OF MIRACLES so far considered have been those
associated with the great shrines of Western Europe that were believed
to house the mortal remains of certain saints. In their cults, devotion
was focussed on a particular place and was inextricably connected with
it. Of such shrines, that of St Thomas at Canterbury has supplied the
largest number of miracles, and in some ways this collection is the
climax of that kind of localized miracle collection. New elements,
however, tended to decentralize and personalize this most traditional of
cults, so that St Thomas emerges as a saint who can be called upon
anywhere by any person devoted to him, even though the place where
his body lay remained important. By the end of the period in question,
this decentralized type of devotion was particularly evident in a series of
miracles that outnumbered even those of St Thomas: the miracles of the
Virgin Mary, which were to dominate the devotion of Europe. The
miracles of St Thomas were the epitome of traditional shrine miracles
and those of the Virgin the clearest instances of the new devotion,
though to some extent they overlap. The miracles of St Thomas were
diffused as well as centralized; those of the Virgin were centralized at
particular shrines as well as diffused. Also, while the cult of St Thomas
had its centre in England, it emerged almost at once in France; likewise
the miracles of the Virgin, which grew up around her shrines in
France, had their counterpart in the early collections of Mary miracles
in England.

Two factors contribute to the universal and unlocalized devotion to
the Virgin Mary. The first of these was that in the twelfth century there
was no need to establish her claim to sanctity by miracles. She was the
first of saints, holding a pre-eminent place in the economy of salvation

132

as the Mother of the Redeemer, from the earliest ages of the church. Her title of 'theotokos' had been in use at least since the fourth century,[1] and her intercession was sought by Christians in the liturgy and in private prayer from a very early date.[2] While the eleventh and twelfth centuries saw an increase in liturgical veneration for her, this was not an innovation but a reaffirmation of that claim to sanctity most firmly established in the church. No miracles were needed to prove her a saint; as St Bernard among others asserted, the basic miracle of all was that she had indeed borne Christ as her Son.[3]

Secondly, the miracles of the Virgin were not primarily localized in her relics. It was generally believed that the Virgin Mary had been assumed into heaven, leaving behind no more than fragments of her clothing. There was no body to be venerated and therefore no central shrine that housed it.

These two factors would seem to make inevitable that devotion to the Virgin be of a universal and personal character. That this was so in the early church and also after the twelfth century is certain, and the literature devoted to the development of Mary miracles in their generalized form is voluminous.[4] But that it should have developed in this way was, at the beginning of this period, by no means inevitable. A large number of the twelfth-century miracles of the Virgin were just as localized as those of other saints. Churches claimed her special patronage as firmly as that of St Cuthbert or St Faith. The absence of her body was partially mitigated by minor relics of clothing or hair; by miraculous relics like drops of her milk; by statues and icons, often miracle working; or simply by the dedication of churches to her. She was 'Notre Dame de Coutances', 'Notre Dame de Rocamadour', 'Notre Dame de Chartres'; she was acclaimed at particular places, especially in France.[5] A large number of the miracles attributed to her are indistinguishable from those performed by the relics of saints at their shrines. Devotion to her, as seen in the miracles, was local as well as universal.

The relationship between the local miracles of the Virgin and her more general miracles illuminates the connection between 'traditional' miracles and 'modern' miracles. Both general and local miracles are combined in *Mariales,* the books filled with devotions to the Virgin, most of all with accounts of her miracles, which were compiled for reading aloud on her feast days.[6] The shrine collections most often combined with general collections were those of Our Lady of Laon, Our

Lady of Soissons, and Our Lady of Rocamadour. I will discuss these collections together with the other major surviving collections of Mary miracles for this period: the miracles of Our Lady of Chartres and the collection at St Pierre-sur-Dives. The later development of general col-tions of Mary miracles lies outside the scope of this book, but the relationship betweeen these and the early shrine collections will be examined.

The first collection, that of Our Lady of Laon, involves a specific use made of certain relics for a brief space of time. The cathedral of St Mary in Laon had been destroyed by fire in 1112, together with a good deal of the property surrounding it, and a rebuilding campaign was at once launched by the newly-installed bishop, Bartholomew. To finance the work he sent some of his clergy on a fundraising tour, with the relics of the church as the chief attraction. A second tour took place a year later. Money was collected, and the miracles that took place around the fere-tory were recorded and later written into a consecutive account; these miracles are known as the miracles of Our Lady of Laon.

During the tour, notes were kept that were rewritten and made into a coherent account of the miracles nearly thirty years later. When Guibert of Nogent was writing his autobiography in 1115, he men-tioned some of the miracles he had heard from the canons, implying that an official and final account of their travels did not exist then: 'We are not writing their travel-book; let them do that for themselves.'[7] Guibert's account of the miracles contains a selection from the stories told in the main collection: 'We are . . . picking out examples useful in sermons'.[8] Only one of the miracles described by Guibert is not found in the canons' account, the story of a woman at Angers, whose wedding ring had been embedded in her flesh for many years. It broke when she placed offerings on the relics during mass.[9] Guibert's account of other miracles differs in some details from the official account. The full record of the miracles was written by Herman, a canon of Laon. He gave separate accounts of the two tours: the first being written in the third person, from information received; the second in the first person plural, as a verbatim report of the canons who went on the journey.[10] The descriptions of the two tours contain much curious and unusual information, relating to matters as varied as the stories of King Arthur in Cornwall and the presence of Englishmen at the school of Anselm of

Laon. The accounts have been examined elsewhere in relation to these matters,[11] and while some points still need further elucidation[12] that may clarify the use Herman made of the material at his disposal, this need not concern our examination of the miracles themselves.

The first tour with the relics began on the Thursday before Pentecost 1112 and ended on 21 September of that year. Eight canons from the community at Laon were sent out: Boso, Robert, Anselm, Herbert, Robert, Boniface, Amisard, and Odo; with them went six laymen: Richard, John Piot, Odo, Lambert, Boso, and Theoderic:[13] 'With us we took the feretory of Our Lady and we carried other containers with relics in them to receive the offerings of the faithful'.[14] They went through Northern France on a fairly leisurely tour. At each stopping place, the feretory was carried into the town or village in procession by the canons. The local clergy would give permission for the relics to be placed in the main church, often on the high altar. The canons and their companions would lodge with local dignitaries while attending the veneration of the relics, which might last two or more days. Local people came and kissed the feretory, prayed before it, and gave money or portable goods as offerings. The sick were brought to the relics and were allowed to lie all night before them. The relics were dipped in water or water and wine, and this liquid was often given to the sick either to drink or wash in, or both. Occasionally, the canons would take a smaller container with the relics inside to a person who was bedridden. Both clergy and local people joined the sick and the canons in public prayer for the sick and in rejoicing over any cures; bells would be rung and a *Te Deum* sung, when a cure was proclaimed. Confession of sin sometimes preceded the prayers of the sick. The offerings made while the relics were in a church belonged to the canons.

This procedure reproduced at each place the rites and ceremonies usual at relic shrines. The miracles also followed the same pattern of vengeance, protection, and cures. On the first tour, one miracle expressed the anger of the Virgin against enemies, two the protection afforded by the relics to their guardians; one captive was set free, nine people—four men, five women—were cured of illnesses. The ill people were those commonly cured at shrines: four cripples, two who were deaf and dumb, one described as 'sick', two women in danger after pregnancies. Benedict, one of the cripples, and Christian, one of the

135

dumb boys, returned with the canons to Laon, offering their services in rebuilding the church in gratitude for their cures, a fact also attested by Guibert of Nogent.[15]

The last three miracles on the French tour took place at Chartres and further illustrate the relationship between portable relics and the churches visited.[16] Chartres was already known for its veneration of the Virgin, and the church was dedicated to her. The canons arrived on the vigil of the feast of the Nativity of the Virgin, the patronal feast of the cathedral. They were received with honour by the bishop and the canons, who were expecting them. The relics were placed on the high altar with great solemnity and made the centre of devotion. Two women were cured, and a young man asserted that Our Lady of Laon had released him from captivity. The bishop, who ordered the *Te Deum* to be sung in thanksgiving for these miracles, appears to have been ready to credit them to the relics from Laon. Since there is here no suggestion of rivalry with relics at Chartres, it seems possible that Chartres had at this time no relics of the Virgin of its own on display. The tradition at Chartres of veneration for the Virgin was well-established. A century earlier, William of Malmesbury credited Bishop Fulbert in particular with working to establish greater reverence for the feast of the Virgin's Nativity.[17] In reward for Fulbert's devotion to the Virgin, she appeared when he was ill and cured him with a drop of her milk. The central relic venerated at Chartres was the Shift of the Virgin. It was said to have been given to Chartres by Charles the Bald, who brought it there from Constantinople. Furthermore, it was said to have been used as a rallying-point during the siege of Chartres in 911. According to these legends, the Shift should have been at Chartres when the canons of Laon appeared with their relics of the Virgin in 1112; and since they arrived on the main festival of the Virgin, it should have been occupying the chief place in the festivities. In other places, lesser saints than Mary had maintained their central place on the celebration of their feast-days, in spite of the presence of the Laon relics. But here, the Shift is not mentioned, while the relics of the hairs of the Virgin were welcomed and put on the high altar. Possibly the Shift of the Virgin at Chartres was not known or only achieved its full potential as a relic after the canons' visit.

The party returned to Laon with considerable funds, enough to continue the rebuilding through the winter.[18] During Lent, however,

136

money ran out and a further, more ambitious tour was planned. This time, the canons were to take the relics to England, which seemed a promising place to beg, since at that time they said England 'flourished in abundant riches, for peace and justice had been established by King Henry, the son of King William'.[19] Another factor encouraged the canons to go to England. Several Englishmen had been pupils of Anselm of Laon and had urged their friends in Laon to visit them at home. Thus, they could expect a welcome in Canterbury,[20] Exeter,[21] Salisbury,[22] and Cornwall.[23] Moreover, such a tour had been undertaken before. Between 1075 and 1087 the relics of St Ouen had been carried to England to collect money for rebuilding the church at Rouen;[24] and in England itself, the relics of St Cuthbert were renowned both for the miracles they occasioned when they were carried about during the Danish invasions and for more recent tours for the collection of funds for rebuilding the church in Durham.[25] For this English tour, the members of the party were not identical with those on the first tour. They included Boso, the leader, and his nephew Robert, the canons Boniface and 'Amisardus clericus' went again; to them was added Robert the Englishman, Ralph, John, and Helinand, who were said to be proficient in learning and chanting. No list is given of laymen, but one was certainly there, the boy Hugellinus, who provoked a fight in Cornwall on the subject of King Arthur.[26]

The party set out on Palm Sunday, 1113 and returned on the Feast of the Nativity of the Virgin in September of the same year. This time, more details are given in the account of the relics that were the focus for the miracles. The feretory contained the relics of the church of Laon among which, in a special container, were the relics of the Virgin. It bore a curious inscription that can be roughly translated as: 'May I be consecrated by the sponge, the cross of the Lord, with the cloth of thy face, also by the hairs of your Virgin Mother'.[27] Guibert of Nogent had seen or been told about the feretory and its inscription. He agreed that it contained part of the robe of the Virgin, the sponge lifted to the lips of the Saviour, and parts of the cross, but he expressed doubt about the 'hairs of the Virgin'.[28] It was these 'hairs of the Virgin' that were the most popular of the Laon relics. 'Hairs of the Virgin' were already known in France and England. A crusader, Ilger Bigod, professed to have found a packet containing the hairs of the Virgin in the Holy Sepulchre during the first crusade; he brought them back to France, and they were distributed among several monasteries including Bec and Maule, a dependency of Evroul.[29] Eadmer also related this story when some 'hairs of the Virgin' were offered to Anselm of Canterbury.[30] It would be in no way surprising if the relics of Laon came from the same source. The pious explanation offered about these relics was that they were the hairs that the Virgin tore out of her head in her grief at the foot of the cross, hairs collected and preserved by St John.[31] What this explanation lacked in historical perspective it made up for in emotive appeal. Not only were these relics of the Mother of God, but they were connected with the Passion of Christ.

The canons took their feretory to Arras, and there an encounter with an old blind goldsmith revealed further details about the feretory itself. After feeling the casket and having it described to him, the goldsmith claimed that he had originally made it himself for Bishop Helinand of Laon, to contain the head of St Walaricus and the relics of St Montanus. He said also that the bishop had told him that Montanus was a saint who went blind and whose sight was restored by the application of milk from the breast of St Cilnia. The cure of illness by milk from the breast of a saint is associated with the Virgin in general collections of Mary miracles.[32] The goldsmith saw the story of St Cilnia as an encouragement to himself, and he prayed before the relics for his sight to be restored, which eventually happened.[33] If this feretory made by the goldsmith of Arras, given a different label and new content, was the one taken on tour by the canons, it may also be the one in an illuminated initial of the Miracles of St Mary of Laon, in a thirteenth-century manuscript.[34] In the initial of the first story, two men are shown carrying a feretory on two long poles; it has three small pinnacles on the lid, with a spire projecting from the centre one of the three; the whole is plated with gold and ornamented with jewels.

On this second tour, the canons first visited Nesle, where a deaf and dumb boy was cured before the relics; like a sick boy cured on the first tour, he wanted to go with the canons, but they allowed him to go only as far as the coast.[35] They went on to Arras, where they encountered the goldsmith, and then to St Omer and Wissant to take ship for England. The miracles on this second tour were cures of illness, miracles of protection, and miracles of vengeance. It is in the latter that the changed ethos of these miracles is most apparent. The cures and the miracles of protection are those already familiar at shrines. The procedure was the same at the feretory as on the first tour. People came and venerated the relics, made offerings, and prayed; in some cases their prayers were answered by miraculous cures. The proportion of men and women remained about equal; the diseased people cured are familiar; a deaf and dumb boy, a paralysed woman, a woman in labour, cripples, the blind, the lame, those with fever, some vaguely diagnosed as 'sick', and a boy who was thought to have been drowned in the thermal springs at Bath.[36] Almost all the people named have been identified, including 'Radulfus pincerna regis' who was Ralph Mortimer, one of the notable followers of William I, William Rufus, and Henry I, and an ancestor of the Earls of March.[37] Generally, however, it was the anonymous townsfolk of the south of England that came to the feretory at Dover, Canterbury, Winchester, Christchurch, Exeter, Salisbury, Wilton, Bodmin, Totnes, and Bristol. As in the cults of St William of Norwich and of St Frideswide at Oxford, the charity exercised in presenting gifts to the shrine enclosing the relics of a saint suggests the increasing wealth of the towns, especially at centres of trade.

In all these cases, the relics formed the kind of centre for devotion familiar at any healing shrine of the period. But the relics did not belong to the countryside; they were essentially foreign and provisional. This fact lay behind the other miracles that took place around the feretory—miracles of protection for the canons and vengeance against their critics. The dangers of the journey increased the need for protection, and the canons turned to the relics of the Virgin for practical help in temporal difficulties in the same way the monks of Fleury or of Conques turned to their patrons for help earlier. The perils of the channel crossing called at once for the use of the relics. The boat was threatened by a pirate ship and the canons produced the relics of the Virgin, which turned the wind and enabled them to escape their attackers.[38] The merchants aboard had promised gifts to the Virgin of Laon during the danger, but when they landed at Dover they went off without making these offerings; Herman states that their goods perished by fire as a result: 'The Just Judge will punish, the Son will punish on behalf of his Mother'.[39]

The canons depended on the hospitality of the towns they visited and on the goodwill of the local clergy; several times this failed them. Twice they were refused the use of the High Altar in a church because of a local festival, and in both cases a local party was formed, composed

139

of merchants, women of position in the community, and men of some influence, who gave the canons lodging and a place to exhibit their relics in defiance of the clergy.[40] This temporal help, which foreshadows the clashes a century later between visiting friars and local clergy, was also supported by prayer to the Virgin, who exercised her protection over those who favoured the canons. The canons were not needlessly provocative, and in one case at least showed concern for local customs. At Exeter, Glutinus a cripple prayed for his cure for ten days before the relics; when he was not cured, the canons questioned him and discovered that he was from the diocese of Salisbury. They then insisted that the Virgin would only heal him on his home ground, and made him return with them to Salisbury, where he was in fact cured ('no one can be cured outside his own diocese').[41] There were dangers from thieves who stole money from the feretory. A young man at Totnes pretended to kiss the feretory and took away coins for a drinking bout; when he was later found hanging in a wood, the canons publicized his death as the retribution of the Virgin.[42] At Bristol, the canons believed that certain merchants plotted to steal the canons themselves and sell them as slaves; a warning from the Virgin as well as temporal advice saved them.[43] There was danger from rival lords at war with one another;[44] there was danger from the weather.[45] In all these hazards the canons demanded the protection of the Virgin, whose relics they carried.

The other side of protection for the canons was vengeance on their enemies. Punishment by the saints was a traditional theme at certain shrines, but here the phrases in which it is expressed give a new tone to the miracles. The phrase 'vindicta Mariae' has already been noted in the punishment of the merchants at Dover who refused to pay what they had promised to the Virgin of Laon.[46] At Christchurch, another severe punishment befell those who refused to welcome the canons and the relics. Herman relates the details with imagination and vigour, describing a dragon with five heads coming out of the sea to burn all the houses except those in which the canons had been sheltered;[47] Guibert of Nogent, in a more sober version of the same event, says the place was struck by lightning.[48] Guibert was closer in time to the events than Herman and gives the more likely explanation; Herman may have supplied details from his recollection of the dragon with seven heads in the book of Revelation, which came out of the sea to devour the woman identified in medieval exegesis with Mary. Through such biblical reminiscence, rejection and disaster is interpreted as punishment in the light of the new style in devotion to the Virgin. She is called upon by the canons to avenge them, but in the account her Son protects his Mother's honour. Mercy belongs to Mary, justice to her Son, a division that has its roots in a popular misunderstanding of that theology of Incarnation so carefully expressed, for instance, by Anselm, particularly in his third prayer to the Virgin.[49]

In September the canons returned to Laon with their gains, 'one hundred and twenty marks, not counting the hangings and various other ecclesiastical ornaments'.[50] The church building was finished, and, as Guibert records, included statues of oxen on the towers to commemorate a miracle in which an ox volunteered to help in the building when some other oxen were exhausted.[51] Pictures of the new church appear in manuscript illuminations. One manuscript written at St Germain early in the thirteenth century includes an illumination that shows Bishop Bartholomew consecrating the church.[52]

The miracles were eventually put into written form by Herman, and in his work they become part of a collection of more general Mary miracles. The miracles were 'traditional' shrine miracles of vengeance, protection, and healing; more than any others, they were concentrated exclusively on the relics themselves. The miracles followed the traditional pattern, especially in the use of water in which the relics were dipped for the cures.[53] This account of a miracle by the relics is typical and could, except for the mention of Mary at the end, come from any shrine of the period: 'He washed the enclosed relics in water and wine and poured the liquid over the head and face of the aforesaid young girl and gave her some of the liquid to drink and ordered her to lie down under the feretory; then bending the knee he began to pray earnestly to Our Lady'.[54]

But Herman had already linked the local miracles of Laon with a wider tradition; in the preface to his book he refers to the *Life of the Virgin* by Hildefonsus, a work full of miraculous incidents from the life of the Virgin Mary, saying that the local miracles were a continuation of those.[55] The relationship of the *Life of the Virgin* by Hildefonsus to the collection of miracles of the Virgin at Laon by Herman is expressed by two illuminated initials in one manuscript. In the first illumination, Bishop Hildefonsus kneels and offers his book to the Virgin; in the

141

second, Herman, with a similar gesture, offers his book to her.[56] This manuscript is one of the *Mariales* in which the *Life* and the *Miracles* at Laon are found together. The *Mariales* were books devoted to the Virgin. They were used for reading in chapel and refectory on her feast days and Saturdays. For the most part they contain her miracles and very often the *Life of the Virgin,* with the Letter of Herman and a preface to it; the Laon miracles appear after the *Life,* as in a Corbie manuscript of the thirteenth century.[57] Miracles from the general collections of Mary miracles, as well as from the collections from Soissons and Roca-madour, follow an arrangement found in other manuscripts. The Laon collection, while essentially a shrine collection, seemed to have enough in it of the new style in Marian devotion to make it acceptable among the general stories. These stories proclaim the personal glory of the Virgin, her power, and her mercy toward those devoted to her.

This less local aspect of the Laon miracles was emphasized both by the 'pilgrimage', in which the relics travelled to people rather than the reverse, and also by the nature of the relics themselves. The hairs of the Virgin were not relics that would suggest, as the whole body of a saint would, that the Virgin 'lived' in her relics. The Laon miracles therefore stood within the main stream of devotion to the Virgin that focussed on her as a saint in heaven rather than on her relics at a shrine on earth, in spite of the many aspects of the Laon miracles that showed a different tendency.

Thirteen years after the canons of Laon returned from their successful tours with their miracle-working relics, a church nearby at Soissons made use of another relic of the Virgin, this time her slipper. Thirty-one miracles were recorded of Our Lady of Soissons; they happened in response to a specific need. In 1128, after an unusually wet summer, there was an outbreak of ergotism, known also as *ignis sacer,* a disease caused by eating rye infected by a fungus.[58] The alarming symptoms are graphically described by Hugh Farsit, a canon of St Jean des Vignes, who composed an account of the miraculous cures that happened in connection with the disease.[59] Ergotism affected most of all the lower classes and was a well-known scourge in northern Europe at that time; it was often followed by pilgrimages to local shrines of the Virgin. These cures gave the Virgin a reputation as a healer, especially among the poor, and gratitude for them is another aspect of the veneration for the Virgin that was also expressed in the desire to take part in church building in her honour.

The miracles at Soissons occupied the late summer of 1128; Hugh Farsit claimed to have been present and to have witnessed daily cures, though he did not write a formal account of the miracles until 1143. The focus of the cures was the slipper of the Virgin, a relic that appears in these miracles but that seems to have no previous history, nor to have excited legends later about its transmission to Soissons. It was produced in a convent whose head at that time was the Abbess Mathilda.[60] A poor girl who worked in the convent was seized with symptoms of the illness; the abbess and a nun held her still and made the sign of the cross over her with the relic; the agony lessened and she was pronounced cured amid general rejoicing.[61] The news of the cure spread and sufferers flocked to the church; Hugh Farsit says that as many as a hundred and three cures were known at that time.

The slipper was a somewhat homely relic of the Virgin and one that appealed to the simple and unlearned, though even among them it was not without its critics. Most would accept the slipper, arguing that since the Virgin would have worn slippers, it was not improbable that one survived; but Boso, a servant who came to Soissons, commented that it could not really be the slipper of the Virgin since it would have fallen to pieces long ago. For this exercise in historical criticism Boso found that his tongue shrivelled up, and he was only cured after kissing the relic and acknowledging its provenance.[62] The relic was kept in the church and could be venerated there at any time; it seems to have been placed on the altar that the sick, *'ut mos est'*, kissed after praying in the church. Candles were offered as well as money, but no lavish offerings are recorded. The procedure was the same as at any thaumaturgic shrine, with the sick lying in the church sometimes for days on end and proclaiming their cures among general rejoicing. The relic was taken up and offered for the personal veneration of the faithful at certain times, a procedure not without risk, since on one such occasion a man bit a piece of out of the slipper for his private use.[63] Other ailments besides ergotism were cured by the relic. Those came who were paralysed; those with tumours, dropsy or stones; the blind, deaf, dumb, cripples, and demoniacs, as at any healing shrine. Outbreaks of plague brought people to the church in the sudden emergency, and the reputation of the Virgin as a healer was established at that place; henceforward, other illnesses would also be brought there for her attention. The cult was focussed on a particular place by the relic it contained. Hugh Farsit says that a star hung over the church, so that heaven glowed through the windows.[64]

These localized shrine cures were included in the *Mariales* alongside the more general Mary miracles. The Soissons miracles are in a small collection that shows the power of the Virgin, and certain aspects of these stories made them acceptable in the context of a more general devotion to her. First, the miracles were performed on behalf of the poor and undeserving, a theme central to the general devotion found in the miracles of the Virgin at this period. Peasants, cowherds, servants, even a man who was not a Christian, came and received cures. A woman who had been a prostitute found herself, like St Mary of Egypt, whose story was often counted among Mary miracles,[65] unable to enter the church until she had repented.[66] Mary was addressed at Soissons as 'Mother of Mercy', a title used for her at Cluny in the eleventh century by a thief turned monk on his deathbed.[67] The second aspect that relates these miracles to the new and more general Marian devotion was the penitential atmosphere of the pilgrimage made to Soissons. A kind of religious hysteria produced processions of the poor—barefoot and beating themselves,[68] confessing their sins and weeping in repentance. The 'holy fire' was seen as an inscrutable punishment by God on the sins of men. The response was personal confession and repentance. Hugh Farsit emphasizes this by elaborating his account with lengthy personal prayers in the new style of devotion that he attaches to the miracles and puts into the mouths of those praying at the shrine. Certain images in the miracles also recall the more personal kind of devotion that was emerging. A dumb man who was cured, for example, said he had seen Christ and St Mary coming toward him and that she had touched his mouth to heal him.[69]

These instances of the power of the Virgin exercised at the prayer of the poor, the sick, and the repentant were accepted as an integral part of the devotion proper to the Virgin. They were stories of local cures, at a specific place, yet they are found alongside general Mary miracles in the *Mariales*. How local they were is illustrated in this collection by a story told of a woman, Gundrada, who was cured at Soissons, but whose story was so much appreciated that it was later told of Chartres. Gundrada lived near Soissons and contracted *ignis sacer* that damaged her face. In most cases, a 'cure' of *ignis sacer* would mean that the disease was arrested, not that the damage was repaired. In this instance, however, Gundrada stayed in the church wearing a heavy veil and praying that the damaged tissue of her face might also be renewed; when this was found to have happened, it was proclaimed as the most resounding part of the cure.[70] The story was told later among the miracles of the Virgin of Chartres with the same details of name, place, and disease, but the most arresting part of the miracle takes place on a later visit of Gundrada to Chartres.[71] This transference of a miracle of the Virgin from one of her shrines to another underlines the importance attached to the two places as locations for veneration of the Virgin, while the fact that the place could be altered points toward a detachment from precise places to a more general devotion. The general miracles of the Virgin, especially those that came from the East, were at first related to specific places, but because they were repeated so often elsewhere, they lost the connection with their original places and could be located anywhere.[72] The more recent stories still retain their original local colour.

The theme of the power of the Virgin as available to all, everywhere and always, expanded from the precise theological devotion of Anselm and St Bernard into the collections of general Mary miracles. But at the same time, the cult of the Virgin remained localized at a surprising number of shrines. John of Coutances urged that Our Lady of Coutances should not be confused with Our Lady of Bayeux.[73] At Rocamadour, the Virgin was venerated as 'Our Lady of Rocamadour'.[74] Thus, on one hand the popularization of the cult of the Virgin among the more simple people led to an acknowledgement of her ubiquitous powers, but on the other hand it domesticated her as the 'Lady' of a certain area, in a way similar to the localization of the older saints in their tombs.

The miracles of St Mary of Rocamadour form a much larger collection than those at either Laon or Soissons and cover a longer space of time. They were recorded in three books, completed by 1172; they cover about twenty years. This collection is the third of the shrine collections of the Virgin to find its place in the *Mariales* of the thirteenth century, and, like them, it had elements of the shrine collections as well as certain non-local elements that allow these miracles to blend with the more general collections of miracles of the Virgin.

The miracles at Rocamadour claimed to be contemporary : 'We are not able to record the whole of the events we see and hear daily at the church of Blessed Mary of Rocamadour'[75]—a claim clothed in biblical language, but intended as a statement of fact. The miracles were recorded at the church by a notary, who is mentioned in the prologue to the second book of miracles: 'The notary was ill during those days so that he was not able to write down the miracles, either in their order or for their content'.[76] Making scedulae at shrines has already been mentioned, and here the same procedure kept the records of day-to-day miracles available for the monk who later composed the official record. The miracle books seem intended for public reading, since the miracles are grouped in sections ending with a doxology and 'amen'; presumably these collections were for use at the feast of the Nativity of the Virgin, the church's main festival, and throughout the octave. These miracles probably were read at other times in Rocamadour, especially on Saturdays, in refectory, and at Vigils.[77]

Records were kept as at a traditional shrine; the miracles, to some extent, were those of a healing shrine. The sick came, prayed, slept if necessary in the church, made offerings, and announced their cures. Specific details of name, place, and disease were recorded. The diseases cured are those already familiar at shrines. Twenty-eight external injuries are cured, including two bites and three broken limbs, the rest being wounds. Other external ailments, such as a fistula of the anus and a polypus of the nose, are cured. Four teeth knocked out in a fight are replaced. These and other such injuries account for only a quarter of the cures. The rest are cures of internal ailments, mainly complaints connected with the nervous system: fever, dropsy, paralysis, skin infections, a hysterical pregnancy, blindness, deafness, and dumbness. Cripples with withered limbs and seven demoniacs were also cured.[78] The cures were obtained by praying in the church, and this was carried out with an unusual degree of participation by both clergy and other pilgrims. The monastic liturgy was closely linked with the cures, as for instance in the cure of a blind woman during the Office of Tenebrae on Maundy Thursday. In this miracle, the blind woman cried out at intervals during the service as her sight was restored. The extinction of the

Tenebrae candles, which happened gradually through the service, balanced the restoration of light to her eyes.[79] The monks were involved in the miracles by their presence in the church at their liturgy, by their hospitality to pilgrims, and by their control of the crowds. Gerard the Sacristan found particular cause for complaint about the difficulties of keeping people in his church in order.[80] Pilgrims usually came in groups: men and women with their households, knights with their retinues, at times a whole village under the leadership of the parish priest.[81] Individuals helped one another, like the 'prince of Lorraine' who helped a poor blind woman into church and stayed to pray for her cure.[82] Animals were often brought along with the pilgrims, and there were cures of oxen, monkeys, and falcons.

The Virgin of Rocamadour could heal the sick; she was, like the saints at traditional shrines, also a great patron exercising protection and retribution. Like St Faith, the Virgin delivered prisoners who prayed to her, and they afterwards brought their fetters to her shrine. Like St Benedict, she exercised her sanctions against those who alienated her property in any way, and thirty-six miracles are devoted to this side of her powers. But here the similarity with the traditional miracles ends. A closer look at the miracles of Our Lady of Rocamadour sets them more surely than those of either Laon or Soissons in the category of general Mary miracles.

The church at Rocamadour was not a shrine. It held no relics of the Virgin and had no claim to special veneration for her beyond the fact that the church was dedicated to her. No sudden need for money as at Laon, no moment of crisis as at Soissons started the fame of the church. The statue later placed above the altar was a result and not a cause of the cult.[83] The legends that linked the Virgin and St Amadour with the place during the lifetime of the Virgin were also twelfth-century creations. In 1166 Ralph Tortaire described the finding at Rocamadour of the incorrupt body of 'S Amadour';[84] legend at once identified him as the husband of St Veronica, a friend of St Peter, a hermit at Rocamadour, and a friend and companion of the Virgin.[85] But the book of miracles of the Virgin ignored the finding of the body of the saint and devotion continued to be concentrated on Mary; S Amadour had significance there only from his association with her. The writer of the miracles finds no other reason for her veneration at Rocamadour than 'eligit': 'She has chosen to favour above all others the church of

Rocamadour'.[86] In nearly all these miracles, the Virgin is addressed as 'Our Lady of Rocamadour' and prayers and thanksgivings were made to her under that title.[87] To this extent the cult was artificial, not caused by the body of a saint at a place, but drawing devotion that already existed elsewhere to Rocamadour.

Another difference between the traditional shrines and the cult at Rocamadour was that most of the miracles happened away from Rocamadour itself. Of the cures recorded, only eleven actually took place at the shrine. Forty-eight occurred elsewhere, and the patients came to Rocamadour afterwards to give thanks; five more were cured on their way there. Local people were accustomed to make yearly visits to the church of the Virgin at Rocamadour and to pray to her when they were at home. When, like Bernard the priest of Quercy, they fell ill at home and prayed to their saint and were cured, they promised some offering in thanksgiving and brought it when next they came to Rocamadour.[88] Miracles are self-perpetuating, and once many such offerings of gratitude had been made on yearly visits, the fame of Our Lady of Rocamadour for miracles was established. Several pilgrimage routes converged on Rocamadour, and the fame of the church spread rapidly.[89]

The fact that most of the cures happened away from the Church is connected with another unusual feature of the cult. Many pilgrims were cured before they came and so had time to construct elaborate offerings appropriate to their situation. In almost every story some tangible offering is mentioned, often of a more imaginative kind than the usual offerings of candles and coins. Wax models of limbs were brought, but to these were added ships, mills, a whole village, a bier, a chalice, a pigeon, and four false teeth modelled in wax or in silver. Such *ex voto* offerings were not unknown at other centres of veneration and were to become more popular later.[90] Here, their number and their elaboration seem directly connected with the distance from which pilgrims came after cures.

The literary presentation of these miracles, however, shows the new forms of Marian devotion most clearly. The writer adds to his narrative long and elaborate prayers that he puts into the mouths of those visiting the shrine. These are the prayers of a monk steeped in the tradition of devotion to the Virgin created by Anselm. They are not brief prayers for help or collects used in corporate worship such as are found in older

collections of miracles, but long effusions of self-abasement full of in-
tricate phrases in praise of the Virgin. The prayers form a literary work,
carefully addressed to the Son through the Mother, in which ex-
pressions of need and personal devotion are worked out at length. These
are not the simple prayers of pilgrims at a shrine, but part of the new
'meditation' school of prayer.[91]

The recipients of the favours of Our Lady of Rocamadour are
likewise very far from the usual clientele of a shrine. They are those
who have no claim on the assistance of the saints. The very poor,
'populus simplex et rusticanus' are well represented; but almost as numerous are the undeserving rich. On the one hand, those who receive
the help of the Virgin are often described as young, pretty, rich, noble.
Knights and their ladies are helped, with their pets—a runaway mon-
key or a hurt falcon. A young knight teases his pregnant wife too far
and causes her to try to kill herself; she is restored by his tears and
prayers to the Virgin.[92] In two stories trial by battle is described and
the outcome reversed by the Virgin; in another case, the outcome of an
ordeal by water is changed for a princess who prays to the Virgin.[93]
On the other hand, the Virgin favours a troubadour, who plays for her
in the church; he prays that she would show him her favour, and she
sends three candles through the air from the altar to stand on his lute
strings.[94] Two boys who disobeyed their elders and swam in a river on
the way to Rocamadour are saved from drowning by her help.[95] She
herself is seen in visions as 'Domina mea': 'Lo! A Lady surrounded by a
marvellously varied beauty . . . she touches him with her own hand as
a sign of maternal affection'.[96] She is portrayed as an arbitrary patron,
ready to answer prayers to her and to her Son, bringing mercy into a
power-dominated society simply because she chooses to do so. She in-
tervenes to save those whom human and divine justice alike condemn,
as mater misericordiae. There is no reciprocal arrangement here by which
the saint as patron protects his own territory and people; on the contrary, stress is laid on how undeserving the suppliants are.

The miracles of Rocamadour hold a central place in the Mariales, and
their tone is increasingly that of the general Marian collections of miracles. It is possible that some direct connection exists between these
miracles and the general collections that originated a little earlier in
England; for instance, the stories collected by Dominic of Evesham
contain, like those told at Rocamadour, instances of the Virgin's con-

trol over the four elements,[97] and both collections include the story of the conversion of St Mary of Egypt.[98] The English knew about Rocamadour: Ralph of Diceto and Benedict of Peterborough both mention the miracles at Rocamadour.[99] Henry II may have visited it;[100] certainly two of his knights asked leave from the Irish wars to go there.[101] Gilbert Foliot visited it.[102] The seal of Rocamadour and that of the shrine of Our Lady of Walsingham are very similar.[103] This similarity points, however, to a general similarity of genre rather than to direct borrowing.

The shrine collections of miracles of the Virgin so far considered have been those associated with collections of more general Mary miracles. These shrines used relics of the Virgin, and their cults were focussed on these relics or on churches dedicated to her. The miracles to some extent have been occasioned by events, such as the plague at Soissons and the fire at the church in Laon. I will now discuss two more shrines of the Virgin in order to complete the picture of this type of miracle. The first of these is the church of Our Lady at Pierre-sur-Dive, where miracles surrounded the rebuilding the church; the second is the cathedral of Our Lady at Chartres, where the miracles draw together all the facets of the cult of the Virgin already discussed and also blend more closely with the collections of general miracles of the Virgin than any collection yet considered.

The miracles of the Virgin at Pierre-sur-Dive were described in 1145 by the monk Haimo in a letter to a dependent monastery at Tutbury in Staffordshire. They were connected with the rebuilding of the church at Dive in that year. Haimo claims that the pattern for the rebuilding operations was the reconstruction at Chartres in 1144: 'Memory and courage alike would fail me if I attempted to write down all the miracles I have deserved to see and hear by which she glorified first Chartres and then our church here'.[104] The first building crusade was started at Chartres in 1144–45, when pilgrims arrived to help rebuild the western towers of the cathedral. They hauled stones up to the site with prayers, penances, and flagellation, and miracles took place in response to the almost hysterical atmosphere of revivalist enthusiasm. In the same year Pope Eugenius III proclaimed the Second Crusade, and the enthusiasm it evoked probably found another outlet in building churches.[105] The rebuilding at Dive with its miracles took place after the first rebuilding at Chartres, but the miracle collection that survives for Chartres is connected with a later rebuilding project in 1194, after a fire. The miracles at Dive will therefore be considered before those at Chartres, both as being earlier in time, and as illustrating only one of the themes of such shrines, that of rebuilding, while the Chartres collection is more complex.

The monastery of Our Lady was founded in the eleventh century at Pierre-sur-Dive by Lesceline and dedicated in 1067 by Maurius of Rouen in the presence of William, Duke of Normandy and King of England. Forty years later it was severely damaged by fire, and attempts to repair it were delayed.[106] In 1145, however, inspired by the rebuilding at Chartres, the monastery began a similar process, with immediate success. Haimo recorded the miracles that took place during the building operations from 28 June, the vigil of the feast of St Peter, patron of the monastery and town, until August 1145. Haimo calls the 'greatest miracle' the ardour with which people of all stations combined to help with the work and then gives twenty-eight chapters of miracles of the Virgin intermingled with the work of reconstruction.

These miracles are all related to the *plaustra,* the carts that conveyed loads of building materials to the church from the surrounding district.[107] Eleven *plaustra* are mentioned, and, though the account is unfinished, it seems probable that there were not many more. During the week of the feast of St Peter, a load of stone was brought from Pierre-sur-Dive itself, followed on the next day by a load of wood. On 2 July, feast of the Visitation, a third *plaustrum* came from S Clemente; the next day, more stones were brought from Pierre-sur-Dive. On Wednesday and Thursday of the same week (4 and 5 July), carts came from Courcy and Bures, and at the end of the week a load was brought from Chartres itself. On 21 July, the vigil of the feast of St Mary Magdalene, local women brought a loaded *plaustrum,* and another cart came during the week loaded with staves. During August two more carts are mentioned, one brought by the young noblemen of Ponthieu and the other by the children of Ecajeul.

Here, as at other Marian shrines,[108] groups of local people banded together, vowing to supply building materials for the church. The gifts were collected and taken to the church on a cart, often pulled along by the donors and accompanied by all concerned with the gift. It was a penitential pilgrimage, with people walking barefoot, flagellating themselves, confessing their sins, and holding services on the way in honour of the Virgin. At the church the carts were unloaded, and the pilgrims entered the church to pray. The sick were also brought on the carts and were taken into the church where they could lie all night before the altar, both the monks and their own companions praying with them, according to Haimo, in an aggressive and demanding tone.[109] If a cure was announced, there was public rejoicing with bells ringing and the *Te Deum* sung. The church did not claim any relic or miraculous statue of the Virgin, and the focus of the cult was simply the high altar of the church dedicated to her. In the last miracle a statue of the Virgin is mentioned: 'At length turning to the statue of the holy Mother of the Lord which was over the altar they began to argue with it as if it were alive'.[110] But here as at Rocamadour, the statue was a result rather than a cause of the cult.

Most miracles in this collection were cures, and they took place inside the church. They concerned people from the district around St Pierre who prayed and made offerings as at other shrines. Here, however, the offerings were central rather than incidental. The names of the people cured, their places of residence, and the details of their illnesses were carefully recorded. The ill people were like those cured at other shrines. Twenty were crippled, four deaf, four blind, three dumb, and four had withered limbs. They were men, women, and children, almost all poor. The protection of the Virgin was exercised toward her pilgrims, especially two who were injured during the actual building operations.[111] Where these miracles differ from those at traditional shrines is in the account of the emotionally charged pilgrimage by which people took part in the rebuilding.

Haimo's inspiration for the record of miracles at St Pierre is from Chartres; twice Haimo tells miracle stories about St Pierre that emphasize the power of Dive at the expense of Chartres. A boy who was deaf and dumb was cured in one ear only at Chartres; his other ear was cured and his dumbness removed after prayer to Our Lady at St Pierre-sur-Dives.[112] Emma, a sick woman from Bayeux, lay ill at Chartres for fifteen days and was cured only when she at last went to pray to Our Lady at St Pierre.[113] Haimo describes the religious emotion at Chartres and at St Pierre in the same terms: 'what groaning, sighing, pleading . . . lacerating, beating of breasts without sparing'.[114] But St Pierre was a pale reflection of Chartres; the most important centre for devotion

152

to the Virgin was there and not at Laon, Soissons, Rocamadour, nor St Pierre-sur-Dives.

The record of the miracles of Our Lady of Chartres that occurred in connection with the rebuilding of the cathedral in 1194 was made at the end of the twelfth century and is preserved in a Vatican manuscript.[115] This was the main, though not the only, source for the version of the miracles of the Virgin in French verse made by Jean le Marchant, c. 1262.[116] The greatest number of miracles at Chartres are cures. Paralysis, dumbness, withered limbs; the blind, deaf, and crippled were cured and these cures recorded with the details of name, place, occupation, and disease. Moreover, like the miracles at St Pierre, a proportion of the miracles at Chartres were grouped around the arrival of *plaustra* with building materials and with the sick. A cart came from Château-Landon and another from Pithiviers loaded with grain to be sold for the benefit of the building work. A load of cement came from Bonneval, a load of staves from Courville; on the feast of the Assumption, a load of stones came from Batilly. As at Dive, the carts were drawn by penitents and with them came the sick who lay all night in the church. The miraculous protection of the Virgin was exercised toward pilgrims, guarding them from dangers and accidents on the way and ensuring a good price for their products at the end.[117] She was not known as a vengeful saint and in fact cured two people said to have been punished by other saints. The story of her punishment of a woman who worked on Saturday is, however, told in detail and follows the theme of one of her most famous miracles, 'Compline', in the general collections.[118]

In all this, Our Lady of Chartres was a traditional saint, with miracles focussed on her shrine and with cures of the sick as her chief claim to fame. The offering of building materials came from the district around Chartres, and therefore expressed the devotion of local people to the saint in their own district. She appeared in a vision to instruct a cured woman to advertise her shrine at Chartres: 'You will tell the faithful that Our Lady of Chartres has done this'. 'Whence it seems', comments the author, 'that she has chosen Chartres to be her special dwelling place on earth'.[119] As at Rocamadour, her 'choice' of the place was made an argument for her veneration there. But there were new elements in this collection, and the first of these was the relic of the Virgin venerated at Chartres. This was the *sacrosancta camisia*, 'the most holy shift which the Virgin wore when she was carrying the Son of God in her womb'.[120] The collection of miracles includes a story of how this relic had been used at the siege of Chartres in 911 as a temporary rallying point for the French against the Normans:

The alarmed citizens trusted neither in courage nor arms or walls, but implored the help of Blessed Mary and the shift of the most glorious Virgin which had been brought from Constantinople by someone for Charlemagne; he put it on a spear and displayed it like a banner in the wind.[121]

Whether or not this legend is of an early date, establishing the presence of the relic at Chartres by the beginning of the tenth century, it does not appear that the shift was continuously used for veneration until the end of the eleventh century. Only then was it invested with its full devotional significance. The shift was a particularly intimate and emotive relic of the Virgin and was used as such. The preface to these miracles describes the papal legate as appealing to the people of Chartres to do penance for whatever sins had caused them to be punished by the burning of their cathedral and to express that repentance by building a fitting church to house the relic of the Virgin, which was produced unharmed from the fire.[122] This combination of such a relic of the Virgin with the theme of personal repentance gave the miracles a background highly charged with emotion.

This emotion was expressed in the miracles by longer, more detailed stories among the accounts of practical cures, which were embellished with prayers and exclamations, groans, tears, sighs. Besides the poor people from the district around Chartres, there were other recipients of these miracles, people who belonged to the world of romance: a knight from Sourday; a young and noble husband; a noble lady from Sully-sur-Loire; a knight from Aquitaine; a young scholar from England. The situations were also those of romance. A knight seduces a girl and cuts out the tongue of a child who might betray him; a young man chooses the Virgin as his mistress, a story contrasting the themes of sacred and profane love; a knight touches his armour with the shift and is protected in battle; children are raised from the dead by the prayers of the Virgin. Some cures followed a familiar pattern: 'We have seen the deaf hear, the blind see, dumb speak again, the lame walk, and we have beheld many cured of illnesses, weaknesses, and various infirmities'.[123] But the new devotion showed in such phrases as: 'I am Mary, your

154

lover, and I have decreed that you shall take me as your best be-loved'.[124] Many of the miracles in this collection took place away from Chartres, and people came to give thanks there, another indication of the decentralization noted previously about Marian cults. The venera-tion of the shift provided a focus at Chartres, but many other elements made devotion to the Virgin more personal, less attached to the shrine, and dependent only upon supplication and the favour of the Virgin.

So far, miracles of the Virgin have been examined in relation to her main shrines in the twelfth century in France. They are mainly cures, similar to cures at the shrines of other saints, localized and specific, taking whatever difference in tone they have from the fact that another vein of Marian devotion was crossing with this one. The shrines so far discussed were flourishing after 1112; between 1100 and 1140 miracle stories associated with the Virgin, which had a different tone al-together, were current in England. Three main collections of such miracles exist. The earliest, made by Anselm of Bury,[125] consists of thirty-six stories about the miraculous powers of the Virgin exercised on behalf of her devotees. The second was made by Dominic of Evesham, prior of the abbey of St Mary at Evesham.[126] The third, by William of Malmesbury, drew upon these two collections, with a few additions.[127]

The dedication of the abbey at Evesham to Mary probably was the basis of the collection made by Dominic, and a miracle about the foun-dation of the abbey rests on an account of a vision of her seen by the swineherd Eaves.[128] The collection made at Malmesbury may also have taken its source of inspiration from the dedication of the monastery to Mary. Many of the miracles in these collections had local points of departure. *HM* 14, for instance, is the story of wine spilt during mass and cleaned up by the Virgin in the monastery of St Michael at Chiusa. But most of these stories have lost any local focus, and the accounts are impatient of such details. These collections are not shrine collections in the sense in which the miracles at Laon, Soissons, Rocamadour, Chartres, and Pierre-sur-Dive are. The details given are not intended to direct devotion to a place but to a person. Nor are the miracles usually concerned with cures. Only two stories in these collections are of cures, and they are told by Anselm of Bury: the stories of 'Mureldis'[129] and 'Foot Cut Off'.[130] The first is a story connected with an individual, perhaps of local repute; the second, significantly, is about a cure of ergotism in France. The rest of these stories do not focus devotion on any particular shrine; they are about the power of the Virgin intervening for individuals, above all for hopeless cases. The story of Eppo the Thief, told with much circumstantial detail of St Faith, St Giles, St Nicholas, and St Thomas of Canterbury, is told thus of the Virgin:

There was once a great robber, the most wicked of men, who thought of nothing but the service of the devil. Yet he had this much good in him that he scrupulously fasted on bread and water during the vigil of the Blessed Mary and when he went out to rob he used to salute her with as much devotion as he was capable of, asking her not to let him die in mortal sin. One day he was caught and hung on the gallows; he hung there for three days and could not die . . . He was taken down from the gallows and said that it was the Virgin who had kept him alive.[131]

When this story was told of other saints, the point was that the saint of a particular place had saved the thief, and that the thief gave thanks at a particular shrine. But in this new telling, any emphasis on locality has disappeared. The place where the miracle took place is omitted, and all attention is focussed on the devotion of this sinner to the Virgin and her mercy toward one devoted to her. This places the miracle in a different setting altogether, though the connection between the stories is clear. This connection can be seen elsewhere, particularly in the collections of Mary miracles called *Mariales*. The shrine miracles of the Virgin at Laon, Soissons, and Rocamadour were included in these books for reading on feasts of the Virgin and especially on Saturdays along with other more general collections. A typical arrangment of this material is found in a thirteenth-century manuscript from Corbie.[132] The letter of Herman to Bishop Bartholomew of Laon is first, followed by the *Liber de Virginitate Sanctae Mariae* and the *Life of St Hildelfonsus;* next appear the miracles of St Mary of Laon, the miracles at Soissons, and the miracles at Rocamadour. Then, after a brief preface, follow the series of miracles of the Virgin known as *HM* and *TS,* interspersed with prayers to the Virgin such as *O Intemerata.*[133] In other collections, the *HM* series is placed between the miracles of Laon and Soissons; *TS* between Soissons and Rocamadour.[134] These collections were for liturgical use and are described in these terms: 'Sermons about the Saturday of St Mary and about the miracles with which the solemnity of the commemoration of the Holy Virgin Mary is supported'.[135] The cures at the three shrines, therefore, were acceptable as part of a book of general Mary miracles.

156

Some of the stories of the powers of the Virgin told at Chartres are incorporated into collections of general Mary miracles, which show most clearly the link between the shrine cures and the general stories. The story of the Siege of Chartres is included in collections of general Mary miracles and is found in the collections of Dominic of Evesham and William of Malmesbury.[136] The vengeance story, in which a woman is rebuked for not observing the period from Saturday vespers to Sunday lauds as devoted to the Virgin, finds its place in general collections as the story called 'Compline'.[137] In the Chartres collection, a very detailed account is given of a young Englishman who was returning home with a present for his betrothed; he was caught up in the excitement of itinerant preaching for the rebuilding of Chartres, gave his present to the Virgin, and became her servant at Chartres. This story, known as 'Betrothed to a Statue', is found in the general Marian collections.[138] The story told at Chartres of a man buried by a fall of earth and kept alive by the power of the Virgin was told elsewhere as a general miracle of the Virgin, though it had been told by Peter Damian in connection with the eucharist rather than the Virgin.[139]

When Jean le Marchant produced his vernacular translation of the miracles of the Virgin of Chartres, he added several stories in this more general vein[140]—the story of Our Lady's chancellor,[141] in which a priest is described as a clerk of Chartres, and the story of the priest of only one mass.[142] Some other miracles found in the general collections are also associated with Chartres. The story called 'Milk' is told of Fulbert of Chartres[143] and the 'Five Gaudes' story is placed by William of Malmesbury in Chartres.[144] Gualterus of Cluny told three Mary miracles that he said he had heard from Godfrey, bishop of Chartres, and all three are found in general Marian collections as 'Bread offered to the Christ Child',[145] 'The Drowned Clerk',[146] and 'Wife and Mistress'.[147] These stories were not localized at the shrine of the Virgin in Chartres, but Chartres was important nonetheless in the growing cult of the Virgin.

How was veneration of the Virgin at local shrines connected with more generalized and untethered devotion to her as a person—the dominant characteristic of Mary miracles in the ensuing centuries? One of the means by which devotion became more general was the liturgical celebration of Mary as the greatest saint of the universal church. Mary could be invoked anywhere and by anyone; the canon of the mass commemorated her first among those whom each mass celebrated; and major festivals of the year were established in her honour as well, such as the Office of the Virgin and the dedication of Saturday to her honour.

The great feasts of the Virgin were the feast of the Annunciation (24 March), the Purification (2 February), the Nativity of the Virgin (8 September), the Assumption (15 August), and the Conception (8 December). Each grew in popularity in the eleventh and twelfth centuries, and miracle stories were told about them. The feast of the Conception of the Virgin, the feast commemorating the moment at which the Virgin Mary was conceived by her parents, was especially popular.

The feast of the Conception had been celebrated in England before the Conquest; after the conquest, like other feasts not known to the Normans, it was threatened with extinction. It was revived in the twelfth century, in those monasteries that held most firmly to Anglo-Saxon traditions: Winchester, Worcester, Ramsey, St Albans, Bury St Edmunds.[148] The feast reflected the interest felt in anything connected with the Virgin Mary—in this case, her origin—an interest also apparent in the attempts at this time to establish the feast of her mother, St Anne.[149] Thus, the feast of the Conception was part of that great wave of enthusiasm for Mary, in which Anselm of Bury played so large a part.[150] The Conception of the Virgin was the subject of theological speculation, and the word 'immaculate' was being added to her name in certain quarters. It was supposed, erroneously, that Anselm of Canterbury had held this view;[151] it was known that St Bernard of Clairvaux opposed it.[152]

Three miracles are connected with this feast. The first is the vision of Abbot Elsin of Ramsey, the abbot of St Augustine's Canterbury when the Normans invaded England. Rumours reached England of a possible Danish attack, and the king sent Elsin to Denmark to pacify the Danes. On his return journey, Elsin and his companions were in danger from a storm at sea; Elsin had a vision of a bishop who told him that they would be safe provided they guaranteed to introduce the feast of the Conception into England with the same texts as those used for the feast of the Nativity.[153] The story is not inconsistent with the career of Abbot Elsin, and he probably promoted the feast later as abbot of Ramsey.[154] The story became well known as part of the liturgical readings for the feast of 8 December. It asserted divine approval for the feast and indeed divine commands about its observance; it also demonstrated the possible rewards for those who kept it. It was not the vision that established the feast, since the story has nothing to do with the earlier feast in England, nor was the vision used by the promulgators of the feast in the twelfth century. Neither Eadmer in his *Tractatus de Conceptione Sanctae Mariae*[155] nor Osbert of Clare in his letters and sermons mentions it.[156] It was a miracle story told after the event to assert the unanswerable claim of the vision that 'God wills it' and to reveal the benefits for those keeping the feast.

A second miracle about the origins of the feast claims to be earlier than the vision of Elsin, but may be a later composition for the liturgy of the feast. It is included in the annals of the church in Aquileia[157] and survives in a fragment of a fourteenth-century collection of stories about devotion to the Virgin and its rewards.[158] The story of Elsin's vision appears to have preceded it, since the lines immediately above refer to the use of the texts of the Nativity of the Virgin for the feast of the Conception. The second story is set in the days of Charlemagne, 'the most illustrious Charles, King of the Franks'. A deacon who used to say the Hours of the Virgin with particular devotion was about to be married; he had a vision of the Virgin, who offered herself as his bride, and added 'if you celebrate annually on December 8th the feast of my Conception, and preach its celebration, you will be crowned with me in the kingdom of my son'. The writer then adds that the man became a monk:

And shortly after that time, by the merits of Blessed Mary ever Virgin, whom he diligently praised and blessed, he was made bishop of the see of Aquileia, and as long as he lived he carefully celebrated the feast of the Conception of the blessed Virgin on that day with its own octave and he preached its celebration everywhere.[159]

Like the Elsin story, this story supports the celebration of the feast with divine commands and promises of benefits. Here the benefits are spiritual rather than temporal, and the command comes directly from the Virgin rather than from another saint. Both stories draw on various collections of Mary miracles. The story of deliverance by the Virgin at sea is found in the miracles of the Virgin of Rocamadour;[160] the apparition of a saint at sea to deliver those in danger is common to many miracle books. The story of the young clerk and the Virgin is based upon the story of the clerk betrothed to the Virgin, found in the collections of general Mary miracles that originated with Anselm of Bury, himself an advocate of the feast of the Conception.[161] Both stories have had added to them the prescriptions about keeping the feast of the Conception; they affirm divine direction and promise divine favour to forward this specific feast. Later, a third story was told about the feast of the Conception. Alexander Nequam was always prevented by illness from lecturing on the *Song of Songs* this feast day, another instance of divine insistence for its observance.[162]

The feast of the Conception, therefore, was given dignity and appeal by the story of Elsin's vision and the tale from Aquileia. The feast so closely connected with the feast of the Conception in Elsin's vision, that of the Nativity of the Virgin, was also more commonly observed in the West after the eleventh century; it was, like the Conception, associated with devotion to the Virgin and curiosity about her origins, and it was put forward in the same circles.[163] A miracle story, less precise in its details, but with the same message as the miracles about the Conception, was told by Honorius of Autun. A hermit would hear celestial music on a certain night each year. At last, when an angel appeared to him, he asked what the music was, and he was told that the angels were celebrating the feast of the Nativity of the Virgin Mary; he told this vision to the pope, who, so the story says, instituted the feast on 8 September.[164] This story is another instance of divine approbation being accorded to a feast whose popularity was increasing, in order to give its observance the highest possible sanction.

Two other feasts of the Virgin that had been known in the East and were introduced at Rome under Pope Sergius (687–701) became more popular in the West in this period. These were the feasts of the Purification (2 February)[165] and the Assumption (15 August).[166] Both were connected with miracle stories. The celebration of the feast of the Purification of the Virgin in the Temple was said to have been instituted as the result of her miraculous intervention in the 'purification' of the city of Constantinople from the plague in 524.[167] As with the story of the vision of Elsin, this miracle is given a precise setting among historical events; and in both cases the stories illustrate favours bestowed by the Virgin. The miracles surrounding the feast of the Assumption have this theme also, but with a more 'spiritual' slant, as was appropriate for a feast of the entry of the Mother of God into heaven. It was a feast whose origins were related with miraculous details from the first,[168] to emphasize its splendour. Peter Damian tells a story told him by the Priest John about the Vigil of the Assumption in Rome. A woman in the crowd claimed to have seen her recently dead godmother, Marozia, who had explained her appearance thus: 'Indeed on this day the Queen of the world prays for us and I with many others am set free from the place of penance'.[169] This idea of the *refrigerium* for souls in Purgatory is told elsewhere about the time between vespers on Saturday and the morning of Sunday, and is related to the dedication of Saturday to Mary;[170] here it has been attached to the specific celebration of the Assumption, to add to its solemnity. A second story was told of the feast of the Assumption and its celebration in Spain. After the mass of that day, a voice was heard saying that the Son of the Virgin was again being crucified by the Jews; this experience led to violence against the Jewish community and the discovery of a wax image, pierced and crowned with thorns. The story was the first in the series collected by Anselm of Bury;[171] as retold by William of Malmesbury, it is given a setting as historically precise as the stories of the Conception and the Purification.[172] Like the rest, it gives supernatural recognition to the liturgical celebration.

Besides these feasts and vigils of the Virgin, the mass itself and the Office of the Virgin as well as various prayers to her were recommended in this period by miracle stories. The stories told about the value of celebrating her mass on Saturday usually contain a priest, otherwise ignorant, who celebrates her Saturday mass regularly and is commended by the Virgin for his devotion, usually with salvation after death.[173] There were variations. Sometimes it was the only mass he knew; sometimes he was specially humble and was refused burial until a revelation from the Virgin revealed his merits; sometimes he was specially sinful and the Virgin had to defend him for his devotion to her alone.[174] The message, however, was always the same. The Celebration of the Saturday mass provided outstanding and indeed unique privileges for the priest who celebrated it.

The Office of the Virgin was a more recent liturgical development in this period. In the tenth century, Berengarius, the bishop of Verdun, was said to have recited her Office privately, prostrate, before Matins each night;[175] at the end of the tenth century, Ulric of Augsburg was renowned for saying her Hours privately daily.[176] In the twelfth century, the Cistercian lay brother Christian of Aumône recited her Hours on a journey, and the text indicates that it was not yet a public celebration among the Cistercians.[177] Peter the Venerable refers to it as still a novel practice at Cluny, where it had been introduced by St Hugh for use in the infirmary.[178] The monk or clerk who celebrated the Hours of the Virgin was given her protection, and, as the second story told of the Conception shows, was the object of her favour.

Saying the *Ave Maria,* the *Salve Regina,* the Sequence of the Virgin, and the Five Joys also was recommended by stories of Mary's favour to those carrying out these devotions. The following is typical of these tales. A sacristan in a certain monastery led an impure life, but he loved the Virgin Mary and said an *Ave* whenever he passed her altar. One night he was drowned on his way home after visiting his mistress; his soul was delivered, at the intercession of the Virgin, from the demons who claimed it, and he was restored to life with space for amendment.[179] These miracles were included in general miracle collections of the Virgin, and directed to these specific devotions.

The theme of this powerful propaganda for the Virgin's feast and devotions to her is part of the general popularity of her cult in this period. The stories offer great rewards, often connected with salvation rather than material benefits, for some simple act of prayer to her. These were universal devotions, untethered by place, and in them all Mary is a figure of mercy without bounds. Where shrine miracles stressed the locality and urged a visit to it, these miracles stressed devotion to a person available to all, anywhere. The stories could be given a very precise location, especially when they concerned the supposed origins of a feast, but these miracles were essentially generalized and popular with all classes. Anyone might undertake liturgical actions, and the stories stress the extent of the power of the Virgin and the lightness of the required devotions for the most heavy sins to be removed. Such stories inevitably were more popular than any others and led straight into the Marian collections of the next century.

With these general collections, the Mary miracles moved into a new phase and came to occupy a central and formative position in the imagination of Europe. It is outside the scope of this book to comment on the Mary miracles of the thirteenth and fourteenth centuries, but some observations should be made about the material as it stands at this crucial juncture between the local and the general cult. Two things in particular ensured that the Mary miracles would expand in popularity,

162

and both have already been discovered in the miracles at the shrines of the Virgin: the unquestioned power of the Virgin as Queen of Heaven and the relationship of that power to every kind of human need. She was infinitely powerful; she was infinitely concerned. Dominic of Evesham says that since she made peace between God and man by bearing Jesus Christ, she is the one best able to aid man in the judgement that is against him.[180] William of Malmesbury asserted that she can answer any prayers for material help, but that her real concern is the care of souls.[181] The fascination of these stories was that they turned on the unpredictable workings of limitless power held in the hands of a woman. Only one thing was demanded, devotion to her involving repentance for her sake and with her aid. In the later romances, these miracles continued to emphasize the triumph of mercy and goodness for the needy in a world of power and strength.

The regal image of the Virgin could draw to itself all the varieties of praise that imagination could muster. But her concern for human need was equally attractive. It seemed from the stories already current that there was no situation in which she would fail to support the weak and despised; everyone was therefore able to identify with the people of the stories in some way. The recipients of the miracles of the Virgin seem, even in this early period, to fall into three groups, of universal interest: knights, young lovers, and sinners. An extreme instance of the care of the Virgin for knights is the story of how a knight missed a tournament through staying to hear her mass on his way there and found that she had taken his place and achieved amazing victories in his name.[182] Stories of her protection of lovers abound and revolve around her readiness to help them meet. The extreme instance of this must be the story of a nun Beatrice, the portress of a convent, who ran away with her lover and later found that the Virgin had taken her place so that she had never been missed.[183] Both of these kinds of stories overlap with the innumerable tales of the favour of the Virgin toward the sinful. The story, already quoted, of how she held up a thief on the gallows until he was taken down alive and freed is typical.[184] Her assistance was most potent of all at the moment of death, when salvation could be secured for the worst sinners by prayer to her.[185] In seventeen stories in the first series of one of the most popular early collections of Mary miracles,[186] those who gain her aid are four ill-living monks, a wicked abbot, a worldly clerk, and three knights who have killed someone in sanctuary.[187] In the second series, out of seventeen tales, there are four worldly and ignorant monks, two unchaste clerks, a thief who prayed to the Virgin whenever he went out to steal, and a peasant who stole his neighbours' land.[188] The protection of the Virgin in almost all these cases gave them assurance of pardon and salvation for their repentance, rather than material benefits in this world.[189]

The collectors of such tales all say that they wrote primarily to glorify the Virgin; but both William of Malmesbury and Dominic of Evesham say they also wrote to benefit 'simple men'. Dominic claims to write for the *simplices* rather than *doctas aures,*[190] in describing the powers of the Virgin who is 'refuge of sinners, perpetual help of all Christians'. William's praise of the Virgin occupies one tenth of his whole book of her miracles; he then explains what effect the miracles may have: 'They are helpful in kindling simple souls to the love of the Lord'.[191] The edification of the unlearned is, as with the use of miracles in sermons, in the mind of the collector of Marian miracles. This does not necessarily mean that the Mary miracles were intended for the peasant and labourer. On the contrary, they seem to have been told especially for the nobility, for such knights and ladies as appeared in their pages. The situations were familiar to the audience, which consisted not of monks or clerics but the unlettered.[192] This audience for miracle stories insensibly moved the miracles out of the exclusively ecclesiastical atmosphere of the shrine collection, the saints' *Lives,* the liturgy, the sermon. When the stories were read in a court or hall, the religious purpose soon merged with the magical elements in romance; the later forms of such stories are of knights devoted to great ladies, rather than to the Queen of Heaven, but the seeds of romance lay in the Mary stories of the earlier period.

The favour of the Virgin was claimed by individuals and families. Thomas Becket, for instance, was popularly held to have had visions of the Virgin and to have employed her to deal with his mending;[193] Fulbert of Chartres and St Bernard were also associated with her for intimate and personal favours. The story of Muriel concerns the wife of Roger Fitzwimund of Fécamp.[194] The family of Miles Crispin claimed a miracle of the Virgin as their unique possession.[195] The emphasis has passed from the glory of the saint at a particular shrine in connection with visible relics, to the interior devotion of individuals to the Virgin. This devotion was older than the localized devotion at the shrines, and it outlasted it; the shrine cures were lost in the wave of popular interest in the wider and yet more personal powers of the Virgin that the general collections displayed. This devotion inverts the usual approach to miracles that happened at shrines, and yet it is not totally different. It dominated the next century and stood apart from shrine-cults:

Society had staked its existence in this world and the next on the reality and power of the Virgin, it had invested in her care nearly its whole capital. . . . she was chosen unanimously by all classes because what man most wanted in the Middle Ages was not merely law or equity but also and particularly, favour.[196]

9

Miracles and Sanctity

THE ACCOUNTS OF MIRACLES so far examined have mainly recorded the saints' posthumous miracles. They include a large number of different kind of events, all of which are intended to illustrate and advertise the saint's power. The stories of miracles at shrines described the individuals who experienced the events, and they were of interest most of all to people who knew the shrines. Such collections were rarely copied and usually exist in the book kept at the shrine, or at most in a few copies made for particular purposes. These collections were as much a part of the cult at a shrine as the *ex voto* offerings. They were placed near the feretory, as a part of the furnishings of the shrine, as a witness to the power of the saint. Certain collections were copied for liturgical use and had, therefore, a wider circulation. This was so with the miracles of saints who were included in the calendar of the church and had a feast day in more than one place, where material was needed for public reading; the miracles of St Faith,[1] St Thomas of Canterbury[2] and the miracles of the Virgin were copied for this purpose, while the miracles of saints of local importance remained at their shrines, or were copied in places associated with the monastery that held the main relics.[3] The miracles of St William of Norwich, for instance, survive in only one known copy,[4] as do those of St Godric,[5] St Frideswide,[6] and St Cuthbert.[7] The miracles of St James at Compostela were widely copied and used on his feast day, while the collection connected with the Hand of St James at Reading survives in one manuscript only.[8]

The posthumous collections of miracles at shrines continued to be the primary source for miracle stories, but by the end of the twelfth century these collections took on a new form. The chroniclers began to write down the miracles of newly dead saints in the form of legal briefs

166

for the purpose of applying for official canonization. Before this change is discussed, however, it is necessary to look at another kind of miracle collection, one closely related to the shrine collections and also to the canonization process. The *Lives* of the saints, as distinct from the record of their posthumous activities, very often included miracles, and they generally reached a wider audience than the shrine collections. The *Life of St Anselm,* for instance, was copied and read in England and on the Continent;[9] the *Life of Hugh of Lincoln* was well known, especially among the Charterhouses;[10] the Cistercian *Lives,* of Aelred[11] and of Bernard,[12] match the popularity of their subjects with the number of mansucripts.

The *Lives* of the saints were sometimes followed by selections of posthumous miracles that served in a general way the same purpose as the canonization miracle collections: proving the sanctity of the miracle worker. The main difference between miracles recorded in a hagiographical context and those recorded in a canonization process lies in the formality of the procedure. The first is an appeal to the hearer or reader to recognize sanctity by the signs of its action; the second is a collection of evidence laid before professional judges for their decision. Miracles recorded in a hagiographical context either follow a pattern traditional in the writing of hagiography or are closely associated with the life of the individual saint. These types cannot always be separated, but for convenience I will examine the hagiographical model first.

In the *Lives* of the saints the miracles that predominate at the beginning of this period and are present throughout link the saint with acknowledged instances of sanctity. Such miracles make a different statement about sanctity from the miracles attributed to a living saint. They connect the primary pattern for the life of a saint—the life of Christ—with the literary record of that life in the Gospels. From the first, the significance of the Christian saints was found in the life and death and resurrection of Christ. The proto-martyr, St Stephen, for instance, was killed 'outside Jerusalem' by the Jews like his master and died with two prayers that were also attributed to Christ at his death (Acts 7:58–60). The miracles at the birth of Christ and other biblical persons in both Old and New Testaments were echoed in the infancy stories of later saints; the deaths of the saints, particularly of the martyrs, were linked with the passion and death of Christ; and in between, there were events called miracles in the Gospel accounts of the life of

167

Christ and his apostles to which the miracles of later saints conformed. These events were called in the Vulgate not *miracula* but *signa et prodigia.* They showed the incursion of the supernatural into the daily life of a saint, thereby authenticating his sanctity with signs, recognized and established, of true Christian holiness.

The importance of this pattern of miracles in the *Lives* of the saints cannot be overstated. The *Lives* of the saints, particularly at the beginning of this period, did not reveal the saint's character or recount his deeds, but showed that supernatural power worked in him according to accepted patterns of sanctity. The need to distinguish Christian miracles from pagan magic was a powerful incentive to find authentication in recognized patterns for the miracles of later saints. Bede's comparison of the miracles of St Cuthbert with the miracles of the prophets, patriarchs, and apostles has already been noted. Sulpicius Severus likewise linked the miracles of St Martin, particularly his raising of the dead, with the miracles of Christ.[13] St Benedict was described by St Gregory as a patriarch able, like Moses, to draw water out of the rock (Exodus 17:1–7);[14] to make iron float, like Elisha (2 Kings 7:4–7);[15] to receive obedience from ravens, like Elijah (1 Kings 16:6);[16] to cause St Maur to walk on water, like Christ and St Peter (Matthew 14:28–29).[17]

Such miracles in the lives of the saints were intended to establish them as Christian saints, powerful and holy according to the scriptural pattern.[18] But by the period under consideration, other models had been interposed between the pattern of the Bible and the life of a saint. The *Lives* of established saints, themselves patterned on the Bible, became in their turn patterns for authenticating the miracles of later saints. Three *Lives* in particular formed the hagiography of the Middle Ages: the *Life of St Antony* by Athanasius;[19] the *Life and Miracles of St Benedict* in the second book of the *Dialogues* by Gregory the Great,[20] and the *Life of St Martin* by Sulpicius Severus.[21] In each case, a double pattern is reflected in later saints' *Lives:* miracles of Scripture, miracles of the established saints. The formative influence of the *Dialogues* of Gregory on later shrines of St Benedict and on the *Life of St Cuthbert* has already been noticed. Desiderius, in his *Miracles of St Benedict,* describes how Apollinarius, abbot of Monte Cassino in the early ninth century, walked on water not only like Christ (Matthew 14:25) and St Peter (Matthew 14:29), but also like St Maur;[22] in the same account of miracles, the rescue of a hammer from the water it fell into explicitly recalls not only Elisha (2 Kings 6:5–7), but also St Benedict.[23] In the *Lives* of the abbots of Cluny, miracles are frequently similar to those of both the Bible and earlier saints' *Lives,* especially St Martin's. The dealings of St Antony of Egypt with demons colour innumerable saints' *Lives,* while these in their turn had their source in the temptations of Christ in the wilderness (Luke 4:1–14).[24]

Two moments in the *Lives* of saints especially were surrounded by these hagiographical miracles: birth and death. Dreams about the birth of saints reflected the dream of Joseph before the birth of Christ or the wonders prefacing the birth of a prophet or John the Baptist. The deaths of the saints were seen in terms of the accounts of the death of Christ and his resurrection; in the case of martyrs, the details of the Passion were recalled, sometimes in great detail.[25] With other saints, the presence of angels, white robes, sweet odours, and heavenly sounds recall the images of the first Easter and the deaths of the early martyrs.[26]

Between these moments of transition from one world to another lay the earthly lives of the saints, in which incursions of the supernatural again echo the Bible and earlier saints' *Lives.* The use of Old Testament types in the New Testament was continued and extended in the *Lives* of the new saints. Moses striking water from the rock in the Wilderness (Exodus 17:5–6) was seen by commentators as a type of Christ, both giving 'living water' to the woman at the well in Samaria (John 4:5–15) and when water and blood flowed from his side on the cross (John 19:34);[27] the type was continued in the provision of water from rock by later saints—St Benedict,[28] St Dunstan,[29] and St Anselm,[30] to mention only a few. The echoes of biblical miracles such as the changing of water into wine are found in accounts of the saints who blessed water and turned it into wine. This was told of Thomas Becket who was said to have turned water into wine at the table of the pope three times.[31] The story was elaborated in the thirteenth century, possibly from a very early vision recounted by William of Canterbury, in which an antiphon was sung in honour of Thomas, containing the lines: 'Our Saviour performed a wonder, when he turned this water into wine'.[32] The later versions made of this an occasion when Thomas was served with water at a meal but by blessing it turned it into wine. The point of the story was not the same as that in the Gospel. Here, the water made wine was intended to disguise Thomas's austerity. The narrative, however, has biblical overtones that link it with the 'first miracle' of Jesus. From this instance it is easy to see how miracles in hagiography develop. A phrase expressing the fact of Thomas's martyrdom in poetic form was taken literally and made into an event in his life, with the Gospel precedent in mind.

These powers exercised by Christ and his immediate followers were not used in precisely the same way by the saints. The parallels are not drawn exactly, since the claim of the saints was not to be great men themselves but deputies of Christ, to whom he had promised power. The wonders that accompanied the births and deaths of the saints were not identical with those at the birth of Christ. The angels, star, and prophetic visions of the first chapters of St Luke are replaced by dreams, lights, and symbols of future sanctity. The cures of diseases in the *Lives* of the saints reflect the list given in the Gospel: 'The blind receive their sight, the lame walk, the lepers are cleansed, the deaf hear, the dead are raised up' (Luke 7:22). When such miracles were attributed to the saints, however, they were not described precisely as in the life of Christ. Where Christ healed the sick directly, saints made the sign of the cross, invoked the Trinity, prayed, or used blessed objects, espe- cially water. Even when St Hugh of Cluny deliberately re-enacted the cure of a paralytic by St Peter (Acts 9:33–34),[33] he used a relic of St Peter's cloak to emphasize both that this was a parallel to the cure related in Acts and also that it was not the same. The assertion behind these differences is that it is still Christ who works miracles through his saints, not that they can work miracles in their own power. Hagio- graphical miracles should not be dismissed as invention; they were of great interest to the reader of the life of a saint, though they did not provide the same kind of information as that found either in miracles the saint performed during his life or after his death. In the case of shrine miracles the interest in the story as recorded lies in the person cured; in the case of miracles in the *Lives* of the saints, the interest of the reader is focussed on the saint himself and his likeness to his pre- decessors. The life of a saint whose history was unknown could be entirely reconstructed from hagiographical models.[34] While the re- cords of miracles at shrines for this period were, generally speaking, a painstaking record of what people believed had happened to them by the power of the saint, miracles in saints' *Lives* cannot be taken at their face value in the same way; nevertheless, when this distinction has been made, they have a special and remarkable value in showing what mattered to readers of accounts of sanctity.

While early saints' *Lives* presented the saints in this predominantly supernatural context, certain *Lives* of saints in the twelfth century came nearer to the modern idea of biography as 'honest and impartial'.[35] There are, of course, hagiographical parts in the *Lives* of saints at all times, but in the twelfth century other elements were stressed. A more personal and intimate style of biography emerged, which still contained miracles, though with a different interest. I have chosen to examine four accounts of twelfth century saints in some detail: the *Life of St Anselm* by Eadmer, the *Life of Aelred of Rievaulx* by Walter Daniel, the *Life of St Hugh of Lincoln* by Adam of Eynsham, and the *Vita Prima S Bernardi*.

The *Vita S Anselmi* has been described as 'the first intimate portrait of a saint in our history'.[36] In two major respects it meets the requirements of modern biography. It is by someone who knew St Anselm personally, and it presents a unified picture of a life not set on the public stage but in private.[37] The public life of St Anselm had been written by Eadmer in the *Historia Novorum in Anglia*; the *Vita S Anselmi* is an anecdotal account of a man who was also a saint, and it is the later work that contains the accounts of Anselm's miracles, 'Anselm's private life . . . his character . . . the setting forth of his miracles'.[38]

The *Vita S Anselmi* is not entirely without echoes of hagiographical miracles, to establish Anselm in the tradition of the Scriptures and the saints. In striking water from the rock at Liberi, his action recalled Moses in the Wilderness as well as St Dunstan;[39] his blessing extinguished fire, calmed waves, ensured a supply of food when needed, all of which echoed the Bible and older saints' *Lives*. John of Salisbury, summarizing Eadmer's work for the canonization appeal, found parallels for Anselm's miracles in the Bible and in the *Lives* of St Benedict, St Martin, St Clement, and St Basil.[40] But Eadmer was not eager to pile up similarities of this kind. A difference in approach is apparent in his story of an event in the life of St Anselm that can be paralleled in the *Life of Odo of Cluny*. John of Salerno records how St Odo crossed a river safely even though his boat had a hole in it and comments that 'the merit of this holy man is manifest, who was able by his prayers to obtain what Peter and Paul and then our father Benedict has previously

merited'.[41] Eadmer described a similar situation, when Anselm crossed
to Wissant in 1097, but here Eadmer draws no parallel with earlier
saints. The main interest in Eadmer's account is in Anselm himself and
his anxiety in case he would have to turn back: 'He finished speaking
and tears stood in our eyes while our hearts were smitten with sorrow at
what we saw and heard'.[42] The miracle only came to Eadmer's knowledge long after the event and was retold as an instance of God's care for
the archbishop, insofar as it has any particular significance in his work.

The rest of the miracles in the *Vita S Anselmi* are of a personal,
self-revealing kind, which reflects the character of the saint himself and
his own virtues rather than linking him with his predecessors. Four of
them are the most personal of all kinds of miracles, visions, and their
source seems to have been Anselm himself.[43] These dream experiences
are not prophetic visions, but remembered dreams, accompanied by
Anselm's own reflections on them, couched in the same kind of language and imagery as his conversation and preaching. The miracles he
performed are presented in the same way, with the emphasis on Anselm
and his attitude to what was asked of him, insofar as it showed his
virtues. When asked to perform cures, he was reluctant and only ready
to give his blessing as a form of prayer for those in need.[44] When a man
asked for the water in which Anselm had washed his hands, proposing
to drink it in order to be cured of fever, Anselm was astonished and
would let him have only the water in which he had washed his hands at
mass on the understanding that any cure that might result was not to
be mentioned.[45] Eadmer was more eager for miraculous results and at
Vienne gave scraps of Anselm's food to the sick who asked for them.[46]
The monks Baldwin and Alexander were even more alert for miracles.[47]
But the miracles in the *Vita S Anselmi* reflected the total character of
Anselm for sanctity, the 'miracle' of his life, though Eadmer saw this as
part of a tradition of biblical sanctity: 'If anyone doubts whether Anselm was inspired by a spirit of prophecy in these incidents, the plain
facts of the case show what is to be believed'.[48] Eadmer made a determined effort to establish Anselm's reputation by posthumous miracles,[49] but his death, like his birth, remained notably lacking in
hagiographical details. The miracles collected by the monk Alexander[50] are not, with four exceptions, miracles of Anselm, but miracles
told by or to Anselm; they reflect neither the patterns of hagiography
nor his personal sanctity, but his interest and that of his friends in a
certain kind of miracle story, told for its edifying content.

The most outstanding personal biography of a saint for the twelfth century, therefore, stressed hagiography less and the miracles connected with personal sanctity of life more. Such miracles were told with an emphasis opposite to that of posthumous shrine miracles and hagiographical miracles. At the shrines, all the interest in a miracle is in the patient and his cure; in hagiography, the interest is in the saint and especially in finding precedents for his action. In this style of saintly biography, the saint himself and his reflections and reactions are central. The same style in biography, though with a stronger bias toward hagiography, can be seen in the *Lives* of two other monastic saints, Aelred of Rievaulx and Hugh of Lincoln. The *Life* of Aelred, abbot of the Cistercian foundation at Rievaulx, was written about fifty years after the *Vita S Anselmi* by a monk who had known Aelred, Walter Daniel. The *Life of St Hugh* of Lincoln was written early in the thirteenth century, by the monk Adam of Evesham, a close companion of Hugh in the last years of his life.

In both these *Lives,* the subject is compared explicitly with biblical and saintly personages of the past. Aelred was presented as a second Daniel, a new Joseph, David, Lot.[51] His staff, like that of Moses, worked wonders.[52] As a child, his face shone with a supernatural light;[53] he was Noah, making his body an ark for the faithful.[54] Walter himself reveals his source for the description of the dead body of the saint as being Sulpicius Severus's *Life of St Martin.*[55] In the case of Hugh of Lincoln, Adam compares his subject to Aaron, Joshua, Daniel, David, Joseph, and St Paul.[56] Both saints are frequently compared by their biographers with St Martin, in accordance with the tradition of the *Life of St Martin* as the paradigm of the life of a monk who also held episcopal or abbatial authority. In the *Life of St Aelred,* the death of St Martin is the model for Walter Daniel's account of the death of Aelred; in the *Life of St Hugh,* the references to Martin are more comprehensive still. Hugh is called 'devoted disciple and imitator of the most blessed Martin'.[57] Martin and Hugh are compared in detail,[58] and a miracle connected with Hugh after his death has this comment: 'The miracle I have just described was no departure from the footsteps of St Martin, but an instance of their close resemblance to each other'.[59]

But in the cases of Aelred and Hugh, both members of the new monastic orders, authenticating miracles were not of central importance to their biographers. The virtues of Aelred, his austerities, his sufferings, above all his charity, were what stood out for Walter Daniel: 'Our father's are great miracles. But bad men can work miracles, even great miracles . . . I marvel at the charity of Aelred more than I should marvel if he had raised four men from the dead'.[60] Those miracles that show the supernatural virtues of Aelred himself predominate in the *Life*. The cures mentioned by Walter are all connected with members of Aelred's own monastery—a monk who became dumb after illness, a shepherd of Rievaulx, a young monk—and depended upon Aelred's order to them as their abbot, 'speak, my brother, in the name of the Lord'.[61] A fourth cure was that of a young man in the neighbourhood of Rievaulx who had swallowed a frog. This tale is more elaborate, and one that is suspect due to its similarity to a miracle attributed to William of York, whom a former abbot of Rievaulx had opposed as a simoniac.[62] The other miracle attributed by Walter to Aelred concerned an abbot who spoke angrily to Aelred and died in agony; Walter later retracted this story, since it reflected upon Aelred in a manner not consonant with Cistercian virtues, though it would have been perfectly acceptable at any older shrine where vengeance from the saints was expected.[63]

St Hugh, like Aelred, is presented by his biographer as the wise, God inspired man who discerns reality and banishes illusion,[64] whose virtues of charity and understanding are central to his life. It is a vivid personal portrait of a man capable of the human reactions of irritation,[65] spontaneous affection, and delight, with an appreciation of animals and birds that recalls the relationship characteristic of hermits and animals.[66] Adam records no miracles about Hugh's childhood; rather he quotes Hugh's own account of a stark and austere childhood, when his father and teachers made him study constantly: 'Little Hugh, little Hugh, I am educating you for Christ, play is not for you'.[67] His death and burial are described in terms of the death of St Martin with wonders and visions. But between birth and death, this biography emphasizes, as did those of Anselm and Aelred, virtues. Adam quotes Hugh himself in support of this preference for virtue rather than miracles:

He thought miracles were the last thing to admire or wish to emulate, although he used to describe very attractively those worked by holy men which he had read or heard about and had a great veneration for them himself.[68]

Adam adds that everyone in Hugh's household believed he performed many miracles, though he does not enumerate them. Twice Adam mentions miracles connected with the Eucharist, and in both cases the stories show Hugh as unequivocally opposed to mere wonders. In the first instance, a clerk told him that he had seen Christ in the form of a child in Hugh's hands at mass; Hugh forbade him ever to mention this again, and Adam later recorded Hugh's opinion more forcibly in another account of the matter: 'What concern is it of yours, if on the occasion you have mentioned and on very many others, the Lord vouchsafed to manifest himself to me in this way'?[69] Later, when Hugh visited France, he met a priest who claimed that the elements of bread and wine had once turned visibly into flesh and blood when he was celebrating the eucharist; he had therefore preserved the chalice containing this behind the altar for veneration. Hugh refused to look at this wonder:

It is not our concern. Why should we gape at a sensory image of this divine gift, when every day we behold by faith this heavenly sacrifice, whole and entire. Let that man look with his bodily eyes on the minute fragment who cannot by faith inwardly behold the whole.[70]

The contrast between the miracles told to identify with earlier saints and the miracles connected with present virtues is summed up in a reply of St Hugh to William de Montibus, who had expressed surprise when Hugh kissed a leper: 'Martin by kissing a leper cleansed his body, but the leper's kiss cleansed my soul'.[71]

The literary tradition of hagiography combined with the record of contemporary miracles finds further expression in both the writings and the accounts of the life of one of the greatest men of the twelfth century, Bernard of Clairvaux. His influence on his contemporaries through his personality and his writings was greater than that of any other churchman of his time, and it is therefore necessary to look more closely at anything that concerns the miraculous in his life and works. In discussing miracles used in sermons, we have already seen that Bernard regarded miracles of the saints as signs of the power of God. It is clear from his works that he belonged to the tradition of Gregory the Great, of Bede, and of Anselm, which saw wonders as subservient to virtue. The miracles of the saints, he says, are to be admired, but it is their virtues that are to be imitated by others. The *mirabilia* that were central for him were the great acts of God, known only to faith. Miracles were chiefly important as converting ordinances, as *signa,* by which men were converted. St Bernard presents this view in his sermon on the monastic saint, St Martin, to an assembly of abbots; he speaks not of his miracles, posthumous or during his life, but of his obedience, his poverty, his charity. His *miracula* and *signa,* he says, are to be wondered at, his *merita* and *virtutes* are to be imitated: 'Consider therefore carefully what is appropriate for you, that is, that which is to be wondered at or that which is to be imitated'.[72] St Martin is to be imitated in his demonstration of the Beatitudes, rather than in his performance of miracles:

Does the word of God then pronounce those blessed who raise the dead, give sight to the blind, cure the sick, cleanse the lepers, heal the paralysed, cast out demons, foresee the future, shine out with miracles, or is it rather those who are poor in spirit, gentle, sorrowful, hungering and thirsting for righteousness, merciful, pure of heart, peacemakers, persecuted for righteousness' sake?[73]

It is in the *Life of St Malachy,* however, that Bernard most clearly sets out his didactic approach to miracles. Malachy of Armagh knew Bernard, shared his ideals of monastic reform, and corresponded with him.[74] Malachy died at Clairvaux on the night of 2 November 1148. Bernard thought him a saint and wrote his *Life;* the two were at one point considered together for canonization.[75] They appeared together in visions later, and Bernard was buried with Malachy at Clairvaux.[76]

In the sermon he preached in chapter the morning after the death of Malachy, Bernard referred to Malachy's miracles only as signs of his sanctity.[77] A few months later, Bernard dictated a *Life of Malachy* to his secretary, Geoffrey of Auxerre. In the preface, Bernard says he wrote at the request of Abbot Cogan of Inislaughan and that much of his information came from Ireland, where all the miracles took place. It is, however, clear that Bernard regarded Malachy as a saint. He describes six instances of prophecy in Malachy's lifetime, four revelations, five 'revenge' miracles, three conversions by miracles, twelve cures, and one resurrection of the dead. He groups them in a hagiographical pattern, to demonstrate that Malachy was proficient in all the ancient kinds of miracles, and says at the end: 'In what kind of miracle common in former days did Malachy not shine?'[78] The miracles are authentication, but even more they reveal the saintly character of Malachy. They have a third function in the narrative. Bernard regarded the lives of saintly men as *condimentum,* a spice added to the life of the world; miracles encourage men toward their own conversion, and give them a 'taste' for holiness: 'It was always thought praiseworthy to record the illustrious lives of the saints so that they could serve as a mirror and good example; they could be a kind of spice to the life of men living upon earth'.[79] Bernard wrote the *Life of Malachy* as the epitome of sanctity, and he saw Malachy's whole life as the real miracle, the full expression of *'fides et cor humanum'*: 'It seems to me that the first and greatest miracle he presented was himself'.[80]

Immediately after Malachy's death, an incident showed in one action the three kinds of miracles so far discussed. Bernard was convinced of the personal, 'biographical' sanctity of Malachy; he had worked miracles when alive, he would continue to do so now he was nearer to God. Bernard therefore took the withered hand of a boy present at the funeral and placed it within the dead hand of Malachy; the boy was cured at once. As Bernard says; 'I laid it on the bishop's hand and he brought it back to life. Surely the grace of healing lived in the dead man; his hand was to the lifeless hand what Elisha was to the lifeless man.'[81] Linking this practical demonstration with the example of Elisha gives the incident a hagiographical aspect. The incident sums up the whole approach of Bernard himself to the miracle: It was an actual, visible cure of a contemporary; it was told to edify the faithful and convince them of the holiness of Malachy and God's power in him; it was set within the tradition of the work of God as recorded in scripture. In combining hagiographical tradition with personal knowledge and assessment of virtue, Bernard is following the same tradition of writing about saints as did Eadmer, Walter Daniel, and Adam of Eynsham.

The main evidence for the miracles worked by Bernard himself during his life is found in the several books of the *Vita Prima.*[82] It is possible to see there a pattern of miracles that corresponds to those in the twelfth-century biographies already discussed: miracles told for hagiographical purposes, to illustrate virtues, and, above all, to present Bernard as *'vir Dei'* throughout his life. The *Vita Prima* was given as evidence for the canonization of St Bernard, and in its second recension it was not only successful, but also earned the praise of the pope for how it had been constructed.[83] Thus it is the epitome of the style of saintly biography that had evolved in the twelfth century and that was required by the formal process of canonization. The aim of showing the virtues of the saint to edify the faithful meant that accounts of miracles and exorcisms would be included, along clearly defined lines of scriptural reminiscence. The absolute holiness of Bernard is emphasized, and previous criticisms of his faults are answered, especially by William of St Thierry.

This theme of absolute holiness runs through the biography: Bernard's birth was surrounded by signs and portents,[84] his youth was a model of goodness, and his virtues were miraculously expressed.[85] He is rarely compared explicitly to other saints, but implicitly to Christ in his earthly life. He is said to have been offered in the church as Samuel was offered to God in the temple,[86] and his visions as a child are compared to those of the young Samuel.[87] The vision he saw as a boy was of the nativity of Christ, and thereafter the model in the mind of his biographers is the life of Christ: as a boy at home with his mother, as a young man with a band of disciples, and finally as the father of monks at Clairvaux, the new apostolic community.[88]

Within this hagiographical framework, the biographers of St Bernard recorded the second type of miracle found in this kind of saint's life—interpretations of actions performed by Bernard himself. William of St Thierry wrote the first book of the *Vita Prima* while Bernard was still alive; these were recollections of a man he had known and believed to be a saint. Geoffrey of Auxerre, who wrote the third, fourth, and fifth books and edited the whole, was Bernard's secretary and responsible more than anyone for accounts of his life and miracles. Both had known Bernard and wrote about him as a monk, in the ethos of Clairvaux, in his private and monastic life. In these accounts they stressed the virtues of Bernard but they also included miracles.

Behind the *Vita Prima* lies an earlier source, also the work of Geoffrey, the *Fragmenta Bernardi*, which was used by William and Geoffrey himself. These notes were completed by 1147[89] and are the earliest record of Bernard of Clairvaux. They contain accounts of twenty miracles, most of which are 'monastic' miracles, typical of the Cistercians: miracles of insight and prophecy; visons; and miracles illustrating the power of the monastic virtues of obedience and poverty. But there are also accounts of cures, of which the first is typical. Josbert de la Ferté, a relative of Bernard, fell seriously ill while Bernard was away from

Clairvaux. His wife sent for the saint, and when he came, he expressed concern most of all for the spiritual state of the man. He promised the family that Josbert would remain alive long enough to make his confession. Bernard then said mass, the man recovered sufficiently to confess his sins and hear his son promise to make restitution on his behalf.[90] This story is told as an event in Bernard's life, and it illustrates his primary concern—not physical cure, but spiritual salvation.

The miracles recorded in the *Vita Prima* of Bernard among his monks are also told with this 'spiritual' intent. Bernard's letter rebuking Robert was said to have been kept dry miraculously during a shower of rain ('He took down the letter while it rained without a single drop of water falling on the sheet') not from vengeance, nor in an event *contra naturam,* but from charity: 'The love which inspired the letter sheltered the parchment and kept the writing and the sheet quite unspoiled'.[91] His prayers at the eucharist enabled a monk to confess his fault;[92] soldiers who visited Clairvaux were converted by his prayers;[93] even flies that infested a church were obedient to his excommunication of them.[94] In the accounts of Bernard's monastic miracles by Herbert of Clairvaux and Conrad of Eberbach, the same theme is dominant: Bernard saw angels standing among the monks during the *Te Deum;* he also saw the disposition of each monk as he chanted the psalms;[95] when he was away from the monastery, he knew in spirit what the novices were doing there.[96] When a monk, Herbert, suffered an attack of epilepsy, Bernard did not offer to cure him, but sat by his side and held his hand until he fell asleep: 'What shall we do, then; come, let us pray'.[97]

This tradition of the 'monastic' Bernard follows from his own opinion of miracles in his writings. Bernard was criticized by his brethren for working material rather than spiritual miracles. In describing the cure of Josbert, William says that Bernard's brother Gerard and his uncle Gaudry protested when Bernard promised that Josbert would live, thinking such a miracle a temptation to pride.[98] His other brother, Guy, joined them in warning Bernard about the danger to pride concealed in his power to work miracles:

They were quite merciless to him, criticizing him severely in spite of his gentle and retiring nature. They misconstrued even his most blameless actions demolishing the wonders he had worked and pressing home their taunts and reproofs until they had often reduced him to tears.[99]

When Bernard came home or visited another Cistercian house, he is said to have ceased his cures, partly to spare the monks the disturbances created by crowds asking for miracles, but also because he recognized that within the cloister the interest of the monks was in a different kind of wonder, the miracles of prayer and salvation. This theme of the 'monastic' Bernard prevailed in the account of his posthumous cult. After his death a cure was reported during his funeral[100] and the brothers were dismayed by the excitement it caused. It was said that the abbot ordered Bernard to stop performing miracles: 'He asked him by virtue of obedience not to perform any more miracles', and Conrad of Eberbach adds 'from that day until now he has never been seen to do any miracles in public'.[101] This may be a pious invention to cover a lack of actual miracles, but it is also indicative of one of the main lines in the picture of Bernard as *vir Dei*.

So far, I have explained how the *Life of St Bernard* corresponds with Bernard's own opinions about miracles and with the type of saintly biography usual among his monastic contemporaries. There is, however, another side to the miracles of St Bernard, which emphasizes a different kind of miracle in biography. The reputation of Bernard as a wonder-worker rests mainly on the sixth book of the *Vita Prima*. It shows Bernard constantly working miracles, healing one sick person after another, during his visit to Germany in 1146–1147. These cures are more like miracles at the shrine of a dead saint than miracles in the life of a saint; they must therefore be considered in some detail.

The *Historia Miraculorum in Itinere Germanico Patratorum* claims to be a first-hand account of Bernard's cures in Germany in 1146–1147, and it is at least as early as the *Fragmenta*. Bernard's companions took notes daily of miracles, and from these they compiled a dossier for each day. These notes and the comments of the contributors were written down in dialogue form under the names of the contributors; an example will make this method clear:

Eberhard: On that day I saw him cure three others who were lame. *Franco:* You all saw the blind woman who came into church and received her sight before the people. *Guadricus:* and a girl whose hand was withered had it healed, while the chant at the offertory was being sung. *Gerard:* on the same day I saw a boy receive his sight.[102]

180

The account falls into three parts, each part covering a different section of the journey.

The first part describes the journey from Frankfurt through Constance to Speyer, from November 1146 to January 1147.[103] Herman, bishop of Constance,[104] is one of the contributors and perhaps the leading spirit in the enterprise. The letter prefacing the account of this first part is by him to Henry, brother of Louis VII, then a novice at Clairvaux,[105] and he takes a leading part in providing the notes. His diocese was involved in the journey and great interest was aroused in it there. The others who wrote accounts of miracles as they witnessed them were also well-known men. With Herman were his chaplain, Eberhard;[106] Philip, archdeacon of Liège and later a monk of Clairvaux;[107] Abbot Baldwin of Chatillon-sur-Seine;[108] Abbot Frowin of Salmansweiler;[109] Gerard of Auxerre and Godfrey, both monks of Clairvaux; two clerks, Otto and Franco. At Cologne they were joined by Alexander of Cologne, later a great man in the Cistercian Order.[110] All these took notes of the miracles and, when they left Speyer, they put them together in a single account.

The second part of the *Historia* records miracles collected in the same way on the return journey from Speyer. They stopped at Cologne from 10 to 13 January and continued through Aix-la-Chapelle, Maastricht, to Liège, where they arrived on 17 January.[111] The membership of the party had changed: Alexander, Bishop Herman, the abbots Baldwin and Frowin, the clerks Otto and Franco had left them, and in their place were Volkmar, a chaplain to Herman, bishop of Castore; Theodore, abbot of Camp; and Hervin, provost of Steinfeld, though the last two were not at the final redaction, which was made at Liège.[112] The final account was sent to the clergy of Cologne from those of the party who remained at Clairvaux: Gerard, Geoffrey, Philip, and Volkmar. The letter sent with it gives three reasons for sending the account: to remind those who had witnessed the miracles of the wonders of the journey, to stir up zeal for conversion in those who had not been there, and to provide a permanent reminder of those things for the clergy of Cologne.[113] These miracles were seen as signs from God to show his approval for the preaching of the crusade that was the purpose of the visit and to convert men, either as crusaders or as monks at Clairvaux.

Bernard's unswerving belief in his cause overflowed in his preaching, drawing crowds to hear him. In many the impact of the experience led to physical healing. Others, including some of those cured, took the cross; a few joined Bernard and returned with him to the novitiate at Clairvaux. Geoffrey mentions thirty such men, including Archdeacon Philip of Liège, Alexander of Cologne, and Volkmar, chaplain to the bishop of Constance.[114]

These cures, then, can be considered as events, as miracles that took place during the three months of the tour of Germany. Bernard himself took an active and even eager part in the cures. He would make the sign of the cross and pray for a cure in the name of Christ or the Trinity. Several times he was interested in the outcome of events and sent his companions to see if the person concerned were really cured.[115] In his letter to Pope Eugenius III, he refers to his cures in Germany:

But perhaps they say, how shall we know if this word comes from the Lord? What signs have you given that we may believe in you? I do not reply to that, spare my modesty. Reply on my behalf and for yourself also, according to that which you have heard and seen or according as God inspires you to answer.[116]

There was an overwhelming demand from crowds for his powers and a confident expectation of them. Often he was lost in crowds, so that his companions could not observe his miracles.[117] Emotion similar to that at the shrines of the Virgin accompanied these scenes, with shouts of 'Christe uns genade', the ringing of bells, weeping, repentance, and also public jubilation.

The number of cures recorded must have been considerably less than those performed, but the records contain two hundred and thirty-five cures of the crippled, one hundred and seventy-two of the blind, as well as cures of the deaf and dumb, demoniacs, and those afflicted with other illnesses. The people came to the saint, and in their veneration of him, they treated him very much as they would treat the relics of a saint at his tomb. These miracles are close to shrine miracles, both in their kind and in their number. The records, however, are less detailed than those at shrines; 'a boy', 'a woman of the town', 'a man' are usually all the designation given, unless the one cured was already known to the party, as was Anselm of Havelberg,[118] or became one of them, as did Philip of Liège.[119] This vagueness may point to the authenticity of the record. The party was among crowds of unknown people, and the difficulty of making notes under such conditions and with an unknown language would result in just the kind of record produced. The single instance of St Bernard raising a dead person to life is included as the climax of the first book.[120]

The third part of the *Historia* differs from the first two sections. It records miracles performed by Bernard as he returned from Liège to Clairvaux, followed by notes of his miracles on his journey a few days later to the Council of Étampes and back to Clairvaux; some details were also added of a later journey to Frankfurt.[121] The material was collected by Geoffrey of Auxerre, probably after the return from Étampes,[122] and sent by him to the bishop of Constance at his request. The party left Liège on 19 January 1147 and reached Clairvaux on 6 February, going through Gembloux, Cambrai, and Chalons and staying at monasteries on the way. Geoffrey gives a daily account of a few miracles, suggesting that these are only samples; in this method the account at once differs from its predecessors. It seems probable that Geoffrey had the help of the novices Philip and Volkmar when he compiled the account in the scriptorium at Clairvaux; otherwise, he gives no indication of his sources beyond his own observations, nor of the composition of the company. From Clairvaux, Geoffrey accompanied Bernard to Étampes; the miracles recounted on this journey are his own observations. The notes given of miracles on the second journey to Frankfurt are also his own work from his own notes. The miracles are retold at greater length with more detail than in the earlier accounts, and the sense of immediate recording is lost.

It seems from this third letter that miracles continued to accompany Bernard wherever he went, and not only during his preaching of the crusade. Geoffrey does not mention such preaching at all, but shows Bernard as a recognized healer, welcomed as such in every place where he came and ready to cure, especially within the context of the eucharist;[123] his reception at Trier, Frankfurt, and Toul is similar, though he was not at these places specifically preaching the crusade. This public miracle-working probably was not confined to three months of Bernard's life. When he visited Milan in 1135 after the Council of Pisa, he was received as a miracle worker, besieged by crowds of the sick. Ernold of Bonnevaux, author of the second book of the *Vita Prima*, a record of Bernard's public life, says that Bernard cured many there, and gives accounts of three exorcisms he performed in the church.[124] Ernold relates these miracles to the papal cause, in support of which Bernard had visited the dissident Milanese; the miracles were signs that God was with both Bernard and the papal cause.

It seems that there were in effect two biographies of Bernard: a monastic *Life,* very similar to the *Lives* of other contemporary saints, in which miracles either linked Bernard with other instances of holiness or illustrated his virtues; and a *Life* of Bernard as a miracle-worker on the public stage, performing miracles that have more in common with shrine miracles than with miracles in saints' *Lives.* This corresponds to a dichotomy that Bernard himself saw in his character:

I am a sort of modern chimera, neither clerk nor lay-man. I have kept the habit of a monk, but I have long ago abandoned the life. I do not wish to tell you what I dare say you have heard from others: what I am doing, what are my purposes, through what dangers I pass in the world, or rather down what precipices I am hurled.[125]

The *Lives* of the saints contain accounts of miracles that differ from miracles recorded in connection with the saints' relics. The chief interest in such *Lives,* however, was not in miracles but in virtue, though miracles, as signs of God's approval of the saint, remained important. By 1215 the combination of miracles and virtues in the *Life* of a saint achieved a more formal structure in the briefs prepared for the official process of papal canonization. It had become customary, and finally obligatory, to obtain the approval of the pope before a saint could be publicly revered. Detailed information as well as reputable witnesses were required in Rome, and such information was subject to assessors appointed by the pope. In the two hundred years we have been considering, about forty candidates were proposed for canonization, four of whom will be examined in some detail to see how miracles were used in this context. First, however, a brief account of the evolution of the process will be necessary.

By the beginning of this period the process of canonization had evolved from the spontaneous veneration of Christians as saints by their local community[126] to the official recognition of them by the local bishop and his synod.[127] The term *canonizare* in the sense of official recognition of a saint began only in the eleventh century;[128] it meant

that the person concerned was enrolled in the calendar of the local
church and his commemoration was thereby sanctioned. The acknowledgement of the saint was often accompanied by the translation of his
relics to a shrine or place of honour in a church. Before the eleventh
century this matter was largely in the hands of diocesan bishops,
though there were instances in which appeal was made to the pope.[129]
From the eleventh century onward it became the custom to ask for
papal recognition of a saint; this custom evolved into appealing for
permission to proceed with the matter. Requests came from local
bishops and were often supported by the ruler of the country concerned. While the pope's permission increased the dignity and authority of the saint and ensured him a wide recognition through the calendar of the universal church, it was primarily a recognition of papal
jurisdiction in this as in other spheres.[130] By 1200 papal recognition of
saints had become the rule, and the requirements for canonization were
therefore formulated.

Miracles were required by the papal courts for canonization; miracles
were usual at translations when the canonization was proclaimed; miracles thereafter formed a part of the *Vita et Miracula* of the saint in
liturgical and para-liturgical reading. The process of reservation to the
papacy had given canonization a precise form; the stages of *petitio, informatio,* and *publicatio* can be distinguished in the first papal canonization, that of Ulric of Augsburg by John xv in 993.[131] It was the second
stage, *informatio,* that dealt with the miracles, and in this period
changes are noticeable in the information sought about them, changes
that correspond to the kinds of miracles already noticed in the *Lives* of
the saints.

The first requirement in canonization was in accord with the assessment of sanctity expressed by Gregory the Great. Miracles should be
edifying to the faithful and linked to the virtues of the person proposed. The second requirement had a new note of efficiency. A close
investigation should be made to see if the miracles were true. The first
requirement, that the lives of the saints should be edifying, corresponds to how the *Lives* of the saints used miracles to link the new
saints with the traditions of hagiography. It is notable that the process
of canonization, as did the twelfth-century *Lives* of saints, continued to
emphasize merits and virtues rather than the effect that wonders might
have on others. Virtues had to be linked with miracles, and miracles, to

be acceptable, had to be shown to be of God—the theme established most of all by Gregory the Great and illustrated in the *Lives* of the saints already examined. In a letter to Hubert Walter, Innocent III states this with particular clarity with regard to the canonization of Gilbert of Sempringham:

To be accepted for a saint among men in the church militant, two things are essential: holiness of life and mighty signs, that is, merits and miracles, so that each may reciprocally bear witness to the other. Separately, merits without miracles or miracles without merits are not fully sufficient to establish saint-hood here on earth.

After a reference to Satan transforming himself into an angel of light and to the 'miracles' worked by the magicians of Pharaoh, he continues:

But when sound merits come first and are followed by notable miracles, they afford a sure proof of sainthood—to inspire in us a veneration for the man whom God by preceding merits and following miracles presents as worthy of veneration.[132]

The miracles demanded were those related to a life of virtue; miracles alone were not sufficient. In a letter to the king of Sweden (later incor-porated into the Decretals of Gregory IX), Alexander III mentions with horror that he has heard the Swedes were venerating a man killed in a drunken brawl; he condemns miracles alleged to come from such a source: 'Even if there were many signs and miracles through him, we cannot permit him to be venerated publicly as a saint without the authority of the church of Rome'.[133] The spontaneous veneration of men as saints, especially after violent death, had produced many cults similar to this, as has been seen. The authority of the Roman see is here said to be necessary for public veneration, a claim established only recently, but already acknowledged. The cult of St William of Nor-wich was limited while he had no official recognition, and a vision relating to Becket shows that he was not accorded full public honour as a saint until he was formally canonized.[134] This insistence on papal recognition of a saint was in part due to the unedifying nature of these small cults with their miracles; the insistence on miracles linked with virtues was a check to credulous popular mistakes.

186

The second requirement urged by papal canonization was concerned with the authenticity of the information offered. Early requests had often been heard in councils[135] and acceded to at once. This meant that there was little opportunity for information to be examined, and the ability to edify was mainly what was required from the *informatio*. Thus, *Lives,* especially of those whose lives were in fact unknown through antiquity, tended to be constructed according to previous models, whether of martyr, confessor, bishop, or monk. But in this period—partly because the number of requests multiplied so that they could not be dealt with during a council but had to be submitted to a committee, with more chance of detailed examination of the material, and partly because interest in the actual details of the saints' lives, especially those of contemporaries, increased—more was demanded in the way of witnesses and evidence. Written accounts had to contain details of miracles and the circumstances in which they took place: name of the person concerned, where he lived, his illness, names of witnesses, when and how he came to the saint, his cure, and names of more witnesses. These requirements were concerned with the post-humous miracles at shrines in the main, the second part of the *Vita*. However, miracles claimed during the life of the saint also needed authentication. Witnesses were required to go to Rome and state the facts in person, or assessors might be sent to examine the witnesses and report on their reliability. The authority of *viri auctorabiles* had always been claimed in asserting miracles. The people whose word could be respected were still those called on in this matter; but also those who said they had actually experienced or witnessed miracles were called upon to give evidence.

These two themes of edification and authenticity in canonization can be seen in the requests for canonization for certain saints already discussed. Four canonizations are of particular interest in this respect: those of Anselm, Bernard, Becket, and Hugh of Lincoln. The first three were proposed for canonization during the pontificate of Alexander III (1159–1181), a period when the process of canonization became clearer and more regulated, the last during the pontificate of Honorius III, when it was in regular use.

Early in 1163, Alexander III was asked to canonize Anselm of Canterbury at the forthcoming Council of Tours. The request for Anselm to be considered came from archbishop Thomas Becket. The year after his election as archbishop, Thomas presented to the pope an account of the life and miracles of Anselm by John of Salisbury, consisting of a summary of Eadmer's work, with the emphasis on miracles. The *Vita* established the virtue of Anselm beyond doubt; and John of Salisbury rearranged the miracles into the traditional pattern of miracles before and after burial; to the posthumous miracles of Eadmer, he adds only one:

Elphege who was widely known, had been born blind, deaf, dumb and lame. And this was well known. Here, just as at the present day, he testified that he received complete cures of all his ills at the tomb of blessed Anselm.[136]

The pope replied, remitting the matter to a council to be called by the archbishop at Canterbury.[137] It seems probable that this council met and that the initial report for the formal canonization procedure was drawn up; the calendar for Christ Church, Canterbury in the mid-twelfth century lists 7 April as the feast of the translation of St Anselm, as well as 21 April as his feast day.[138] The matter lapsed, however, during the archbishop's exile, and the popularity of Anselm in Canterbury was eclipsed by the martyrdom of Becket himself. The papal canonization of Anselm was not officially reported until his name was included in the Roman martyrology of 1568.[139] The twelfth-century procedure, as far as it went, shows the place of miracles at that time. A formal request was made by the archbishop; the documents he sent attested the virtues and the miracles; the pope asked for assessment to be made in England, presumably by the interrogation of witnesses, as in other cases. Eadmer's *Vita Anselmi* established virtue, and for this there need be no more witnesses; it was the miracles that were to be examined and established.

The second canonization demanded by the English of Alexander IIII was the canonization of Becket. As soon as the news of the archbishop's death spread, stories of miracles began, and Thomas was acclaimed a martyr by popular consent. In 1171 John of Salisbury wrote to his friend the bishop of Poitiers, giving an account of the martyrdom; he says that the pope would already have been asked to proclaim him martyr, but that no one was allowed to take ship for Rome without the king's consent.[140] There was a firm belief in England and France that Thomas was a saint; there was equally a conviction that he should not be publicly venerated as such without papal permission. In the vision already mentioned, the monk who refused to sing an antiphon in honour of Becket says, 'it was not correct to do so, for he had not yet been inscribed officially in the list of martyrs'.[141] The pope appointed two legates, Albert and Theodwin, to examine the case of Thomas Becket, and on 10 March 1173, he wrote to them to say that he had received their report and enrolled Thomas as a saint. Two days later he sent the bull *Gaudendum est* to the Chapter at Canterbury and the bull *Redolet Anglia* to the clergy and people of England: the latter describes the examination of the miracles by the legates.[142] At this time, the accounts of miracles collected by Benedict and William were the main evidence presented for the canonization; the various *Lives* of St Thomas came after the canonization, not before.[143] It was, therefore, the miracles that the legates examined, and it was for them and for the martyrdom that Thomas was canonized; the evidence of a life of outstanding virtue was not in this case required or available.

The canonization of Bernard of Clairvaux was also proposed to Alexander III before the Council of Tours, in 1163; the *Vita Prima Bernardi* in its first recension was presented and possibly also Bernard's own writings. The initiative for canonization came, as was usual, from those who possessed the body of the saint, in this case the abbot of Clairvaux, who by this time was Geoffrey of Auxerre, the compiler of the *Vita*. No list survives of the applicants, though it is probable that the Cistercian abbots and Cistercian bishops, such as Peter of Tarantaise[144] and Henry of Rheims,[145] and the cardinal Henry Moricotti,[146] were among them. With such a weight of authority behind the request and an extensive *Vita* to be considered, it might have seemed certain that the canonization would go forward at once. However, the pope rejected the petition for the moment. Geoffrey of Auxerre, who had been present at the Council, at once began to revise the *Vita Prima*, omitting some of the stories most clearly taken from the stock of hagiography,[147] softening any slighting references to the great,[148] omitting certain prophecies, revising the style, and adroitly avoiding giving exact references to events that were doubtful.[149] For a while, it seemed that this *Life* would be replaced by a *Vita Secunda* composed by Alan of Auxerre,[150] but with the appointment of Gerard as abbot of Clairvaux, Geoffrey again prepared to present a request for canonization with his own revision of the *Vita Prima*. This time the advocates were the abbot of Clairvaux and Fromund, the bishop of Veroli, formerly a Cistercian. A letter from Tromund of Chiaravalle[151] to Gerard of Clairvaux tells of the progress of the cause and its final success, with a celebration of the first mass in honour of St Bernard by the pope himself.[152] It is noteworthy that in the letters by which the canonization was announced, there is mention only of the merits and virtues of Bernard, his austere life, his teaching, and his example rather than of posthumous miracles. In this case, the pope accepted the evidence offered of a life of outstanding virtue with the miracles that happened while Bernard was alive, without posthumous evidence of more than visions. The great number of cures in the *Historia Miraculorum* may have taken the place of accounts of posthumous cures, as the required 'signs' of the approval of God.

Hugh of Lincoln was canonized by Honorius III twenty years after his death in 1200. He had been respected as a saintly man in his lifetime and his funeral was an occasion of great splendour, attended by the kings of England and Scotland and the archbishops of Canterbury, Dublin, and Ragusa.[153] Once the case for his canonization had begun, it continued smoothly and is, like the case of Gilbert of Sempringham,[154] a classic instance of the formal process of canonization in action for this period. The case was presented by the whole English hierarchy and the pope at once appointed Stephen Langton and John, abbot of Fountains,[155] as his representatives to inquire into the matter. They met at Lincoln and received a large number of testimonies to miracles from which they selected thirty-six to include in their report. Of these, five were alleged to have happened during Hugh's life, two at his funeral, and twenty-nine at his tomb.[156] By far the largest number of these posthumous cures were cures of madness, the second most numerous being cures of paralysis. The names, lengths of illnesses, cures, and witnesses were carefully attested and sworn. A typical instance is the cure of John Ancaster. The witnesses were named and the cause of the illness explained:

John of Ancaster and his father and certain others said upon oath that this John had been insane for a month . . . he added that this sickness had come upon John because of overwhelming grief when all his goods were destroyed in war.

His cure is then recounted: 'His father took him back to the tomb of the aforesaid bishop and after a few days he came away cured'.[157] A record of such cases had been kept at the tomb, and in many instances the recipients were still available to swear to their cases. The cures alleged during Hugh's lifetime demanded further investigation, and there are letters from Abbot Richard of Walton and a canon of Holy Trinity, London, who had examined witnesses to the cure of Roger Colhoppe on behalf of the commission in Lincoln;[158] from the abbot of Sawtrey and the prior of Huntingdon about the cure of a child who swallowed a piece of iron;[159] and from the chapter at Berwick, who attested to the cure of one Mathilda.[160] The miracles of St Hugh were mostly posthumous and had been recounted by Gerald of Wales;[161] his virtues were well attested by the *Magna Vita* of Adam of Eynsham; and together with the report of the commission, these were considered in Rome. Canon Reimund, archdeacon of Leicester and a kinsman of St Hugh, was present together with Hugh the Chaplain and Theobald. The bull of Honorius III proclaimed the canonization, and in it he makes a statement that summarizes the stage the legal process had reached and accounts for the details discussed here. Alexander III had asked for evidence of both virtues and miracles; Innocent III asked for witnesses to present themselves to swear to such miracles in person; Honorius III, in the case of St Hugh, said that miracles are the deciding point in a case of official canonization.

Virtue, then, was the basic requisite for sanctity, and this was to be established beyond all possible doubt by an account of the life of the saint. Without this account the case could not even begin. The need for the *Life* to be edifying to other Christians was central, and in this the canonization process was in line with the twelfth-century emphasis on the biography of saints. But what made it certain that a person could be proclaimed a saint was the evidence of God's approval of him in miracles. The canonization process insisted more and more on evidence and witnesses for these miracles, with full details. These miracles had to be both edifying and authenticated, and this double pressure had the result of producing fairly stereotyped lists of miracles, almost all of which were cures. Cures could be attested; they were also counted as more edifying than accounts of acts of vengeance by the saints. This precision about the place of miracles and the kind of miracles in the life and after the death of a saint marks a new stage in the use of miracles for the official recognition of sanctity.

10
Monastic Miracles

THE MIRACLE COLLECTIONS and saints' *Lives* discussed so far have been 'monastic' in the sense that they were written by monks and clerics, but other kinds of miracle collections also can be called 'monastic'. These are collections that related specifically to monastic ideals and observances. Such collections interested a limited audience. They were not new in the twelfth century. Two of the books suggested in the *Rule of St Benedict* for community reading, the *Conferences* and *Institutes* of Cassian, as well as the *Lives of the Desert Fathers*,[1] contain accounts of miracles of monasticism. The *Dialogues* of Gregory and, in particular, his account of St Benedict, became the miracle book of the Black Monks. Its influence on later monastic collections has already been seen. Monastic miracles were known, too, at Cluny, where they were told in the *Lives* of the abbots. Monasteries would tell miraculous stories about their foundation and about some of their saintly members. In the twelfth century there were collections of miracles about contemporary monastic life. These modern miracle books are found mostly among the Cistercians, but one major collection came from the abbey of Cluny—the *De Miraculis* of the abbot, Peter the Venerable.

The complete text of the *De Miraculis* consists of sixty miracle stories collected by Peter the Venerable over several years and put together in various versions.[2] A nucleus of nine miracles can be discerned,[3] to which the rest were added, including the miracles connected with Matthew of Albano, which form the basis of the second book.[4] Later the *De Miraculis* became one of the most popular sources for *exempla*, and for this reason similar stories were added to the work of Peter the Venerable under his name, notably seven accounts of visions.[5]

The *De Miraculis* was monastic propaganda on several levels. It was, first of all, like Gregory's *Dialogues,* a collection of stories for the encouragement of the monks themselves. It was put together for circulation after the schism of Pons,[6] to which two stories refer,[7] when Peter the Venerable was convalescent after an illness.[8] The abbot's first concern was to restore unity and confidence among his own monks. Thus, there are stories of heroic virtue rewarded by God among monastic contemporaries. For instance, the collection includes the story of the monk Gerard, 'a monk of purity and simplicity of life',[9] renowned for his emotional style of devotion and for the visions with which he was rewarded.[10] Peter the Venerable presents a picture of Cluny familiar in Cluniac hagiography, as a camp besieged by demons held at bay by the fidelity of the brethren to their common observances.[11] Palms of victory were ready for the faithful monk at his death,[12] and angels in white came to conduct him to heaven.[13] The observance of charity kept the demons out of the monastery.[14]

Secondly, the miracles were a defence for Cluny against outsiders. The nuns at Marcigny were praised for their insistence on observing their enclosure even in opposition to the order of a bishop, for which they were rewarded by miraculous delivery from fire.[15] Princes who threatened the lands of Cluny were portrayed as being in hell for their sins.[16] Above all, the miracles asserted the continuing value of Cluniac observances in opposition to stirrings of monastic reform in Europe. The connection between St Bernard's *Apologia* and Letter 28 of Peter the Venerable, defending Cluniac observances, has not been established;[17] but there is certainly a connection between Letter 28, written around 1130 after the schism of Pons,[18] and the *De Miraculis.*[19] They assert the same principles of monastic stability: charity, right order, and discretion. In the letter these themes are presented as a defence against criticism, in the *De Miraculis* they are supported by miracles of divine favour. One of the stories seems to be directed against an accusation made by St Bernard himself against Cluny. In 1122 the prior of Cluny, Bernard d'Utelle, visited Clairvaux and was instrumental in removing Robert, Bernard's nephew, from Clairvaux and installing him at Cluny.[20] A letter of St Bernard on the subject, itself the subject of a miracle,[21] presented the protests of the Cistercians against this transference. In the *De Miraculis,* some years later, Peter the Venerable includes a story of a monk of Cluny, John the Italian, who was tempted to leave Cluny by one claiming to be the abbot of a less exacting abbey, who promised him an easier life and honours, as Bernard claimed the Cluniacs had promised Robert.[22] In Peter's story, the integrity of John overcomes the temptation, which is seen to be of the devil, by reliance on stability and the prayers of the brethren: 'I cannot in any way leave here, for the enclosure of the monastery forbids it and the brethren surround me in multitudes'.[23] The message is plain. If a brother is tempted to leave his monastery, whether at Cîteaux or Cluny, the onus is on him to resist this himself and not trust in the influence of his abbot.

Thirdly, the stories in the *De Miraculis* were propaganda for certain policies and doctrinal issues that concerned Peter the Venerable. The miracles he puts first and to which he says he attaches most importance[24] are those concerned with the eucharist, asserting either the change in substance in the elements after consecration or the necessity for purity in a priest.[25] This support of clerical morality was no doubt part of Peter the Venerable's monastic and pastoral conviction; it was also a major part of the reform connected with Gregory VII. The miracle stories about the Cardinal Bishop Matthew of Albano,[26] a firm supporter of the Gregorian cause, form the main part of the second book of the *De Miraculis* and offer further propaganda for that party in the church.[27] Some stories urge the value of private confession of sins;[28] others justify the practice of prayers for the dead, a theme of contemporary interest and also a source of revenue at Cluny.[29]

The miracles told by Peter the Venerable are not selected for their wonder; nor does he try to present a complete record of miracles of any kind. These are didactic tales, set down in detail in the familiar phraseology of St Gregory the Great, 'to build up faith and conduct'.[30] Peter carefully gives the source from which he heard the story, relying on the traditional *vires auctoribiles,* and tells the stories with much edifying detail of name, place, and behaviour. The miracles are not usually cures of illness,[31] but visions of rewards and punishments, and in this sense they belong to the kind of miracle stories used in preaching. They are stories of heroic virtue in individuals, of divine favours toward people connected with Cluny, or known to Peter's acquaintances. They always show the action of God in contemporary life. The tradition of miracles among the Black Monks continued in the *De Miraculis,* while the interest in visions and especially visions of the eucharist and of the dead point to new content in the collection that links it more closely with other collections of the times.

The miracle collection of the Black Monks was soon matched by those of monks of the new orders, and in particular by the Cistercian collections. While the *Lives* of Cistercian saints, such as the *Life of Christian of Aumône,* are packed with miracles, other collections contain miracles relating to aspects of Cistercian life itself. The paradigm collection for the Cistercians was the *Three Books of Miracles* of Herbert of Clairvaux[32] and the *Exordium Magnum Cisterciense,* possibly by Conrad of Eberbach. The *Exordium* is to some extent based on Herbert's work.[33] A later Cistercian collection, that of Caesarius of Heisterbach,[34] belongs partly to this monastic tradition but also to the wider tradition of miracles used as *exempla* in preaching.

Herbert of Clairvaux collected his miracles into three books around 1178, twenty years after the death of St Bernard. The work contains over a hundred miracle stories connected with the early days of the Cistercian order.[35] The sources for these tales go back to the foundation of the Order, with stories of Stephen Harding, Alberic, and St Bernard. Herbert had been a novice at Clairvaux and was later chaplain to Henry, abbot of Clairvaux,[36] where he heard stories from the first generation Cistercians. Like the miracles recorded by Peter the Venerable, these stories are not new; they belong to a monastic tradition of miracles, but were related to the particular interests of the Cistercians. Name, place, and event are given for each story, setting it in a Cistercian context, with details about content and source. As with Peter the Venerable's collection, these stories are primarily about miraculous dreams and visions, very different from the terse stories connected with shrines. Like the miracles of Peter the Venerable, they are propaganda for an Order, the inward-looking miracles of a specific group, giving warning and encouragement to the monks about various aspects of their 'new' way of life.

The collection contains miracles of recruitment. It was held that God had made known his will to many Cistercians by direct revelations in which they were told to become Cistercians or from which they inferred that this was the case. Alexander of Cologne, for instance, claimed that he was converted from a life of learning as a canon to Cîteaux not only by the words of St Bernard and the dreams he had had, but also by eating a piece of fish over which St Bernard had prayed that he would become a Cistercian.[37] Another story of this kind was told by several writers and held a special place in the Cistercian world—the story of the reapers of Clairvaux. Renaldus, one of the first generation of monks at Clairvaux, saw three women whom he identified as Mary, Mary Magdalene, and Elizabeth walking among the brethren who were getting in the harvest at the abbey and wiping the sweat from their foreheads. This story of the involvement of saints or angels in monastic work has a long history; here it is used to show God's approval for manual labour[38] and the Virgin Mary's special interest in Clairvaux.[39] But this story was primarily a story of conversion: Renaldus was confirmed in his Cistercian vocation by it.[40] Herbert of Clairvaux and Conrad of Eberbach both included the story in their books of miracles.[41] Caesarius of Heisterbach[42] was told the story by Gerard, abbot of Heisterbach, on a journey from Walberg to Cologne before he became a monk. He placed it in the first section of his account of miracles of conversions for the benefit of others and claimed that it had caused him to become a Cistercian himself. Miracles of conversion were of special interest to the Cistercians and to later preachers when they showed the value of turning from academic to monastic life. These collections take from the *Vita Prima* a story of how St Bernard converted the students of Paris not by words but by tears.[43] A particular instance of this kind of story is that of Master Serlo who became a monk at La Charité-sur-Loire in the mid-twelfth century.[44] He claimed that he had abandoned his academic life in Paris as a result of a vision of a pupil who appeared to him wearing a cloak covered with phrases learned in the schools: 'It was written over with sophistries and those idle investigations with which I used to waste my time'.[45] The pupil added that he was burning with heat from the weight of the cloak and allowed a drop of his sweat to burn Serlo's hand; Serlo afterwards showed this burn as proof of his experience.[46] Many elements in the story are to be found in earlier monastic stories.[47] This story was very popular later with preachers, offering an illustration of the dangers of scholastic learning, but it is found first as an instance of the conversion of a Cistercian.

Not only did stories show how God directed men toward the Order; miracle stories also confirmed the practices of the monks, especially in controversial areas. Their observance of prayer at night was commended by signs of divine approval. The liturgy of the monks was seen to involve angels, who stood by the Cistercians singing the *Te Deum*.[48] Demons waited for the monk who sang his Office without attention.[49] The simplicity of the Office, the fervour of the monks in choir, and their attention to what they were singing all receive the accolade of visions from heaven. So also does the liturgy itself. Knowledge of the mass was held in high esteem, even among the lay brothers, and there are stories of lay brothers who were taught the mass of the Holy Spirit when asleep,[50] and of the lay brother, 'an uneducated man, which had never learned either to sing or read',[51] who learned the chant of *Alleluia* in a vision and sang it on his death-bed. While the theme of rejection of secular learning persisted, as in the dream of the lay brother Christian of Aumône, who saw demons chanting *'sic et non'* in a parody of a scholastic debate,[52] the Cistercian approach to the value of other kinds of learning is illustrated in these visions, which are at variance with the older monastic traditions of the Desert Fathers to which the Cistercians so often referred.[53]

Miracles of divine encouragement also accompanied the monks in their much-criticized practice of silence.[54] Their poverty was said to be blessed by God with miraculous rewards.[55] Their fasting was seen to receive supernatural aid. A novice who dosed himself privately with medicine to help manage the austerities of the diet one day saw the Virgin Mary standing at the entrance to choir, giving all except him medicine of her own.[56] Manual work, especially that of the lay brothers, was aided by the saints; in one case, a brother saw Jesus Christ helping him goad the cows home to Clairvaux.[57]

The private prayer of the monks was seen to be rewarded with extravagant visions, often of the kisses and embraces of Christ or the Virgin Mary.[58] Personal confession was also presented in visions as essential to the Cistercian way of life.[59] But the greatest space in these collections is given to the death of the saints. The death of the Cistercians was seen as the moment of their entry into heaven, and in many revelations they are seen among the elect, not subject to purgatorial fire.[60] Those who left the Order were called apostates; the faithful Cistercians received crowns of glory and were taken to heaven by angels, where they were sheltered under the cloak of the Virgin.[61] The determined emphasis in these stories on the abundance of heavenly rewards, which balanced the austerities of Cistercian observances, is propaganda directed toward the Cistercians themselves. The incidence of suicide, madness, and apostasy was high among the Cistercians, and even in these two miracle collections there are instances of negative response to stress beyond endurance. Ministering to this psychological state seems to have included the use of miracle stories to show the rewards in heaven, the help of God on earth, or the terrors in store for failures. This kind of shock treatment was apparently applied by St Bernard himself[62] and by the first novice master at Clairvaux, Achard,[63] in the first days of the Order.

The compiler of the *Exordium Magnum Cisterciense* (1186–1193) borrowed a great deal of material from Herbert's less sophisticated collection. He is first of all concerned with the increase of what he called *negligentia,* a vice he saw creeping into later generations of his Order.[64] This concern with slackness was familiar in other contexts, notably in the treatises of Peter Damian;[65] here, it is applied to the Cistercians, who are urged by the example of the miracles granted to their predecessors to imitate them in fervour and discipline.

There was, however, another use for Cistercian miracle propaganda, and the writer of the *Exordium* was concerned with more than encouraging the Cistercians. He was thinking of another audience— the Black Monks, now critics of the Cistercians: 'For the black monks of the order do not cease to criticize the monks of our order'.[66] His book is a reply to Black Monk polemic. He includes the early documents of the Order to show that the Cistercians had from the first 'the approval of men', that is, of the ecclesiastical authorities;[67] he then produces the Cistercian miracles as proof of 'the approval of God'. He hopes thus to provide a 'two-branched candlestick' to shed light on the darkness of those who accuse the Order.[68]

A distinctive mark of the twelfth-century Cistercian miracle collections is that they are miracles not of the holy individual but of the holy Order. It is not the great feat of individual asceticism that is rewarded by God, but the keeping of corporate rules within the Order's daily life. The Cistercians had their holy men, particularly their holy abbots, but even such men as Stephen Harding and Alberic are seen only within the context of the Order.[69] The miracles of the Order are seen within an even more specialized context. The author of the *Exordium Magnum* recounts the emergence of the Cistercians as the proper end of the monastic tradition, which he says began with Christ himself, St John the Baptist, the apostles, and the early monks—Antony,

Pachomius, and Basil.[70] He then selects incidents from the lives of Western monks, for instance Benedict, Odo, Odilo, and Hugh of Cluny,[71] showing that they were 'true' monks and that they observed customs for which the Cistercians are now being criticized by their successors. The later miracles are taken from the *Life of St Bernard* and the records of the early monks at Clairvaux and Cîteaux, especially the lives of the lay brothers. The effect is to present the Cistercians as the monks who follow the most ancient customs of the church, not innovators, but preservers of what had been obscured, secure in the authority of history.[72] With this perspective, the Cistercians could see themselves as approved by God; they saw such approval expressed by miracles and visions. And so their miracle collections became an extensive apologia for their way of life, with the whole fabric of their observance set forth in terms of the miraculous.

While the main collections of miracles connected with monastic life came from the Cistercian Order or from Cluny, there were miracles connected with the lives of other religious founders such as St Gilbert of Sempringham, St Romuald among the Camaldoli, and St Stephen among the Grandmontines.[73] But these showed the holiness of individuals rather than of an Order, and do not form distinctive miracle collections.

Some miracle stories were told to express the approval of God for the new orders. Peter the Venerable, for instance, praised the Carthusian Order and supported this praise by an account of a miracle among the brothers, adding: 'I have been told by many of the number of miracles which have taken place in that holy order'.[74] A certain young lay brother of exemplary life and devoted to the Virgin Mary, one night had a vision in which demons in the form of pigs burst into his cell, followed by a demon like a giant who threatened to carry the monk off; at his prayers, the Virgin appeared, dispersed the demons, and consoled the brother, praising his way of life as well as his devotion to her.[75] Caesarius of Heisterbach told several miracle stories about members of the Premonstratensian Order, not in defence of their observances but as edifying miracles related to certain subjects such as confession or the eucharist.[76] Miracle stories were also told about hermits, such as Wulfric of Haselbury, Godric of Finchale, and Symeon of Trier.[77] In these stories they appear as men of God, renowned for the individual feat of asceticism or prayer, and endowed with miraculous

199

powers of foresight. These stories praise certain individuals rather than defending a way of life. It is of interest to note that the miracles of these heroic individuals were recorded by members of established communities; in the case of Wulfric, by a Cistercian of Ford,[78] for Godric, by a monk of Durham,[79] and for Symeon (an Eastern hermit who settled at Trier and died there), by a monk of the community that protected him during his life.[80]

Sometimes miracle stories are used within the established Benedictine framework for strictly polemical purposes. The *Chronicle* of Jocelyn of Brakelond[81] provides two instances of this use of miracles. In the first case, Jocelyn describes a fire that broke out at the shrine of St Edmund in 1198. He begins his account with the impressive remark that 'the glorious martyr St Edmund desired to terrify our convent and to teach it that his body should be guarded with greater reverence and care'.[82] He then explains that the fire was caused by the carelessness of the custodians and extinguished by the efforts of the monks. The negligence was hushed up, though the damage led to extensive repairs and rebuilding in the name of St Edmund for the honour due to him. Jocelyn, and, according to him, Abbot Samson, saw this mundane event, whose immediate causes were no mystery, as a miraculous sign from God. Jocelyn thought it a sign that St Edmund should be better honoured, while Abbot Samson thought it a judgement on the slackness of the monks.[83] Thus, in this account it is possible to see several layers of interpretation for an event called a miracle. The immediate causes of the disaster were well known, but disregarded; the question asked about it was 'why'; and it was answered from two points of view according to the interests of two parties.

In the second instance, the two interpretations clashed more forcibly. The abbot was told that a certain man had dreamed of St Edmund lying hungry and naked outside the church, claiming that his shrine was not well guarded.[84] This neutral event was seized by the abbot, who interpreted it as a warning from God against the lack of charity among the monks. In a spirited rejoinder, however, the monks said they considered the vision to mean that they, 'the naked limbs of St Edmund', were being unjustly despoiled by their abbot. Thus, rival factions called events miracles and interpreted them to support their own views and conduct; as soon as the events were known as miracles, they were open to use as propaganda for opposing parties.

11
Miracles and Events

THE FOREGOING DISCUSSION of monastic miracles indicates the extent to which interpretation could affect the record of events. But what was the connection between record and event? This question, impossible to answer and largely irrelevant as regards miracles in the Middle Ages, is nevertheless worth exploring in this attempt to understand the complexities of accounts of medieval miracles. In shrine collections the relationship was by no means simple; in the *Lives* of the saints tradition and the process of canonization came into play; while in monastic records propaganda predominated. How flexible were such records? To what extent and in what manner was it possible to alter material?

Miracle stories are found in historical writings, which are not primary sources for miracles, but at a second remove draw upon all the sources so far discussed. They include miracles as part of historical events and as exotic and inexplicable wonders. The first use of miracles, as part of events, was didactic. These stories were told to assert divine approval, usually for ecclesiastical or secular politics: St Aldhelm was said to have returned a sword to Athelstan in battle so that he was able to defeat his enemies;[1] grants made to the shrine of St Cuthbert by William the Conqueror were said to be the direct result of the panic miraculously caused in him when he visited Durham;[2] the victory of Henry II over Malcolm of Scotland was seen as the result of the miraculous intervention of St Thomas after the king's penance at his tomb.[3]

But this detection of the hand of God in political events was set within a wider view of history itself as propaganda, in which the rise and fall of nations were signs from God to men. Medieval historians looked to classical historical writing, the sequence of sacred history, and the work of God in contemporary affairs for examples to benefit the reader. They followed the historians of Greece and Rome in seeing history as a quarry for examples, historical writing as an art that formed a branch of rhetoric.[4] Robert of Torigny justified his chronicle as 'recorded for the imitation of those that follow after', and he adds, 'historical writers and moralists pursue the same plan, they praise virtue, they censure vice, and so they admonish us to love and fear God'.[5] Orderic Vitalis concurred with these sentiments:

I will give a true account of the different events, both prosperous and adverse, which have happened in the course of thirty years, and will record them simply, for the benefit of future generations. For I believe there will be some men after me like myself, who will eagerly peruse the events and transitory acts of this generation in the pages of the chroniclers, so that they may unfold the past fortunes of the changing world for the edification or delight of their contemporaries.[6]

William of Malmesbury interpreted an escape of the Empress Mathilda as a 'miracle' not because of any supernatural intervention, but because it seemed to him an edifying instance of the justice of God manifest in affairs.[7]

With this conviction that historical events were to be recorded for the instruction of future generations went the understanding of history as a continuation of the history of salvation recorded in the Bible. Historians were apt to preface their accounts of contemporary events with a summary of events in the Old and New Testaments, and in the early Church. Orderic Vitalis, for instance, summarized events from the birth of Christ to the coming of the Holy Ghost in the first book of his *Ecclesiastical History* and in the second book summarized what he knew of the early Church.[8] He was eager to advise his readers to look for edifying historical instances in the Bible, as the prototype of historical writing: 'Meditate on the books of the Old and New Testaments, and from them heap up examples to teach you what to shun and what to pursue'.[9] Robert of Torigny refers in his chronicle to the histories of Jerome, Eusebius, and Prosper,[10] before coming to his own times. Ralph of Diceto began his historical account with stories from first-century Rome.[11] Writers of monastic annals, such as those of Dunstable[12] and Waverley,[13] began their accounts with the year one. In these records contemporary writers discovered an abundance of miracles and wonders. Orderic Vitalis made a separate summary in his history of the miracles of Christ and added to them the miracles of former saints such as Evroul, Judoc, and William.[14] Ralph of Diceto included in his account the dream of Constantine, the miracles surrounding the invention of the Cross, and the miracle of the Seven Sleepers of Ephesus.[15] Miracles were received from the past as part of the record of history.

Those who recorded contemporary events had inherited a tradition in which miracles were a natural part of historical records. Miracles were of particular value to them for rhetorical purposes. But the historian rarely found first-hand evidence for miracles in his own times. Some writers recorded contemporary miracles from sources known to them without apparent difficulty: William of Malmesbury, for instance, filled the *Gesta Pontificum* with miracle stories that he continued up to his own day. Henry of Huntingdon scoured England to obtain reliable records of the miracles of the English saints, both past and present.

The crusade historians were particularly alert for miracles and saw a crusade as a major miracle of the times in itself. One event especially was recorded in accounts of the first crusade, and it is a useful example of the connection between miracles and their records in historical writings. When the Christian armies were besieged at Antioch, at a moment of acute discouragement, a lance said to be the lance that had pierced the side of Christ on the Cross was produced to restore morale. Together with visions of the military saints Demetrius, George, and Mercury,[16] the lance conveyed the message that God's miraculous power was with the Christians. The message was eminently successful, and this side of the story has survived in the chronicles of the crusade.[17] A more prosaic side to the matter, however, was recognized even at the time.[18] Power politics among the crusaders surrounded the finding of the lance; it was a pawn in the struggle for leadership between the Count of St Gilles and Bohemund. A visionary, Peter Bartholomew, dreamed that he had found the Holy Lance in Antioch and told his vision, among other tales, to the chaplain of the Count of St Gilles, Raymond d'Aguilers. The Count seized the opportunity and took Peter Bartholomew into his care, under the personal protection of his chaplain.[19] The Count then planned excavations to 'find' the lance and appears to have controlled them with such finesse as to leave little doubt that he had also caused the lance that was eventually found to be placed in position.[20] The Count advertised himself owner of the Holy Lance; his ownership was rejected, along with his authority, by peers.[21] The consensus of the leaders at Antioch was at first against the lance. Ralph of Caen saw the lance as the chief cause of division between the two leaders. (It was, perhaps, more a symptom of their conflicting ambitions.) Bishop Arnulf [22] was said to have rejected it because he doubted the reliability of Peter Bartholomew and suspected him of being in collusion with the Count; and he thought it highly improbable that the Holy Lance could be in Antioch.[23] The Bishop of Puy had a more personal reason for rejecting the relic: Peter Bartholomew's vision of it had also included a condemnation of the sins of the Bishop by St Andrew.[24] That the lance was already acclaimed as a relic elsewhere may also have been known to those present.[25] But despite all these objections to the use of the Lance, the enthusiasm of the army was in its favour; it was produced as a banner and was a deciding factor in the subsequent victory:

And so that man found the Lance, as he had foretold, and they all took it up with great joy and dread, and throughout all the city there was boundless rejoicing. From that hour we decided on a plan of attack.[26]

The attack resulted in the defeat of Karbuqa and the relief of Antioch. A curious irony is that the credit for producing the lance went, together with power in Antioch, to the opponent of the Count, Bohemund. Thus, a prosaic event was both known and recorded in detail, while at the same time a miraculous view of it was given, which survived as the dominant interpretation.

Such contemporary events were called miracles by some writers, but at least one historian found no great wonders to record of his own times: 'If new wonders were openly wrought in these days, I would endeavour to give a faithful report of them in my annals . . . but in these wicked times the splendid miracles of the saints naturally cease'.[27] Orderic Vitalis does in fact record contemporary miracles; his lament is connected with a recurrent problem of theology rather than with a falling off in actual miraculous happenings. It is a question of how events are to be perceived and interpreted after the death and resurrection of Christ. Are miracles to be regarded as a prolongation of New Testament signs and wonders in a redeemed world, as in the days of the first Adam? Or are they signs of divine encouragement in especially dark days of unbelief, appropriate to unbelievers, as a promise of the 'city which has foundations, whose builder and maker is God' (Hebrews 11:10)? This is a perennial question, found in Gregory the Great's *Dialogues* and unresolved in Newman's essay on miracles twelve centuries later.

Chronicles written toward the end of the twelfth century contain fewer miracles than earlier ones, but this may be due to an increasing classification of material, so that miracles were dealt with in other records, particularly in the *Lives* of the saints and the shrine collections. Thus, the annals of Worcester do not include an account of the miracles of St Wulfstan; they refer to his death and his translation and give an example of his miracles, but the full record of the miracles of the saint is in the *Vita Wulfstani*.[28] Similarly, William of Newburgh mentions his visit to St Godric of Finchale whom he saw in extreme old age, but he does not recount his miracles, presumably because they were to be found in the works of Reginald of Durham.[29] The miracles of St Anselm were given a place in the *Vita Anselmi* rather than in the account of his public life in the *Historia Novorum in Anglia*.

Miracles stories in histories were, then, primarily meant to be edifying. But they were also included because of the strangeness and unusual nature of these narratives, which might attract the reader. In ecclesiastical histories the proper illustrative material was the miracles of the saints; in secular histories there was a wider field. The contrast between stories in ecclesiastical and secular histories can be seen particularly clearly in the works of William of Malmesbury. In the *Gesta Pontificum* William includes miracles of the saints, whether in the lengthy account of the miracles of St Aldhelm, the patron of his own house of Malmesbury, or in brief stories such as that of St Werberga of Chester and her geese.[30] But when he wrote his secular history, the *Gesta Regum,* he illustrated it with a wide range of *mira* and *prodigia* rather than with miracles of the saints. What stand out in his secular history are anecdotes of rulers, instances of the valour or perfidy of kings. He inserts material that can be called miraculous in the form of dramatic visions, like that of the hell of the Carolingians[31] or the other-worldly journey of Maurilius of Fécamp.[32] Sometimes the wonders are associated with great men, as in the description of miracles connected with the English royal house that leads up to the miracles of Edward the Confessor and provides a watershed between the account of England under the Anglo-Saxons and England under the Normans.[33] Some-

times there are *mira* associated with a famous place, as in the account of
the wonders of Rome, or with a famous but mysterious person, as in the
account of wonderful magical powers possessed by Pope Sylvester II.[34]

The *mira* used by William of Malmesbury in the *Gesta Regum* and by
other historians cover a wide range of events. They record 'counter-
miracles', that is, wonders attributed to demons—*prestigia inferna* as
opposed to *miracula superna*.[35] They mention miracles performed by
heretics, like the heretics of the Périgord,[36] or by impostors claiming
to be saints, such as St Nicholas and St Andrew;[37] or they mention
wonders such as those ascribed to Eon d'Étoile.[38] Other wonders were
attributed to fairies, like the provision of a fairy banquet for a man
walking the moors at night.[39] A greater number were connected
neither with the world of demons nor of fairies, but with the afterlife.
The chronicles contain two kinds of stories concerning the world beyond death: visions of heaven and hell, the most famous being Orderic's account of the Hunt of Herloquin;[40] and stories of ghosts. These
occupy the attention of William of Newburgh in particular, and his
history contains five stories of ghosts haunting the countryside, tales he
says are unparalleled in his own reading of ancient authors.[41] Similar
stories had a great attraction for Walter Map; had he been writing a
history instead of a book for entertainment, he would certainly have
included many of the prodigies that occupy a large place in his *Nugae
Curialium*.[42] Walter Map makes a clear distinction between miracles of
the saints, of which he was often sceptical, and prodigies of the natural
world, for which he had an avid curiosity.

Brief stories of curious contemporary events, *prodigia et mira*, supply
for writers of secular histories the interest found by writers of ecclesiastical histories in miracles alone. Common to both kinds of historical
writing, however, are the *mira* of signs and omens in the natural world.
Wonders observed in the heavens were recorded with great interest:
comets, eclipses, unusual cloud formations, strange lights, different
colours, as well as storms and lightning. Comets in particular assumed
a political significance, as in the case of Halley's comet that appeared in
1066.[43] Wonders and prodigies on earth also supplied the chronicler
with material. Unnatural births are recounted by Gerald of Wales in
his account of Ireland just before he turns to the miracles of the Irish
saints.[44] William of Newburgh recorded the arrival of two mysterious
green children in a village in East Anglia, and gave an account of
phenomena such as a toad found alive in a rock.[45]

These wonders provided a large proportion of material in chronicles. They were carefully observed and described. The question was then posed as to what they signified. A specific answer was not always given; for instance, the entry 'cometa apparuit' occurs in chronicles frequently with a date, but no further significance is attached to it.[46] When John of Worcester described the details of an unusual glow in the sky in Hereford in 1130, he drew no specific conclusion about its significance: 'What they said, I have written; may the grace of Christ save us'.[47] On other occasions, definite conclusions were drawn. A strange configuration of stars might be specifically linked with an outbreak of plague, the plague being seen as a punishment sent by God for the sins of men, the strangeness in the heavens as a warning of this judgement.

These wonders were interpreted by historians at various levels. Strange events would be noted, along with their effects, which might then be interpreted. A shooting star might, for some, foretell disaster such as a famine or plague, which in turn might be held to indicate the anger of God for specific sins. This connection of events was the usual approach of historians to omens and indeed to any miraculous material they recorded in this period. Some, however, like Roger of Hoveden and Gerald of Wales, hesitated. William of Newburgh was particularly reluctant to look for layers of significance unless he was sure that the events were really mysterious. He records his doubts about the green children in East Anglia, when others greeted them as a sign and prodigy from another world:

Though it is asserted by many, I have long been in doubt about this matter and deemed it ridiculous to give credit to a circumstance supported by no rational foundation or at one of a very mysterious character, yet at length I was so overwhelmed by the weight of so many and such able witnesses that I have been forced to believe and wonder at this matter which I have not been able to comprehend or unravel by any power of the intellect.[48]

In his account of the death of three men in a lime pit, he is equally hesitant, and suggests that they were overcome by fumes from the lime, rather than that they died mysteriously as a punishment for their sins.[49] Others before William knew perfectly well how certain events occurred, but they were far more interested in the significance of the events as miracles than their mechanical construction; William hesitates about adopting the supernatural significance of the event where natural causes are known.

Miracles were, then, open to a great variety of interpretation. In some instances miracles were deliberately used as propaganda, notably in the policies of the Gregorian Reform, where miracles attached to the lives of supporters of Gregorian policy and miracles connected with specific issues, such as simony and celibacy, were used both to advance the cause and to oppose it. In secular politics, miracles were used to forward national and dynastic interests, one instance being the use of the legend of the Royal Touch, by which the kings of France and then of England claimed to cure scrofula. This raises the question of how far it was regarded as proper to tamper with the records of miracles. Whether miracles were staged or manipulated by tricks does not usually appear in the records and cannot be verified. Were changes made deliberately in the records of miraculous events, with a specific end in view?

Notable changes might occur for quite different reasons. New material could be added by a later witness as, for instance, in the miracles added to those of Edward the Confessor by Osbert of Clare.[50] Sometimes a writer might change his opinion of the mechanics of a miracle, as in the case of a phenomenon at sea variously described by Roger of Hoveden on his two visits to the Mediterranean.[51] A change could be made simply because of a mistake in a manuscript; for instance, Dominic of Evesham states in his version of the Mary miracle at the Siege of Chartres that the Normans were struck blind by the sight of the relic, because of a misreading of *caesis* for *caecis.*[52] Again, additions and expansions of a story were made for purely literary reasons, for instance, by using a more elaborate style or adding speeches in the first person or prayers, as in the miracles of Our Lady of Rocamadour.

Deliberate changes in the content of miracle stories seem to have been made for three reasons. The first is the desire to claim the surest possible authority for witnesses to miracles. Events can be described, but miracles need to be witnessed and proved. Eye-witnesses were at a premium, especially those to whom miracles happened. Withbert, who claimed to have been cured of blindness by St Faith, became a dependant of her shrine at Conques, and his story was the pivot of the miracle collection there; it was in his interest to elaborate and improve his story as he told it. When Bernard of Conques came to write it down, Withbert told him that his eyes had fallen out of their sockets, two birds had carried them away, later returned them, and inserted them into his eye sockets after several years had elapsed.[53] Almost all collections, whether of miracles at shrines or in saints' *Lives,* include one miracle that happened to the writer of the collection and these were given some prominence, as, for instance, in the case of the cure of Prior Philip by St Frideswide,[54] a story twice as lengthy as the rest.

The concern of persons involved in the miracles to elaborate their own stories and give them the authority of personal involvement is one side of this demand for witnesses. The other is the claim that stories were told by 'good and trustworthy men', especially those of high ecclesiastical position. This improvement on stories by sharpening the details of their provenance is especially noticeable in the two versions of the *Miracula Anselmi*. The author of both, the monk Alexander,[55] allowed himself considerable latitude between the two versions. In one instance, the cure of a blind man, reported by Eadmer and by Alexander as a presumed miracle, is turned in Alexander's second version into a miracle observed by himself;[56] in another case, he makes a general phrase into a precise statement that the monk Eustace had told his story to St Anselm in the presence of Alexander.[57] In four other cases, the authority for believing a story is made more precise, and said to be that of St Hugh of Cluny.[58] Anselm's own authority is claimed for other miracles, as a great and holy man who ought to be believed.[59]

Another authority urged for miracles, especially for those where contemporary evidence was lacking, was the Bible. St Amadour, whose body was unearthed at Rocamadour in the twelfth century,[60] was given a past in the New Testament as a hermit who helped the Holy Family on their flight into Egypt. The relic said to be 'the hairs of the Virgin' was brought from the Holy Sepulchre to Europe by the crusader Ilger Bigod and presented as the hairs that the Virgin tore out of her head at the foot of the Cross, hairs that were collected and preserved by the Apostles.[61] When he presented some of them to Anselm of Canterbury, he gave the story this scriptural authority, though he glossed over the theft.[62] Relics were peculiarly subject to this invention of authorities, and Guibert de Nogent commented scathingly on the practice.[63]

Another addition to miracle collections was the theme of 'pious theft';[64] stories of how miracle-working relics were stolen from their original shrines and taken to their present ones were assertions about the genuineness and authority of the relics. The relics of St Benedict claimed by Fleury were supported by a story of this kind of theft, circumstantial in all its details, and including a dream about the matter by a pope.[65] The relics of St Scholastica were said to have been stolen with those of St Benedict, and the Fleury account says they were taken to Le Mans.[66] It is possible, however, that the relics of St Scholastica received notice first when Queen Richela asked for their translation in 873, and the story of their translation with the bones of St Benedict may be an attempt to give the Le Mans relics that authority. Another kind of authority came from visions: St Benedict appeared to Prior Richard at Fleury to assert that his relics were indeed there.[67] The Virgin appeared in a vision to claim the miracles at Chartres and to assert that she was to be venerated there.[68]

The second change in miracle collections was the transference of miracles among saints to enhance their glory or the glory of a particular shrine. Gregory of Tours had said that all the saints have all their miracles in common and what was said of one could equally well be said of another.[69] Thus, for instance, a woman Gundrada was cured of the plague and its effects in a particularly striking way at Soissons;[70] the story is found, complete in all its details, in the collection of miracles of Our Lady at Chartres, with the single exception that it was claimed for the Virgin at Chartres as well as at Soissons.[71] The similarity between the miracles at Chartres and at Pierre-sur-Dive has already been noticed. The saint might change; the place might change, as in the Mary miracle of the Jewish Boy, who was said to have been thrown into the furnace at Pisa, Pavia, Bourges, and Constantinople.[72] Instances of this exchange of miracles among saints for the local glory of a shrine could be multiplied indefinitely. Local loyalty is the basis of such transferences.

The third element in the recasting of miracle stories involves the predilections and intentions of those who wrote them down. Miracles were increasingly used in preaching and instruction, and the influence of what was presented as edifying had its effect. For instance, the monastic influence of Aelred of Rievaulx on the miracles recorded of Edward the confessor turned the last of the Anglo-Saxon kings, who unfortunately had no heir, into a monastic saint by choice devoted to chastity. The story of the silence of Odo of Cluny, originally told as proof of his personal austerity, became among the Cistercian writers an argument to support Cistercian rules of silence.[73] As devotion to the Virgin grew, so miracles were transferred from other saints to her,[74] and in no case was her intercession said to be without effect. The desire to interest an audience caused writers to add wonder to wonder and emphasize the marvelous aspects of their stories.

In addition to being subject to the changes inevitable for any literary work in transmission, miracle stories were altered in detail in any number of ways. They record the intervention of God in human affairs, but how, where, when, and to what effect could vary. Miracles were not copyright; they were part of a general world view and belonged to an essentially subjective kind of truth. Where they were later used and invented as part of romance, they reached their limits as creative images. The miracles of the Virgin and the miracles of the Holy Grail were only 'true' in the sense of being consistent with their context and embodying certain truths that could best be apprehended through them—contextual truths that are a long way from simple associations of events and records.

Finally, there is a kind of miracle story that seems to contradict the serious view of miracles so far suggested: the *joca sanctorum. Joca* are not 'jokes' at the expense of miracles. Miracles were not mocked, though false claims were ridiculed. No one, as far as the records go, was amused by the possibility of divine intervention in human affairs. Miracles were, however, inserted into discourses to arouse interest and attention, and thus became entertainment. As tales about human situations, often involving well-known people, they had the appeal of gossip. As tales about the mysterious otherworld of the saints, they had the appeal of the unexpected and novel. But they were not in themselves subjects for laughter.

The *joca* of the saints show a less austere side of the saint's character, even after death. They continue the theme, found in the *Lives* of the saints, of the virtues of *hilaritas,* by which saints were shown to be men who could be amused and cheerful.[75] Odo of Cluny, for instance, was said to have made his companions 'laugh till [they] cried, and were unable to speak to one another'.[76] Wulfric of Haselbury, a grim and forbidding hermit, smiled over a man who wanted by a miracle to speak French as well as English.[77] Aldhelm of Malmesbury entertained the local people by songs and jokes until they were prepared to listen to his more serious remarks.[78] The tradition of folly in the church is illustrated in every age and place and was not absent from the eleventh- and twelfth-century texts. Pleasantries are even seen in the posthumous miracles of the saints. In certain shrine collections *joca* show the saint to be concerned with trivia. The application of powers of sanctity to trivial incidents was a subject of mirth as well as edification; these stories were not 'jokes' in the modern sense of the word, but a way of express-

ing the relationship between the saint and his or her devotees in terms
appealing to all. These *joca* occur in two of the collections already discussed, one from the 'traditional' shrine of St Faith, the other from the
twelfth-century shrine of St Thomas at Canterbury.

Bernard of Angers records ten *joca* of St Faith, and his continuator
one. Bernard says these stories appealed to the *rusticus intellectus* rather
than the learned and scholarly audience he had in mind for the collection. In almost all the *joca* St Faith appears as a pretty young girl with a
taste for jewelery, using blandishments and ruses to obtain trinkets
from her devotees. She was seen, for instance, by Bernard, abbot of
Beaulieu, asking for two golden doves;[79] by Arsendis, wife of Count
William of Toulouse, demanding a pair of gold and jewelled
bracelets.[80] She insisted on receiving rings from William of Auvergne,[81] from Avigenna, second wife of Austrin of Conques,[82] and
from an unnamed pregnant woman.[83] Richarde, widow of Count
Raymond of Millau, was made to contribute a golden brooch. Bernard
mentions a further quantity of rings, pins, bracelets, and jewels that
decorated the shrine and had been obtained by the saint at her own
suggestion. Among the *joca,* Bernard also includes St Faith's help in
finding a lost psalter, filling an empty wine skin, recovering a straying
hawk; *joca* was also the word used for the punishment delivered by the
saint against those who tried to steal gold from her shrine, or a trumpet
from her band, or who wanted too much profit from the sale of candles
at her shrine.[84]

In these stories, the power of the saint is brought to bear on trivia
and the sense of incongruity may have been heightened by the contrast
between the grotesque and forbidding statue and the demands of a girl
for jewellery. The stories nearly always relate to objects of interest to
those who were not monks—hawks, jewels, gold, riches of all
kinds—and this may be an indication that, as with miracles of the
Virgin, there was an audience of a non-theological bent for such tales.
The *rusticus intellectus* mentioned by Bernard when he is introducing the
joca is perhaps simply non-literate, rather than lower class.[85] *Joca*
aroused the contempt of certain scholars in Chartres who jeered at Bernard for believing them. It was this strand of 'secular' interest in the
miracles of saints that developed into romances later. Here, in an
eleventh-century collection, miracles were used to arouse interest
among laymen and even to give them amusement, although this use is
also viewed with suspicion by churchmen.

The *joca* were meant as 'serious jokes' by their compilers. They were to be edifying as well as amusing. The *Miracles of St Thomas of Canterbury* by Benedict of Canterbury included certain *ludi:* 'I include certain games played by the martyr, or rather, a few serious games, for even his games were serious'.[86] In the first of these stories, surprise makes the stories *joca*. Devotees of St Thomas lack money to offer him and are miraculously provided with some. Incongruity provides the amusement in a later story told *ad risum*. Beatrice, a child in Ramsholt, and her smaller brother were told to take care of a large cheese; while they were playing they hid it and forgot where it was. They prayed to St Thomas, who appeared in a dream to both of them and revealed the cheese. Edric, their parish priest, told the story in Canterbury: 'This miracle aroused as much joy and mirth as admiration'.[87] So did stories told of hawks cured or restored to their owners by St Thomas, stories that were related to the early life of the saint and his interest at court in hunting and hawking.

Many of the *joca* of St Thomas involve the water of St Thomas, which was carried off in wooden boxes from which it often leaked away, an endless source of surprise to those who looked for it. On one occasion, a shepherd who worked for Richard, a farmer in Essex, brought a box of the water of St Thomas into a room where his master was entertaining friends. Richard at once improvised a test, announcing that if the box were found to be dry, he would take it as a sign that the shepherd was dishonest. The box was opened and was seen to be dry, whereupon the man admitted his dishonesty with the cheese and butter accounts; Benedict says that everyone present was highly diverted by his embarrassment and that the box was hung up in the church in memory of such a 'merry miracle'.

Such stories were in no way directed against the theory of miracles, but the application of the tremendous powers of heaven to secular and trivial matters apparently caused mirth. Such stories contributed to the loosening of the connection between miracle stories as records of serious events and as literary accounts that aroused interest in a wider audience.

Epilogue

AT THE END OF THIS STUDY of the records of medieval miracles in the Middle Ages, it is proper to draw some conclusions. These are necessarily tentative, since the book claims only to be a preliminary approach to one portion of a vast, complex, and unstable mass of material. The complexity of the material and its diversity have made the task at all stages a delicate one, and it has seemed at times to become an analysis of layers of culture throughout medieval society. Perhaps the first conclusion that can be drawn is that the records of miracles in the Middle Ages are not merely bizarre sidelights to the religion of the period. They provide, rather, a way to approach the ordinary day-to-day life of men and women in all kinds of situations and in all ranks of society, and serious historians must take them into consideration. In the study of history, miracle material has been largely ignored or dismissed in favour of documents such as charters, grants, wills, letters, tracts, and chronicles; the skeleton these provide needs to be fleshed out from other sources, of which miracle stories are the most important and least used.

This material, however, does not have the definite contours of historical documents and is therefore particularly difficult to use. The word 'miracle' covers a wide spectrum of events, each with its own context and interpretation. The first record of a 'miracle' includes a certain amount of interpretation of events, which increases with every repetition and rearrangement of the tale in other contexts. But this variation in itself is of great value, and not only for the historian. For it makes us recognize that our usual definition of 'miracle' as the direct intervention of God in the normal running of events is a narrow and modern concept, which had little meaning before the sixteenth century at the earliest. A cause-and-effect universe, with its exclusive interest in 'how' things happen, in the mechanics of events, is then recognized as only one way of thinking about reality. A more subtle and varied understanding of the world and of the place of man within it—and of the relationship of all creation, including man, to God—is there for rediscovery. Certainly the records of medieval miracles can suggest a new approach to the records of miracles in the Bible, an area in which demythologizing long ago reached a dead end.

It should be clear from this discussion of miracles that they are intimately associated with the society in which they take place, and therefore as subject to change as any other record of events. The miracles of the earlier period were subject to certain economic and social pressures and were in themselves a response to certain needs that in a later period altered; acts of power for protection and vengeance, for instance, were replaced by miracles of mercy and cures, in a society for which these were appropriate. Still later records of miracles, particularly in the fourteenth and fifteenth centuries, show different traits again, some of which are more familiar than those of the earlier formative period under discussion. What can only be called the vulgarization of miracles belongs to this later period and is significantly bound up with the decline of that unified and interiorized understanding of reality that is found in the monastic tradition of East and West from the fourth century to the fourteenth.

The later chapters of this book have included some discussion of the use of miracle stories as propaganda in various contexts. This raises the question of the relationship between event and record of event in miracle stories, and it may be that for some readers it will seem that I have avoided a direct answer to the question of whether miracles 'really' happen. It seems to me that such a question is beyond the scope of a historical work; it belongs to theology and especially to philosophy. I can only repeat my observation, that there is rarely deliberate fraud in the records of miracles in this early period. Those who recorded or acclaimed a 'miracle' believed in it. People believed that they had experienced or witnessed certain events, and they recorded what they thought had happened. This is not a guarantee, of course, that the events were what the participants supposed them to be. The essence of a miraculous event insofar as it relates to the action of God is unverifiable, especially after a lapse of time. All that can be said is that here are events that caused wonder and that were interpreted by sincere and truthful men as signs of the action of God within human affairs. Something was thought to have happened; the rest is interpretation.

The questions usually posed in relation to miracles have to do with their external strangeness, their unpredictability, their wonder. Some of the material discussed here presents a deeper and more interior understanding of reality. From the time of Augustine and Gregory the Great, there was in certain writers a concentration on the significance of miracles rather than on their marvellousness. Miracles were understood in the setting of a world that was seen as an extension of man and not apart from him, his desires, and his needs. Over against this unified creation was a world within a world, the 'mystic heaven' of God and the saints and miracles were one kind of connection between the two. The immense influence of Gregory the Great in formulating this fundamental medieval world view cannot be overstated, and it is being increasingly discussed by both historians and theologians. In his picture of St Benedict of Nursia in the *Dialogues,* praying in his cell and beholding the whole world gathered up in a single ray of light, Gregory was recording no mere wonder; it is an image of the union of man with God in, as he says, an 'inner light' that gave the perspective of heaven to the whole of creation. This ability to see reality in its totality as created and re-created by God removed miracles from the realm of simplistic wonder tales. In their Christian context they were signs of humanity redeemed, signs of the last age, of the ending of time in the single moment of redemption to which all things were to be related. On a more popular level, St Gregory offered men that most reassuring of all miracles—the glory of God revealed in the faces of the saints. The world was the antechamber of heaven, and he made sure that his readers understood that they had friends at court who would intercede for them in their needs and difficulties. This familiarity with the saints and the increasing desire to be in physical, practical contact with them by visiting the place where their bodies lay created the great shrines and pilgrimage routes of the Middle Ages. These remained, in however distant and confused a way, an image of men within the household of faith, exiles continually returning to their home country of heaven. In this context, the miracles of the saints were simply the ordinary life of heaven made manifest in earthly affairs, chinks in the barriers between heaven and earth, a situation in which not to have miracles was a cause of surprise, terror, and dismay.

The records of miracles in the Middle Ages have their moments of greatness but they are by no means consistently to be seen as the subtle and spiritual accounts they became in the hands of Augustine, Gregory, Bede or Anselm. The great men exchanged miracle stories in their letters and conversations; they wove them into their sermons and treatises; their biographers assure us that they also performed miracles in their lives. But alongside these great signs of the Kingdom there are innumerable accounts of little miracles, small events shot through with significance for the ordinary man, and it is with one of these that this introduction to medieval miracle stories can best be concluded. It is a story translated from a document in Canterbury Cathedral Library (Charta Antiqua C 1303) and is dated 27 July 1445. It is of interest in several ways. The subject of the miracle is a cripple, a poor man, Alexander of Aberdeen. He made a vow of pilgrimage at a local shrine of the most popular of later medieval saints, Mary, and went to the saint whose miracles form the most famous collection in existence, St Thomas of Canterbury. Moreover, after his cure Alexander went on to yet another shrine, this time the Holy Blood of Wilsnak, an indication of yet another kind of devotion that increased in this later period. Wilsnak was a small town near Wittenberg. When in August 1383 the parish church there burned down, the parish priest alleged that he had found in the ruins three consecrated hosts marked with drops of blood. These were placed in a shrine and the new church became a centre of pilgrimage. In 1412 the archbishop of Magdeburg condemned the cult and caused the shrine to be closed. It was reopened in 1446, a year after the visit of Alexander, a fact that indicates the continued repute of the shrine in spite of official censure. On Alexander's return to Canterbury, his account of his cure by St Thomas was supported by the oath of some of his countrymen, and the document itself is a formal letter vouching for the genuineness of the miracle, a normal procedure in this period. Thus Alexander links devotion to the Virgin, to St. Thomas, and to the eucharist with the moment of his cure. The letter includes inflated rhetoric about the glory of the miracle, but for Alexander, as for so many like him, it was the event itself, rather than its significance for others, that mattered:

To all the sons of holy mother church to whom this document shall come, from John, by divine permission prior of Christ Church, and the chapter of the same place, greetings; you ought always to glory in the merits of the saints. Since any Christian worshipper of the divine majesty is bound to glory in the wonderful power of God, 'let him that glories, let him glory in the Lord' the Apostolic words proclaim. We are moved to give glory in praise of the divine majesty everywhere in mouth and in mind, for God always and everywhere works wonders in his saints and shines in miracles. Wherefore, since recently in our holy church in Canterbury, the metropolis of all England, we are experiencing a great and very wonderful miracle performed by the divine power through the holy martyr of God, Thomas of Canterbury, we must glory when the whole wide world does not cease to exult with us in praise of him who moves and exalts all the quarters of the globe with his heavenly gifts. For since Alexander, son of Stephen, from the town of Aberdeen in Scotland being twenty-four years old, suffered great pain from his feet that from birth were disgustingly worm-eaten, crippled with hidden ulcers in them; he made a vow at the pilgrimage place of the Virgin Mary, blessed of God, called Segitis, and after undertaking the toil of a high cart, having other aids to his weakness, he knelt on his weak knees at the shrine of the holy Martyr Thomas and before the eyes of all men the glorious athlete of God restored his feet and soles so that he threw away his hated crutches on the second day of May before this was written; and for the next three days the same Alexander by the mercy of God was able to kick the ground lightly with joy and was able to walk away firmly and in good health. We were assured of the truth of this event with full supporting evidence when the aforesaid Alexander made a pilgrimage to the Holy Blood of Wilsnak, which he did in fulfilment of a vow and then came to the shrine of St Thomas the martyr, walking and healthy. We, therefore, not wishing the glory of the glorious martyr Thomas to lie hidden under the shadows of ignorance, desired to place it on the candle-stick of faith so that it should shed light on all the faithful of Christ in praise of the divine majesty, and therefore the aforesaid Alexander took an oath on the sacrament in our presence that the miracle was a genuine cure and to this was added the oath of other worthy men, the nobleman Alexander Arat, Robert son of David, and John son of Thomas, who suddenly arrived as if by the clemency of divine providence from the same town in Scotland. On the aforesaid day of the month of May they took the oath in our presence in the holy church of Canterbury as the law requires and we have published it solemnly as a cause for general rejoicing. We therefore beseech all to whom this letter shall come to praise God worthily in his saints and join in rejoicing to Him who has adorned his own church, united to him as a bride with various shining miracles by the merits of the holy martyr Thomas in his church in Canterbury to the confusion of heresy and error. Given at Canterbury in our chapter on the twenty-seventh day of July, 1445. In witness whereof our common seal is appended to this present writing.

Abbreviations

Acta SS	*Acta Sanctorum Bollandiana*, ed. J. Bollandus *et al.*, 61 vols, Antwerp, Brussels, etc., 1643– (in progress)
Anal. Boll.	Analecta Bollandiana
Becket	*Materials for the History of Archbishop Thomas Becket*, ed. James C. Robertson, 7 vols, Rolls Series, 1875–85
BHL	*Bibliotheca Hagiographica Latina*, 2 vols, and supplement, Brussels, 1911
Bibl. Clun.	*Bibliotheca Cluniacensis*, ed. M. Marrier, Paris, 1614
Bibl. Nat.	Bibliothèque Nationale, Paris
Bodleian	Bodleian Library, Oxford
Brit. Lib.	British Library, London
CCSL	Corpus Christianorum Series Latina, Turnholt, 1954–
CCSM	Corpus Christianorum Series Medievalis, Turnholt, 1954–
CSEL	Corpus Scriptorum Ecclesiasticorum Latinorum, Vienna, 1866–
DACL	*Dictionnaire d'Archéologie Chrétienne et de Liturgie*, ed. F. Cabrol, H. Leclercq, *et al.*, 15 vols, Paris, 1865–1907
DNB	*Dictionary of National Biography*
EHR	*English Historical Review*
Gallia Christiana	*Gallia Christiana*, 16 vols, Paris, 1715–1865

Gesta Pontificum	William of Malmesbury, *De Gestis Pontificum Anglorum Libri Quinque,* ed. N. E. S. A. Hamilton, *Rolls Series,* 1870
Gesta Regum	William of Malmesbury, *De Gestis Regum Anglorum Libri Quinque,* ed. W. Stubbs, *Rolls Series,* 1887, 1889, 2 vols
Jaffé	P. Jaffé, *Regesta Pontificum Romanorum,* 2nd ed., ed. G. Wattenbach, S. Löwenfeld, F. Kaltenbrunner, P. Ewald, 2 vols, Leipzig, 1885–87
Mansi	J. D. Mansi *et al., Sacrorum Conciliorum Nova et Amplissima Collectio,* 55 vols, Venice, Florence, 1759–1962
MGH Epp.	Monumenta Germaniae Historica, Epistolae
MGH Merov	Monumenta Germaniae Historica, Scriptores rerum merovingicarum
MGH SS	Monumenta Germaniae Historica, Scriptores
PG	*Patrologiae cursus completus: series graeca,* 161 vols, ed. J. P. Migne, Paris, 1857–66
PL	*Patrologiae cursus completus: series latina,* 221 vols, ed. J. P. Migne, Paris, 1844–6
Rev. Bén.	*Revue Bénédictine*
RHC	*Recueil des historiens des Croisades*
RHC Arm.	*Recueil des historiens des Croisades. Documents Arméniens,* 2 vols, Paris, 1869–1906
RHC Hist. Occ.	*Recueil des historiens des Croisades, Historiens occidentaux,* 5 vols, Paris, 1845–95
RS	Rolls Series. Chronicles and memorials of Great Britain and Ireland during the Middle Ages, published under the direction of the Master of the Rolls (London, 1838–96)
TRHS	*Transactions of the Royal Historical Society*

Notes

INTRODUCTION

1   J. H. Newman, 'Essay on the Miracles Recorded in Ecclesiastical History', *The Ecclesiastical History of M. l'Abbé Fleury*, pp. xiff.

2   David Hume, *An Inquiry Concerning Human Understanding*, Section 10, *Of Miracles* in *The Philosophical Works of David Hume*, 4:138ff.

3   *Chronica Magistri Rogeri de Houdene*, 4: xiv–xxiv (ed. W. Stubbs).

4   Instances of miracles were cited in this period from both Old and New Testaments, but the word *miraculum* was not used in the Vulgate to describe them; where *miraculum* is used (Exodus 2:10; Numbers 26:10; 1 Sam. 14:15; Job 33:7; Is. 21:4; Is. 29:23; Jer. 23:32; Jer. 44:12), it does not convey the sense of miracle. The words used for events later called miracles in the Vulgate were *signa, virtus, prodigia, mirabilia, paradoxia*, which translate various words in both Hebrew and Greek. *Miraculum* was more commonly used in pagan sources, though cognates were used there also. This points to the different concepts that were eventually combined under the word miracle, a prehistory not without significance for its use in this period. For recent discussion of the etymology and cognates of *miraculum* see R. Grant, *Miracle and Natural Law*, pp. 153–220. There is also an admirable summary in 'The Vocabulary of Miracle', *Miracle*, ed. C. Moule, pp. 235–38.

5   E.g. the definition of miracle given in the *New Catholic Encyclopedia*, 'a miracle is an extraordinary event, perceptible to the senses, produced by God in a religious context as a sign of the supernatural'. Few of the miracles here discussed would fulfil all of these requirements.

6   *De Civitate Dei* 21. 9 (PL 41. 724). English trans. by H. Bettenson, *The City of God* (London, 1972).

CHAPTER ONE

1   *Epistle* 102, p. 549 (*PL* 372).

2   *Sermon* 247 (*PL* 38. 1158).

3   *De Trinitate* 3. 7 (Bettenson, p. 140; *PL* 42. 875–76). Discussed by R. Grant, *Miracle and Natural Law*, pp. 218–19.

4   *De Civitate Dei* 22. 8 (Bettenson, pp. 821–27; *PL* 41. 766–72). The Miracles of St Stephen were copied separately also and circulated later as an independent work; the MS tradition is discussed by A. Wilmart, *Miscellanea Agostiniana,* vol. 2 (Rome, 1931), pp. 279–97.

5   'For how can an event be contrary to nature when it happens by the will of God, since the will of the great creator assuredly is the nature of every created thing? A portent therefore does not occur contrary to nature but contrary to what is known of nature'. *De Civitate Dei* 21. 8.

6   *De Utilitate Credendi* 16. 34 (Bettenson, p. 43; *PL* 42. 90).

7   *De Cura pro mortuis Gerenda* 16. 19 (Bettenson, p. 653; *PL* 40. 606–7).

8   *De Civitate Dei* 21. 8 (Bettenson, p. 773; *PL* 41. 722): 'hence the enormous crop of marvels, which we call 'monsters', 'signs', 'portents', or 'prodigies'.

9   *De Conceptu Virginali* 2. 11 (Bettenson, p. 154). The italics are mine.

10   Ibid., p. 153.

11   Ibid., p. 154.

12   E.g. Albertus Magnus *Summa de Creaturis, Opera Omnia,* 34:318 (ed. A. Borgnet): '*triplicem causam, scilicet naturalis, cuius principium est natura; et voluntarius, cuius principium est voluntas; et divinus cuius principium est Deus'.* 'There are three modes of action according to three kinds of causation, that is, naturally, by the principle of nature; or willingly, by the principle of the will; or supernaturally, by the principle of God'.

13   *Expositio in Hexameron* 3. 7 (*PL* 178. 746).

14   *Theologia Christiana* 3. 128–29, p. 243 (ed. E. M. Buytaert OFM, CCSM, 1969).

15   For the influence of the *Timaeus* see E. Gilson, *History of Christian Philosophy in the Middle Ages*, pp. 139–40; M. Chenu, *Nature, Man and Society in the Twelfth Century*, pp. 64ff.

16   W. Jansen, ed., *De Septem diebus et sex operum distinctionibus, Der Kommentar des Clarembaldus von Arras zu Boethius De Trinitate* (Breslau, 1926), pp. 106–12.

17 'Omnia enim quae sunt vel opus Dei sunt, vel naturae, vel naturam im-
   itantis hominis artificis', *Platonis Timaeus interprete Chalcido cum eiusdem
   commentario*, p. 73 (ed. J. H. Waszink).

18 *Notae super Johannem secundum magistrum Gilbertum*, London, Lambeth
   Palace, MS 360, fol 32r. Quoted by M. Chenu, p. 40.

19 *Quaestiones Naturales*, ed. M. Müller, *Beiträge zur Geschichte der Philosphie
   des Mittelalters*, 1934, p. 58

20 Ibid., 4, p. 8.

21 *De erroribus Guilielmi de Conchis* (PL 180. 339–40).

22 Gerald appears to have made three visits as a student to Paris in the
   mid twelfth century, cf. Gerald of Wales, *Gemma Ecclesiastica, Opera Omnia*, preface to vol. 1, pp. xiv–xv (ed. J. S. Brewer).

23 E.g. *Gemma Ecclesiastica*, pp. 161–64, on the punishments which befell
   blasphemers, and *Topographia Hibernica*, where he comments that the
   miracles of the Irish saints were particularly severe since the land had few
   castles to give protection against wrongdoers and the power of the saints
   was therefore the more necessary.

24 *Topographia Hibernica*, pp. 74–75.

25 Ibid., pp. 126–27.

26 E.g. *De civitate Dei* 21. 7 (Bettenson, pp. 769–70; *PL* 41. 720).

27 Ibid., 31.7, p. 769.

28 The miracles of the Old Testament are grouped around Moses, Aaron,
   Elijah, and Elisha. These were endlessly discussed in the early church and
   the Middle Ages, both as patterns for later miracles and as signs of the last
   age.

29 The conjuring of the spirit of Samuel for Saul by the witch of Endor was a
   continual cause of dispute among Christians. Apologists tried to explain
   it as a trick of ventriloquism, but those eager to conjure spirits used it to
   warrant their activities; cf. L. Thorndyke, *A History of Magic and Experimental Science*, 2:448–49, 469–71.

30 E.g. Iambilicus's discussion of miracles in his *Life of Pythagoras*, pp.
   72–73 (trans. T. Taylor); and Philostratus's *Life of Apollonius of Tyana*,
   1:4–5 (trans. J. S. Phillimore).

31 *De Civitate Dei* 10. 9 (Bettenson, p. 281; *PL* 286).

32 Ibid., (Bettenson, pp. 283–84; *PL* 288).

33 Christian apologists denied the existence of pagan gods, classing their
   supposed actions as deceits of demons; the twelfth-century revival of
   learning brought with it interest in the gods of antiquity, but the same

formal prohibition remained, e.g. a hermetic text, the *Liber Toc,* called the *Book of Venus* was included by Albert the Great in a list of forbidden astrological texts: A. Borgnet, ed., *Toz Graeci, de stationibus ad cultum Veneris', Speculum Astronomicum,* vol. 10, p. 641.

34 Burchard of Worms, *Decretorum Libri* 20 (*PL* 140. 960–3).

35 Ibid.

36 See Thorndyke for a list of manuscripts containing 'Egyptian Days' (pp. 695–96).

37 Sulpicius Severus, *Vita S. Martini* 23. 5, pp. 280–82 (ed. J. Fontaine); Gregory the Great, *Dialogues,* 2. 8, pp. 95–96.

38 Bede *Vita S. Cuthberti* 9, p. 184 (ed. B. Colgrave).

39 Ibid., 3, pp. 160–64.

40 For a recent study of the continued use of charms in medieval medicine see S. Rubin, *Medieval English Medicine*, pp. 70–97.

41 *Les Miracles de S. Benoît* (ed. E. de Certain). E.g. Christian the Sacristan demanded from St Benedict the return of goods stolen from his shrine: 'Believe me, if you don't give me back your bracelets, I won't light a single candle to you again.' (1. 26, p. 59).

42 Cf. the vengeance miracles of the Merovingian saints recorded by Gregory of Tours' *Miracula et opera minora* as an example of the *saevitas Dei* that wreaked as much damage on the recipients as any amount of magical ill-wishing could have done.

43 E.g. John of Salisbury uses the doctrine of occult virtues as virtually indistinguishable from the *'semina seminorum'* of Augustine; *Polycraticus* 2.2g, pp. 475a–476d (ed. C. C. J. Webb).

44 'Natural medicine' is used here to cover all the methods of healing that used the four elements and stones, plants, and animals in cures.

45 E.g. Marbod of Rennes (1035–1123), *Liber lapidum seu de gemmis* (*PL* 171. 1757–80) is a fund of information about the properties of gems.

46 *Physica* (*PL* 197. 1125–1352).

47 *Etymologies* (*PL* 82. 310–60). This account was repeated by later writers, for instance, Rabanus Maurus (*PL* 110. 1097–110); Burchard of Worms (*PL* 140. 839–51). John of Salisbury made it the basis of his discussion of magic (*Polycraticus* 2. 27, pp. 143–161).

48 *Polycraticus* 2. 28.

49 Ibid., 1, p. 66.

50 Ibid.; cf. Augustine, *De Civitate Dei* 22. 8 (Bettenson, p. 822; *PL* 766).

51 Ibid.; cf. St Gregory the Great, *Dialogues* 2. 3, p. 81.

52 Ibid.; cf. Symeon of Durham, *Capitula de Miraculis et Translationibus* 21, pp. 361–62 (ed. T. Arnold).

53 *Polycraticus* 2. 1, pp. 66–67.

54 Ibid., 29, p. 166.

55 Ibid., 15, pp. 88–94.

56 *Gesta Pontificum* 3. 118, p. 259, note 6.

57 Osbern, *Vita S. Dunstani*, p. 81 (ed. W. Stubbs).

58 *Gesta Regum* 2. 2, 167–72, pp. 193–203.

59 E.g. the condemnation of the miracles of the heretics in the Périgord, *Annales de Morgan*, pp. 15ff (ed. H. R. Luard).

60 *Becket* 2. 11, 43, p. 91.

61 As is done for instance by C. G. Loomis, *White Magic: An introduction to the folklore of Christian Legend*.

62 For an admirable summary of the superstitions attached to these rites, with bibliography, see K. Thomas, *Religion and the Decline of Magic*, pp. 36–40.

63 Private confession to a priest was made obligatory by the Fourth Lateran Council XXII, Mansi, 21:1007–10; it was urged much more frequently upon the faithful, as a private matter.

64 The 'matter of the sacrament' in confession was of course the sins of the penitent; the question discussed in this period was whether it was essential to make oral confession of sins and to whom; it was agreed that contrition of heart for the person concerned was what was most needed: e.g. Gratian *Concordantia discordantium canonorum, De Paenitentia (Decreti secunda pars Causa)* 33. qu. 3, 89 (*PL* 187. 1562) and Peter Lombard, *Sententiae* 4. 17. (*PL* 192. 880–85).

65 The doctrine of the eucharist in the early church is fully discussed by Darwell Stone, *A History of the Doctrine of the Holy Eucharist*, vol. 1, chapters 1 and 2.

66 *Sermon* 272 (*PL* 38. 1246–7).

67 The Roman Rite as used in this period is discussed by E. Bishop, 'The Genius of the Roman Rite', *Liturgica Historica*, pp. 1–20.

68 *Orationes* 3. 3, p. 10; *Prayers and Meditations of Saint Anselm*, trans. B. Ward (Harmondsworth, 1973), p. 101.

69 *Speculum De Mysteriis Ecclesiae* (*PL* 177. 362).

70 Cf. Darwell Stone, 1:103–9.

71 *De Corpore et Sanguine Domini* 14, pp. 14–15 (ed. Bede Paul OSB, [Turnholt, 1969]).

72 Ibid., pp. 85–92. Several of these were added in the twelfth century.

73 Lanfranc, *De Corpore et Sanguine Domini* (*PL* 150. 411).

74 *Disputationes* 99, p. 287.

75 Caesarius of Heisterbach *Dialogus Miraculorum* 9. 3 (ed. J. Strange). English translation by E. Scott and C. C. S. Bland, *The Dialogue on Miracles,* 2 vols (London, 1929), 2:110.

76 Ibid., 5 (Scott, p. 170). For a discussion of the various images under which Christ was seen in the sacrament see P. Browe, *Die Eucharistischen Wunder des Mittelalters.* The development of the theme of Christ seen at the eucharist is elaborated by L. Sinanoglou, "The Christ Child as Sacrifice', *Speculum* 48 (1973): 491–509. It is of some interest for the popularization of this theme to note its use in fiction a little later, e.g. as the central vision of the Grail in the *Quest of the Holy Grail,* trans. P. M. Matarasso, pp. 276–77.

77 Gerald of Wales *Gemma Ecclesiastica,* pp. 162–64. Peter the Venerable also recounts instances of the host vanishing from the hands of a sinful priest as a judgement on him: *De Miraculis* 1. 2 (*PL* 189. 852–53).

78 A story of bees protecting a stolen host is found in Peter the Venerable, *De Miraculis* (*PL* 189. 851–52). It is told in many places in the twelfth and thirteenth centuries: cf. G. Constable, 'The Manuscript Works of Peter the Venerable', *Petrus Venerabilis 1156–1956,* Studia Anselmiana 40, ed. G. Constable and J. Kritzeck (Rome, 1956), pp. 219–74.

79 Caesarius, 9. 48.

80 Cf. N. Herrmann-Mascard, *Les Reliques des Saints*, pp. 173–74.

81 Guitmund, *De Corporis et Sanguinis Domini Veritate Tres Libre* 2 (*PL* 149. 1449–50).

82 *Vita Magna S. Hugonis* (ed. and trans. D. Douie and H. Farmer, 2 vols [London, 1961–2], 2:92–94).

83 Ibid., 2:86.

84 E.g. a case remitted to Peter Damian concerned a woman who had stolen part of the host for magical purposes, *De Variis Miraculosis Narrationibus* (*PL* 145. 571–73).

85 Mansi, Fourth Lateran Council xx, 21:1007. The open veneration of the relics of the saints was also forbidden: Mansi, 62, 21:1045–51.

86 A general introduction to the subject of ordeals is by Frederico Patetta, *Le ordalie*. A more recent study is Hermann Nottarp, *Gottesurteilstudien*, Bamberger Abhandlungen und Forschungen, 2 (Munich, 1956). In a recent unpublished paper, 'Trial by Ordeal: the Key to Proof in the Early Common Law', P. Hyams suggested that the move away from the ordeal was the result of changed social needs rather than a move away from the supernatural.

87 The views of Peter the Chanter and his circle are discussed by J. W. Baldwin, *Merchants, Masters and Princes*. A more concise account is given by the same writer in 'The Intellectual Preparation for the Canon of 1215 against Ordeals', *Speculum* 36 (1961): 613–36.

88 Peter the Chanter (+1197) constantly referred to the problem of ordeals in his lectures; his most comprehensive treatment of it is in the *Verbum abbreviatum* (PL 205. 226–33). For ordeals as tempting God, see *Verbum* 226, 542.

89 *Verbum* 233–548.

90 Mansi, 22:106–7. There had already been prohibition of the use of the ordeal in the trial of heresy, by Innocent iii (*PL* 216. 502).

CHAPTER TWO

1 See B. Smalley, *The Study of the Bible in the Middle Ages* for the background to this discussion of the commentators. See also Roger E. Reynolds, *The Ordinals of Christ from their Origins to the Twelfth Century* (Berlin, 1978).

2 *Commentariorum in Exodus* (PL 108. 9).

3 Anselm of Laon (died 1117). 'Anselm was certainly responsible for the *Gloss* on St Paul and the Psalter, probably for that on the Fourth Gospel', B. Smalley, p. 60.

4 *Biblia Sacra Cum Glossa Ordinaria* 5. 1195.

5 *De Doctrina Christiana* 3. 15 (PL 34. 74).

6 *Commentary on St John's Gospel* (PL 169. 277 and 276).

7 The *sententia* and *quaestiones* emerged in the mid-twelfth century as a new and freer method of exposition; the *quaestiones* could be separated from the text upon which it was based and circulated separately as more systematic teaching. Cf. B. Smalley, pp. 66–83.

8   *Glossa Ordinaria* 6, 67–68.

9   Peter Lombard, *Libri Quatuor Sententiarum* 18. 6 (*PL* 192. 688).

10 R. M. Martin, ed., *Quaestiones de Divina Pagina,* vols 13, 18, 21, 25 (Louvain, 1932), 2:18.

11 J. Marichez, ed., *Les 'Disputationes de Divina Pagina'* (Louvain, 1932), pp. 210–11.

12 *De Mirabilibus Sacrae Scripturae* 111. 8 (*PL* 35. 2197). Several writers have discussed the authorship of this work. E.g. J. F. Kenney, *The Sources for the Early History of Ireland,* pp. 275ff. and P. Grosjean, 'Sur quelques exégètes irlandais du VIIe siècle', *Sacris Erudiri,* vol. 7 (1955), pp. 67–98. They conclude it belongs to the Irish school of exegetes in the seventh century. A forthcoming edition of the text by Fr Gerard McGinty OSB will include some discussion of the text itself; I am grateful to Dom Gerard for permission to consult his text and for discussion of it.

13 Cf. J-Th. Welter, *L'Exemplum dans la littérature religieuse et didactique du moyen age,* pp. 9–34.

14 *Homilies on Ezekiel* 11. 7 (*PL* 6. 1014, 1300).

15 *De Civitate Dei* 22. 9 (Bettenson, pp. 825–27; *PL* 41. 770–71).

16 Ibid., 827.

17 *3rd Sermon on the Vigil of the Nativity of the Lord, Opera Omnia,* 4:216–17 (eds. J. Leclercq et al.).

18 *Sermon on St Martin, Opera Omnia,* 5:407.

19 Ibid.

20 *Sermon on St Victor, Opera Omnia,* 6:30–31.

21 Sermon 5, *De Oneribus* (*PL* 195. 378–79).

22 *Liber de Commendatione Fidei* (*PL* 204. 606 and 604).

23 Sermon 3, *Mariale* (*PL* 211. 725).

24 *De Bone Religiosi status et Variarum Animantium Tropologia* (*PL* 145. 776). The translation of *sacramentum* in this passage is fraught with difficulties, cf. J. de Ghellinck, 'Les Anteniens', *Spicilegium sacrum Lovaniense, Études et Documents* 3 (Louvain and Paris, 1924) and C. Mohrmann, *Études sur le Latin des chrétiens,* pp. 233–44. I have used 'sacrament' in its basic meaning of outward and visible sign of an inward and spiritual grace and use this note to correct the overtones inherent in this word.

25 *Sermon on the Vigil of St Benedict* (*PL* 144. 546–47).

26 Guibert of Nogent, *Liber quo ordine sermo fieri debeat* (*PL* 156. 24).

27 Caesarius *Dialogus Miraculorum* 4. 36. 1, p. 205.

28 Guibert *Ordine sermo* 25.

29 James of Vitry *Life of St Mary of Oignies* (Acta SS, June 28, p. 547).

30 Cf. Jean Leclercq, 'Le Sermon, acte liturgique', *La liturgie et les paradoxes chrétiens*, pp. 205−27.

31 Fulbert of Chartres (*c.* 960−1028) *Sermones ad Populum* (PL 141). *De Nativitate Beatissimae Mariae Virginis* 323ff.

32 A legend found in the Latin recension of the *Life of St Basil* by Amphilocius, bishop of Iconium.

33 The bibliography of this legend is given elsewhere (pp. 256−7). The version given by William of Malmesbury, *Miracles of the Virgin,* has an extensive conversation between Theophilus, the Devil, and the Virgin.

34 *PL* 141. 323.

35 *De Civitate Dei* 22. 8 (Bettenson, p. 824; *PL* 768).

36 Philip the Prior *Miracles of St Frideswide* (Acta SS, Oct. 8, p. 568).

37 William of Malmesbury, *Miracles of the Virgin,* 1:271 (ed. P. Carter). 'The composer of this work loves our Lady from the depths of his heart'.

38 *Becket*, 1:282−83.

39 *De Civitate Dei,* 21. 8 (Bettenson, p. 771; *PL* 721).

40 Abbot Samson, *Miracles of St Edmund, Memorials of St Edmund's Abbey,* 1:143 (ed. T. Arnold).

41 Another reason for believing the miracles of a saint is given by Osbern, whom William of Malmesbury was later to criticize as too credulous. Osbern thought they should be believed by all who want their own accounts of miracles to be believed, *Memorials of St Dunstan*, p. 129 (ed. W. Stubbs, RS, 1874).

CHAPTER THREE

1 Ireneus, *Adversus Haereses* 2. 31 (*PG* 7.824).

2 Acta SS, Oct. 3, pp. 288−89. Cf. L. Saltet, *Étude Critique sur la Passion de Sainte Foy et de Saint Caprais*.

3 Ibid., pp. 289−92. *Fragmentum Passionis Metricae* (ed. E. Dümmler, Neues Archiv, vol. 10 [1885], pp. 337−38). Cf. *La Chanson de Sainte Foy* (ed. P. Alfaric).

4 Acta SS, Oct. 3, pp. 294−99. The argument about the composition of the account of the translation, its date, and its probability is still unresol-

ved. The present state of opinion is stated by P. Geary, *Furta Sacra,* pp. 169–74. What matters for this discussion of miracles is that for this period the miracles connected with St Faith were at Conques not Agen; the reference to miracles at Agen in the *Translatio Metrica* (Acta SS, Oct. 3, p. 290) is general, not specific.

5   *Liber Miraculorum Sancte Fidis,* 1. 13, p. 47 (ed. A Bouillet).

6   *Miracles of St Faith* 1. 13.

7   Ibid., 2. 26, p. 66.

8   For the background to the miracles of St Faith among the independent nobility, see G. Duby, *La Société aux XIe et XIIe siècles dans la région Mâconnaise* (Paris, 1971).

9   *Miracles of St Faith* 1. 28, pp. 54–55.

10   Ibid., 1. 31, p. 76.

11   *HM* 6; Dexter, pp. 20–21. The miracle of Eppo the Thief, with references, will be discussed below, p. 156.

12   *Miracles of St Faith* 1. 30, p. 74–76.

13   Ibid., 2. 12, pp. 120–27.

14   The connections between Spain and Conques are discussed by M. Defourneaux, *Les Français en Espagne aux XIe et XIIe Siècles*; the pilgrimage route was only one link among several.

15   'Then the most precious body of blessed Faith, virgin and martyr, was buried with honour by Christians in the valley popularly called "Conques" and above it the Christians built a most beautiful basilica in which even to the present day the Rule of St Benedict is kept to the glory of God. There many benefits are bestowed upon those who are well and those who are sick at the threshold of the best of fountains and there are more miracles than I could relate. *Codex Calixtinus* 1:365.

16   Acta SS, Oct. 3, pp. 283ff. Cf. Dugdale, *Monasticon Anglicanum* 1:415–16, for donations of Ralph Fitzwalter and his wife to the new foundation. Two charters of Henry I to Horsham St Faith are printed in *Birmingham Historical Society Journal* (1973): 16–21.

17   *Miracles of St Faith* 2. 4, pp. 100–101.

18   Ibid., *Letter to Fulbert,* p. 1.

19   Cf. N. Herrmann-Mascard, *Les Reliques des saints,* pp. 159–60 for the requirement of relics for altars.

20   *Miracles of St Faith* 1. 24, pp. 49–50.

21 Ibid., 1. 13, p. 47.

22 Ibid.

23 Ibid., p. 3.

24 Ibid.

25 Ibid., 1. 1, pp. 8–9.

26 'A Prayer to St Benedict', *Opera Omnia 3*. 61–64 (*Prayers and Meditations of St Anselm,* trans. Benedicta Ward [London, 1973; reprinted 1979], p. 199).

27 *Dialogues* 2. 1, p. 72.

28 Ibid., p. 71.

29 For a detailed analysis of the miracles recorded by St Gregory, see Pierre Boglione, 'Miracle et merveilleux religieux chez Grégoire le Grand, Théorie et Thèmes', pp. 11–102.

30 *Dialogues* 2. 34, p. 128.

31 Ibid., 37, p. 133.

32 Desiderius, *Dialogi de Miraculis Sancti Benedicti,* prologue, pp. 1116–17 (ed. G. Schwartz and A. Hofmeister).

33 Ibid., 2. 13, p. 1133; *Dialogues of St Gregory* 2. 6, p. 89.

34 Desiderius, 1. 2, pp. 1118–19.

35 Ibid., 2. 12, pp. 1132–3

36 Ibid., 1. 9, pp. 1123–4.

37 Ibid., 8, p. 1122.

38 Ibid., 1. 1–12, p. 1124.

39 Ibid., 2. 16, p. 1135.

40 Ibid., 2. 8, p. 1131.

41 Peter Damian, *De Bono Suffragiorum* (PL 145. 564).

42 *Chronica Monasterii Casinensis* 3. 28, pp. 716–17.

43 Peter the Deacon, *Historia Relatio de Corpore S Benedicti Casini* (Acta SS March 3, pp. 288–89). For a fuller discussion of the relics of St Benedict see Paul Meyvaert, 'Peter the Deacon and the Tomb of St Benedict', *Benedict, Gregory, Bede and Others*, pp. 3–70. A recent examination of the relics now at Fleury has been undertaken and its results will be published.

44 *Vetera analecta*, pp. 211–12 (ed. J. Mabillon) and Paul the Deacon *De*

gestis Langobardorum (*PL* 95. 621–22). For the possible influence of Einhard's *Translatio SS Marcellini et Petri* on the rewriting of these accounts, see P. J. Geary, *Sacra Furta; Theft of Relics in the Central Middle Ages* (1978), pp. 143–7.

45 For the tradition about the translation of the relics of St Scholastica, see Walter Goffart, 'Le Mans, St Scholastica, and the Literary Tradition of the Translation of St Benedict', *Rev. Bén.* 77 (1967): 107–41.

46 Adrevald, 'Translatio S Benedicti', *Les Miracles de Saint Benoît,* pp. 13–14 (ed. E. de Certain). Hereafter referred to as *Miracles of Benedict.*

47 *Miracles of Benedict* 1. 15–17, pp. 37–42. It seems that part of the relics were returned.

48 Ibid., 7. 15, p. 274.

49 Ibid., 1. 26, p. 60; St Benedict is elsewhere compared with Moses, 2. 10, p. 112.

50 Ibid., 1. 23, p. 52; 1. 29, p. 66; 1. 30, pp. 66–68; 1. 32, pp. 69–70; 1. 36, pp. 78–79; several cures are also noted in cap. 31, pp. 68–69.

51 Aimon of Fleury was born in Périgord of a noble family; he was a child-oblate at Fleury under abbot Amalbert (979–985) and was taught by Abbo. He was with Abbo when the latter was murdered at La Réole. He dedicated his two books of miracles to Gauzelin, Abbo's successor, and says that he would have liked to continue the record. He later wrote the *Lives of the Abbots of Fleury* and died *c.* 1008. Cf. *Histoire littéraire de la France,* 6:38.

52 *Miracles of Benedict* 7. 15, p. 276.

53 Andrew of Fleury entered the abbey under Abbot Gauzelin, whose life he wrote.

54 *Miracles of Benedict* 6. 2, pp. 218–21.

55 Ibid., 4. 10, 11, pp. 187–91.

56 Cf. Jean Leclercq, 'Violence and the Devotion to St Benedict in the Middle Ages', *The Downside Review* 310 (October 1970): 344–61.

57 *Miracles of Benedict* 3. 5, pp. 138–41; 5. 15, p. 213.

58 Ibid., 4. 9, p. 186.

59 Ralph Tortaire, b. 1063, monk and poet, cf. *Histoire littéraire de la France* 7:102, 125.

60 Hugh of St Mary, son of a local knight also called Hugh; he had a brother Cleopas, see plate 4, p. 55.

61 *Miracles of Benedict* 4. 4, p. 179.

62 Ibid., 9. 7, p. 370, i.e. the Feast of the Annunciation, 25 March 1114.

63 *Chronica Monasterii Casinensis*, p. 741.

64 Peter Damian *Sermon for the Vigil of St Benedict* (PL 144).

65 Udalric *Consuetudines Cluniacensis* 1. 34 (PL 149. 637).

66 John of Salerno *Life of St Odo* (*Bibl. Clun.* 51–52).

67 'Vita Sancti Cuthberti Anonymi', *Two Lives of St Cuthbert*, bk. 4, vol. 13, p. 130.

68 Ibid., 15, p. 134.

69 I have discussed at greater length Bede's treatment of miracles in an article 'Miracles and History: a Reconsideration of the Miracle Stories in Bede', *Famulus Christi,* ed. G. Bonner (Durham, 1976), pp. 70–76.

70 'Vita Sancti Cuthberti Prosaica', *Two Lives of St Cuthbert*, 23:232.

71 Eadmer *Life of St Anselm*, pp. 165–67 (ed. R. W. Southern).

72 B. Colgrave and R. A. B. Mynors, eds., *Ecclesiastical History of the English People* 4:446.

73 The *Vita Metrica S Cuthberti* by Bede adds nothing to the picture of Cuthbert's miracles. The reference to Bede himself in the prologue should be taken in a metaphorical sense: 'of these there is one which happened to myself, as I have already told you, in the guidance *(curatio)* of my tongue while I was singing of his miracles' (*PL* 94. 575), in spite of Reginald's later assumption that this was a physical cure of a speech impediment; Reginald of Durham, *Libellus de Admirandis Beati Cuthberti Virtutibus* 76, pp. 158–60.

74 Symeon of Durham 'Historia de Sancto Cuthberto', *Opera Omnia,* pp. 196–215 (ed. Thomas Arnold). The 'Historia' is discussed as an historical source by E. Craster, 'The Patrimony of St Cuthbert', *EHR* 69 (1954): 177–99, where he also identifies the places mentioned and comments, 'The list of wills which formed the gift does read like a mutilated version of a genuine land-boc' (p. 180).

75 'Historia', Osbert and Ella, pp. 201–2; Halfdune, pp. 202–3; Onalafbald, p. 209.

76 Ibid., p. 202.

77 Symeon of Durham, 'Historia Dunelmensis Ecclesia', *Opera Omnia* 1, p. 96 (ed. T. Arnold). The value of Symeon as an historian is discussed by H. S. Offler, *Medieval Historians of Durham* (Durham Inaugural Lecture, 1958).

233

78 'Historia Dunelmensis Ecclesia', p. 107.

79 Ibid., p. 95. The restoration of monks to St Cuthbert's cathedral provides the theme of the book, which begins with a reference to it and ends with the death of William of St Carilef in 1096.

80 'Historia Translationis', *Symeonis Dunelmensis Opera et Collectanea*, pp. 158–201 (ed. H. Hinde). It is discussed in *The Relics of St Cuthbert*, ed. C. F. Battiscombe. The presence of Symeon is attested by Reginald, p. 84.

81 'Historia Translationis', 19, pp. 197–98.

82 *Chronicon Abbatiae de Evesham and anum 1418*, pp. 323–24, 335–36 (ed. W. D. Macray).

83 *Gesta Regum* 2. 207, p. 260.

84 Ibid., 121, pp. 127–28.

85 Feasts of St Cuthbert had a prominent place in the church in Durham; his death was celebrated with an octave on 20 March, an early translation on 4 September. 'The chief stages of the enrichment of the liturgy provided for the saint to coincide with periods following his more famous translations', C. Mohler, *The Relics of St Cuthbert*, pp. 155–192.

86 Reginald of Durham 68, pp. 138–40.

87 Ibid., 36, pp. 78–79. Elfred is described in cap. 26, pp. 59–60. Other instances of St Cuthbert warning guardians of the shrine of impending danger are 37, pp. 80–81; 51, pp. 106–8.

88 Ibid., 16, pp. 197–201.

89 Ibid., 35, pp. 77–78; 97, pp. 215–17.

90 Ibid., 19, pp. 37–41. In 1172, when again lots were cast between three English saints to find which was the most powerful, St Thomas of Canterbury had replaced St Etheldreda, while St Cuthbert remained among the three, with St Edmund (112, pp. 248–54).

91 Queen Margaret of Scotland gave a copy of the Gospels bound in silver to the shrine; an illuminated *Life of St Cuthbert* was also kept there, and the *Lindisfarne Gospels*. The book-learning of Northumbria is reflected in several of the miracles, for instance, on two occasions people (a knight and a boy) are described as finding learning difficult and trying to escape it, only to be encouraged by St Cuthbert (Reginald, 73, p. 173; 76, pp. 158–60).

92 Ibid., 89, pp. 188–93.

93 Ibid., 112, pp. 248–55. The pilgrims to St Cuthbert were largely upper-class, including the young man from Norway. Nobles, bishops, kings, and archbishops patronized the shrine, a tradition beginning with St Cuthbert and his close association with the royal house of Northumbria and continued because of the needs of the guardians of the shrine for protection later. When the relics of St Cuthbert were examined in 1104, his coffin contained the relics also of King Oswald and King Ceolwulf, as well as Bishops Aidan, Eadalbert, Eadfrith, and Ethelwold, and those of Bede. See article by J. Raine, *Dictionary of Christian Biography*. There is a parallel here with the shrine of St Edmund of Bury, another Anglo-Saxon saint patronized by royalty; *Miracula S Edmundi, Memorials of St Edmund's Abbey* (ed. T. Arnold, RS, vol. 1, pp. 107–209).

94 Ibid., 99 and 100, pp. 219–23.

95 E.g. ibid., 67, p. 134, a candle with a wick composed of sixty-six threads. In the *Miracles of St Cuthbert on Farne*, (ed. E. Craster) a candle is mentioned 'the height of a person' (cap. 8, p. 17) and one whose wick was long enough to encompass a house and had to be twisted into two wicks (cap. 12, p. 19).

96 Reginald, 26, p. 57.

97 Ibid., 44, pp. 90–91.

98 Ibid., 25, p. 56.

99 Farne is an island four miles off the North coast, northeast of Bamburgh. It was occupied by hermits from Durham for centuries, of whom Reginald mentions Aelric, Aelwin, and Bartholomew. The miracles printed by E. Craster, *The Miracles of St Cuthbert on Farne*, pp. 5–9, are taken from the MS Harley 4843 in the British Library. For the later history of hermits on Farne, see H. D. Farmer, *The Hermit of Farne* (London, 1961).

100 Reginald, 2 and 3, pp. 10–12.

101 Ibid., 12, p. 19. 'Vita Anonymi' 2. 7, pp. 89–90.

102 Cf. R. B. Dobson, *Durham Priory 1400–1450* (Cambridge, 1973), pp. 314–15.

103 *Gesta Pontificum* p. 276.

CHAPTER FOUR

1   Thomas of Monmouth, *The Life and Miracles of St William of Norwich* 2. 13, p. 97 (ed. and trans. A. Jessopp and M. R. James).

2   Ibid., 15, pp. 111–12. John de Cheyney, son of Robert Fitzwalter, died as sheriff of Norwich in 1146; the family held Norwich Castle for the king and also protected the interests of the Jews in Norwich. The Jew Eleazar was murdered by Sir Simon de Novers who was deeply in his debt; ibid., pp. xxxiii–xxxiv.

3   Ibid., 2. 12, pp. 136–45.

4   Ibid., 4. 1, pp. 165–67. Elias was prior of Norwich 1146–1150 as successor to William Turbe, who became bishop of Norwich at that date.

5   In spite of Thomas's endeavours, the liturgical celebration of St William never spread further than Norwich. St William is mentioned twice in the *Ormesby Psalter* (Bodleian, MS Douce 366), once in the calendar, where the Passion of St William Martyr of Norwich is given three days before Easter Day (fol. 3r), and once in the second litany (fol. 210r). It is probable that these sections were added to the Psalter and originated in Norwich. Representations of St William are noted in M. R. James, pp. lxxxv–lxxxviii; he notes only one outside East Anglia.

6   Ibid., 1. 8, pp. 29–30. Aelward Ded, a wealthy citizen of Norwich, died 1149.

7   Ibid., 1. 17, p. 49.

8   Ibid., 2. 7, p. 84.

9   Ibid., 8, p. 85.

10 Ibid., 1. 4, pp. 18–19. Thomas draws a parallel between Christ being sold for silver to the Jews and William's mother receiving silver for her son; it is tempting to see this simply as a literary idea, but it is not necessarily without factual basis.

11 Ibid., 14, pp. 40–41.

12 The body was translated from Thorpe Wood to the monk's cemetery in 1144; *Miracles of St William* 1. 18, 19, pp. 50–55. It was taken from the cemetery to the Chapter House in 1150; 3. 1, pp. 116–25. From there it was taken to the south side of the high altar in the church in 1151; 5. 1, pp. 185–86; it was finally transferred to its own chapel in 1154; 6. 1, pp. 221–22.

13 Ibid., 4. 8, p. 174.

14 Ibid., 3. 11, pp. 135–36. Lady Mabel was a benefactor of the monastery. For information on the Bec family in Norwich see 'Bek', *DNB*.

15 Ibid., 4. 8, pp. 172–74.

16 Ibid., 3. 12, p. 140.

17 Ibid., 1. 2, p. 12.

18 Ibid., 3. 12, p. 139.

19 Ibid., 7, prologue, p. 262.

20 Extracts show this in the register of the diocese of Norwich, quoted by M. R. James, for 1277 to 1442; ibid., pp. lxxxii–lxxxiv.

21 *Miracles of St William*, 1. 18, pp. 51–52.

22 Ibid., 2. 3, pp. 66–67.

23 Ibid., 3. 1, pp. 123–24.

24 Ibid., 2. 6, pp. 78–79.

25 Ibid., 3. 5, p. 129.

26 Ibid., 8, p. 133.

27 Ibid., 28, pp. 159–60.

28 Ibid., 9, pp. 135–36.

29 E.g. the Lady Legarda, formerly wife of William of Apulia, who lived near the church of St Mary Magdalene and tended the sick (ibid., 1. 9, pp. 31–32). On the association of St Mary Magdalene with hospitals see V. Saxer, *Le culte de Marie Madeleine en occident des origines à la fin du moyen âge*. The tradition of anchoresses in Norwich continued into the fourteenth century with the best known of them, the author of *Revelations of the Divine Love*, ed. E. Colledge and J. Walsh, *A Book of Showings to the Anchoress Julian of Norwich*, 2 vols, Studies & Texts 35 (Toronto, 1978).

30 *Miracles of St William* 6. 9, pp. 231–33. Philip de Bella Arbore, a knight from Lorraine, was excommunicated by the archbishop of Trier for the murder of his brother, and his penance was imposed by Pope Eugenius III (1145–1153).

31 Ibid., 7. 11, p. 271.

32 Ibid., 1, pp. 263–64.

33 Ibid., 18, pp. 284–86.

34 Ibid., 3. 29, pp. 160–61; 7. 19, pp. 289–93.

35 Ibid., 6. 1, p. 221: 'as the wonder-working power of the holy martyr William was so frequently manifested in such great miracles, he began to be waited upon by unusually large crowds, and since the place where he lay was not adapted to this enormous throng and pressure . . . it was suggested . . . that a fit place be found for the martyr where he might rest in greater honour and the people might approach his tomb without risk'.

36 Ibid., 6. 6, pp. 226–28.

37 Gregory of Tours, *De Virtute S Martini, Miracula et opera minora* 2. 51, p. 626 (ed. B. Krusch).

38 *Miracles of St William* 4. 10, p. 181.

39 Ibid., 7. 18, p. 288.

40 Ibid., 2. 4, pp. 67–68.

41 Ibid., 7. 18, p. 286. Robert may be the brother of St William?

42 The use of English in connection with a new saint is sometimes held to show that he was not yet officially canonized. Cf. *Becket* 1. 2, pp. 150–51 where this is said; here it seems to show only the girl's ignorance of Latin.

43 Herbert of Losinga, +1119, bishop of Norwich and founder of Norwich Priory. Cf. 'Henry de Losinga', *DNB;* Dugdale, *Monasticon Anglicanum,* 4:1 and 2.

44 *Miracles of St William* 1. 1, p. 10.

45 Ibid., 5. 11, p. 202.

46 Ibid., 4. 3, pp. 168–69.

47 Dugdale, *Monasticon Anglicanum* 3:635–37.

48 *Miracles of St William* 7. 7, pp. 267–68.

49 Ibid., p. lxxxv.

50 Ibid., prologue, pp. 2 and 6.

51 *The Anglo-Saxon Chronicle,* ed. and trans. D. Whitelock, D. C. Douglas, and S. L. Tucker, refers to the death of St William: 'Jews of Norwich bought a Christian child before Easter and tortured him with all the torture that Our Lord suffered, and on Good Friday hanged him on a cross on account of Our Lord and then buried him', p. 200. Jocelyn of Brakelond wrote an account of the death of the child Robert of Bury which has not survived, *Chronicle of Jocelin of Brakelond,* p. 16 (ed. H. E. Butler). M. R. James gives seven instances of children supposed to have been killed in this manner after the story of St William was composed. *Miracles of St William,* pp. lxxiv–lxxvi.

52 Reginald of Durham, *Libellus de Vita et Miraculis S Godrici, heremitae de Finchale*, p. 269 (ed. J. Stevenson).

53 *Life of St Godric* 2, pp. 24–25; 4, pp. 28–30. Godric was presented by H. Pirenne as the typical self-made man of the new merchant class, *Medieval Cities*, pp. 120–24.

54 *Life of St Godric* 5, 6, 7, pp. 30–38.

55 Ibid., 12, 14, 15, pp. 152–58.

56 Ibid., 20, p. 66. The Bishop of Durham, Ranulf Flambard (1099–1128) granted the lands of Finchale to the prior and convent of Durham after Godric had settled there, *The Charters of Endowment, Inventories and Account Rolls of the Priory of Finchale*, ed. James Raine, Surtees Society (London, 1937), p. 201; this was confirmed by Hugh Pudsey, p. 21. Finchale had a sequence of hermits there, and was used in the fourteenth century as a rest-house for the monks of Durham (cf. R. B. Dobson, *Durham Priory*, pp. 310ff.).

57 The prior of Durham was Germanus, 1163–1189; he described his relationship with Godric in warm terms and valued his opinion, *Life of Godric*, prologue, pp. xviii–xix.

58 The relationship of the 'new' hermits to communities is fully discussed by Henrietta Leyser, 'The New Eremitical Movement in Western Europe, 1000–1150' (unpublished B.Litt. thesis, Oxford, 1966). The function in society of a 'new' hermit such as Wulfric of Haselbury has been discussed by Henry Mayr-Harting, 'Functions of a Twelfth-Century Recluse', *History* 60 (1975): 337–52. See also my article, 'The Relationship between Hermits and Communities in the West, with Special Reference to the Twelfth Century', *Solitude and Communion*, ed. A. M. Allchin (Oxford, 1977), pp. 54–63.

59 *Life of Godric* 16, pp. 69ff.

60 *The Psalter of St Jerome*, consisting of the first verses of each psalm only, was a great favourite of Godric; it is mentioned twice in the *Life of Godric* 9, pp. 42–43; 92, pp. 200–201.

61 Ibid., 77, pp. 175–76.

62 Ibid., 123, pp. 246–47; 137, pp. 263–64; 141, pp. 270–71; 155, pp. 293–94. Two Cistercian abbots visited Godric's tomb later, *Miracles of Godric* 171, p. 430.

63 *Life of Godric* 58, pp. 135–36.

64 Ibid., 166, pp. 315–17. When Reginald at first asked Godric to give him leave to write his *Life*, he refused; some years later the hermit of his

own accord gave Reginald information about his early life and finally approvd the *Life* on his death-bed.

65 The preface of Germanus's *Life* is printed in *Life of Godric,* appendix to preface, pp. xvii–xviii.

66 Printed in Acta SS, May 5, pp. 70ff. It is dedicated to Thomas prior of Finchale who died in 1196.

67 John of Ford, *Wulfric of Haselbury.*

68 *Miracles of Godric* 10, pp. 333–481.

69 Ibid., 10, p. 350.

70 Ibid.

71 *Life of Godric* 57, pp. 132–34.

72 The ideas about the early days of monasticism in Egypt that were current among the Cistercians, for instance, were coloured by their own expectations and interests; see my article 'The Desert Myth', *One Yet Two,* ed. B. Pennington (Kalamazoo, 1976), pp. 183–200.

73 *Life of Godric* 13, pp. 52–53.

74 The *Cantus S Godrici* has been widely discussed; the verses of this unlettered seaman have been held to stand at the beginning of Middle English poetry, Cf. J. Zupitza, 'Cantus beati Godrici', *Englische Studien* 11 (1888): 401–32; J. W. Rankin, 'The Hymns of St Godric', *PMLA* 38 (1923): 699–711. Three of his verses are recorded in the *Miracles,* an invocation of Mary, a prayer to the angels, and one to St Nicholas. It is significant that these unliterary rhymes were revealed to Godric by the saints, whereas the songs of Caedmon, held to be the beginning of Anglo-Saxon poetry, were revealed to him also in a dream. It is in both cases the nature of poetic inspiration that is being described. The words and music of the song taught to Godric by Mary appear in Brit. Lib., MS Harley 322, printed in *Life of Godric,* p. 288.

75 Called the 'angel of Monks' and therefore depicted with wings in iconography.

76 *Life of Godric* 43, pp. 102–3.

77 Ibid., 49, pp. 114–15.

78 Ibid., 170, pp. 327–32.

79 Ibid., p. 329.

80 *Miracles of Godric* 23, pp. 368–70.

81 Ibid., 1, p. 372. It is possible that the miracles that follow are transcripts of *scedulae,* perhaps not made by Reginald himself.

82 Ibid., e.g. 128, p. 411 where a candle is made to the size of a child.

83 The cures follow the pattern familiar at healing shrines, both because of the pattern of cures inherited from the Bible, and because of the stereotype of diagnosis of illness in the period.

84 *Miracles of Godric* 177, pp. 434–35; see also *Life of Godric* 143, pp. 418–19; 176, p. 434.

85 The places named in the miracles have been identified by J. Stevenson in his edition of the *Life of Godric.* For application of these details in terms of geographical distance see R. Finucane, 'The Posthumous Miracles of Godric of Finchale', *Transactions of the Architectural and Archaeological Society,* vol. 3, (Durham, 1975), pp. 47–49.

86 *Miracles of Godric* 169, pp. 427–28.

87 Ibid., 33, p. 381.

88 Ibid., 95, p. 403.

89 Ibid., 23, p. 369.

90 Ibid.

91 Ibid., 2, p. 373.

92 William of Newburgh, *Historia* 2. 20, pp. 149–50.

93 *Gesta Pontificum* 4. p. 315.

94 Sir Frank Stenton, 'St Frideswide and her Times', *Oxoniensia* 1 (1936): 103–12.

95 Dugdale, *Monasticon Anglicanum,* 2:143.

96 Foundation charter of Ethelred (spurious), *Cartulary of the Monastery of St Frideswide at Oxford,* ed. Spencer Robert Wigram, 2 vols (Oxford, 1895), 1:2–6.

97 *Miracula S Frideswidae,* Bodleian MS Digby 177; edited with some errors Acta SS, Oct. 8, pp. 568ff.

98 Ibid., p. 569.

99 In some cases it appears that doctors had made patients worse, e.g. John Chadlington, who went to St Frideswide in order to recover from a blood-letting, *Miracles of Frideswide,* 40, p. 577.

100 Ibid., 13, pp. 570–71.

101 The days on which miracles occurred are vaguely stated in this collection, 'about this time' being fairly common.

102 *Miracles of Frideswide* 10, p. 570 and 64, p. 581.

103 Ibid., 47, p. 579.

104 Ibid., 74, p. 582.

105 Ibid., 5, p. 569.

106 Ibid., 6, p. 569.

107 Ibid., 7, p. 569.

108 Ibid., 10, p. 570.

109 Ibid., 8, p. 569.

110 Ibid.

111 Ibid., 104, p. 587. For these bottles, see Section Two.

112 John Peshall, *The Ancient and Present State of the City of Oxford* (Oxford, 1773), p. 321.

113 *Miracles of Frideswide,* 64, p. 581.

114 Ibid., 97, p. 586. Melancholy was often held to be insanity and treated, as in this case, as such; e.g. *Miracles of St Thomas* 11, 43, p. 204; Peter Damian, *De Variis Miraculosis Narrationibus* (*PL* 145. 575–76).

115 *Miracles of Frideswide* 31, pp. 574–75.

116 Ibid., 80, p. 584.

117 Ibid., 110, pp. 588–89.

118 Ibid., 105, 106, pp. 587–88.

119 Ibid., 8, p. 569.

120 Ibid, 51, p. 579: 'a clerk who fell ill while in Oxford for study'; a rare mention of a student in Oxford at this time.

121 Ibid., 9, pp. 569–70.

122 Ibid., 30, p. 574.

123 Ibid., 64, p. 581.

124 Ibid., 10, p. 570.

125 William of Herdulesley, in *Miracles of Frideswide* 11, p. 570.

126 Ibid., 102 and 103, p. 587.

127 These are all toward the end of the collection, and seem intended to form a climax to it.

128 Ibid., 74, pp. 582–83.

129 Ibid.

130 'Miracles of St Ithemar' (ed. Denis Bethell, Anal. Boll., vol. 89 [1971], pp. 421-37). Ithemar was bishop of Rochester c. 644-655; Acta SS, June 10, pp. 294–95. This was a local cult, with a collection of sixteen miracles that covered the first year after it was established in the twelfth century; St Ithemar appeared in visions and healed the sick; water poured over the foot of a cross was also given to the sick to drink at the tomb.

131 Her collect runs as follows: 'Almighty and eternal God, author of virtue and lover of virginity, grant we beseech thee, that we may be commended by the merits of St Frideswide thy virgin which were pleasing to thee, and whose life of chastity deserved to win thy favour' (Roman missal, 1527).

132 Acta SS, Oct. 8, p. 547. *Cartulary of the Monastery of St Frideswide* 2, p. 384.

133 Dugdale, *Monasticon Anglicanum*, 2:166–67.

CHAPTER FIVE

1 The collections made by Benedict and William are printed in *Materials for the History of Thomas Becket, Archbishop of Canterbury*, 7 vols, ed. J. C. Robinson. Vol 1 contains the miracles collected by William; vol 2 contains those collected by Benedict.

2 Benedict *Passio S Thomae* (Becket 2:1–19); cf. *Quadrilogus* (Becket 4:386–88).

3 Benedict, 'which I have mentioned in my account of the passion' (4. 37, p. 209); 'which we saw that he had when he fell in the church' (4. 52, p. 220).

4 Ibid., 1, prologue, p. 26.

5 Ibid., 1. 1, pp. 27–28. Three visions in which an author was urged by a saint to write is a familiar pattern in hagiography, cf. Thomas of Monmouth and his zeal for three visions before writing the *Miracles of St William of Norwich* 3. 1, pp. 116–21.

6 Benedict tells of a plot to carry off the body; Benedict 2. 26, pp. 77–78.

7 The cure of William a priest of London took place in the crypt, whence he was admitted by special permission; ibid., 1. 12, p. 42.

8 The last date mentioned by Benedict is the fire at Rochester that took place in 1177; ibid., 4. 6, p. 186.

9 William of Canterbury, *Vita S Thomae* (Becket 1:1–136); cf. also *Quadriologus* (Becket, 4:266ff).

10 More than 80 miracles appear in both accounts; these have been compared in detail in E. Abbot, *St Thomas of Canterbury*, 2:76–273.

11 Letter from Odo, abbot of Battle (*Becket* 2, note A, 48).

12 Gervase of Canterbury, *Opera Historica,* p. 230 (ed. W. Stubbs).

13 Benedict 1, prologue, p. 26.

14 William 1. 5, pp. 144–45.

15 Ibid., 4, pp. 143–44.

16 Ibid., 11, pp. 150–51.

17 Ibid., 12, 13, and 14, pp. 151–54.

18 Benedict 4. 64, pp. 229–34; William 2. 5, pp. 160–62.

19 A. P. Stanley, *Historical Memorials of Canterbury*, pp. 104–5.

20 The wall was built, according to Benedict, very close to the tomb, but with holes (shown in the miracle window) for pilgrims to touch the stone inside. He recounts moments of intense excitement among the pilgrims when the sick would put their heads or even their whole bodies inside the outer covering; in one instance it was feared that the wall would have to be taken down to extract an enthusiastic but stout person (Benedict 2. 31, p. 82).

21 Benedict was himself appointed for this work.

22 Benedict 2. 6, pp. 60–61.

23 Ibid., 2. p. 698; there are many records of the visit of Louis VII and his offerings at the shrine, but I have so far found no mention of the *Regale* until its removal by Henry VIII.

24 Ibid., 2. 53, pp. 101–2; William 3. 58, p. 311.

25 Benedict 6. 2, p. 263; William 3. 3, pp. 258–61.

26 Benedict 2. 45, p. 92.

27 For illustration of such coils, see B. Rackham, *The Ancient Glass of Canterbury Cathedral.*

28 Benedict 4. 62, pp. 226–27. In the case of Robert of Rochester, restored after being drowned in the Medway, his mother offered a thread of silver: 'Then the mother, when she had by invocation of the martyr entrusted her son to him, promising to give a thread of silver the length of her son to the martyr for the life of her child'.

29 E. E. Woodruff, 'The Financial Aspects of the Cult of St Thomas of Canterbury', *Archaeologia Cantiana,* vol. 44 (1932), pp. 13–33.

30 *Customary of the Shrine of Becket,* Brit. Lib., Additional MS 59616.

31 'The poor who were running to and fro soon worshipped him with devo-

tion, and with great reverence kissed his hands and feet. Some took rags, others cloths, and dipped them in the fountain of holy blood which flowed copiously over the floor, showing their devotion and reverence for the new martyr'. (*Becket* 3. 6. 13, p. 519). The parallel drawn by Herbert Bosham between the poor who followed Christ and those who approached the body of St Thomas weakens his testimony to the fact, but does not annihilate it.

32 William 6. 140, p. 524.

33 Benedict 2. 29, p. 138.

34 William 2. 37, p. 196.

35 Leviva, a woman with dropsy, was advised in a vision of St Thomas to drink herbs and go to sleep; ibid., 2. 4, p. 160.

36 M. R. James, *The Ancient Libraries of Canterbury and Dover*, pp. 55–62.

37 E.g. William displays an interest in the work of the doctors he professes to despise; William 4. 20, pp. 332–34. In the case of Robert of Brompton, he describes his previous attempts to find a cure: 'He had merely weakened himself by using many potions, pills, decoctions, plasters and oils'; William 2, 32, p. 187.

38 W. Urry, *Canterbury under the Angevins*, pp. 23–79.

39 William 4. 21, pp. 334–36. Simon, a mason in Derby, contracted leprosy while in the employment of Archbishop Roger of York; he applied to St Thomas for a cure, but was told in a vision of St Thomas to ask the archbishop of York to cure him since he claimed jurisdiction over him; eventually, Simon was cured at Canterbury, after acknowledging the rights of the metropolitan see.

40 Herbert of Bosham, *Libro Melorum* (*Becket* 3:546–48).

41 William 2. 91, p. 251; Benedict 3. 45, pp. 149–50.

42 The cure of William de Broc, brother of Robert de Broc, a central figure in the murder of Becket, apparently took place within a year of the archbishop's death; he had suffered from fever for four years and went to Canterbury when he heard of the cures there; after drinking the water three times, he was cured; Benedict 2. 17, p. 128.

43 Benedict, for instance, believed that the miracles that proclaimed Thomas a saint confirmed the position of Alexander III as pope; ibid., 1, prologue, p. 24.

44 Ibid., 1. 2, p. 29.

45 William 1. 1, pp. 139–43; 1. 12, pp. 151–53.

46 The archbishop had a dream while at Pontigny, in which he saw the Cardinals trying to tear out his eyes as he pleaded his cause before the Pope, *Garnier* 11.3590; Grim, *Vita S Thomae* (*Becket* 2:143). This was later elaborated into a detailed prophecy of the manner of his death, William, *Vita S Thomae* (*Becket* 1:52); Fitzstephen, *Vita S Thomae* (*Becket* 3:83); Gerald of Wales (*Becket* 2:283–84), quote from *De Vitis Sex Episcoporum Coetaneovum.*

47 William 2. 56, pp. 217–19.

48 Benedict 4. 37, p. 208.

49 William 6. 3, pp. 410–11.

50 Ibid., 46, p. 534.

51 William quotes a letter of John of Salisbury to the monks of Christ Church; ibid., 6. 57, pp. 458–63. Cf. Letter 323, *Letters of John of Salisbury*, ed. W. J. Millor and C. N. L. Brooke, 2 vols (Oxford, 1979), 2:795–99.

52 William 6. 25, pp. 437–38, for the archbishop from the East; William 6. 66, pp. 466–67 for two pilgrims from Norway.

53 David Knowles, 'Archbishop Thomas Becket, the Saint', Canterbury Cathedral Chronicles, vol. 65 (1970), p. 18.

54 See H. Delehaye, *Sanctus* for a full discussion of the meaning of 'martyr' and 'saint' in the early church.

55 E.g. seven days after the murder, a monk of Lewes saw St Thomas raised to the glory of the apostles; Benedict 3. 41, pp. 31–32. On the night of the murder, Fitzstephen says all called upon Thomas as a saint; *Becket* 3:148. Three days later, Emma, wife of Robert, a knight in Sussex, was cured of blindness, calling upon 'Saint Thomas, precious Martyr of Christ'; Benedict 1. 8, p. 38.

56 For an admirable discussion of the causes of the popularity of the cult of St Thomas and the criticism that was made of it, see B. Smalley, *The Becket Conflict and the Schools*, especially 'The Martyr'.

57 Anon. 5 *Vita S Thomae* (*Becket* 4: 199).

58 Anon. 1 *Vita S Thomae* (*Becket* 4:79); 'heremita' is used here in its original sense of 'ascetic'.

59 Grim 2, p. 442.

60 Thomas of Cantimpre (1255), *Becket* 2:292–95; Caesarius, *Dialogus, Miraculorum* 2, pp. 5–6, where the story is linked with a Mary miracle 'Priest of Only One Mass'.

61 Roger of Hoveden, *Chronicle*, pp. 11–12 (ed. W. Stubbs); Arnold of Lübeck,

Vita S Thomae (*Becket* 2:290–91).

62   Grim 2, pp. 356–61.

63   *Garnier's Becket*, trans. Janet Shirley (London, 1975), pp. 96–103.

64   Benedict 3. 31, pp. 139–40; 'I admit my disbelief'.

65   Ibid., 2. 43, p. 91.

66   Caesarius of Heisterbach records a debate held in Paris between Peter the Chanter and Master Roger, about the sanctity of St Thomas: 'Some said he was a lost soul as a betrayer of his country; others said that he was a martyr as a defender of the church. . . . For master Roger swore that he had been worthy of death, even if not of such a death, judging the constancy of the saint to be mere obstinacy. On the other hand, Peter the Chanter swore that he was a worthy martyr of God, since he had been killed for the liberty of the church.' The various opinions about Becket are admirably discussed by Beryl Smalley, *The Becket Conflict*.

67   Benedict 1. 8, pp. 37–38.

68   Ibid., 9, pp. 39–40.

69   Ibid., 10, pp. 40–41.

70   Ibid., 13, pp. 42–44.

71   Ibid., pp. 44–45.

72   Ibid., 14, pp. 46–47.

73   Ibid., 15, pp. 47–48.

74   Pope Alexander's interdict and anathema was issued on Maundy Thursday 1171; the cathedral was reopened at Easter; *Becket* 7. 7, p. 474.

75   Letter 305, *Letters of John of Salisbury*, p. 737.

76   Guernes de S-Maxence, *Vie de Saint Thomas*, 11:5885–5893 (ed. E. Walberg). English translation: *Garnier's Becket*, p. 157.

77   For an instance of a cure at Canterbury and thanksgiving there in the fifteenth century, see *Charta Antigua*, Canterbury Cathedral Archives 1303. A formal recognition of the cure was by then made in public and in writing. See Epilogue, pp. 217–18.

78   *Miracles of Benedict* 8, pp. 308–9.

79   *Miracles of William* 3, p. 162.

80   *Miracles of Frideswide*, p. 570.

81   Gregory of Tours, *De Virtutibus S Martini* 1. 2, p. 626.

82   Fitzstephen 3, p. 148.

83 Anon. 1 4, p. 78.

84 Herbert of Bosham 3, p. 519.

85 Fitzstephen 3, pp. 149–150.

86 The parallel is drawn by many writers and implicit in all accounts of the martyrdom; Benedict 1. 12, p. 43.

87 Ibid., pp. 42–43.

88 Ibid., 2. 2, pp. 58–59. Godfrid the Baker appears to have been ungrateful for the benefits received from this cure and the later cures of two other children in the family; in the spring of 1188, he is described as ringleader in a faction in which the servants of the cathedral took sides against the monks; the document is quoted by W. Urry, p. 162.

89 Benedict 1. 22, p. 54.

90 Ibid., 3. 22, pp. 134–35.

91 Ibid., 23, p. 135.

92 Ibid., 1. 17, pp. 49–52.

93 Ibid., 3. 20, pp. 131–32. A parallel could be drawn between the miracles of the blood of St Thomas and the miracles concerning the Eucharistic species. Both seem to take on a life of their own and to react to the intentions of those handling them in a visible manner.

94 Ibid., 1. 19, pp. 52–53. Dr Urry has identified him as William 'presbyter de Burenis' who held land near St Margaret's church in Canterbury; *Canterbury Under the Angevins,* p. 184.

95 Benedict 3. 40–42, pp. 145–48. The girdle of St Anselm of Canterbury had been used seventy years earlier for cures, but no lasting tradition was established; *Life of St Anselm,* pp. 163–68.

96 Canterbury Cathedral Archives, Eastry Correspondence 4. 11 and 12.

97 Claims were made in the fifteenth century in Rome that various relics from St Thomas were kept there; they were mentioned by Capgrave but later erased from his manuscript. Bodleian, MS Bodley 423, fol. 384. *Erasmus,* p. 49 (ed. and trans. J. G. Nicols).

98 Benedict 4. 47, p. 216.

99 Caesarius 2, p. 140.

100 Mansi, vol 22, Canon 232, 1049.

101 *PL* 200. 900.

102 Ibid., 901.

103 The principal feast of St Thomas is the day of his death, 29 December; his translation is kept on 7 July. For a discussion of para-liturgical texts composed from the twelfth century onwards in honour of St Thomas see Denis Stevens, 'Music in Honour of St Thomas', Canterbury Cathedral Chronicle, vol. 65 (1971), pp. 61–66.

104 William 1. 11, p. 150.

105 This is one example of the close connection between England and Sicily. The conflict between Henry II and Becket had been followed with intense interest in Sicily; in 1177, William II married a daughter of Henry II; churches were dedicated to Becket in Sicily as early as 1179. The impressive mosaic at Monreale was constructed c. 1170. E. Kitzinger, The Mosaics of Monreale (Palermo, 1960), plate 96.

106 Miracles of William 3. 29, p. 160.

107 Christ Church held a 'managium' in Norwich rendering 10 shillings a year; see Urry, p. 36.

108 Miracles of William 7. 19, pp. 289–94. The date given is 15/16 January 1172.

109 Reginald, Miracles of St Cuthbert 19, pp. 37–41. The story was told to Reginald by the canons who were ejected from Durham in 1083.

110 Ibid., 117, pp. 248–54.

111 Ibid., 125, pp. 270–71.

112 Ibid., 126, pp. 271–72.

113 Ibid., 116, pp. 261–62.

114 Reginald, Life of Godric 116, pp. 236–39.

115 John of Ford, Life of Wulfric of Haselbury, pp. 78–79.

116 Miracles of Godric 22, pp. 366–68.

117 Ibid., 52, pp. 391–92.

118 Ibid., 23, p. 378.

119 Ibid., 38, p. 382.

120 Ibid., 44, p. 384.

121 Ibid., 75, pp. 397–98; 80, p. 398; 109, p. 409.

122 Benedict 2. 52, pp. 97–101.

123 Ibid., 51, pp. 96–97.

124 Miracles of Frideswide 12, p. 570.

125 Ibid., 35, p. 575.

126 Ibid., 76, p. 583.

127 Ibid., 106, p. 587.

128 Ibid., 98, p. 586.

129 Ibid., 104, p. 587.

130 Benedict 2. 16 and 17, pp. 67–68.

131 Ibid., 65 and 66, pp. 109–12.

CHAPTER SIX

1   The priority of the Compostela manuscript is fully discussed and established by P. David, 'Le manuscrit de Compostella et le manuscrit d'Al-
cabaca', *Études sur le Livre de S Jacques attribué au Pape Calixtus II*, pp.
1–41.

2   Jeanne Vielliard, ed., *Guide du Pèlerin de S Jacques de Compostella* (Paris,
1950), Appendix 1, p. 126.

3   *Guide for Pilgrims* 9. 17, p. 118.

4   Walter Muir Whitehill, ed., *Liber Sancti Jacobi, Codex Calixtinus,* 2 vols.
Vol 2 contains the *Liber Miraculorum* 17, p. 282. Cf. R. W. Southern and
F. S. Schmitt, eds., *Memorials of St Anselm*; *De Miraculis,* pp. 196–268
and 22, p. 207, where any mention of the feast is omitted.

5   The exceptions to this are three miracles taken from the *De Miraculis,* cf.
pp. 214–15.

6   Cf. *Études,* 'Les Livres Liturgiques et le Livre des Miracles', pp. 1–73.

7   The exception seems to be *Liber S. Jacobi,* Miracle 3, pp. 263–64, where a
woman threatens to kill herself unless St James restores her son to life; but
even here it was her husband who had originally prayed to St James for a
son, and it is the son who is the recipient of the miracle.

8   Ermengaud d'Urgel (1065–1092) was captured during the wars between
Alphonsus IV and Almoravides; this miracle was recorded at Compostela
on the Feast of the Translation of St James, 30 December, *Miracles of St
James* 1, pp. 26–32.

9   Ibid., 11, p. 273. Bernard was captured in 1105 and imprisoned at Cor-
zano; he took his chains with him and deposited them at Compostela.

10 Ibid., 15, pp. 275–76. He visited Compostela later; the record of this
miracle includes the comment that he was saved by a miracle and not 'as
some say' by the swiftness of his horse 'which was valued at only 20
solidi'.

250

11 Ibid., 20, pp. 286–86. Count of Forcalquier in High Provence (1100–1110).

12 Ibid., 9, pp. 271–72. The knight finally visited Compostela with money as an offering for the rebuilding of the cathedral.

13 Ibid., 10, pp. 272–73.

14 Ibid., 16, pp. 276–78; cf. *De Miraculis* 21, pp. 196–200.

15 Ibid., 4, pp. 265–66.

16 Ibid., 21, p. 286. Guibert of Burgundy had been paralysed for 14 years; he visited Compostela with his family, but did not stay in the church; it was while he slept at the inn that he had a vision of St James and woke cured.

17 Ibid., 12, pp. 273–74. This man was cured by the application of a cockle-shell from Compostela to his throat. The shells became the symbol of the pilgrims of St James; they were at first taken from the seashore by pilgrims but soon were manufactured in lead and sold under the authority of the archbishop. They are mentioned in a sermon attributed to Pope Calixtus II, *Codex Calixtinus* 1, p. 153.

18 *Miracles of St James* 18, pp. 282–83; cf. Anselm, *De Miraculis* 23, pp. 208–9. Pons of S. Gilles, Count of Toulouse, and his brother Bertrand, sons of William III Taillefer, Count of Toulouse 1037–1061.

19 *Miracles of St James* 17, p. 278. The message was for Girinus Calvus, Lord of Donzy; he is known through documents at Savigny where he was a benefactor: 'Cartulaire de l'abbaye de Savigny', ed. A. Bernard, *Collection de documents inédits sur l'histoire de France* (Paris, 1853), nos 780, 815, 819, 830, 834, 906, 923.

20 *Miracles of St James* 9, p. 271. A bishop returning from Jerusalem in 1102, 19, pp. 283–84. A 'Greek bishop' settled in Compostela called 'Stephen'.

21 Compostela was made an archiepiscopal see by Calixtus II in 1120; U. Robert, ed. *Bullaire de Calixtus II* (Paris, 1891), p. 216. The claim to precedence over the see of St Peter in virtue of the seniority of St James among the apostles was never made good.

22 The military saints, SS Demetrius, George, and Mercury, appeared to the crusaders to encourage them against the infidel; cf. *Gesta Francorum*, p. 69 (ed. R. Hill).

23 *Codex Calixtinus* 1. 19, pp. 283–85.

24 Ralph Glaber, *Historia IV*, 7, (*PL* 142. 628–29). See also *Vita B. Morandi* in *Bibl. Clun.* 501–03.

25 Appointed by Pope Urban II, 5 December 1095.

26 For the attribution of the collection to Pope Calixtus see P. David, *Études* 4, pp. 10–11 and R. W. Southern, 'English Origins of the Miracles of the Virgin', pp. 207–8.

27 *Guide for Pilgrims,* p. 108.

28 *Miracles of St James* 18, pp. 282–83.

29 Ibid., 4, p. 265 and pp. 400–401.

30 Ibid., p. 1.

31 *Dicta Anselmi* 21, 22, and 23.

32 *De Miraculis,* pp. 196–207.

33 *Miracles of St James* 16, pp. 276–77.

34 Cf. Odo of Cluny 'Life of Gerald of Aurillac', *Bibl. Clun.* 66–114.

35 *Miracles of St James* 17, p. 281.

36 Ibid., pp. 20–21.

37 *Guide for Pilgrims* 11, pp. 122–24, 'that pilgrims of St James are to be received'.

38 J. Laford, *Les Vitraux de l'église de S Ouen de Rouen* (Paris, 1970), pp. 94ff. For a discussion of the pilgrimage routes see *Les Peregrinacions a Santiago de Compostella,* 3 vols (Madrid, 1948–1949).

39 Cf. *Codex Calixtinus* 1, pp. 48–49. Sermon including a list of diseases cured at the shrine.

40 Ibid., 'History of the Translation', pp. 289–94.

41 K. Leyser, 'Frederick Barbarossa, Henry II and the hand of St James', *EHR* 356 (1975): 481–506.

42 Cf. D. Bethell, 'The Making of a Twelfth-Century Relic Collection', *Popular Belief and Practice,* ed. Derek Baker (Cambridge, 1972), pp. 61–72.

43 'This relick was inclosed in a case of gold; of which is was stript by Richard I, but, in compensation, King John granted the abbey a mark of gold to be paid annually at the exchequer, which Henry III afterwards changed to ten marks of silver'; C. Coates, *The History and Antiquities of Reading*, p. 247.

44 *Miracles of St James* 20, pp. 14–15.

45 Ibid., 14 and 26, pp. 11–12; 18.

46 Ibid., 11, pp. 10–11.

47 Ibid., 18, pp. 13–14.

48 Dugdale's *Monasticon* 4:44.

49 Compostela is frequently named as a place to which penitents were sent to fulfil their penances. Cf. *Codex Calixtinus,* the sermon *Veneranda Dies,* pp. 144–45.

50 W. J. Moore, *The Saxon Pilgrims to Rome and the Schola Saxorum.*

51 R. Valentini and G. Zucchetti, *Codici topografici della Citta di Roma,* pp. 29–47.

52 R. Vielliard, *Recherches sur les origines de la Rome Chrétienne* (Mâcon, 1941).

53 For evidence that the Roman pilgrimage declined during the thirteenth century, see J. Sumption, *Pilgrimage,* pp. 226–27.

54 *Chronicon Monte Cassino,* p. 590.

55 Gregory of Tours *De Gloria Martyrum,* pp. 503–4.

56 These *brandea* were probably the earliest form of Christian relics; cf. Cyril of Jerusalem *Catechesis* 18. 16; 19. 7 (*PG* 33. 1071). For later use of *brandea,* cf. Guibert of Nogent *De Vita Sua* 3. 18, p. 219. They are discussed by Delehaye, *Les origines de la culte des martyrs,* p. 116.

57 Valentini and Zucchetti, *Codici topografici,* pp. 29–47.

58 Gregory I *Registrum* 6. 6, 1, p. 385; 7. 23, p. 468.

59 Sigebert of Gembloux, *Vita Theodosii I Mettensis episcopi.*

60 Gregory I *Registrum* 7. 23, p. 468.

61 *Translatio SS Alexandri et Justini* 15, pp. 286–88.

62 *Translatio S Sebastiani* 15, pp. 379–91.

63 Acta SS, Sept. 7, pp. 471–72.

64 Raynaldus *Life of St Hugh* 2, 10 (Acta SS, Apr. 3, p. 658).

65 Anselm and his companions were in Lyons, December 1103 to April 1105; Eadmer *Historia Novorum* 157–64. They visited Cluny and proceeded to Rome.

66 Anselm *De Miraculis,* pp. 238–40.

67 Anselm *Opera Omnia* 3, pp. 30–33 (ed. F. Schmitt).

68 *Vita Prima S Bernardi* 1, 10 (*PL* 185. 254B).

69 For a full discussion of the penitential pilgrimage see J. Sumption, *Pilgrimage,* pp. 98–113.

70 Bull *Antiquorum* of Boniface VIII, *Régistres* 3875 (ed. A. Thomas et al., Bibliothèque des Écoles Françaises d'Athènes et de Rome, vol. 2, pp. 922–23).

71 Gregorii VII *Registrum* (MGH Epp., *Selectae* 2, ed. E. Caspar, pp. 201–8).

72 Acta SS, April 2, pp. 665–73, for St Leo's Roman posthumous miracles.

73 Acta SS, May 6, pp. 113–43.

74 Lipsius, *Acta apost. apocr.* 1 (1891, 1–22).

75 Hubert Dauphin, *Le Bienheureux Richard*, p. 379.

76 The veneration of the holy places in Jerusalem took a more immediate turn in devotion in the fourth century under the influence of St Cyril of Jerusalem and St Helena; this is reflected in the account of the visit paid by Etheria there; *Itinera Hierosolymitana saeculi iv–viii* (ed. P. Geyer, CSEL, 1898, pp. 35–101).

77 I am indebted to Canon Edward Every for a prolonged and informative correspondence about the Holy Fire and its history.

78 The main accounts of the Holy Fire can be found in *RHC: Continuator of William of Tyre*, 2:508; *Tudebode Imitatus et Continuatus*, 3:385–87; Fulcher of Chartres, *Historia Hierosolymitana*, 3:385–87; *Gesta Francorum Hierosalem Expugnantium* 47–49, 3:524–26; Baldric of Dol *Historia Ierosolimitana* 1, 4:13; Guibert of Nogent, *Gesta Dei per Francos* 41, 4:255–56; Albert of Aquitaine, *Historia Hierosolymitana* 12, 33, 4:712–13; Anonymi Rhenori, *Historia et Gesta Ducis Gotfridi* 37, 5:513–14; and in *RHC Arm.:* Matthew of Edessa, *Récit de la Première Croisade* 25, 1:54–55, 61–63.

79 Quoted by Baldric of Dol, *Historia Ierosolymitana* 4:13.

80 The Armenians and Syrians tried to keep Easter a week after the Greeks and Latins at the Holy Sepulchre; it was agreed (in the eighteenth century) to keep it on one date.

81 Matthew of Edessa 25, p. 67.

82 Ibid., p. 63.

83 Fulcher of Chartres, *Hist. Hierosol.*, pp. 385–87.

84 Hugh of Flavigny *Chronicle* (PL 154. 247); H. Dauphin, pp. 291–92.

85 *Gesta Dei per Francos,* p. 255.

86 *The Pilgrimage of the Russian Abbot Daniel to the Holy Land,* trans. C. M. Wilson (London, 1888), pp. 74–75.

87 Letter of Gregory IX to Herard of Lausanne, 9 March 1238; Oderic Raynald, *Annales ecclesiastici* (Lucca, 1747), 2:195.

88 Cyril of Scythopolis, *Life of St Mary of Egypt*, in *Life of St Cyriacus*, ed. Schwartz (Leipzig, 1939), pp. 17–19. The Latin text best known in the West in the Middle Ages is the translation by Peter the Deacon, *PL* 72. 671–90.

89 *Miracles of St William*, pp. 280–82.

90 *Miracles of Rocamadour*, p. 165.

91 *Miracles of Godric*, pp. 54–58.

92 *The Pilgrimage of the Abbot Daniel* 3, p. 5.

93 Ibid., 6, p. 8.

94 Ibid., 90, p. 70.

95 *Codex Calixtinus* 1, lessons for 25 July, p. 44.

96 A visitor to both the Holy Sepulchre and to Rocamadour was struck by the absence of *ex voto* offerings in the former and their abundance in the latter; he thought that the offerings proclaiming miracles at Rocamadour must be frauds, since he could not believe that a local shrine had more miracles to its credit than the Holy Sepulchre; *Miracles at Rocamadour* 111. 2, pp. 288–92.

97 Hugh of Flavigny *Chronicle* (*PL* 154. 246); Dauphin, pp. 228–29.

98 *Pilgrimage of Abbot Daniel* 96, p. 93.

99 Besides the meditation of Richard of St Vannes already quoted, see Hugh of Flavigny *Chronicle* 11 (*PL* 154. 393).

100 *Saxon Chronicle* 1031; cf. William of Malmesbury *Gesta Regum* 1, p. 221.

101 Roger of Hoveden *Chronicon*, p. 26 (ed. W. Stubbs).

102 E.g. the pilgrims to St Frideswide who asked for cures before longer pilgrimages.

103 Sequence for the mass of Easter Day, *Victimae Paschali Laudes*, attributed to Wipo; cf. J. Julian, *Dictionary of Hymnology*, 2 vols (London, 1892) 2:1222–24.

CHAPTER SEVEN

1 William of Canterbury (*Becket* 1:289–90; 5:385–86).

2 Ibid., 3: 304.

3 Guibert of Nogent, *De Pignoribus Sanctorum* (*PL* 156. 621).

4 Werric, *Vita Domini Alberti Leodiensis Episcopi*, 26, pp. 139–68. The contrast between the two cults is also discussed by B. Smalley, *The Becket Conflict*, pp. 208–15.

5 *Vita Domini Alberti Leodiensis Episcopi*, p. 168.

6 Ibid., pp. 156–66.

7 William of Newburgh, *Historia Rerum Anglicarum*, 1:82–84 (ed. R. Howlett).

8 Ibid., 4, 8, p. 311.

9 Roger of Hoveden, *Chronicon* 3, p. 170 (ed. W. Stubbs).

10 William of Newburgh 1. 19, pp. 60–64.

11 Ibid., p. 61, 'he who shall come to judge the living and the dead and the world by fire'.

12 Ibid., 5. 20–21, pp. 466–73.

13 Ibid., p. 473.

14 Roger of Hoveden, *Chronicon* 4, 5.

15 Ralph of Diceto, *Opera Omnia* 2:143 (ed. W. Stubbs).

16 Ordericus, *Ecclesiastical History* 4. 2, p. 347 (ed. M. Chibnall).

17 William of Malmesbury, *Gesta Regum* 1, p. 253.

18 Roger of Hoveden, *Chronicon* 4. 24.

CHAPTER EIGHT

1 The title 'theotokos' ('God-bearer') was defended by the Council of Ephesus (431) and the Council of Chalcedon (451) as the proper title for Mary.

2 For discussion of this see H. Barré, *Prières anciennes de l'occident à la Mère du Sauveur*.

3 Bernard 'Sermon for the Vigil of the Nativity of the Lord', *Opera Omnia*, 4:216–27 (ed. J. Leclercq et al).

4 The pioneer study of medieval miracles of the Virgin is by A. Mussafia; it appeared in five parts in *Sitzungsberichte der kaiserlichen Akademie der Wissenschaften in Wien*, Phil.-hist.Kl. as *Studien zu den mittelalterlichen Marienlegenden:* part 1 in Vol. 113 (1886); 2 in Vol. 115 (1887); 3 in Vol. 119 (1889); 4 in Vol. 123 (1890); 5 in Vol. 139 (1898). His identification of two series of miracles as *HM* and *TS* will be used hereafter to identify

them. An index of Mary miracles arranged according to their incipits appears in Anal. Boll., 21 (1902) by A. Poncelet, *Miraculorum B.V. Mariae quae saec. vi–xv latine conscripta sunt.* Other studies and editions include T. F. Crane, *Liber de miraculis sanctae Dei genetricis Mariae*, a re-edition with notes of a collection printed by Bernhard Pez at Vienna in 1731; E. F. Dexter, *Miracula sanctae virginis Mariae*, an edition of Chicago MS 147, hereinafter referred to as Dexter; H. Kjellman, *La Deuxième Collection Anglo-Normande des Miracles de la Sainte Vièrge et son original latin*, edited from Brit. Lib., Royal MS 20.b.14; R. W. Southern, 'The English Origins of the Miracles of the Virgin', *Medieval and Renaissance Studies* 4 (1958): 176–216; E. F. Wilson, *The Stella Maris of John of Garland;* and P. Carter's edition of William of Malmesbury's *Miracles of the Virgin.*

5   Cf. John of Coutances, 'Miracula Ecclesiae Constantiensis', pp. 367–83 (ed. E. A. Pigeon).

6   H. Barré, 'Un plaidoyer monastique pour le samedi marial', *Rev. Bén.* 76 (1967): 375–99.

7   *De Vita Sua* 3. 13 (*PL* 156. 940). There is an English translation, *Self and Society in Medieval France, the Mémoires of Abbot Guibert of Nogent,* trans. with introduction by John F. Benton.

8   *PL* 940.

9   Ibid., 939–40. The breaking of metal bonds at shrines is a commonplace; often they were fetters bound on as a penance, which broke at the touch of a relic; cf. *Miracles of William,* pp. 12–13.

10 Herman, *De Miraculis S Mariae Laudunensis* (*PL* 156. 961ff).

11 E.g. J. S. P. Tatlock, 'The English Journey of the Canons of Laon', *Speculum* 8 (1933): 454–85; Simone Marinet, 'Le voyage des Laonnais en Angleterre en 1113', *Mémoires de la fédération des sociétés d'histoire et d'archéologie de l'Aisnel,* vol. 9 (1963), pp. 81–92.

12 E.g. the reference to 'William' as archbishop of Canterbury in 1113 remains unsatisfactory, but see Tatlock, *Speculum* 8 (1933): 463–64, and see note 20 below.

13 Herman *De Miraculis* 968.

14 Ibid.

15 Guibert 3. 7, miracle 4, cols 939–40.

16 Herman *De Miraculis* 972.

17 William of Malmesbury, *Miracles of the Virgin,* 2:369 (ed. P. Carter).

18 Herman *De Miraculis* 973.

19 Ibid.

20 Ibid., 977. The host was 'William', here called archbishop of Canterbury, and said to have been well known to the canons from his stay in Laon as a pupil of Anselm; Herman says he taught the sons of Ralph, the king's chancellor there. Cf. Tatlock, 'The English Journey', pp. 463–64. There was in fact a vacancy at Canterbury from the death of Anselm, 21 April 1109 until the appointment of William de Corbeil in February 1123. It may be that Herman substituted the name of 'William' as being a recent archbishop of Canterbury.

21 Herman, *De Miraculis* 982. Archdeacon Robert Chichester, another pupil of Anselm of Laon, was their host here; he became bishop of Exeter 1138–1155; *Gervase of Canterbury* 1. 106, 138.

22 Herman, *De Miraculis* 983. Roger, bishop of Salisbury, welcomed them, since his nephews Alexander and Nigel had been taught by Anselm of Laon. They were later bishops of Ely and Lincoln; cf. Tatlock, 'The English Journey', pp. 461–62.

23 Herman, *De Miraculis* 983. They were received by Algard, Canon of Bodmin, a pupil of Anselm of Laon, later bishop of Constance (1132–1151); *Gallia Christiana* 11, p. 874.

24 Vacandard, ed., *Livre Noire de S Ouen de Rouen*, Anal. Boll., 20 (1901), pp. 164–76.

25 Reginald of Durham, *Miracles of St Cuthbert* 35, pp. 77–78.

26 Herman, *De Miraculis* 983. It seems that this is the earliest known reference in England to Arthur as still living. The next (sceptical) reference is in *Gesta Regum*, p. 342.

27 Herman, *De Miraculis* 973: 'Spongia, crux Domini, cum sindone, cum faciali, Me, sacrat, atque tui Genitrix et virgo capilli'.

28 Guibert 3. 12. 938: 'A splendid little reliquary which contained part of the robe of the Virgin Mother and of the sponge lifted to the lips of the Saviour and of his cross. Whether it contained some of the hair of Our Lady I do not know. It was made of gold and gems and verses written on the gold told of the wonders within'.

29 Ordericus Vitalis, *The Ecclesiastical History*, 5:170 (ed. M. Chibnall).

30 Eadmer, *Historia Novorum in Anglia*, pp. 179–81 (ed. M. Rule). In this version, Ilger Bigod was given the relics by the patriarch of Antioch; in the version by Orderic, he stole them.

31 The lack of historical perspective illustrated here is notable in hagiography in general; cf. H. Delehaye, *Les légendes hagiographiques*.

32 *TS* 11; Dexter, pp. 54–57; cf. William of Malmesbury, *Miracles of the Virgin* 2, p. 375.

33 Herman, *De Miraculis* 975.

34 Bibl. Nat., MS Lat. 17491, fol. 91ᵛ.

    Herman, *De Miraculis* 975.

36 Ibid., 986.

37 Tatlock, *Speculum* 8 (1933): 458–61.

38 Herman, *De Miraculis* 975–77.

39 Ibid., 977.

40 Ibid., 980–81.

41 Ibid., 982–83.

42 Ibid., 985; cf. Guibert 941.

43 Herman, *De Miraculis* 985–86. *Miracula S Wulfstani*, pp. 43–44, mentions the slave trade at Bristol (ed. R. R. Darlington).

44 Herman, *De Miraculis* 969–70.

45 Ibid., 971.

46 Ibid., 977.

47 Ibid., 981.

48 Guibert 940–41.

49 Anselm, *Opera Omnia* 3, prayer 7, pp. 18–20.

50 Herman, *De Miraculis* 987–88.

51 Guibert 941. The carved oxen outside the cathedral still commemorate this miracle.

52 Bibl. Nat., MS Lat. 12593, fol. 45ᵛ.

53 Herman, *De Miraculis*. This water is mentioned in nearly every cure.

54 Ibid., 969.

55 The Marian works of Hildefonsus of Toledo are discussed by H. Barré, *Prières anciennes de l'occident à la Mère du Sauveur,* pp. 30–33.

56 Bartholomew, Bishop of Laon (1113–1150); *Gallia Christiana* 9:528–32.

57 Bibl. Nat., MS Lat. 12593, fols 8ʳ–10ʳ.

58 L. Bourgin, *La chaire française au XIIe siècle d'après manuscrits*, pp. 365–68.

59 Hugh Farsit, *Libellus de Miraculis Beatae Mariae* (PL 179. 1777ff).

60 Hugh Farsit wrote up his account of the miracles immediately after her death, 13 December 1143.

61 Hugh Farsit 3. 1779–80.

62 Ibid., 12. 1786.

63 Ibid., 5. 1780. The risk of damage to relics by those venerating them was not unusual; cf. *Life of St Hugh*, 2:169–70 (ed. H. Farmer and D. Douie).

64 Hugh Farsit 4. 1779. The title 'stella maris' applied to the Virgin stems from this light, by which she was held to be a 'star' to those in danger on the seas of this world.

65 The story of Mary of Egypt was introduced into the cycle of Mary legends in the West by Dominic of Evesham; the earliest surviving Greek account is in the *Life of St Cyriacus* by Cyril of Scythopolis (mid-sixth century); cf. William of Malmesbury *Miracles of the Virgin* 2, pp. 551–58.

66 Hugh Farsit 22. 1792–93. A different version of this is found in the *Miracles of St William of Norwich* 7, pp. 279–82; the comparison with the story of St Mary of Egypt is made there explicitly.

67 Hugh Farsit 1781–82. John of Salerno *Vita Odonis* (*PL* 133. 71–72).

68 In this period self-flagellation in western Europe was found among the hermits of Camaldoli; cf. Peter Damian (*PL* 145. 415–17, 1002); E. G. Forstemann, *Die christlichen Geisslergesellschaften* (Halle, 1828).

69 Hugh Farsit 1785.

70 Ibid., 1781–82.

71 *Miracles de Notre Dame de Chartres*, p. 508 (ed. A. Thomas).

72 'Theophilus', the most popular of Mary-miracles in the twelfth century; it resembles the Faust legend and has been widely discussed as such; cf. William of Malmesbury *Miracles of the Virgin* 2, p. 315 for references.

73 John of Coutances, *Miracula Ecclesiae Constantiensis*, pp. 370-72.

74 E. Alb, ed., *Miracles de Notre Dame de Rocamadour*, p. 63.

75 Ibid., Bk. 2, prologue, p. 163.

76 Ibid., p. 167.

77 Lessons for the Saturday Office of St Mary; e.g. Bibl. Nat., MS Lat 18309.

78 The cures have been analysed from a medical point of view by M. Serres, 'Étude Medicale', *Le Livre des Miracles de Notre Dame de Rocamadour*, pp. 45–95.

79 *Miracles de Rocamadour* 2. 36, p. 245.

80 Ibid., 1. 34, p. 129.

81 Ibid., 2, pp. 72–75.

82 Ibid., 22, pp. 110–12. Simon, son of Duke Matthew of Lorraine, who became a monk in 1205.

83 For a discussion of the statue of St Mary at Rocamadour see Marcel Durliat, 'Marie dans l'art du sud-ouest de la France et de la Catalogue de N.D. de Rocamadour aux XIe et XIIe siècles', *Le Livre des Miracles,* pp. 157–71.

84 Ralph Tortaire, *Hist. Litt. de la France,* vol. 13, p. 407.

85 *Miracles de Rocamadour,* Introduction, pp. 21–42. For such reconstructions of legends concerning biblical persons see Delehaye, 'The development of Legend', *Legends of the Saints,* pp. 12–59.

86 *Miracles de Rocamadour* 1, prologue, p. 63.

87 E.g. 'Domina Rupis Amatoris' 1. 2, p. 75.

88 Ibid., pp. 72–75.

89 Cf. Jacques Juillet, 'Lieux et chemins', *Le Livre des Miracles,* pp. 25–45.

90 *Ex voto* offerings in the form of models of human limbs and organs date from pre-Christian times; such offerings are still made at shrines such as that of St Joseph in Montreal. Such wax figures were discovered in the tomb of Bishop Edmund Lacy in Exeter Cathedral in 1943, see U. Radford, 'The Wax Images found in Exeter Cathedral', *The Antiquaries Journal* 29 (1949): 164–68.

91 E.g. *Miracles de Rocamadour* 1. 7, pp. 85–86.

92 Ibid., pp. 83–87.

93 Ibid., 36, pp. 132–35. The Infanta Sancha of Navarre, wife of Gaston v of Béarn.

94 Ibid., 34, pp. 128–30.

95 Ibid., 1, pp. 70–71. Illustrated in Bibl. Nat., MS Lat. 17491, fol. 103^v, 'How two young men fell in the water and were unharmed'.

96 Ibid., 2. 35, p. 245.

97 Cf. J. Jennings, *Prior Dominic of Evesham and the Survival of English Tradition after the Norman Conquest* (B.Litt. Thesis, Oxford, 1958).

98 *Miracles de Rocamadour* 1. 5, pp. 79–82; *Dominic of Evesham,* pp. 195–99.

99 Ralph of Diceto, *Imagines Historiarum, The Historical Works of Master Ralph de Diceto, Dean of London,* 2:377 (ed. W. Stubbs).

100 Benedict of Peterborough *Gesta Henrici II,* ed. W. Stubbs (RS, 1827), 1, p. 7. Henry II fell ill while in France and visited Rocamadour on 27

September 1170. This visit is not mentioned in the *Miracles*.

101 *Miracles de Rocamadour* 1. 45, pp. 148–49.

102 Ralph of Diceto, *Imagines Hist.* 1:339.

103 John Dickinson, *The Shrine of Our Lady of Walsingham*, p. 112 and plate 6.

104 Haimon, *Lettre de L'abbé Haimon sur la construction de l'église de S Pierre-sur-Dive*, 1:113–39 (ed. L. Delisle).

105 Cf. P. Alphandéry and A. Dupont, *La Chrétienté et l'idée de Croisade*.

106 Haimon, p. 124, 'but after an interval of many years'.

107 In this discussion of the *plaustra* I am indebted to M. Jean-Claude Richard's unpublished thesis for the *Ecole des Chartres*, 'Les Miracles composés en Normandie au XI et XII siècles' (Paris, 1975).

108 Chartres was the prototype for this kind of endeavour; cf. Haimon, p. 124 and *Chronique de Robert de Torigni*, p. 508 (ed. L. Delisle).

109 Haimon, pp. 138–39. The bullying tone used toward the saint is found in many miracle collections; e.g. St Faith, St Benedict, St Cuthbert.

110 Ibid., p. 138.

111 Ibid., p. 124 (Andrew) and p. 125 (Odo).

112 Ibid., pp. 131–34.

113 Ibid., pp. 129–30.

114 Ibid., p. 123.

115 Vatican, MS Regina 339, printed by A. Thomas, *Les Miracles de Notre Dame de Chartres, Bibl. de l'école des Chartres*, vol. 42.

116 Jean le Marchant, *Le Livre de Notre Dame de Chartres*, ed. M. G. Duplessis.

117 *Miracles at Chartres*, pp. 514–15.

118 'Saturday' *TM* 16; Dexter, 48–51; *Miracles at Chartres*, pp. 531–36.

119 *Miracles at Chartres*, pp. 537–38; cf. also p. 509: 'she has chosen this church to be her special dwelling place on earth'.

120 Ibid., p. 509.

121 Siege of Chartres; cf. William of Malmesbury, *Miracles of the Virgin* 2. pp. 362–66; Carter notes that the compiler of the Chartres collection adds William's version of this story to the twenty-six Mary miracles he has collected; *Miracles at Chartres*, p. 549.

122 *Miracles at Chartres*, p. 509.

123 Ibid., p. 513.

124 Ibid., p. 530.

125 Mussafia, 115, 1888, for these lists. They are discussed by R. W. Southern, 'The English Origins of the Miracles of the Virgin', and attributed to Anselm of Bury.

126 J. J. Jennings, 'Prior Dominic of Evesham and the Survival of English Tradition after the Norman Conquest', pp. 145–203.

127 William of Malmesbury, *Miracles of the Virgin.*

128 *Dominic of Evesham,* pp. 116–17.

129 *HM* 17; Crane, pp. 19–20; Dexter, pp. 31–32.

130 *TS* 2; Crane, pp. 20–21; Kjellman, pp. 141–46. For a different view of the source of this miracle, see William of Malmesbury *Miracles of the Virgin* 2, pp. 585–91.

131 Johannes Herolt *Promptuarium Discipulis de Miraculis Beate Marie Virginis,* a fifteenth-century collection of one hundred Mary miracles. This story was also told specifically of Our Lady of Rocamadour, 1. 13, pp. 97–99.

132 Bibl. Nat., MS Lat. 12593.

133 Cf. A. Wilmart, *Auteurs spirituels et textes dévots du moyen âge latin,* pp. 474–504.

134 E.g. Bibl. Nat., MSS Lat. 2333A and 2873.

135 Cf. *Scriptorium Bulletin Codialogique,* vol. 24 and 22 (1968).

136 Dominic of Evesham, pp. 178–80; William of Malmesbury *Miracles of the Virgin* 2, pp. 357–68.

137 Two Mary miracles pursue this theme of leaving Saturday as a day dedicated to the Virgin: 'Compline' and 'Saturday'.

138 *Miracles at Chartres,* pp. 528–31.

139 Ibid., pp. 517–19; Peter Damian, *De Bono Suffragiarum* 5, (PL 145. 567–68).

140 Jean le Marchant, *Miracles de Notre Dame de Chartres.*

141 Ibid., pp. 184–88; *HM* 3; Dexter, pp. 18–19.

142 Jean le Marchant, pp. 204–5; *HM* 9; Crane, p. 12; Dexter, p. 24.

143 *TS* 11; Dexter, pp. 54–55; Kjellman, pp. lvii–lviii.

144 *HM* 4; Dexter, p. 19. For a discussion of this devotion see A. Wilmart, 'Les Méditations d'Étienne de Salley sur les Joies de la Vierge Marie', *Auteurs Spirituels,* pp. 330ff; William of Malmesbury, *Miracles of the Virgin* 2, pp. 474–78.

145 Gualterus of Cluny (*PL* 156. 572).

146 *HM* 2; Dexter, pp. 17–18; Crane, pp. 4–6.

147 Cf. T. Crane, *Romanic Review* 2 (1911): 247–48.

148 The early origins of the feast in England are discussed by E. Bishop, *Liturgica Historica*, pp. 238–49. More recent discussions are found in S. J. P. van Dijk, 'The Origins of the Latin Feast of the Conception of the B.V.M.', *Dublin Review* (1954): 251–67, 428–42; R. W. Southern, 'English Origins of the Miracles of the Virgin', pp. 194–99; William of Malmesbury *Miracles of the Virgin* 2, pp. 397–406.

149 Osbert of Clare writing to Simon, bishop of Worcester *c.* 1137 sent lessons he had composed for the feast of St Anne; *Letters of Osbert of Clare*, ed. E. W. Williamson, pp. 77–79. Some chants in honour of St Anne from Burgundy in the twelfth century are edited by A. Wilmart, *Auteurs Spirituels*, pp. 46–55, but the feast was little known in the West until the fourteenth century. In the East, the feast of St Anne on 9 December to some extent replaces the Western feast of the Conception on 8 December.

150 The collection of Marian miracle stories for which he was responsible contains a large number of stories advocating feasts of the Virgin or prayers in her honour: *HM* 9, *Mass of the Virgin; HM* 12, *Hours of the Virgin; HM* 1, *Advent; HM* 5, the *Five Gaudes; HM* 2, 3, 6, 11, the *Ave Maria; TS* 15, *Conception; TS* 16, *Saturday.*

151 The Provincial Council of Canterbury in 1228 attributed the institution of the feast of the Conception to St Anselm and partly to a confusion with his nephew, Anselm of Bury, who was in fact responsible for promoting the feast.

152 *Letters of St Bernard*, Letter 174, vol. 7. 1. 388, letter to the canons of Lyons; in this protest against the feast, he mentions the vision of Elsin 'profertur scriptum supernae, ut aiunt, revelationis'.

153 Dexter, pp. 37–38. William of Malmesbury's enlarged account derives from this; cf. William of Malmesbury *Miracles of the Virgin* 2, pp. 397–406. The 'bishop' who delivers the message to Elsin is presumably St Nicholas, as Edmund Bishop suggests, a saint connected both with the Virgin and with mariners.

154 Cf. R. W. Southern, *English Origins of the Miracles of the Virgin*, p. 197.

155 The tract, 'De Conceptione sanctae Mariae' was at first attributed to St Anselm. Its authorship as a late work of Eadmer was established by H. Thurston and T. Slater, *Eadmeri monachi Cantuariensis tractatus de Conceptione sanctae Mariae* (Freiburg, 1904). He mentions that this feast was kept in former times, but does not refer to the vision of Elsin.

156 Letters 7 and 13, *Letters of Osbert of Clare*, pp. 65–68, 79–80.

157 J. B. M. Rubeis, *Monumenta ecclesia Aquileiensis*, pp. 456–57.

158 Bodleian, MS Rawlinson D. 894, fols 54ᵛ–55ʳ.

159 *Monumenta ecclesia Aquileiensis,* p. 456. The date for the institution of the feast of Aquileia is *c.* 920.

160 *Miracles de Rocamadour;* e.g. pp. 69–71. Assistance to those in danger at sea accounts for the largest number of miracles devoted to one kind of need in this collection.

161 *HM* 16; Dexter, pp. 30–31; Crane, pp. 18–19; Wilson, pp. 161–66.

162 Brit. Lib., Royal MS 5.A. VIII, fol. 148ʳ.

163 This feast was observed in the East at least from the seventh century: cf. two sermons by St Andrew of Crete (*c.* 660–740), *PG* 97. 805–843. It is found in some manuscripts of the *Gelasian* and *Gregorian Sacramentaries* before the eleventh century.

164 Honorius of Autun *Sigillum Sancte Marie* (*PL* 172. 517).

165 This feast is first described by Egeria on her visit to Jerusalem in the fourth century, and celebrated on 14 February; J. Petre, ed. and trans., 'Etherie, Journal de voyage', *Sources Chrétiennes* 51 (Paris, 1968): 206. See also a sermon by Gregory of Nyssa (*c.* 330–395), *PG* 46. 1151–82. Its introduction to the West is discussed by E. de Moreau, 'L'Orient et Rome dans la fête du 2 février', *Nouvelle Revue Théologique* 62 (1935): 5–20. See also D. de Bruyne, 'L'Origine des processions de la chandeleur et des rogations à propos d'un sermon inédit', *Rev. Bén.* 34 (1922): 14–26.

166 The date for the feast of the Dormition of the Virgin varied in the East between 18 January and 15 August; the Emperor Maurice ordered the later date to be observed (582–603). The corporal assumption of the Virgin was first asserted in the West in the writings of Gregory of Tours, who used an account attributed to Melitos of Sardis; by 847 it was a feast of the universal church, when Pope Leo ordered it to be observed with an octave. The doctrine was not, however, officially promulgated until the bull *Munificentissimus Deus* of Pius XII, 1 November 1950.

167 William of Malmesbury *Miracles of the Virgin* 2, pp. 611–19.

168 Cf. M. R. James, *The Apocryphal New Testament*, pp. 194–227.

169 Peter Damian *De Variis Apparitionibus et Miraculis* (*PL* 145. 586–87).

170 The Mary legend *TS* 16, *Saturday,* related the story of an icon in Constantinople that unveils itself in her honour from Friday to Saturday; Dexter, pp. 48–49; Crane, p. 78; William of Malmesbury *Miracles of the Virgin* 2, pp. 600–603.

171 *TS* 1, *Toledo;* Dexter, pp. 39–40.

172 William of Malmesbury's historical settings for miracles of the Virgin is examined by P. Carter, cf. *Miracles of the Virgin*, especially 2, pp. 330–33 for this miracle.

173 Peter Damian *De bono suffragiorum* (*PL* 145. 564); a slightly different version is found fifty years later as *HM* 9, 'Priest of Only One Mass'; Crane, p. 12; Dexter, p. 24; Carter 2. 490–94.

174 The versions of this miracle are summarized by H. L. D. Ward, *Catalogue of Romances in the Department of Manuscripts in the British Museum*, 3:607.

175 *Chronicle of Hugh of Flavigny*, p. 365 (ed. G. H. Pertz).

176 Gerhard, *Vita S Oudalrici*, p. 389 (ed. G. H. Pertz).

177 J. Leclercq, 'Le Texte complet de la vie de Christian de l'Aumône', Anal. Boll., 61 (1953), pp. 21–52; 'since permission had not yet been given to sing the Hours of the Blessed Virgin publicly', p. 41.

178 Bernard of Cluny *Ordo Cluniacensis sive Consuetudines*, ed. M. Hergott, *Vetus disciplina monastica* (Paris, 1726), 1, 23, p. 189. Cf. *Statuta Petri Venerabilis*, ed. G. Constable, *Consuetudines Benedictinae Variae, Corpus Consuetudinum Monasticarum* T. 6 (Sieburg, 1975), cap. 60, *De Horis Beatae Mariae in Ecclesia Infirmorum*, pp. 90–91.

179 *HM* 2; Dexter, pp. 1117–18; Crane, pp. 4–6; William of Malmesbury *Miracles of the Virgin* 2, pp. 417–22.

180 Dominic of Evesham, *Miracles of the Virgin*, ed. J. J. Jennings, p. 148.

181 William of Malmesbury, *Miracles of the Virgin* 2, p. 494.

182 Caesarius, *Dialogus Miraculorum* 7. 38. 2, pp. 49–50.

183 Ibid., 2. 42–43.

184 *HM* 6; Dexter, pp. 20–21; Crane, pp. 8–9; William of Malmesbury *Miracles of the Virgin* 37.

185 The many versions of this theme are summarized in William of Malmesbury, *Miracles of the Virgin* 2, pp. 420–22. The prayer most usually said was the *Ave Maria;* for an account of the gradual development of this prayer, see H. Barré, 'Les premières prières mariales', *Prières Anciennes.*

186 Mussafia, *Studien zu den mittelalterlichen Marien legenden*, 119 (1889), p. 59 for the lists *HM* and *TS*.

187 *HM* 1 (Hildefonsus); 2 (Drowned Sacristan); 3 (Clerk of Chartres); 6 (Eppo the Thief); 7 (Monk of St Peter's); 8 (Unchaste Pilgrim); 11 (Rustic Who Removed Landmarks).

188 *TS* 4 (Penitent Monk); 8 (Drowned Sacristan); 9 (Devil in Three Shapes); 11 (Milk); 12 (Three Knights); 15 (Leofric).

189 Dominic of Evesham, *Miracles of the Virgin*, p. 147.

190 Ibid., p. 150.

191 William of Malmesbury, *Miracles of the Virgin* 1, p. 121.

192 For the audience for legends of the saints, see R. Aigrain, *L'Hagiographie, ses sources, ses méthodes, son histoire,* pp. 78–86, 141–46.

193 Caesarius *Dialogus Miraculorum,* 7. 4. 2, pp. 5–6.

194 *TM* 17; Crane, pp. 19–20; Dexter, pp. 31–32. Nothing has been discovered about Muriel and Roger Fitzwimund.

195 *PL* 150. 935–36.

196 Henry Adams, *Mont S Michel and Chartres*, p. 289.

CHAPTER NINE

1 *Miracles of St Faith,* pp. xiv–xxxvi. The *Miracles of St Faith* were also widely known and copied in a metrical version that includes some mention of her miracles, Acta SS, Oct 8, pp. 826–28.

2 The *Miracles of St Thomas* did not attain anything like the popularity of his *Lives,* though some were copied after accounts of his *Life.* The complete surviving manuscripts of the miracles by William and Benedict are mentioned in *Becket* 1:xxx–xxxiv, 2:xxiv–xxvii.

3 E.g. the manuscript of the *Miracles of St Faith* edited by A. Bouillet, *Codex Selestadiensis,* was copied from the version of the miracles kept at the shrine in Conques and sent to a related house; *Miracles of St Faith,* p. xxiv.

4 *Miracles of St William,* pp. l–lxi; a full description of the manuscript is given by M. R. James; he dates it as *c.* 1200, 'a copy very near to the time of the autograph of the author' (p. liii).

5 *Miracles of Godric,* see preface, pp. xv–xvi, for an account of the manuscripts of the *Life;* Bodleian Laud Misc. 413ff.; pp. 102–16 contain the manuscript transcribed; it was probably written at Durham from Reginald's autograph.

6 *Miracles of Frideswide,* Bodleian, MS Digby 177.

7 Reginald, *Miracles of St Cuthbert,* pp. xiv–xviii.

8 *Miracles of St James.* For an indication of the popularity of the miracles found in the *Codex Calixtinus,* see P. David, *Études,* part 1, pp. 47–48. The *Miracles of the Hand of St James* survives in a manuscript at Gloucester, Cathedral Library, MS 1, fols 171^r–175^v, a thirteenth-century manuscript 'perhaps deriving from Reading abbey or its dependent priory at Leominster in Herefordshire'; Brian Kemp, 'The Miracles of the Hand of St James at Reading', Berkshire Archaeological Society (1961), 1.

9 These manuscripts and their diffusion are discussed by R. W. Southern, *The Life of St Anselm*, pp. viii–xxv.

10 D. Douvie and H. Farmer, ed. and trans., *Life of St Hugh of Lincoln*, 1:xlix–liv.

11 F. M. Powicke, ed. and trans., *Life of St Aelred of Rievaulx*, pp. xxvii–xxxii.

12 The complex problem of the manuscripts of the *Vita Prima Bernardi* has been discussed at length by A. Bredero, *Études sur la Vita Prima S Bernardi* (Rome, 1950); reprinted *ASOC* 17 (1961): 3–72, 215–260; (1962): 5–59.

13 Sulpicius Serverus, *Vita S Martini* 3, pp. 133–35 (ed. and trans. Jacques Fontaine). 'The account of the life of the bishop of Tours and abbot of Marmoutiers is that of a true successor of the apostles; deeds and words copy and prolong the actions and teaching of Christ in the course of his public life'.

14 *Dialogues* 2. 5, pp. 88–89.

15 Ibid., 6, p. 89.

16 Ibid., 8, pp. 91–92.

17 Ibid., 7, pp. 89–90.

18 Cf. Paulinus of Nola, *Vita de S Ambrogio,* p. 50 (ed. M. Pellegrino): 'You have asked me, venerable Father Augustine, to take up my pen to write about the blessed Ambrose bishop of the church of Milan, just as the blessed bishop Athanasius and priest Jerome wrote the lives of the holy men Paul and Antony who lived in the desert, for the venerable bishop of Tours'.

19 St Anthanasius, *Vita S Antonii* (*PG* 26. 835–978). For the influence of the *Life of St Antony* in the Middle Ages, see J. Leclercq, 'S Antoine dans la tradition monastique médiévale', *Antonius Magnus, 356–1956 A.D.,* ed. B. Steindle, pp. 229–48.

20 For the influence of the *Dialogues,* see Pierre Boglione, 'Miracle et nature chez Grégoire le Grand', *Cahiers d'Étude Médiévales* 1 (Montreal, 1974): 11–102.

21 The influence of the *Life of St Martin* is discussed in 'Saint Martin et Son Temps', *Studia Anselmiana* 46 (Rome, 1961): 175–187.

22 Desiderius, p. 1118.

23 Ibid., pp. 1133–34; *Dialogues* 2. 6, p. 89.

24 *Life of St Antony, PG* 26. 845–852; cf. Eadmer *Life of St Dunstan,* pp. 164–65, 167, 182–83 (ed. W. Stubbs).

25 E.g. the account of the death of Becket; *Becket* 3:517, Herbert of Bosham *Vita S Thomae:* 'O death of Christ, O death of the Lord Christ, that is the pattern, this is the copy'.

26 Images of light and sweet smells, with heavenly visitors clothed in white, are present in accounts of the death of saints in the early church; they are repeated in many places in this period; one instance serves for many: 'He saw in his sleep two beautiful young men whose faces and clothes shone with radiance, who strewed copiously as it were lilies, roses, and violets, and many kinds of flowers' (*Exordium Magnum Cisterciense* 1. 23, 122).

27 E.g. *Life of St Patrick;* for a detailed comparison between St Patrick and Moses, see the preface by Colgan to the *Vita Secunda* and *Vita Quarta* in *The Four Latin Lives of St Patrick,* ed. L. Bieler (Dublin, 1971), pp. 47–48.

28 *Dialogues* 2. 5, 88–89.

29 Eadmer *Life of St Dunstan,* p. 204.

30 *Life of St Anselm* 2. 31, 107–9.

31 Roger of Hoveden *Chronicon,* 2:11–12 (ed. W. Stubbs). Arnold of Lübeck *Chronicon Slavorum,* quoted in *Becket* 2:290.

32 William, 1. 2, pp. 150–51.

33 Raynaldus *Life of St Hugh of Cluny* (PL 159. 997–98).

34 The practice of composing *Lives* from hagiographical types has been discussed by H. Delehaye, *Legends of the Saints,* pp. 1–40. The practice was parodied even in the Middle Ages; cf. P. Lehmann, *Die Parodie im Mittelalter* (Munich, 1922), pp. 240–45. An excellent example of the life of a saint constructed from the minimum of evidence is given by C. W. Jones, *Saint Nicolas of Myra, Bari and Manhattan* (Chicago, 1979).

35 Samuel Johnson, *The Idler,* no. 84, eds. W. J. Bate, J. M. Bullett, L. F. Powell (London and Yale, 1963), p. 263.

36 R.W. Southern, *St Anselm and His Biographer,* p. 332.

37 'The business of the biographer is . . . to lead the thoughts into domestick privacies and display the minute details of daily life'. Samuel Johnson, *The Rambler,* no. 60, ed. W. J. Bate and A. B. Strauss, (London and Yale, 1969), 1:321.

38 *Life of St Anselm,* Bk 1, preface, p. 1.

39 Ibid., 2, pp. 107–9.

40 John of Salisbury *Vita S Anselmi* (*PL* 199. 1012, 1027, 1031, 1037).

41 John of Salerno *Life of St Odo* (*Bibl. Clun.*, p. 48).

42 *Life of St Anselm* 2. 24, pp. 99–100. Eadmer observed the tears, Baldwin the miracle.

43 Ibid., 1. 2, pp. 4–5; 1. 7, pp. 11–13; 1. 10, p. 18; 1. 21, pp. 35–36; 1. 15, pp. 24–25.

44 Reluctance of saints to perform miracles is a constant theme in hagiography; here it is used as such but also as an instance of Anselm's personal approach to such requests.

45 *Life of St Anselm* 1. 32, pp. 57–58. The use of water in which a saint had washed his hands has been noted also in the life of the non-monastic, non-clerical saint, Gerard of Aurillac, by Odo of Cluny, *Bibl. Clun.*, 92.

46 *Life of St Anselm* 2. 40, pp. 117–18.

47 The sources for the *De Miraculis* are the monks Alexander, Baldwin, and Eustace, not Eadmer.

48 *Life of St Anselm* 1. 18, p. 28.

49 Ibid., pp. 154–70.

50 *De Miraculis*, pp. 196–269.

51 Walter Daniel, *Life of St Aelred*, 2:5, 9 (ed. and trans. F. M. Powicke).

52 Ibid., 23. 32. The power of the staff of the saints is discussed by C. Plummer, *Vitae Sanctorum Hiberniae* (Oxford, 1910), p. clxxv.

53 'Letter to Maurice', *Life of St Aelred*, p. 71.

54 *Life of St Aelred* 40. 48.

55 Ibid., 61. 62, and 'letter to Maurice', pp. 76–77: 'Or again in the Life of St Martin, purer than glass, whiter than milk' (cf. Sulpicius Severus, *Vita S Martini*, 1. Ep. 3, p. 342).

56 *Magna Vita S Hugonis*, ed. and trans. D. Douie and H. Farmer. St Hugh is compared to Aaron, Joshua, Daniel (1. 12, 37), David (1. 14, 42), Elisha and Elijah (4. 6, 33; 4. 9, 44), Enoch (4. 9, 44), Jacob and Israel (4. 9, 44), John the Baptist (4. 10, 51), Job (5. 10, 132), Joseph (1. 14, 42), Nehemiah and Solomon (2. 5, 63), Samuel (1. 2, 8), Tobias (5. 2, 81), John the Evangelist (1. 13, 39; 3. 12, 124), Mary of Bethany (1. 10, 30), St Paul (2. 11, 81).

57 Ibid., 1. 7, 24.

58 Ibid., 5. 17, 199–201.

59 Ibid., 19, 223–24.

60 'Letter to Maurice', p. 78.

61 *Life of St Aelred* 35. 43.

62 Ibid., 35. 46–47; cf. *Miracles of William of York*, 2:531–43 (ed. J. Raine).

63 Ibid., 37, 44–45, and 'Letter to Maurice', p. 68.

64 The theme of the *vir dei* who is able to discern reality from falsehood is a theme well known in pagan and Christian hagiography. Apollonius of Tyana's *Life* of Philostratus and his *Life of Pythagoras* are filled with marvels in which the holy man is the one who knows what is true despite appearances. The *Saying of the Desert Fathers* further illustrate this point, and in saints' *Lives* through this period the virtue of discernment is highly prized and illustrated as miraculous.

65 *Life of St Hugh of Lincoln* 3. 12, p. 124: 'I am more astringent and biting than pepper, and when I am presiding at chapter the least thing rouses me to anger'.

66 Ibid., 3. 6, 7, 104–9. St Hugh is often represented with a swan in statues and paintings.

67 Ibid., 1, 2, 8.

68 Ibid., 3, prologue, 90.

69 Ibid., 5. 18, 216. The first account of the miracle is in Book 5, 3, p. 85, where the brother of Adam of Eynsham relates his vision; he later as a monk of Eynsham saw a famous vision of the next world. Cf. Introduction, 1. viii–ix.

70 *Life of St Hugh of Lincoln* 5. 4, 95.

71 Gerald of Wales *Vita Hugonis, Opera Omnia* 7. 1. 8, p. 108 (eds. J. S. Brewer, J. F. Dimock and G. F. Warner).

72 All references to St Bernard's writings are to the *Omnia Opera*, ed. J. Leclercq et al., vols 1–7 (Rome, 1961–1967). All references to the *Vita Prima S Bernardi* are to *PL* 185, with the additions and criticisms of the text offered by A. Bredero, *Études sur la Vita Prima S Bernardi* (Rome, 1950), reprinted *ASOC* 17 (1961): 3–72 and 215–60; (1962): 5–59.

73 *Sermon on St Martin* 5, p. 407.

74 Malachy is described by Bernard as a close friend, 'The saint was one of his closest friends' (*Vita S Malachiae*, ed. Leclercq, prologue, 3. 309). But

their actual contact was slight: Malachy visited Clairvaux on his way to Rome in March 1140 and on his return journey in August 1140; he was there in October 1148 and died there on 2 November. Mellifont was a foundation from Clairvaux, and monks passed from one monastery to the other. There are four letters from Bernard to Malachy between 1140 and 1148. Their common concern with reform drew them together and it is in the light of this rather than that of a close affection that their 'friendship' should be seen; St Bernard, *Letters*, 341, 356, 357, ed. Leclercq, 8: 282–83, 300, 301–02; a fourth letter concerning the relationship of St Malachy to the Cistercian Order is printed by J. Leclercq, 'Deux épîtres de S. Bernard et de son secrétaire', *Studien und Mitteilungen zur Geschichte des Benediktiner Ordens* 68 (1957): 228.

75 The request for the canonization of St Bernard in 1173 included the request for the canonization of Malachy, since St Bernard had regarded him as a saint; this was not acceptable and he was not included in the next request, *Epistola Tromundi, PL* 185. 626. Malachy was canonized by Clement III in 1190, *PL* 204. 1466.

76 E.g. *Exordium Magnum Cisterciense*, 4. 22, pp. 249–50 (ed. B. Griesser).

77 *Sermon on the Death of St Malachy*, 5:417–23.

78 *Life of St Malachy*, 3. 29. 66, 370.

79 Ibid., prologue, p. 307.

80 Ibid., 19. 43, 348.

81 Ibid., 31. 75, 378. At the funeral of St Malachy, Bernard used a collect for a saintly bishop in place of the collect for the dead.

82 *PL* 185. 226–415. The *Vita Secunda* (*PL* 185. 468–522) and the *Vita* by John the Hermit (*PL* 185. 531–50) rely for information on the *Vita Prima* and its sources. Other miracles of St Bernard are found in Herbert of Clairvaux *De Miraculis* (*PL* 185. 454–67) and the derivative work, *Exordium Magnum* 2. 1–20, pp. 98–118.

83 *PL* 185. 226.

84 *Vita Prima Bernardi* 1. 227–28.

85 Ibid., 230–31.

86 Ibid.

87 Ibid., 228.

88 Ibid., 231–32.

89 *Les Fragmenta de Vita et Miraculis S Bernardi par Geoffroy d'Auxerre*, ed. R. Lechat, Anal. Boll. (1932): 84–122. William's death in 1148 gives the last date at which the manuscript could have been sent to him: it is

probable that he had it in 1147 when he began to write; Hueffer and Vacandard suppose the *Fragmenta* to have been composed in 1145: G. Hueffer, *Der heilige Bernard von Clairvaux*, p. 48; Vacandard, *Vie de S Bernard*, 1. 22.

90 *Fragmenta* 19, 99–100; cf. *Vita Prima Bernardi* 1, cols 252–53.

91 Ibid.

92 Ibid., 256.

93 Ibid., 257.

94 Ibid., 256.

95 *Exordium Magnum* 2. 4, p. 101.

96 Ibid., 11, 12, pp. 104–6.

97 *Vita Prima Bernardi* 254.

98 Geoffrey records how he once tried to change a message of Bernard's which sounded to him too arrogant and how he was rebuked by Bernard: 'I did not say that, what I said was, whoever tastes this will be cured'. (*PL* 185. 315).

99 *Vita Prima Bernardi* 253.

100 *Exordium Magnum* 2. 20. p. 116.

101 Ibid., p. 117.

102 *PL* 185. 374. The *Historia Miraculorum* exists in far fewer manuscripts than the *Vita Prima*. It follows the *Vita Prima* in eleven manuscripts between the twelfth and fifteenth centuries and is found on its own in four more; Bredero, *Études*, pp. 223–24. The differences between the versions in these manuscripts are explained by A. Bredero in terms of subsequent history of each of the three parts. It is certain that the collection of each letter and the three together were all made at Clairvaux toward the middle of the twelfth century, while those involved or named were still alive and concerned in its production. There seems to be no possibility that this unique document is in any way a forgery, and it must be taken as what it claims to be, a first-hand eye-witness record of the miracles, especially the cures, effected by Bernard during his life.

103 For the chronology of Bernard's journeys see 'Tables chronologiques', *Bernard de Clairvaux*, Commission d'Histoire de l'Ordre de Cîteaux, pp. 568–619.

104 Herman Bishop of Constance; see *Gallia Christiana* 5. 45. 913; and G. Hueffer, *Die Wunder des hl. Bernhard und die Kritiker*, in *Historisches Jahrbuch* (Munich, 1889), pp. 769ff.

105 This letter is printed in *Thesaurus anecdotorum novus* 1, ed. Martène (Paris, 1717), p. 399.

106 Eberhard, *'capellanus meus'*, accompanied the bishop only on this first part of the journey; he later became a monk at Clairvaux.

107 Philip archdeacon of Liège, monk at Clairvaux after the journey; cf. *PL* 196. 1623.

108 Baldwin was abbot of Châtillon-sur-Seine, and became bishop of Noyen; cf. *PL* 186. 1371.

109 Abbot Frowin of Salmansweiler and Thierry of Vieux Camp were distinguished in the Cistercian Order, cf. Janauschek, *Originum Cisterciensium*, p. 50.

110 Alexander of Cologne, 'canonicus doctorque famosissimus', *Exordium Magnum Cisterciense*, p. 93, became a monk at Clairvaux in 1146, abbot of Grandesilvae 1149, abbot of Cîteaux 1149–1168.

111 *CHOC, Bernard de Clairvaux*, p. 605.

112 *Vita Prima Bernardi* 387.

113 Ibid.

114 Ibid., 401.

115 Ibid., 375; Philip and Gerard mention Bernard's comments on the cures they had witnessed.

116 *De Consideratione*, 3. 412–13.

117 *Vita Prima Bernardi* 388.

118 Ibid., 384. This was at Speyer after Christmas 1146, when Anselm was cured of a headache by Bernard's touch; Anselm praised the Cistercian order in his *Dialogi, PL* 188, col. 1156. He was a Premonstratentian and bishop of Havelberg 1129–1155, and Archbishop of Ravenna till his death in 1158.

119 'Philippus noster' is often referred to in these letters; he disposed of his goods before the return from Liège and became a monk at Clairvaux; it was he who later sent the complete *Historia Miraculorum* to Samson of Rheims.

120 *Vita Prima Bernardi* 384–85. This story is retold at length in some, though not all, of the manuscripts of the *Exordium Magnum*, pp. 113–15. It concerns the armour-bearer of Duke Conrad, who doubted the powers of Bernard and fell from his horse; Bishop Herman tells the story briefly in the *Historia,* Conrad of Eberbach expands it, drawing out details of a resurrection of a dead man, where Herman had described the fall of the

man from his horse as a warning not to speak against Bernard, leaving open the question whether he was dead or stunned.

121 Bernard visited Étampes and returned to Clairvaux; he went to Trier 27 March and thirteen days later to Frankfurt. *CHOC,* p. 607.

122 It seems probable that Geoffrey put together his notes about these visits after the return to Clairvaux in April 1147.

123 The liturgical setting of the miracles recurs throughout this section; it seems possible that this was the normal procedure with Bernard on his visits outside monasteries; the sick would wait until after mass and ask for his touch then.

124 Bernard's reception at Milan, for instance, had no connection with the crusade yet evoked miracles after the mass (*PL* 185. 276).

125 Letter 250, 8:147.

126 Summarized by P. Delehaye thus: 'The cult of a martyr . . . was simply arranged. When a Christian had died for the faith, the whole community which he represented before the judge and the tribunal was moved; his name was on the lips of everyone. So that he could be buried with honour, his brothers collected his precious remains. The date of such a great event remained clear in their memories and each year to commemorate him they all met with the bishop presiding before the stone that lay over the relics of the martyr'; *Sanctus,* p. 163.

127 For a thorough discussion of the increase of episcopal canonization from the ninth century to the twelfth, see E. Kemp, *Canonization and Authority in the Western Church,* especially pp. 36–55.

128 Ibid., p. 58, where the first instance of its use is quoted from the *Life of St Simeon of Padolirone,* Acta SS, July 6, p. 324. This request to Rome was for support in elevating the body and placing it in a church for public veneration.

129 E. Kemp, *Canonization and Authority,* p. 57. St Severinus and St Ulric of Augsburg are the only instances mentioned of possible papal canonization before the eleventh century.

130 Ibid., p. 59. For the claims of the papacy to canonize as of right: 'non solum est permissus, sed etiam apostolica jussione jussus', *Liber Primus Miraculorum S Adelhardi,* MGH SS 15, 2. p. 862. The 'order' given here is to translate the body of the saint. The translation was followed by cures: 'the lame, the deaf, the dumb, the crippled and the blind were at once cured'. This request was no more than an appeal for support in the process of venerating the body of the saint, as with St Simeon of Padolirone.

131 T. Klauser, *Die Liturgie der Heiligsprechung,* p. 91.

132 Text in *Le Livre de S. Gilbert,* ed. R. Foreville, pp. 33–34. English translation C. R. Cheney, *Selected Letters of Pope Innocent III*, pp. 27–28.

133 *PL* 200. 1259. The stages by which this letter passed into papal legislation are traced by S. Kuttner, 'La Reserve papale des droits de canonization', *Revue Historique de droit français et étranger,* 4th series, 17 (1938): 196–99.

134 *Becket* 1:150.

135 E.g. Jaffé Loewenfeld, *Regesta Pontificum Romanorum* 1:3848, 4112, 4219, 5677.

136 John of Salisbury, *Vita S Anselmi* (*PL* 199. 1040).

137 *PL* 200. 235.

138 Bodleian, Additional MS C.260, fol. 2^v. This is discussed by R. W. Southern, *Saint Anselm,* pp. 339–400.

139 21 April 'Sancti Anselmi episcopi Cantuariensis et confessoris', *Roman Martyrology.*

140 *PL* 199. 359.

141 *Becket* 1:150.

142 *PL* 200. 900–901.

143 Cf. F. Walberg, *La Tradition Hagiographique de S Thomas Becket*.

144 Peter of Tarantaise; cf. *Vita* by Godfrey of Hauteville, Acta SS, May 2, pp. 320–45.

145 Henry, brother of Louis VII, had been a recipient of a copy of the *Historia Miraculorum.* He became archbishop of Rheims in 1162.

146 Henry Moricotti became a cardinal in 1153 and acted as papal delegate under Alexander III in France and Germany.

147 E.g. the story of how Bernard sucked his mother's breasts with modesty (cf. Bredero, *Études,* p. 35).

148 Alan of Auxerre in the preface to the *Vita Secunda* accuses Geoffrey of lack of respect toward the great in his account of St Bernard (*PL* 185. 469).

149 For a discussion of the literary revisions see Bredero, *Études,* pp. 19–26. He also claims that in the second revision Geoffrey deliberately omitted detailed information which could be checked, to avoid having witnesses called who would be unreliable; Bredero, pp. 87–88.

150 *PL* 185. 470–523. The *Vita* was never used in the canonization process nor in the liturgical readings connected with Bernard; in fact, after the death of Abbot Pons, it fell into oblivion; only twelve manuscripts of it are known; cf. Hueffer, *Der Heilige Bernard von Clairvaux,* 1:148–49.

151 *PL* 185. 626.

152 Ibid., 627.

153 The canonization of St Hugh is clearly set out in the documents in Brit. Lib., MS Cotton Roll 13.27, a dossier containing the letters about it; this has been edited by Hugh Farmer, 'The Canonization of St Hugh of Lincoln', Lincolnshire Architectural and Archaeological Society, vol. 6 (1955–1956), pp. 86–117.

154 The documents for this process have been admirably assembled by R. Foreville, *Le Livre de S Gilbert*.

155 John II, abbot of Fountains 1211, till made Bishop of Ely 1220. William of Cornhill was also appointed by the Pope as an assessor but he had already left for the Holy Land and did not function in the proceedings.

156 *Canonization of St Hugh,* pp. 95–104.

157 Ibid., p. 102.

158 Ibid., pp. 107–08; cf. *Life of St Hugh of Lincoln* 5. 9, pp. 124–26.

159 *Canonization of St Hugh,* pp. 109–10; cf. Gerald of Wales 7. 176–77, 190–91.

160 *Canonization of St Hugh,* pp. 110–11; cf. Gerald of Wales, 7. 124–26.

161 Gerald of Wales, vol. 7, *Vita S Hugonis* and *Legenda Hugonis,* 39–42, 67–147. Both lives were presented to Stephen Langton in 1214 for this inquiry.

CHAPTER TEN

1 *Rule of St Benedict,* 73, p. 261 (ed. and trans. Justin McCann [London, 1952]). The place of miracles in the literature of early monasticism requires separate consideration. Accounts of miracles were a part of early monastic writing, though always within the context of miracle as 'sign'. For a more detailed discussion see the introduction to my forthcoming translation of the *Exordium Magnum Cisterciense* (Kalamazoo, 1982).

2 The history of the growth of the collection of miracles in *De Miraculis* has been traced by G. Constable, 'The Manuscripts of Works by Peter the Venerable', *Petrus Venerabilis 1156–1956, Studia Anselmiana,* vol. 40 (Rome, 1956), pp. 219–42. While stressing the need for a critical edition, Mr Constable says of the printed text in *Bibl. Clun.,* cols 1247–1338 (reprinted in *PL* 189. 851–954): '[it] is sufficiently accurate for most purposes of content and style' (p. 220). The text of *PL* 189 will, therefore, be used here.

3   The earliest manuscript version of the *De Miraculis* (late twelfth century) is cited by Mr Constable as MS St Omer, Bibliothèque municipale, 238 (pp. 22–23). He gives the nucleus of the collection as: prologue, col 851; miracles in Book 1: cap. 1, cols 851–53; 2. 853–54; first two parts of 8. 861–62; 22. 889–91; 23. 891–94; 25. 895–98; 26. 898–900. This includes two miracles about the eucharist; one about holy water; the virtues of the monk Gerard; the obedience of the nuns of Marcigny; and three stories about the deaths of sinners. The later additions concern demonic apparitions and the power of the monks of Cluny to oppose them, a theme prevalent in Cistercian miracles from the point of view of Cîteaux and Clairvaux.

4   *De Miraculis* 2. 3–9. 914–20; 11. 921–22. Dom Séjourne thought this the nucleus of the work, *Dictionnaire de Théologie Catholique*, ed. Vacant and Mangenot (Paris, 1933), 12: 2078; Mr Constable has shown that it was a separate work, added to the *De Miraculis* later ('Peter the Venerable, p. 227).

5   G. Constable, 'Peter the Venerable,' p. 221; they are regarded here as not belonging to the final text of *De Miraculis,* though attributed to Peter the Venerable by later writers.

6   The invasion of Cluny by Pons took place in 1125, his trial and condemnation 1125–1126.

7   *De Miraculis* 2. 12–13. 921–26.

8   Peter the Venerable was in Rome in 1125–1126 in connection with the schism of Pons. He was ill and recovered at the monastery of Sauxillanges before his return to Cluny; ibid., 1. 6. 858–61.

9   Ibid., 8. 862–71.

10 His visions at the eucharist were typically twelfth century: Christ on the Cross, with Mary Magdalene and Mary the Virgin; he also wept copiously. Cf. *De Miraculis* 864.

11 E.g. Ibid., 1. 15. 980–81, for the quotation from St Hugh of Cluny's vision on Christmas Eve.

12 Ibid., 8. 869. For a discussion of the rewards in heaven in the *De Miraculis,* see Denise Bouthillier, 'L'Univers religieux de Pierre le Venerable d'après le De Miraculis', pp. 387–415.

13 *De Miraculis* 1. 20. 886–88.

14 E.g. ibid., 12. 876.

15 Ibid., 22. 889–91.

16 Ibid., 11. Bernard le Gros. The seven stories of apparitions of the dead included by Peter the Venerable mark a departure from the tradition of monastic miracles and have much in common with Cistercian miracles. The continual references to the violence and conflict in both society and the cloister continue the picture seen in the miracles of St Benedict at Fleury.

17 'The Date and Character of Letter 28', *The Letters of Peter the Venerable*, ed. G. Constable, 2: 270–74, Appendix E. The text of Letter 28 is 1:52–101.

18 Ibid., 2:274: 'the position of Letter 28, which is well attested by the manuscripts, points to a date some time in the 1130s'.

19 The date of the *De Miraculis* cannot be reduced to any one year; the additions and redactions no doubt occupied many years. The separate existence of the *Life of Matthew of Albano* c. 1139 is attested in Letter 129 (ed. G. Constable, 2:184 and note).

20 Robert de Châtillon, Bernard's cousin, was frequently called his 'nephew' because of the disparity of ages. For Bernard's account of his defection, see Letter 1, *Opera Omnia*, 7:1–11 (ed. Leclercq).

21 *Vita Prima S Bernardi* (PL 185. 255–56).

22 *De Miraculis* 1. 13. 876–77.

23 Ibid., 877.

24 Ibid., prologue, 851: 'In order not to keep the reader in suspense any longer, I will begin with the most important section, that is, what I have been able to hear about the miracles connected with the body of the Lord which have been done in modern times'.

25 Ibid., 1. 1, 2, 3. 851–56. The miracle of the bees and the host appears in many forms, including versions by Herbert of Clairvaux (*PL* 185. 1374); Gerald of Wales, *Gemma Ecclesiastica*, in *Opera Omnia* 2:42–43; Caesarius of Heisterbach, *Dialogus Miraculorum* 9. 8. 2, pp. 172–73 (ed. J. Strange). The vanishing host story was told to Peter the Venerable by the bishop of Clermont and appears in Caesarius 2. 5. 1, pp. 64–67, on the authority of Bishop Conrad of Halberstadt. The third story is also well-known elsewhere, and so also is the story of the man sustained by the host when trapped underground (Peter the Venerable 2. 2. 911–12); it is found in Peter Damian, Caesarius, and later *exemplaria*.

26 Matthew was born c. 1085 near Rheims, studied under Anselm of Laon, became a canon, then monk and later prior at S Martin-des-Champs, c. 1110. He assisted Peter the Venerable in his reforms at Cluny 1122–

1123, defended Peter the Venerable during the trial of Pons in Rome 1126, was made cardinal bishop of Albano by Pope Honorius II, died Christmas Day 1135; Ursmer Berlière, 'Le cardinal Matthieu d'Albano (*c.* 1085–1135)', *Rev. Bén.* 18 (1901): 113–140; 280–303. Other studies are listed by G. Constable, *Letters of Peter the Venerable,* 2:96–97.

27 As cardinal, Matthew accomplished various missions for Honorius II and Innocent II; it was his influence which prevailed upon Cluny to oppose the anti-pope Anacletus. Cf. U. Berlière, pp. 134–36.

28 E.g. *De Miraculis* 1. 6. 858–59.

29 The number of apparitions of the dead in the *De Miraculis* has been noted above; this seems to be a special interest of Peter the Venerable, possibly inherited from his predecessor Saint Hugh. For an instance of liberal alms to Cluny in payment for prayers for the dead, see C. J. Bishko, 'Liturgical Intercession at Cluny for the King-Emperors of Léon', *Studia Monastica* 3 (1961): pp. 53–76.

30 *De Miraculis* 2. prologue. 907.

31 The 'cure' effected by Peter the Venerable himself is typical of his interests; Ibid., 1. 6. 858–60; this is a psychological cure for delusions, in which a monk persecuted by a demon in the shape of a horse was gradually liberated after confession to the abbot.

32 *De Miraculis* by Herbert of Clairvaux (*PL* 185. 1271–1384). Herbert was born in Spain, became a monk at Clairvaux under Abbot Fastred (1157–1162). He became archbishop of Sardinia later.

33 Conrad of Eberbach *Exordium Magnum Cisterciense* (ed. Bruno Griesser). Griesser suggests that Conrad, a monk of Clairvaux, wrote the first five books under Abbot Garnerius (1186–1193) and that he wrote the last two books at Eberbach, from 1206 to 1221. The relationship between Herbert's work and that of Conrad is set out in related columns by Griesser, pp. 36–37. The authorship of this work is only tentatively proposed.

34 Born at Cologne *c.* 1180, Caesarius became a novice at Heisterbach *c.* 1198; he was master of novices and prior and died 1220.

35 Griesser, however, suggests that there were originally one hundred and fifty: 'Herbert von Clairvaux und sein Liber miraculorum', *Cistercienser-Chronik*, vol. 54 (1947), N F 2.

36 Henry, seventh abbot of Clairvaux 1176–1179; Marilier, 'Catalogue des abbés de Cîteaux pour le XII siècle', *Cistersienser-Chronik*, vol. 55 (1948), p. 37.

37 Alexander of Cologne, converted 1146; abbot of Grandisilvae, 1149; abbot of Cîteaux 1168–78. *Vita Prima S Bernardi*, (*PL* 185. 348); Herbert *De Miraculis* 1331; Conrad 1. 33, p. 93.

38 Manual labour for monks was a central topic of dispute between the Cistercians and their critics; the materials on both sides of the debate are summarized by C. Holdsworth, 'The Blessings of Work: A Cistercian View', *Sanctity and Secularity,* ed. Derek Baker (Oxford, 1973), pp. 59–77.

39 For the cult of the Virgin at Clairvaux, see J. Leclercq, 'Marie Reine dans les sermons de Saint Bernard', *Collectanea* 26 (1964): 265–76.

40 Herbert, *De Miraculis* 1. 1. 1273–76.

41 *Exordium Magnum Cisterciense* 3. 13, pp. 176–79.

42 Caesarius, *Dialogus Miraculorum* 1. 17. 1, p. 24. The story is the same as that in Herbert and Conrad, but in place of St Elizabeth, Caesarius identifies the third saint as St Anne.

43 *Vita Prima S Bernardi (PL* 185. 327). Herbert *De Miraculis* 2. 18. 1327–28. *Exordium Magnum* 2. 13, pp. 106–8.

44 Gerald of Wales, *Speculum Ecclesiae,* in *Opera Omnia,* 4:104ff. Discussed by M. B. Hareau, 'Mémoire sur les récits d'apparitions dans les sermons du moyen âge', *Mémoires de l'Institute de France* (Paris, 1876) 28:239–64. It was later used by James of Vitry, *Exampla ex Sermonibus Vulgaribus* 31. 12–13 and note, pp. 145–46 (ed. T. Crane).

45 James of Vitry says Serlo showed the burn when he told the story during the lifetime of James himself (*Exempla ex Sermonibus* 31. 13).

46 See M. B. Hareau, *Mémoire* for other instances. Physical sensations in a person who dreams of hell are attested in Bede in the vision of Drythelm: Bede, *Ecclesiastical History,* p. 499.

47 Discussed in Hareau, *Mémoire,* pp. 242–45.

48 *Exordium Magnum* 2. 3, p. 100.

49 Ibid., 4, p. 101.

50 Herbert *De Miraculis* 1. 22. 1304; *Exordium Magnum* 4. 15, p. 240.

51 Herbert *De Miraculis* 1. 17. 1292–93; *Exordium Magnum* 4. 16, pp. 241–42.

52 *Vie de Christian d'Aumône,* p. 25.

53 Cf. the Eastern hermit, Symeon, who settled at Trier; he refused with indignation to believe that such instruction given him in a dream came from God; Eberwine, *Vita S Symeonis* (Acta SS, June 1, pp. 89–101). For further discussion of this contrast between the Cistercians and the Desert Fathers, see my article, 'The Desert Myth', pp. 183–200.

54 *Exordium Magnum* 1. 6, pp. 54–55. Conrad cites the silence of Odo of

Cluny as an example of true monastic behaviour; cf. *Vita S Odonis*, cap. 32, *Bibl. Clun.* 37–38.

55 The poverty practised by St Stephen Harding was noted especially by both Herbert and Conrad: Herbert *De Miraculis* 2. 23, 24. 1332–33; *Exordium Magnum* 1. 22–28, pp. 80–84.

56 Herbert *De Miraculis* 3. 14. 1365–66; *Exordium Magnum* 3. 21, pp. 199–200.

57 Herbert *De Miraculis* 1. 15. 1291–92; *Exordium Magnum* 3. 18, pp. 190–94.

58 Conrad tells a story of St Bernard being embraced by the Crucified (*Exordium Magnum* 2. 7, pp. 102–3) a theme later illustrated in art. The emotional involvement of the Cistercians in prayer especially with the Virgin Mary reached almost pathological extremes; cf. A. van Iterson, 'L'Ordre de Cîteaux et le coeur de Marie', *Collectanea* 20 (1958): 291–312.

59 Conrad and Herbert both have stories of the punishment meted out to those who do not confess fully; Caesarius of Heisterbach has stories in this category throughout his work, and especially in the first sections, *De Conversione, De Contritione, De Confessione,* and *De Tentatione.*

60 Two stories of the visions of a Cistercian novice at Stratford Langthorne illustrate this theme. In one it is promised that a dead Cistercian will go to heaven as soon as the litany has been said over his body; in the other, that no Cistercian will stay more than thirty days in purgatory; London, Lambeth Palace, MS 51, fol. 123^r, printed by C. Holdsworth, 'Eleven Visions connected with the Cistercian Monastery of Stratford Langthorne', *Cîteaux T.*, vol. 13 (1962), pp. 196–212.

61 Caesarius *Dialogus Miraculorum* 7. 59. 2, pp. 79–80.

62 *Exordium Magnum* 2. 5, p. 101.

63 Ibid., 3. 22, pp. 201–03.

64 Ibid., 1. 9: 'what are we about, into what negligence, alas, is our monastic observance falling, to what vices does it lean?'

65 Peter Damian *De Perfectione Monachorum* (*PL* 145. 291–94).

66 *Exordium Magnum* 1. 10, p. 61.

67 His first chapters are based on the *Exordium Parum* and the *Carta Caritatis;* cf. *Les plus anciens textes de Cîteaux,* ed. J. Bouton and J. Van Damme (Achel, 1974) for the latest work on these texts.

68 *Exordium Magnum* 1. 10, p. 61.

69   The stories given about the founders of the Order by Herbert and Conrad are extremely selective; cf. ibid., 1, for Alberic, Stephen, Fastred.

70   The prologue makes the continuity clear; ibid., prologue, p. 48.

71   The Cluniac abbots are presented as reformers and implicitly compared with the new reformers, the Cistercians; ibid., pp. 54–60.

72   Conrad refers to Anselm of Havelberg and his account of early monasticism; ibid., 3, p. 51; *Dialogus Anselmi* 1. 10 (*PL* 188. 1156).

73   *Le Livre de St Gilbert de Sempringham,* ed. R. Foreville (Paris, 1943), pp. 42–82; *Life of St Romuald* by Peter Damian (*PL* 144. 953–1008); *Life of St Stephen* (*PL* 204. 1045–72).

74   *De Miraculis* 2. 28. 943–45.

75   Ibid., 29. 946–49.

76   Caesarius *Dialogus Miraculorum* 3. 22. 1, p. 138; 4. 62. 1, p. 228; 7. 59. 2, pp. 79–80; 12. 47 and 49. 2, pp. 354–55.

77   'Wulfric of Haselbury', ed. M. Bell, Somerset Record Society, vol. 47 (1932); *Life of St Godric,* ed. J. Raine, Surtees Society, vol. 20 (1845); *Life of St Symeon* (Acta SS, June 1, pp. 89–101).

78   John, abbot of the Cistercian abbey of Ford in Devon, founded 1136 from Waverley.

79   Reginald, a monk of the Benedictine house at Durham.

80   Eberwine, a Benedictine of Trier.

81   *Chronicle of Jocelyn of Brakelond,* p. 106 (ed. H. E. Butler).

82   Ibid., pp. 106–9.

83   Ibid., p. 110.

84   Ibid., p. 111.

CHAPTER ELEVEN

1   William of Malmesbury *Gesta Regum* 2. 131, p. 208.

2   Roger of Hoveden 1. 127.

3   Gervase of Canterbury *Opera Historica*, pp. 248–49 (ed. W. Stubbs).

4   The model of classical historians for the Middle Ages is discussed by R. W. Southern, 'Aspects of the European Tradition of Historical Writ-

ing: 1. The Classical Tradition from Einhard to Geoffrey of Monmouth', *TRHS,* 5th ser. (1970): 1–35.

5   Robert of Torigny, *Chronicle,* preface (*PL* 160. 421).

6   Orderic, *Historiae Ecclesiasticae* 9. 190.

7   *Historia Novella,* p. 77.

8   Orderic, books 1, 2.

9   Ibid., 7. 108.

10 Robert of Torigny (*PL* 160. 421–22).

11 Ralph of Diceto, *Abbreviationes Chronicorum,* pp. 37–55 (ed. W. Stubbs).

12 'Dunstable Chronicle', *Annales Monasticii,* 3:3 (ed. H. R. Luard).

13 'Waverley Chronicle', *Annales Monasticii,* 2:129; 'the years of the Incarnation are counted as beginning from the day of the birth of the Lord'.

14 Orderic 4–7.

15 Ralph of Diceto, pp. 74–75, 76, 85.

16 *Gesta Francorum* 69; St Mercurius and St Demetrius are represented in Greek iconography as a Christianized version of Castor and Pollux. St George was honoured as the patron of knights.

17 E.g. Ibid., 65.

18 Fulcher of Chartres suspected that this 'discovery' was a fraud: 'he found the lance which had perhaps been hidden by deceit' (*PL* 155. 843).

19 Peter Bartholomew was from Provence, a pilgrim of repute as a visionary. He had five visions of St Andrew and was shown the place where the lance was buried; he communicated this to Raymond d'Aguilers. Peter later offered to confirm the validity of the lance by walking through fire, an ordeal from which he emerged injured and later died (ibid., 592ff).

20 Such was the opinion of several men at the time; e.g. Ralph of Caen, *Gesta Tancredi,* 3:677 (*RHC*).

21 Ibid. p. 678.

22 Arnulf, bishop of Martirano, later patriarch of Jerusalem.

23 *Gesta Tancredi,* p. 678.

24 Adhémar, bishop of Le Puy, nevertheless carried the lance into battle for that part of the army under the Count of St Gilles (*Gesta Francorum,* p. 68).

25 The Holy Lance was among the imperial treasures at Constantinople in the tenth century; in 1241, it was given to St Louis and preserved in the Saint-Chapelle. Other parts of the lance are claimed among the imperial insignia of the Holy Roman Empire to the present day a special feast of the Holy Lance was kept in Germany on the Friday after Easter Day.

26 *Gesta Francorum,* pp. 57–58; Raymond d'Aguilers (*PL* 155. 612).

27 Orderic 7. 214.

28 William of Malmesbury, *Vita Wulfstani.*

29 William of Newburgh 2. 20. 150.

30 *Gesta Pontificum* 4. 172, pp. 308–9.

31 *Gesta Regum* 2. 111, pp. 112–16.

32 Ibid., 268; 448–49.

33 Ibid., 201–26; 343–81.

34 Ibid., 193–203.

35 Ibid., 204, 351.

36 'Annals of Margam', *Annales Monastici*, 1:15.

37 'Annals of Winchester', *Annales Monasticii*, 1:74–76.

38 William of Newburgh 1. 19. 60–64.

39 Ibid., 28. 86.

40 Orderic 4. 237–51.

41 William of Newburgh 5. 22–25.

42 Walter Map, *De Nugis Curialium.*

43 Halley's comet appeared ten times after 1066, the latest appearance being 1910. It was observed and recorded widely in 1066 and almost universally linked with the Norman Conquest; for a list of over twenty instances, see F. A. Freeman, *The History of the Norman Conquest of England,* 5 vols (Oxford, 1869), 3:640–44, note M.

44 *Topographia Hibernica* 21–27. 108–113.

45 William of Newburgh 1. 28. 85.

46 E.g. 'Annales de Theokesberia', *Annales Monasticii*, 1:46.

47 John of Worcester, *Chronicle 1118–1140* (ed. J. R. H. Weaver, *Anecdota Oxoniensia* [Oxford, 1908]).

48 William of Newburgh, 1. 27. 82–84.

49 Ibid., 5. 33. 85.

50 Cf. Marc Bloch, 'La Vie de S Édouard le Confesseur par Osbert de Clare', Annal. Boll., vol. 41 (1920), pp. 5–131.

51 Roger of Hoveden, p. 159.

52 Discussed by P. Carter (William of Malmesbury *Miracles of the Virgin* 2. 363).

53 *Miracles of St Faith* 1. 1, pp. 5ff.

54 *Miracles of Frideswide* (Acta SS, Oct. 7, p. 589).

55 Alexander was a monk of Christ Church, Canterbury, and a member of the household of Archbishop Anselm after his return from exile in 1100. He is accepted as the author of the *Miracula S Anselmi;* see *Memorials of St Anselm*, p. 20.

56 For Eadmer's version of the story see *Vita Anselmi* 2. 53, p. 131; for Alexander's two versions see *Memorials of St Anselm*, pp. 245–46.

57 *De Miraculis* 35, pp. 227–30.

58 Ibid., 22, p. 200; 28, p. 215; 32, p. 221. The changes in detail in the story of the simoniac bishop who was unable to say the words *Spiritus Sanctus* vary considerably between the two versions by Alexander, see *Memorials of St Anselm* 22–23 for a discussion of this.

59 Ibid., 46, 47, 48, pp. 249–57.

60 *Miracles of Rocamadour,* Introduction, pp. 22–24. 'St Amadour' appears to have derived his name from the place and not vice versa.

61 Orderic 5. 9, p. 171.

62 Eadmer *Historia Novorum in Anglia*, pp. 179–81 (ed. M. Rule).

63 Guibert of Nogent *De Pignoribus sanctorum* (PL 156. 607–80).

64 The theme of 'Furta Sacra' has recently been discussed by Patrick Geary in his book of that name. His handlist of relic thefts for 800–1100 makes clear how frequent were instances of this kind of 'authentication' of relics (pp. 183–90).

65 *Miracles of Benedict.* A thorough discussion of the evidence for the translation of the relics of St Benedict is found in P. Meyvaert, 'Peter the Deacon and the tomb of St Benedict', p. 65. See also P. Geary, pp. 145–49.

66 Walter Goffart, 'Le Mans, St Scholastica and the Literary Tradition of the Translation of St Benedict', *Rev. Bén.* 77 (1961): 107–41. For more recent discussion, see *Studia Monastica* 1980.

67   *Miracles of Benedict,* BR. 7. 15, p. 274.

68   *Miracles of Chartres,* pp. 537–38.

69   Gregory of Tours, *Liber Vitae Patrum, Miracula et opera minora,* pp. 662–63.

70   Hugh Farsit, *Miracles of Our Lady of Soissons (PL* 179. 1778).

71   *Miracles of Chartres,* p. 507.

72   For a list and discussion of the various versions of this legend, see William of Malmesbury *Miracles of the Virgin* 2. 527–29.

73   *Vita S Odonis* 1. 32 (PL 133. 67ff); *Exordium Magnum,* pp. 54–55.

74   E.g. the story of a pilgrim restored to life by St James, when repeated by William of Malmesbury, is attributed to the power of the Virgin; cf. R. W. Southern, *The Making of the Middle Ages,* pp. 240–41, for this and other examples.

75   This aspect of humour found its extreme expression in the 'Fools for Christ' in both East and West; cf. John Saward, *Perfect Fools* (Oxford, 1980).

76   John of Salerno, *Life of St Odo (Bibl. Clun.* 35).

77   John of Ford, *Life of Wulfric of Haselbury* (ed. M. Bell, Somerset Record Society, vol. 47 (1932), p. 123).

78   *Gesta Pontificum* 5. 190, p. 336.

79   *Miracles of St Faith* 1. 16, pp. 51–53.

80   Ibid., 19, pp. 55–57.

81   Ibid., 21, pp. 58–59.

82   Ibid., 22, pp. 59–60.

83   Ibid., 20. pp. 57–58.

84   Ibid., 2. 10, p. 118; 1. 17, p. 53; 1. 23, pp. 60–62; 1. 24, p. 60.

85   Ibid., 1. 23, p. 60.

86   *Becket* 2. 4. 38, 209.

87   Ibid., 3. 51. 153–55.

Bibliography

PRIMARY SOURCES

ABELARD, PETER. *Commentaria in Epistolam Pauli ad Romanos.* Edited by E. M. Buytaert. Turnholt: 1969.

—. *Theologia Christiana* and *Introductio ad Theologiam. PL* 178.

Acta Sanctorum Ordinis S Benedicti. Edited by L. d'Achery and J. Mabillon. 9 vols. Paris: 1668–1701.

ADAM OF EYNSHAM. *Magna Vita S Hugonis.* Edited and translated by D. L. Douie and H. Farmer. 2 vols. London: 1961–1962.

ADAM OF PERSIÈGNE. *Mariale. PL* 211. 109–97.

ADELARD OF BATH. *Quaestiones Naturales.* Edited by M. Muller. Munster: 1934. English translation by H. Gollancz. London: 1920.

AELRED OF RIEVAULX. *De Oneribus. PL* 195. 361–502.

—. *Vita Aedwardi Regis. PL* 115. 740ff.

ALAN OF LILLE. *Summa de arte praedicatoria. PL* 210.109–97.

ALBERTUS MAGNUS. *Opera Omnia.* Edited by A. Borgnet. 38 vols. Paris: 1890–1899.

Anglo-Saxon Chronicle. Revised, edited, and translated by D. Whitelock, D. C. Douglas, and S. I. Tucker. London: 1961.

Annales de Margam. Edited by H. R. Luard. London: RS, 1864.

ANSELM OF CANTERBURY. *Opera Omnia.* Edited by F. S. Schmitt. 6 vols. Edinburgh: 1946–1961.

ANSELM OF HAVELBERG. *Dialogues.* Edited and translated by G. Salet. *Sources Chrétiennes,* 118. Paris: 1966. (Also in *PL* 188. 1156ff.).

ANSELM OF LAON. *Glossa Ordinaria.* In *Biblia Sacra cum Glossa Ordinaria.* Paris: 1617.

AQUINAS, THOMAS. *De Potentia*. Edited by P. M. Pession. Quaestiones Disputatae, vol. 2. Turin and Rome: 1949.

—. *Opera Omnia, jussu edita Leonis XIII P.M. cura et studio fratrum Praedicatorum*. 15 vols. Rome: 1882–1930.

ATHANASIUS. *Vita S Antonii*. PG 26. 835–978.

AUGUSTINE OF HIPPO. *De Civitate Dei*. Edited by B. Dombart and A. Kaib. 2 vols. CCSL. Turnholt: 1955. (Also in *PL* 41).

—. *De Cura Pro Mortuis Gerenda*. Edited by J. Zycha, CSEL. Vienna: 1900. (Also in *PL* 40).

—. *De Doctrina Christiana*. Edited by J. Martin. CCSL. Turnholt: 1962. (Also in *PL* 34).

—. *De Genesi ad litteram*. Edited by J. Zycha.CSEL. Prague: 1894. (Also in *PL* 34).

—. *De Trinitate*. Edited by W. J. Mountain and F. Glorie. 2 vols. CCSL. Turnholt: 1968. (Also in *PL* 42).

—. *De Utilitate Credendi*. Edited by J. Zycha. CSEL. Prague: 1891. (Also in *PL* 42).

—. *Letters*. Edited by A. Goldbacher. 4 vols. CSEL. Vienna: 1895–1923. (Also in *PL* 40).

—. *Sermons*. PL 38–39.

BALDWIN OF FORD. *Liber de Commendatione Fidei*. PL 204.

BARDON. *Vita et Miracula S Anselmi*. Acta SS, Mar. 2, p. 655. (Also in *PL* 148. 907–40).

BEDE. *Ecclesiastical History of the English People*. Edited by B. Colgrave and R. A. B. Mynors. Oxford: 1969.

—. *Vita Metrica S Cuthberti*. PL 94. 575–96.

—. *Vita Sancti Cuthberti Prosaica*. Edited by B. Colgrave. In *Two Lives of St Cuthbert*. Cambridge: 1940.

BENEDICT OF PETERBOROUGH. *Chronicles of the Reigns of Henry II and Richard I, A.D. 1169–1192, known commonly under the name of Benedict of Peterborough*. Edited by W. Stubbs. 2 vols. London: RS, 1867.

—. *Miracula S Thomae Cantuariensis*. In *Becket*. Vol. 2, pp. 21–281.

BERNARD OF CLAIRVAUX. *Opera Omnia*. Edited by J. Leclercq et al. Rome: 1956.

Biblia Sacra cum Glossa Ordinaria. J. Keerberge. 1617.

Bibliotheca Cluniacensis. Edited by M. Marier. Paris: 1614.

BIELER, L., ed. *The Irish Penitentials.* Scriptores Latini Hiberniae, 5. Dublin: 1963.

BOUTON, J., and J. VAN DAMME. *Les Plus Anciens Textes de Cîteaux.* Achel: 1974.

BUDGE, W. *Miracles of the Blessed Virgin Mary.* London: 1933.

BURCHARD OF WORMS. *Decretorum Libri.* 20. *PL* 140.

CAESARIUS OF HEISTERBACH. *Dialogus Miraculorum.* Edited by J. Strange. 2 vols. Cologne: 1851.

Capitula de miraculis et translationibus S Cuthberti. In *Opera Omnia* by Symeon of Durham. Edited by T. Arnold. London: RS, 1885.

CHALCIDIUS. *Timaeus a Calcidio translatus commentarioque instructus.* Edited by J. H. Waszink. In *Plato latinus.* Vol. 4. London and Leiden: 1962.

Chanson de Sainte Foy. Edited by P. Alfaric. Paris: 1926.

Chronicon Abbatiae de Evesham ad annum 1418. Edited by W. D. Macray. London: RS, 1863.

Chronicon Monasterii Casinensis. MGH SS, 7.

CONRAD OF EBERBACH. *Exordium Magnum Cisterciense.* Edited by B. Griesser. Rome: 1961.

Consuetudines Benedictinae Variae. Edited by G. Constable. Corpus Consuetudinum Monasticarum T, 6. Sielburg: 1975.

CRANE, T. F. *Liber de miraculis sanctae Dei genitricis Mariae.* Ithaca: 1925.

CYRIL OF SCYTHOPOLIS. *Life of St Cyriacus. PL* 73. 671–90.

DANIEL, RUSSIAN ABBOT. *Vie et pèlerinage.* In *Itinéraires Russes en Orient* (Paris: 1889). Edited by Khitrowo. English trans.: Pilgrim Text Society, vol. 4. London: 1895.

——. *Pilgrimage of Daniel.* Translated by C. W. Wilson. London: 1888.

De Mirabilibus Sacrae Scripturae. PL 35. 2151–220.

DESIDERIUS. *Dialogi de Miraculis Sancti Benedicti.* Edited by G. Schwartz and A. Hofmeister. MGH, 32, 1934.

Deuxième Collection Anglo Normande des miracles de la Sainte Vierge et son original latin. Edited by H. Kjellman. Paris and Uppsala: 1922.

DUGDALE, W. *Monasticon Anglicanum.* 6 vols. London: 1817–1830.

EADMER. *De Conceptione Sanctae Mariae.* Edited by H. Thurston and T. Slater. Freiburg: 1904.

—. *Historia novorum in Anglia*. Edited by M. Rule. London: RS, 1884.

—. *Vita S Anselmi, archiepiscopi Cantuariensis*. Edited by R. W. Southern. 1962. Reprinted. Oxford: 1972.

EINHARD. *Vita Karoli Magni Imperatoris*. Edited by L. Halphen. Paris: 1938.

ERASMUS, DESIDERIUS. *Pilgrimages to St Mary of Walsingham and St Thomas of Canterbury*. Edited and translated by J. G. Nicols. London: 1875.

ETHERIA. *Peregrinatio Loca Sancta, Itinera Hierosolymitana Saeculi*. 4–8. Edited by P. Geyer. CSEL, 39. 1898.

FLORENCE OF WORCESTER. *Chronica*. Edited by B. Thorpe. English Historical Society. 2 vols. 1848, 1849.

FOREVILLE, R., ed. *Le Livre de Saint Gilbert de Sempringham: Un procès de canonisation à l'aube du xiiie siècle (1201–1202)*. Paris: 1943.

Four Latin Lives of St Patrick. Edited by L. Bieler. Scriptores Latini Hiberniae. 8. Dublin: 1971.

FULBERT OF CHARTRES. *Sermones ad Populum*. PL 141. 317–340.

Gallia Christiana. 16 vols. Paris: 1715–1865.

GARNIER. *Vie de S Thomas*. Paris: 1922.

GAUTIER OF CLUNY. *De Miraculis S Mariae*. PL 173. 1379–86.

GERALD OF WALES. *Opera Omnia*. Edited by J. S. Brewer, J. F. Dimock, and G. F. Warner. 8 vols. London: RS, 1861–1891.

GERARDUS SILVAE MAIORIS. *Vita S Adelardi*. Acta SS, Jan 1, pp. 3ff.

GERVASE OF CANTERBURY. *Opera Historica*. Edited by W. Stubbs. London: RS, 1879.

Gesta Francorum et aliorum Hierosolymitanorum. Edited by R. Hill. London: 1962.

GLABER, RALPH. *Historiae*. Edited by M. Prou. Paris: 1886.

GRATIAN. *Concordantia discordantium canonorum*. PL 187.

GREGORY I. *Magni Dialogi*. Edited by U. Moricca. Fonti per la storia d'Italia, 57. Rome: 1924.

—. *Registrum Epistolarum*. Edited by P. Ewald and L. M. Hartmann. 2 vols. MGH Epp., 1–2. Berlin: 1891–1899.

GREGORY VII. *Registrum*. Edited by E. Casper. MGH Epp., 2. Berlin: 1920–1923.

GREGORY, MASTER. *De Mirabilibus urbis Romae*. Edited by M. R. James. *EHR* 32 (1917): 531–34.

GREGORY OF TOURS. *Historia Francorum.* Edited by B. Krusch and W. Levison. MGH Script. rerum Merov., 2nd ed. Hanover: 1951.

—. *Miracula et opera minora.* Edited by B. Krusch. MGH Merov., Hanover: 1885.

GREGORY THE GREAT. *Opera Omnia. PL* 77.

GUERNES DE S-MAXENCE. *Vie de Saint Thomas.* Edited by E. Walberg. London: 1922.

GUIBERT OF NOGENT. *De pignoribus sanctorum. PL* 156. 607–80.

—. *Gesta Dei per Francos. RHC, Hist. Occ.,* 4. 115–263.

—. *Histoire de sa vie (1053–1124).* Edited by G. Bourgin. Paris: 1907.

Guide du Pèlerin de Saint-Jacques de Compostelle. Edited by Vielliard. 4th ed. Macon: 1969.

GUITMUND OF AVRANCHES. *De Corporis et Sanguinis Domini Veritate Tres Libri. PL* 149.

HADDAN, A. W., and W. STUBBS, eds. *Councils and ecclesiastical documents relating to Great Britain and Ireland.* 3 vols. Oxford: 1869–1871.

HAIMON. 'Lettre sur la construction de l'église de Saint-Pierre-sur-Dive, en 1145'. Edited by L. Delisle. In *Bibliothèque de l'école des Chartes.* 5th Series. Vol. 1. 1860.

HELINANDUS. *Chronicon. PL* 212.

HENRY OF HUNTINGDON. *Historia Anglorum.* Edited by T. Arnold. London: RS, 1879.

HERMAN, CANON OF LAON. *De Miraculis S Mariae Laudunensis. PL* 156. 961–1020.

HEROLT, JOHANNES. *Promptuarium Discipulis de Miraculis Beate Marie Virginis.* Translated by C. G. Coulton and E. Power as *Miracles of the Blessed Virgin Mary.* London: 1928.

HILDEBERT OF LE MANS. *Life of St Hugh of Cluny.* In *Bibl. Clun.,* cols 414–39. (Also in *PL* 159. 857–92).

HILDEFONSUS OF TOLEDO. *Liber De Virginitate S Mariae. PL* 96. 43–48.

HILDEGARD OF BINGEN. *Causae et Curae.* Edited by Paul Kaiser. Lipsiae: 1908.

—. *Opera. PL* 197.

—. *Physica. PL* 197.

Historia Compostellana. Edited by H. Florez et al. 51 vols. *Espana sagrada,* 20. Madrid: 1754–1879.

Historians of the Church of York. Edited by J. Raine. 3 vols. London: RS, 1879–1894.

HONORIUS OF AUTUN. *Sigillum Sancte Marie. PL* 172.

HUGH FARSIT. *Miracles of the Virgin of Soissons. PL* 179.

HUGH OF FLAVIGNY. *Chronicle.* MGH SS, 8. 288–502. (Also in *PL* 154. 393.)

HUGH OF ST VICTOR. *Didascalicon de studio legendi.* Edited by C. H. Buttimer. Washington: 1939.

——. *Speculum Ecclesiae. PL* 177.

HUMBERT, CARDINAL. *Adversus Simonicos. PL* 143.

IAMBLICHUS. *Life of Pythagoras.* Translated by K. Raine and G. M. Harper. In *Thomas Taylor the Platonist, Selected Writings.* London: 1969.

INNOCENT III. *Letters of Innocent III.* Edited by C. Cheney, R. G. and W. G. Semple. London: 1955. (Also in *PL* 216).

IRENAEUS, ST. *Adversus Haereses libri quinque. PG* 7. 433–1224.

ISIDORE OF SEVILLE. *Etymologies. PL* 82.

JACQUES DE VITRY. *Exempla et sermones vulgares.* Edited by T.F. Crane. Publications of the Folk-Lore Society, 26. London: 1890.

JAMES, M. R. *The Apocryphal New Testament.* Oxford: 1924.

JEAN LE MARCHANT. *Le Livre de Notre Dame de Chartres.* Edited by M. G. Duplessis. Paris: 1855.

JENNINGS, J. 'Prior Dominic of Evesham and the Survival of English Tradition after the Norman Conquest'. B. Litt. Thesis, Oxford: 1958.

Joca monachorum: Das mittellateinische Gespräch Adrian und Epictitus nebst verwandten Texten. Edited by W. Suchier. Tübingen: 1955.

JOCELYN OF BRAKELOND. *Chronicle.* Edited by H. E. Butler. London: 1949.

JOHN OF COUTANCES. *Miracula Ecclesiae Constantiensis.* Edited by E. A. Pidgeon. In *Histoire de la Cathédrale de Coutances,* pp. 369–83. Coutances: 1876.

JOHN OF FORD. *The Life of Wulfric of Haselbury.* Edited by M. Bell, Somerset Record Society, 47. 1932.

JOHN OF GARLAND. *Stella Maris.* Edited by E. F. Wilson. Medieval Academy of America, 45. Cambridge, Mass.: 1946.

JOHN OF SALERNO. *Life of St Odo.* In *Bibl. Clun.,* cols. 13–56. (Also in *PL* 133. 43–86.

JOHN OF SALISBURY. *Opera Omnia. PL* 199.

—. *Policraticus.* Edited by C. J. Webb. 2 vols. Oxford: 1909. (Also in *PL* 199. 385–829).

JOTSALDUS. *Life of St Odilo of Cluny. PL* 142. 897–940.

LANFRANC. *De Corpore et Sanguine Domini. PL* 150.

LEHMANN, P. *Die Parodie im Mittelalter.* München: 1922.

Letters of Osbert of Clare. Edited by E. W. Williamson. Oxford: 1929.

Liber de miraculis sanctae Dei genetricis Mariae. Edited by T.F. Crane. Ithaca: 1925.

Liber Miraculorum Sancte Fidis. Edited by A. Bouillet. Collection des Textes pour servir à l'étude et l'enseignement de l'histoire, 21. Paris: 1877.

Liber Sancti Jacobi. In *Codex Calixtinus.* Edited by Walter Muir Whitehill. 2 vols (Vol. 1 transcription, Vol. 2 music). Compostela: 1944

Life of Christina of Markyate. Edited by C. H. Talbot. London: 1959.

Livre des Miracles de Notre Dame de Rocamadour. In *Livre de la deuxième colloque de Rocamadour.* Rocamadour: 1972.

MABILLON, J., ed. *Vetera analecta.* 2nd ed. Paris: 1723.

MCNEILL, J. T., and H. M. GAMER, eds. *Medieval handbooks of penance.* A translation of the principal 'Libri Penitentiales' and selections from related documents. New York: 1938.

MANSI, J. D. *Sacrorum Conciliorum Nova et Amplissima Collectio.* 53 vols. Florence et alloca: 1759–1927.

MARBOD OF RENNES. *Liber lapidum sue de gemmis. PL* 171.

Materials for the History of Thomas Becket, archbishop of Canterbury. Edited by J. C. Robertson and J. B. Sheppard. 7 vols. London: RS, 1875–1885.

Memorials of St Anselm. Edited by R. W. Southern and F. S. Schmitt OSB. Auctores Britannici Medii Aevi, 1. London: 1969.

Miracles de Notre Dame de Chartres. Edited by A. Thomas. Bibl. de l'école des Chartres, vol. 42. Paris: 1881.

Miracles de Notre Dame de Rocamadour au XIIe siècle. Text and translation by E. Albe. Paris: 1907.

Miracles de S Benoît. Edited by E. de Certain. Société de l'histoire de France. Paris: 1858.

Miracles of St Dunstan. Edited by W. Stubbs. London: RS, 1874.

Miracles of St Faith. Edited by A. Bouillet. Paris: 1897.

Miracles of St Maiolus of Cluny. In *Bibl. Clun.,* cols 1787ff.

Miracles of St William. In *The Life and Miracles of Saint William of Norwich.* Edited and translated by A. Jessopp and M. R. James. Cambridge: 1896.

Miracula Beati Caroli Magni. PL 98 1362–64.

Miracula B. Egidii. MGH SS, 12. 316–23. (Also in Anal. Boll., vol. 9, pp. 393–422. 1890.)

Miracula S Frideswidae. Acta SS, Oct 8, pp. 568–89.

Miracula S Wulfstani. In *Vita S. Wulfstani.* Edited by R. R. Darlington. Camden Society. 3rd series. Vol. 11. London: 1928.

Miracula Sanctae Virginis Mariae. Edited by E. F. Dexter. University of Wisconsin Studies in Social Science and History, vol. 12. Wisconsin: 1927.

ODILO OF CLUNY. *Life of St Adelaide.* In *Bibl. Clun.,* cols 367ff. (Also in *PL* 142. 983–92).

ODO OF CLUNY. *Life of St Gerald of Aurillac.* In *Bibl. Clun.,* cols 67ff. (Also in *PL* 133. 639–710).

ODO OF DEUIL. *De profectione Lodovici VII in orientem.* Edited by H. Waquet. Documents relatifs à l'histoire des croisades, 3. Paris: 1949.

ORDERICUS VITALIS. *Historiae Ecclesiasticae Libri Tredecim.* Edited by A. le Prevost and L. Delisle. Société de l'Histoire de France. 1838–1855. Reprint. 5 vols. London and New York: 1965.

—. *The Ecclesiastical History.* Edited and translated by M. Chibnall. Books 3–13, vols 2–6. Oxford: 1969–1978.

OSBERN. *Vita S Dunstani.* In *Memorials of St Dunstan.* Edited by W. Stubbs. London: RS, 1874.

OTTO OF FREISING. *Gesta Frederici Imperatoris.* Edited by B. de Simson. Hanover: 1912.

PASCHASIUS RADBERTUS. *De Corpore et Sanguine Domini.* Edited by Bede Paul. Turnholt: 1969.

PAUL OF BERNRIED. *Vita S Gregorii VII. PL* 148. 39–114.

PAUL THE DEACON. *De Gestis Langobardorum. PL* 95. 433–672.

PAULINUS OF NOLA. *Vita di S Ambrogio.* Edited by M. Pellegrino. Rome: 1961.

PETER DAMIAN. *Opera Omnia. PL* 144 and 145.

PETER LOMBARD. *Sententiae. PL* 192.

PETER THE CHANTER. *Verbum abbreviatum. PL* 205.

PETER THE DEACON. *Historia Relatio de Corpore S Benedicti Casine.* Acta SS, Mar 3, pp. 288–97.

PETER THE VENERABLE. *De Miraculis. PL* 189. 851–954.

—. *Letters.* Edited by G. Constable. 2 vols. Harvard: 1967.

PETER WILLIAM. *Miracula Beati Egidii.* MGH SS vol 12, pp. 316–23.

PHILIP, PRIOR OF ST FRIDESWIDE'S. *Miracula S Frideswidae.* Acta SS, Oct 8, pp. 567–90.

PHILOSTRATUS. *Life of Apollonius of Tyana.* Edited by C. Jones. London: 1952.

PSEUDO AUGUSTINE. *De Mirabilibus Sacrae Scripturae. PL* 35.

Quest of the Holy Grail. Translated by P. M. Matarasso. Harmondsworth: 1969.

RABANUS MAURUS. *Commentariorum in Exodum. PL* 108.

RALPH OF CAEN. *Gesta Tancredi in Expeditione Hierosolymitana. RHC* 3, pp. 677ff.

RALPH OF DICETO. *Imagines Historiarum; Abbreviationes Chronicorum.* In *The Historical Works of Master Ralph de Diceto, Dean of London.* Edited by W. Stubbs. 2 vols. London: RS, 1876.

RALPH THE MONK. *Life of Peter the Venerable. PL* 189. 15–28.

RAYMOND OF AGUILERS. *Historia Francorum. RHC Occ.,* 3. 231–309.

RAYNALD, ODERIC. *Annales Ecclesiastici.* Edited by J. D. Mansi. 15 vols. Lucca: 1747–1756.

Regesta Pontificum Romanorum. Edited by Jaffé-Loewenfeld. 1888. Reprint edited by Gray. 1956.

REGINALD OF DURHAM. *Libellus de Admirandis Beati Cuthberti Virtutibus.* Surtees Society. London: 1835.

—. *Libellus de Vita et Miraculis S Godrici, Heremitae de Finchale; appendix miraculorum.* Edited by J. Stevenson. Surtees Society, vol. 20. London: 1847.

Registrum Epistolarum. Edited by P. Ewald and L. M. Hartmann. 2 vols. MGH Epp. 1887–1889.

Règle de S Benoît. Edited and translated by A. de Vogüë and Jean Neufville. 6 vols. *Sources Chrétiennes,* 182–86. Paris: 1971–1972.

ROBERT DE TORIGNI. *Chronique.* Edited by L. Delisle. 2 vols. Société de l'Histoire de Normandie. Rouen: 1872–1873. (Also in *PL* 160).

ROBERT OF MELUN. *Quaestiones of Divina Pagina.* Edited by R. M. Martin. Louvain: 1932.

—. *Sententie.* Edited by R. M. Martin and R. M. Grant. 2 vols. Louvain: 1947–1952.

ROGER OF HOVEDEN. *Chronica Magistri Rogeri de Houedene.* Edited by W. Stubbs. 4 vols. London: RS, 1868–1871.

RUPERT OF DEUTZ. *Commentaria in Evangelium S Joannis. PL* 169. 201–827.

SAMPSON, ABBOT. *Miracles of S Edmund.* Edited by T. Arnold. In *Memorials of S Edmund's Abbey.* Vol. 1. London: RS, 1890.

SIMON OF TOURNAI. *Les 'Disputationes de Divina Pagina'.* Edited by J. Warichez. Louvain: 1932.

Statutum Odilonis pro Defunctis. PL 142. 1037.

STEPHEN OF AUTUN. *Tractatus de Sacramento Altaris. PL* 172.

SUGER, ABBOT OF ST-DENIS. *De Consecratione ecclesiae S Dionysii.* In *Oeuvres Completes.* Edited by A. Lecoy de la Marche. Société de l'Histoire de France, pp. 211–38. Paris: 1867.

SULPICIUS SEVERUS. *Vita S Martini.* Edited by J. Fontaine. 3 vols. *Sources Chrétiennes.* Paris: 1967.

SYMEON OF DURHAM. *Capitula de miraculis et translationibus* in *Opera Omnia,* edited by T. Arnold. London: RS, vol. 2, 333–62.

SYMEONIS DUNELMENSIS. *Opera et Collectanea.* Edited by H. Hinde. Surtees Society, 1. 1868.

Thesaurus novus anecdotorum. Edited by E. Martine and U. Durant. 5 vols. Paris: 1717.

THIERRY OF CHARTRES. *De Septem Diebus et sex operum distinctionibus.* Edited by W. Jansen. In *Der Kommentar des Clarembaldus von Arras zu Boethius De Trinitate*. Breslau: 1926.

THOMAS OF MONMOUTH. *The Life and Miracles of St William of Norwich*. Edited by A. Jessopp and M. R. James. Cambridge: 1896.

Translatio S Sebastiani. MGH SS, 15. 379–91.

Translatio SS Alexandri et Justini. MGH SS, 15. 286–88.

UDALRIC. *Consuetudines Cluniacensis*. PL 149. 643–779.

VEILLIARD, J. *Guide du Pèlerin de Saint-Jacques de Compostelle*. Compostela: 1950.

Vita Aedwardi. Edited by F. Barlow. London: 1962.

Vita et Miracula Sanctorum Juvensium. Edited by Wattenbach. MGH SS, vol 11, pp. 84–103.

Vita Prima S Bernardi. PL 185.

Vita Sancti Cuthberti Anonymi. Edited by B. Colgrave. In *Two Lives of St Cuthbert*. Cambridge: 1940.

WALTER, DANIEL. *Vita S Aelredi*. Edited and translated by F. M. Powicke. 1950. Reprint. Oxford: 1978.

WALTER MAP. *De Nugis Curialium*. Edited by M. R. James. Oxford: 1914.

WERRIC. *Vita Domini Alberti Leodiensis Episcopi*. MGH SS, vol 25, pp. 139–68.

WIBERT. *Sancti Leonis Vita*. PL 143. 457ff.

WILLIAM OF CANTERBURY. *Miracula S Thomae Cantuariensis*. In *Becket* 1, pp. 137–546.

WILLIAM OF CONCHES. *Glossae super Platonem*. Edited by Edward Jeaneau. *Textes Philosphiques du Moyen Âge*, 13. Paris: 1965. (Also in *PL* 172. 245–52).

WILLIAM OF MALMESBURY. *De Gestis Pontificum Anglorum*. Edited by N. Hamilton. London: RS, 1870.

—. *De Gestis regum Anglorum*. Edited by W. Stubbs. 2 vols. London: RS, 1887–1889.

—. *Historia Novella*, ed. K. R. Potter. London: 1955.

—. *Miracles of the Virgin*. Edited by P. Carter. 2 vols. D. Phil. thesis, Oxford: 1959.

—. *Vita S Wulfstani*. Edited by R. R. Darlington. Camden Society, 11. 3rd series. 1928.

WILLIAM OF NEWBURGH. *Historia Rerum Anglicarum*. In *Chronicles of the*

Reigns of Stephen, Henry II and Richard I. Edited by R. Howlett. 2 vols. London: RS, 1884–1889.

WILLIAM OF ST THIERRY. *Opera Omnia.* PL 180. 205–727.

WILLIAM OF TYRE. *Historia rerum in partibus transmarinis gestarum. RHC Hist. Occ.,* 1.

SECONDARY SOURCES

ABBOTT, E. A. *St Thomas of Canterbury: His death and miracles.* 2 vols. London: 1898.

ADAMS, H. *Mont S Michel and Chartres.* New York: 1933.

AGRAIN, R. *L'Hagiographie, ses sources, ses méthodes, son histoire.* Paris: 1953.

ALPHANDERY, P., and A. DUPONT. *La Chrétienté et l'idée de Croisade.* 2 vols. Paris: 1854–1859.

Antonius Magnus. Edited by B. Steindle. Rome: 1956.

AMPHILOCHIUS, BISHOP OF ICONIUM. *Life of St Basil.* Acta SS, June 14, p. 423.

BALDWIN, J. W. *Masters, princes and servants: the social views of Peter the Chanter and his circle.* 2 vols. Princeton: 1970.

BARON, R. *Études sur Hugues de S Victor.* Paris: 1963.

BARRÉ, H. *Prières anciennes de l'occident à la Mère du Sauveur.* Paris: 1944.

BATTISCOMBE, C. F. *The Relics of Saint Cuthbert.* Oxford: 1956.

Bernard de Clairvaux. Commission d'Histoire de L'Ordre de Cîteaux. Paris: 1953.

BISHOP, E. *Liturgica Historica.* Oxford: 1918.

BLOCH, M. *Les Rois Thaumaturges.* 1925. Reprint. Paris: 1961. (English translation, *The Royal Touch:* 1961.)

BOGLIONE, P. 'Miracle et merveilleux religieux chez Grégoire le Grand, theorie et thèmes'. Ph.D. dissertation, Montreal, 1974. First part printed as 'Miracle et nature chez Gregoire le Grand'. In *Epopées, légendes et miracles.* Montreal: 1974.

BOISSARADE, J. *Europii Sardiari vitas sophistrum et fragmenta histriarum.* Amsterdam: 1822.

BONSOR, W. *The Medical Background of Anglo-Saxon England: A Study in History, Psychology and Folklore.* London: 1963.

BOURGIN, L. *La chaire française au XIIe siècle d'après les manuscrits.* Paris: 1879.

BOUTHILLIER, D. 'L'Univers religieux de Pierre le Vénérable d'après le De Miraculis'. Ph.D. dissertation, Montreal: 1975.

BREDERO, A. *Études sur la Vita Prima S Bernardi.* Rome: 1950. Reprinted in *ASOC* 17 (1961): 3–72, 215–260; (1962): 5–59.

BREWER, E. C. *A Dictionary of Miracles.* London: 1884.

BROWE, PETER. *Die Eucharistischen Wunder des Mittelalters.* Breslauer Studien zur hist. theol. WF Bd 4, 1. Breslau: 1938.

BROWN, W. N. *The Indian and Christian Miracles of Walking on the Water.* Chicago: 1928.

CHAMARD, F. *Les Reliques de S Benoît.* Paris: 1882.

CHENU, M. D. *Nature, Man, and Society in the Twelfth Century.* Chicago: 1968.

Cluniac Monasticism in the Central Middle Ages. Edited by N. Hunt. London: 1971.

COATES, C. *The History and Antiquities of Reading.* London: 1802.

COHN, N. *The Pursuit of the Millennium: Revolutionary millennarians and mystical anarchists of the Middle Ages.* 2nd ed. London: 1970.

COURCELLE, P. *Recherches sur les Confessions de Saint Augustin.* Paris: 1950.

COWDREY, H. E. J. *The Cluniacs and the Gregorian Reform.* Oxford: 1970.

CRANE, T. F. *Medieval Sermon Books.* New York: 1883.

CROMBIE, A. *Augustine to Galileo; a History of Science 400–1650.* London.

DAUPHIN, H. *Le Bienheureux Richard, Abbé de Saint-Vanne.* Louvain: 1946.

DAVID, P. *Études sur le livre de S Jacques attribué au Pape Calixtus II.* 4 vols. Lisbon: 1946–1949.

DE FOURNEAUX, M. *Les français en Espagne au XIe et XIIe siècles.* Paris: 1949.

DELEHAYE, H. *Les Legendes hagiographiques.* 2nd ed. Brussels: 1905.

—. *Les origines de la culte des martyrs.* 2nd ed. Brussels: 1933.

—. *Sanctus. Essai sur le culte des saints dans l'antiquité.* Brussels: 1927.

DE ROCHAS, A. *L'art des thaumaturges dans l'antiquité.* 2nd ed. Paris: 1922.

DICKINSON, J. *The Shrine of Our Lady of Walsingham.* Cambridge: 1956.

Dictionnaire d'archéologie chrétienne et de liturgie. Edited by F. Cabrol, H. Leclercq, H. I. Marov. 15 vols. Paris: 1907–1951.

DUBY, G. M. C. *La Sociéte aux xie et xiie siècles dans la région Mâconnaise*. Paris: 1953.

DU CANGE, C. *Glossarium mediae et infirmae latinitatis*. 10 vols. Niort: 1883–1887.

DUHEM. *Système du Monde*. Paris: 1913.

EHNMARK, E. *Anthropomorphism and Miracle*. No. 12. Arsskr.: 1939.

—. *The Idea of God in Homer*. Uppsala: 1935.

ERICKSON, C. *The Medieval Vision: Essays in History and Perception*. Oxford: 1976.

Famulus Christi. Edited by G. Bonner. Durham: 1976.

FARMER. D. H. 'English Hagiography'. B.Litt. thesis, Oxford: 1967.

FINUCANE, R. *Miracles and Pilgrims: Popular Beliefs in Medieval England*. London: 1977.

FOLZ, R. *Études sur le culte liturgique de Charlemagne*. Paris: 1950.

—. *Le Souvenir et la légend de Charlemagne dans l'empire germanique médiéval*. Paris: 1950.

FRANZ. A. *Die Kirchlichen Benediktionen im Mittelalter*. Freiburg-im-Breisgau: 1909.

FRIDRICHSEN, A. *Le problème du miracle dans le christianisme primitif*. Paris: 1925.

Gallia Christiana. Paris: 1715–1865, vols 1–16.

Gallia Christiana novissima, Paris: 1899–1920, vols 1–7.

GEARY, P. *Furta Sacra: The Theft of Relics in the Central Middle Ages*. Princeton: 1978.

GHELLINCK, J. DE. *Le Mouvement théologique du XIIe siècle*. 2nd edition. Brussels: 1848.

—. *Spicilegium sacrum Lovaniense*. Études et Documents, 3. Louvain/Paris: 1924.

GILSON, E. *Duns Scotus*. London: 1952.

—. *History of Christian Philosophy in the Middle Ages*. London: 1972.

—. *La Philosophie de S Bernard*. Paris: 1934.

GONSETTE, J. *Pierre Damien*. Paris: 1956.

GRAHAM, R. *S Gilbert of Sempringham*. London: 1901.

GRANSDON. A. *Historical Writing in England c. 550–c. 1307.* London: 1974.

GRANGE, J. *Le Miracle d'après Saint Augustin.* Brignais: 1938.

GRANT, R. M. *Miracle and Natural Law.* Amsterdam: 1952.

GRÉGOIRE, R. *Les Homélaires du Moyen Âge.* Rome: 1966.

GREGOROVIUS, F. *History of the City of Rome in the Middle Ages.* 8 vols. London: 1894–1902.

GUIBERT OF NOGENT. *Self and Society in Twelfth-Century France: The Memoires of Abbot Guibert of Nogent.* Translated by J. F. Benton. New York: 1969.

HÄRING, W. *Life and Works of Clarembald of Arras, a Twelfth-Century Master of the School of Chartres.* Toronto: 1965.

HASKINS, C. H. *Studies in the History of Medieval Science.* Harvard: 1924.

HERRMANN-MASCARD, N. *Les Reliques des saints: formation coutumière d'un droît.* Paris: 1975.

HERZOG, R. *Die Wunderheilungen von Epidauros.* Leipzig: 1931.

HESSEY, J. A. *Sunday and Its Origin, History, and Present Obligation.* Bampton Lectures. Oxford: 1860.

Histoire littéraire de la France. Edited by the Congrégation de S Maur. Paris: 1773.

HUEFFER, G. *Der heilige Bernard von Clairvaux.* Münster: 1886.

HUME, DAVID. *An Enquiry Concerning Human Understanding.* In *The Philosophical Works of David Hume.* Edinburgh: 1842.

HUNT, N. *Cluny under Saint Hugh, 1049–1109.* London: 1967.

JAMES, M. R. *The Ancient Libraries of Canterbury and Dover.* Cambridge: 1903.

—. *A Descriptive Catalogue of the Manuscripts in the Library of Sidney Sussex College, Cambridge.* Cambridge: 1895.

JANAUSCHEK, C. *Originum Cisterciensium.* Vienna: 1877.

JEDIN, K., K. S. LATOURETTE and J. MARTIN. *Atlas zur Kirchengeschichte.* Freiburg: 1970.

JONES, C. W. *Saints' Lives and Chronicles in Early England.* New York: 1947.

KEMP, E. *Canonization and Authority in the Western Church.* Oxford: 1948.

KENNEY, J. F. *The Sources for the Early History of Ireland.* Reprint. Irish University Press, 1968.

KER, N. R. *Medieval Libraries of Great Britain: A List of Surviving Books.* 2nd ed. London: 1964.

KLAUSER, T. *Die Liturgie der Heiligsprechung.* Münster: 1938.

KNOWLES, D. *Thomas Becket.* Reprint. London: 1970.

LAFORT, J. *Les Vitraux de l'église de S Ouen de Rouen.* Paris: 1970.

LAMBERTINI, P. *De Servorum Dei Beatificatione et Beatorum Canonizatione.* Bologna: 1734–1738.

LEA, H. C. *A History of Auricular Confession and Indulgences in the Latin Church.* 3 vols. London: 1896.

LECLERCQ, J. *La Liturgie et les paradoxes chrétiens.* Paris: 1963.

—. *Pierre Damien.* Rome: 1960.

LEFRANC, A. *Le Traité des Reliques de Guibert de Nogent.* Paris: 1896.

LEROY, L. *Histoire des pelerinages de la Sainte Vierge en France.* 3 vols. Paris: 1873–1875.

Life of St Odo of Cluny and Life of St Gerald of Aurillac. Translated by E. G. Sitwell. London: 1958.

LLEWELLYN, P. *Rome in the Dark Ages.* London: 1970.

LOOMIS. C. G. *White Magic: An Introduction to the Folklore of Christian Legend.* Cambridge, Mass.: 1948.

MABILLON, J. *Annales ordinis S Benedicti.* 5 vols. Paris: 1703–1713.

MACDONALD, A. S. *Berengar and the Reform of Sacramental Doctrine.* London: 1930.

MCGINLEY, L. J. *Form Criticism of the Synoptic Healing Narratives.* Woodstock, Md.: 1944.

MASON, A. J. *What Became of the Bones of St Thomas?* London: 1920.

Medieval Scribes, Manuscripts and Libraries: Essays Presented to N. R. Ker. Edited by M. B. Parkes and A. G. Watson. London: 1978.

Medieval Scribes, Manuscripts and Libraries: Essays Presented to N. R. Ker. Edited by M. B. Parkes and A. G. Watson. London: 1979.

MEER, F. *L'Atlas de l'Ordre Cistercien.* Amsterdam: 1965.

MEYER, K., ed. *Aislinge Meic Conglinne.* London: 1892.

MEYVAERT, PAUL. *Benedict, Gregory, Bede, and Others.* London: 1977.

MOHRMANN, C. *Études sur le Latin des chrétiens.* Rome: 1958.

MOORE, W. J. *The Saxon Pilgrims to Rome and the Schola Saxorum.* Freiburg: 1937.

MOULE, CHARLES, ed. *Miracle.* London: 1965.

MOULTON, J. H., and G. MILLIGAN. *The Vocabulary of the Greek New Testament.* London: 1929.

MUSSAFIA, A. *Studien zu den mittelalterlichen Marienlegenden.* Sitzungsberichte der kaiserlichen Akademie der Wissenschaften in Wien. Phil. hist. Kl. 113, 115, 119, 123, 139 (1886, 1887, 1889, 1890, 1898).

NEWMAN, J. H. 'Essay on the Miracles recorded in Ecclesiastical History'. Introduction to a translation of *The Ecclesiastical History of M. l'Abbé Fleury.* Oxford: 1842.

NOCK, A. D. *Conversion.* Oxford: 1933.

NOTTHARP, HERMANN. *Gottesurteilstudien. Bamberger Abhandlung und Forschungen* 2 (1956).

OURSEL, R. *Les pèlerins du moyen âge: les hommes, les chemins, les sanctuaires.* Paris: 1963.

——. *Les Saints Abbés de Cluny.* Paris: 1960.

PATETTA, F. *Le ordalie.* Turin: 1890.

Petrus Venerabilis. Edited by G. Constable and J. Kritzeck. *Studia Anselmiana* 40 (1956).

PHILIPPORT, G. *Les Légendiers latins et autres manuscrits hagiographiques.* Belgium: 1977.

PIRENNE, H. *Medieval Cities: their origins and the revival of trade.* Princeton: 1925.

PONCELET, A. 'La plus ancienne vie de S Géraud d'Aurillac (d. 909)', Anal. Boll., 14 (1895), pp. 89–107.

RACKHAM, B. *The Ancient Glass of Canterbury Cathedral.* London: 1949.

RAUSCHEN, G. *Die Legende Karls des Grossen im 11. und 12. Jahrhundert.* Leipzig: 1890.

RICHARDSON, A. *The Miracle Stories of the Gospels.* London: 1942.

RICHARDSON, H. G. *The English Jewry under the Angevin Kings.* London: 1960.

ROBINSON, M. W. *Inspiration and Revelation in the Old Testament.* Oxford: 1946.

RUBEIS, J. B. M. *Monumenta ecclesia Aquilejensis.* Strasbourg: 1740.

RUBIN, S. *Medieval English Medicine.* London: 1974.

RUPIN, E. *Roc-Amadour: étude historique et archéologique.* Paris: 1904.

RYAN, J. *Peter Damian.* London: 1956.

SACKUR, E. *Cluny.* Paris: 1892.

Saint Martin et Son Temps. Studia Anselmiana 46 (1961).

SALTET, L. *Étude Critique sur la passion de Sainte Foy et de Saint Caprais.* Paris: 1899.

SAXER, V. *Le Culte de Marie Madeleine en occident des origines à la fin du moyen âge.* 2 vols. Paris: 1959.

SMALLEY, B. *The Becket Conflict and the Schools: A Study of Intellectuals in Politics in the Twelfth Century.* Oxford: 1973.

—. *The Study of the Bible in the Middle Ages.* 1952. Reprint. Oxford: 1964.

SOUTHERN, R. W. *The Making of the Middle Ages.* 1953. Reprint. London: 1968.

—. *St. Anselm and His Biographer: a study of monastic life and thought, 1059–c. 1130.* Cambridge: 1963.

SPAHR, K. G. *Robert de Molesumne.* Washington: 1944.

STANLEY, A. P. *Historical Memorials of Canterbury.* London: 1904.

STONE, DARWELL. *A History of the Doctrine of the Holy Eucharist.* 2 vols. London: 1909.

SUMPTION, J. *Pilgrimage: An Image of Mediaeval Religion.* London: 1974.

THIERS, J-B. *Traité des superstitions qui regardent les Sacramens.* 1679. 5th edition. Paris: 1941.

THOMAS BECKET. *Actes du colloque International de Sedières, 19–24 Août 1973.* Edited by Raymonde Foreville. Beauchesne: 1976.

THOMAS, K. *Religion and the Decline of Magic. Studies in Popular Beliefs in Sixteenth- and Seventeenth-Century England.* London: 1971.

THORNDYKE, L. *A History of Magic and Experimental Science.* 8 vols. New York: 1913–28.

TURNER, V. and E. *Image and Pilgrimage in Christian Culture.* Oxford: 1978.

URRY, W. *Canterbury Under the Angevins.* London: 1967.

VACANDARD, E. *Vie de S Bernard.* 2 vols. 4th ed. Paris: 1910.

VALENTINI, R., and G. ZUCCHETTI. *Codici topografici della Città di Roma.* 4 vols. Rome: 1940.

VAN HOVE, A. *La Doctrine du Miracle chez S Thomas Aquinas.* Paris: 1927.

VIDIER, A. *L'Historiographie à S-Benoît-sur-Loire et les Miracles de S Benoît.* Paris: 1965.

WALBERG, E. *La Tradition hagiographique de S Thomas Becket.* Paris: 1929.

WALSH, J. J. *Medieval Medicine.* London: 1920.

WARD, H. L. D. *Catalogue of Romances in the Department of Manuscripts in the British Museum.* 3 vols. London: 1893.

WATKINS, O. D. *A History of Penance.* London: 1920.

WEINREICH, O. *Antike Heilungswunder.* Giessen: 1909.

WELTER, J-TH. *L'Exemplum dans le littérature religieuse et didactique du moyen âge.* Paris: 1927.

WENGER, A. *L'Assumption de la Vierge.* Paris: 1955.

WILMART, A. *Auteurs spirituels et textes dévots du moyen âge latin.* 1930. Reprint. Paris: 1971.

—. *Miscellanea Agostiniana.* Rome: 1931.

WOLFSON, H. A. *Philo.* Cambridge: 1947.

WRIGHT, T. *St Patrick's Purgatory.* London: 1844.

ARTICLES

BALDWIN, J. W. 'A Debate at Paris over Thomas Becket between Master Roger and Master Peter the Chanter'. *Studia Gratiana* 11 (1967): 121–26.

—. 'The Intellectual Preparation for the Canon of 1215 against Ordeals'. *Speculum* 36 (1961): 613–36.

BARRÉ, H. 'Un plaidoyer monastique pour le samedi marial'. *Rev. Bén.* 77 (1967): 375–99.

BAYNES, N. H. 'The Supernatural Defenders of Constantinople'. Anal. Boll., 67 (1949): 165–77.

BERLIÈRE, V. 'Le Cardinal Matthieu d'Albano, *c.* 1085–1135'. *Rev. Bén.* 18 (1901): 113–40, 280–303.

—. 'Les pèlerinages judiciaires au moyen âge'. *Rev. Bén.* 7 (1890): 520–26.

BETHELL, D. 'The Making of a twelfth-century relic collection'. In *Popular Belief and Practice. Papers read at the ninth summer and tenth winter meetings of the Ecclesiastical History Society,* edited by G. Cuming and D. Baker. Studies in Ecclesiastical History 8. Cambridge: 1972.

BOUTHILLIER, D. 'La Tradition manuscrite du *De Miraculis* de Pierre le Vénérable: Bilan d'une première recherche', *Revue d'histoire de Textes*, 6. Montreal: 1976.

BROWN, P. 'Eastern and Western Christendom in late antiquity: a parting of the Ways'. In *The Orthodox Church and the West*. Edited by D. Baker. Oxford: 1976.

—. 'Society and the Supernatural: A Medieval Change'. *Daedalus* (1975): 133–51.

CONANT, K. 'Cluny Studies'. *Speculum*, July, 1975: 383–90.

—. 'The History of Romanesque Cluny as clarified by Excavations and Comparisons'. *Monumenta* 7 (1971).

DELEHAYE, H. 'Les premiers "libelli miraculorum" '. Anal. Boll. 29 (1910): 427–34.

—. 'Les Recueils antiques de miracles de saints'. Anal. Boll. 43 (1925): 5–85; 305–25.

—. *Loca Sanctorum*. Anal. Boll. 47 (1930).

DE MELEY, F. 'La Sainte Lance'. *Notes et Études archéologiques*. In *Riant's Excuviae Sacrae Constantinopolitanae*, vol. 3. Paris: 1904.

DE VOOGHT, P. 'Les Miracles dans la vie de S Augustin'. *Recherches de théologie ancienne et médiévale* 11 (1939): 5–16.

DIMIER, A. 'Mourir à Clairvaux'. *Coll. Ord. Cist. Ref.* 17 (1955): 272–75.

DIMOCK, J. F. 'The Metrical Life of St Hugh'. *Rev. Bén.* 34 (1922): 120–26.

FARMER, D. H. 'The Canonization of St Hugh of Lincoln'. *Lincolnshire Architectural and Archaeological Society*, vol. 6, pt. 2 (1955–1956): 86–117.

FINUCANE, R. 'The Posthumous Miracles of Godric of Finchale'. *Transactions of the Architectural and Archaeological Society of Durham and Northumberland* 3 (1975): 47–50.

—. 'The Use and Abuse of Medieval Miracles'. *History* 60, February 1975.

'Fragmenta de Vita et Miraculis S Bernardi par Geoffroy d'Auxerre'. Edited by R. Lechat. Anal. Boll. (1932): 84–122.

Fragmentum Passionis S Fidis metricae. Edited by E. Dümmler. *Rev. Archiv.* 10 (1958).

GOFFART, W. 'Le Mans, St Scholastica and the Literary Tradition of the Translation of St Benedict'. *Rev. Bén.* 77 (1967): 107–41.

GRIESSER, B. 'Ein Himmeroder Liber Miraculorum und seine Beziehungen zu Caesarius von Heisterbach'. *Archiv. für mittellateinische,* KG 4 (1952): 257–74.

—. 'Herbert von Clairvaux und seine Liber miraculorum'. *Cistercienser-Chronik* 54 (Belgium, 1947).

GROSJEAN, P. 'Sur quelque exegètes irlandais du viie siècle'. *Sacris Erudiri* 7 (1955): 67–98.

HAREAU, M. B. 'Mémoire sur les récits d'apparitions dans les sermons du moyen âge'. *Mémoires de l'Institut de France* 28 (1876): 239–64.

HARMENING, DIETER. 'Fränkische Mirakelbücher'. *Würzburger Diözsan-Geschichtsblätter* 28 (1966).

HENNESSY, W. 'Maconglinny's Vision: a humorous satire'. *Frazer's Magazine* N.S. 13, Sept. 1873, pp. 298–323.

HOLDSWORTH, C. 'The Blessings of Work: the Cistercian View'. *Studies in Church History* 10 (1973): 59–76.

—. 'Eleven Visions connected with the Cistercian monastery of Stratford Langthorpe'. *Cîteaux* t. 13 (1969): 196ff.

HUEFFER, G. 'Die Wunder des hl. Bernhard und die Kritiker'. *Historisches Jahrbuch* (München: 1889), 769ff.

KEMP, BRIAN. 'The Miracles of the Hand of St James at Reading'. *Berkshire Archaeological Society* (1961): 1–19.

KUTTNER, S. 'La Réserve papale des droits de canonization'. *Revue Historique de droit français et étranger* 4th Series 17 (1938).

LECLERCQ, J. 'Monachisme et pérégrination du ixe à xiie siècle'. *Studia Monastica* 3 (1961): 33–52.

—. 'Le texte complet de la Vie de Christian de l'Aumône'. Anal. Boll. 61 (1953): 21–52.

—. 'Violence and the Devotion to St Benedict in the Middle Ages'. *Downside Review,* October 1970, pp. 344–61.

LEYSER, K. 'Frederick Barbarossa, Henry II and the Hand of St James'. *EHR* 356 (1975): 481–506.

'Livre Noire de S Ouen de Rouen'. Edited by E. Vacandard, Anal. Boll. 20 (1901): 164–76.

MAGNIEN, E. 'Le pèlerinage de S Jacques de Compostela et l'expansion de l'ordre de Cluny'. *Bull. Hisp.* 63 (1957), 3, pp. 3–17.

MARILLIER, J. 'Catalogue des abbés de Cîteaux pour le xiie siècle'. *Cistercienser-Chronik* 55 (1948).

MAYR-HARTING, H. 'Functions of a Twelfth-Century Recluse', *History* 60, October 1975.

'Miracles of St Cuthbert on Farne'. Edited by E. Craster. Anal. Boll. 70 (1952).

Miracles of St Ithemar. Edited by D. Bethell. Anal. Boll. (1971): 421–39.

MORRIS, C. 'A Critique of popular religion. Guibert of Nogent on the relics of the saints'. In Cuming and Baker, op. cit., pp. 55–56.

MURRAY, A. 'Was Doubt possible in the Middle Ages?' An unpublished paper delivered at the Studies in Church History Conference in Oxford, 1967.

NIEMAYER, G. 'Die Miracula S Mariae Laudunensis des Abtes Herman von Tournai'. *Deutsches Archiv.* 27 (1971): 137–74.

PONCELET, A. 'Index Miraculorum B.V. Marie quae saec. vi–xv latine conscripta sunt'. Anal. Boll. 21 (1902).

—. 'Vie et Miracles du Pape S Leon IX'. Anal. Boll. 25 (1906): 258–97.

RADFORD, U. 'The Wax Images found in Exeter Cathedral'. *The Antiquaries Journal* 29 (1949): 164–68.

RANKIN, J. W. 'The Hymns of St Godric'. *PMLA* 38, no. 4, Dec. 1923, pp. 699–711.

ROUSSET, P. 'La croyance en la justice immanente a l'époque féodal'. *Le Moyen Âge* 54 (1948): 235ff.

RUNCIMAN, S. 'The Holy Lance found at Antioch'. Anal. Boll. (1950) 68: 197–209.

SCHMANDT, R. H. 'The Election and Assassination of Albert of Louvain', *Speculum* 42 (1967): 639–60.

SCHMITT, F. S. 'Neue und alte Hildebrand—Anekdoten aus dem *Dicta Anselmi*'. *Studia Gregoriana* 5, Rome: 1856): 1–18.

SIGAL, P-A. 'Maladie, Pèlerinage et Guérison au XIIe siècle: Les Miracles de Saint Gibrien à Reims'. *Annals.* 24 (1969): 1522–39.

SINANOGLO, L. 'The Christ Child as Sacrifice'. *Speculum* 48 (1973): 491–509.

SOUTHERN, R. W. 'The English Origins of the "Miracles of the Virgin' ''. *Medieval and Renaissance Studies* 4 (1958): 176–216.

TATLOCK, J. S. P. 'The English Journey of the Canons of Laon'. *Speculum* 8 (1933): 454–85.

THOMPSON, R. *Geoffrey of Wells. De Infancia Sancti Edmundi. Rev. Bén.* (1977); 25–43.

—. 'Two Versions of a Saint's Life from St Edmund's Abbey: Changing Currents in XIIth-Century Monastic Style'. *Rev. Bén.* (1974): 383–408.

URRY, W. 'Some notes on the two resting places of St Thomas Becket at Canterbury'. *Thomas Becket: Actes du Colloque International de Sedières 19–20 Août 1973.* Edited by R. Foreville. (Paris: 1973).

VAN DIJK, P. 'The Origins of the Latin Feast of the Conception of the Blessed Virgin Mary'. *Dublin Review* (1954): 251–67, 428–42.

Visio monachi de Eynsham. Edited by H. Thurston. Anal. Boll. 22 (1903): 225–319.

Vita B. Davidis Monachi. Edited by Ambrose Schmeider. Anal. Sacri Ordinis Cisterciensis (1955), 2:27ff.

WILMART, ANDRÉ. 'La Tradition des Grands Ouvrages de S Augustin'. *Miscellanea Agostiniana* 2 (Rome: 1931): 279–97.

Index

A

Aaron, 22, 173
Abbo, abbot of Fleury, 47
Abel, 98
Abelard, Peter, 5
Abingdon, 87
Achard, novice master at Clairvaux, 198
Ada, countess of Huntingdon, 64
Ada, woman of Norwich, 73
Adalbert, archbishop of Hamburg-Bremen, 115
Adalhard of Corbie, St, 34
Adam, 5, 20, 22, 73, 204
Adam of Eynsham, 171, 173–5, 177, 191
  Life of St Hugh of Lincoln, 167
Adam of Norwich, 73
Adam of Persiègne, 26
Addoc, 81
Adelard of Bath, 6–8, 23
  Quaestiones Naturales, 6
Adelarius of Fleury, 47
Adelicia, 108
Adelitha, 87
Adlusa, 107
Adolph, priest, 16
Adrevald, monk of Fleury, 46, 47
  Translation of St Benedict, 47
  Miracles of St Benedict, 47
Aelfleda, abbess of Whitby, 60
Aelred of Rievaulx, St, 25, 30, 63, 77, 78, 167, 173, 174, 210
Aelward Ded, 70
Agen, 36, 37
Agnes, daughter of Bondo Bloc, 73
Agnes of Karelton, 107
Agnes of Norwich, 73
Aidan, St, 63
Aigulf, monk of Fleury, 46
Aimar, prior of St Pancras, 70

Aimon, monk of Fleury, 47, 48
  Miracles of St Benedict, 47
Aix-la-Chapelle, 181
Alan of Auxerre, 189
Alan of Setchy, 72
Alberic, St, 195, 198
Albert, legate, 104, 189
Albert of Louvain, bishop, 128, 129
Aldhelm, St, 201, 205, 211
Alexander I, Pope, 118
Alexander III, Pope, 89, 96, 186–9, 191
Alexander of Aberdeen, 217, 218
Alexander Arat, 218
Alexander, monk of Canterbury, 172, 209
Alexander of Cologne, 181, 182, 195
Alexander Nequam, 160
Alexius, legate, 83
Algar, Prince, 83, 84
Almoravides, 112
Amadour, St, 147, 209
Amans, St, 41
Amisard, canon of Laon, 135, 137
Ancaster, John, 190
Andrew, St, 204, 206
Andrew of Fleury, 46, 48, 49
  Miracles of St Benedict, 48
Angers, 134
Anglo-Saxons, 117, 205
Anne, St, 158
Anno, St, 27
Anselm of Bury, 155, 158, 160, 161
  Miracles of the Virgin, 155
Anselm of Canterbury, St, 4, 5, 14, 43, 60, 111, 113, 114, 119, 138, 141, 145, 148, 158, 169, 171, 172, 174, 175, 187, 188, 205, 209, 217
  De Conceptu Virginali, 4
  Prayer before receiving the Body and Blood of Christ, 14

Anselm of Havelberg, 182
Anselm of Laon, 21, 22, 134, 137
Anselm, canon of Laon, 135
Ansfrid, 72
Antioch, 203, 204
Antony of Egypt, St, 79, 169, 198
Antony, monk cured by St Benedict, 45
Apollinarius, abbot of Monte Cassino, 168
Apollo, 44
Apostles, 117, 209
Appleby, 107
Aquileia, 159, 160
Aquinas, St Thomas, 1, 2
Aquitaine, 48, 50, 154
Argentan, 98
Aristotle, 6
Armenians, 121, 122
Arnold of Lübeck, 99
Arnold de Monte, 110
Arnulf, bishop, 204
Aronisde, monk of Conques, 37
Arras, 138
Arsendis, 212
Arthur, King, 28, 134, 137
Athanasius, St, *Life of St Antony*, 168
Athelstan, St, 201
Audrey, 102
Augustine of Hippo, St, 1–5, 7–11, 14,
    21–4, 29–31, 216, 217
    De Civitate Dei, 3, 29
    De Doctrina Christiana, 21
    De Genesi ad Litteram, 3
    De Trinitate, 3
    De Utilitate Credendi, 3
Austrin of Conques, 212
Auvergne, 41
Avigenna, 212
Azaliza of London, 100

B
Balaam, 22
Baldwin I, 122
Baldwin, monk of Canterbury, 119, 172
Baldwin, abbot of Chatillon-sur-Seine, 181
Baldwin, abbot of Ford, 25
Banbury, 87
Bartholomew, Peter, 203, 204
Bartholomew, hermit of Farne, 65
Bartholomew, bishop of Laon, 134, 141, 156
Basil, St, 171, 199
Bath, 139
Batilly, 153
Beatrice, nun, 163
Beatrice, child in Ramsholt, 213

Beauvais, 127–9
Bec, 138
Becket, St Thomas, 12, 30, 31, 34, 64, 76,
    81, 82, 85, 86, 89–109, 116, 127–9, 132,
    156, 164, 166, 169, 170, 186–9, 201,
    212, 213, 217, 218
Bede, the Venerable, 42, 56–61, 63, 88, 110,
    175, 217
    Ecclesiastical History of the English People, 56
    Life of St Cuthbert, 10, 56
    Metrical Life of St Cuthbert, 56
Benedict, cripple cured by relics from Laon,
    135
Benedict of Nursia, St, 10, 12, 26, 42–56,
    63–5, 68, 77, 84, 91, 117, 147, 168, 169,
    171, 192, 199, 209, 210, 216
Bendict, monk of Canterbury, 30, 89–94, 96,
    98, 99, 101, 109, 189, 213; abbot of
    Peterborough, 150
    Miracles of St Thomas, 89
Berengar of Tours, 15
Berengarius, bishop of Verdun, 161
Berkeley, witch of, 131
Berkshire, 100
Bernard of Clairvaux, St, 7, 24–6, 107, 119,
    133, 145, 158, 164, 167, 175–80, 182–4,
    187, 189, 190, 193–6, 198
    *Historia Miraculorum in Itinerere Germanico
    Patratorum*, 180
    Life of St Malachy, 176, 177
    Vita Prima S Bernardi, 171, 177, 178, 179,
    183, 189
Bernard of Angers, 22, 39, 40–2, 212
    Miracles of St Faith, 37
Bernard, abbot of Beaulieu, 212
Bernard of Conques, 39, 208
Bernard, priest of Quercy, 148
Bernard, knight freed by St James, 112
Bernard d'Utelle, prior of Cluny, 193
Berwick, 106, 191
Besançon, 113
Bethlehem, 15
Bidick, 81
Bigod, Ilger, 137, 209
Binsey, 83
Black Monks, 192, 194, 195, 198
Bodmin, 139
Bohemund, 203, 204
Bondo Bloc of Norwich, 73
Boniface, canon of Laon, 135, 137
Bonneval, 153
Boso, canon of Laon, 135, 137
Boso, servant visiting Soissons, 143
Botilda, 72, 74
Bourges, 98, 210

Brendan, St, 63
Bristol, 87, 139, 140
Brittany, 48, 108
Brustins, Hugh, 127
Buckingham, 87
Bures, 151
Burgundy, 112, 113
Bury St Edmunds, 105, 158

C

Caesarius of Heisterbach, 27, 28, 103, 104,
    195, 196, 199
    Dialogus Miraculorum, 27
Calixtus II, Pope, 110, 111, 113–15, 123
Camaldoli, 199
Cambrai, 183
Cana, 21
Canterbury, 13, 51, 73, 77, 85, 89–91,
    93–6, 100–9, 112, 113, 116, 117, 129,
    137, 139, 188, 189, 212, 213, 217, 218
    Cathedral Library, 217
    Christ Church, 90, 91, 94, 105, 188, 218
    Trinity Chapel, Canterbury Cathedral, 104,
    105
Canute, 124
Caprais, St, bishop, 36
Carloman, 46
Cassian, John, 192
    Conferences, 192
    Institutes, 192
Castor and Pollux, 118
Catherine of Aragon, 88
Cecilia of Bothdale, 107
Chalcidius, Commentary on Plato's *Timeus,*
    5, 6
Chalons, 183
Charlemagne, 40, 110, 154, 159
Charles the Bald, 136
Chartres, 39, 136, 145, 150–5, 157, 208,
    210, 212
Château-Landon, 153
Château-Gordon, 101
Chaucer, Geoffrey, 109
Chiusa, 155
Christ, 3, 10, 14–17, 20, 21, 23–7, 30, 37,
    47, 52, 65, 71, 76, 81, 82, 100, 102, 104,
    105, 110, 120, 122, 124, 125, 133, 137,
    139, 141, 149, 154, 157, 161, 163,
    167–70, 174, 175, 178, 182, 197, 198,
    202–4, 207, 218
Christchurch, 139, 140
Christian of Aumône, 79, 161, 197
Christian, monk of Fleury, 47, 69
Christian, boy cured by relics from Laon, 135

Cilnia, St, 138
Cistercians, 24, 26, 28, 78, 162, 178, 192,
    193, 195–9
Cîteaux, 194, 195, 199
Clairvaux, 176, 178, 179, 181–3, 193,
    195–7, 199
Clavijo, 122
Clement, St, 171
Cleopas, knight, 55
Clermont, 40, 121, 122
    bishop of, 98
Clifford, Rosamund, mistress of Henry II, 130
Cluniacs, 50, 194
Cluny, 43, 50, 51, 111, 113, 114, 119, 144,
    162, 169, 192–4, 199
Cogan, abbot of Inislaughan, 176
Coimbra, 112, 113
Colbern of Norwich, 72
Colhoppe, Roger, 191
Cologne, 34, 181, 196
Compostela, 39, 77, 84, 102, 110–15, 117,
    120, 124, 125, 166
Conques, 36–42, 44, 46, 47, 51, 56, 69, 75,
    76, 139, 208
Conrad of Eberbach, 26, 179, 180, 195, 196
    Exordium Magnum Cisterciense, 26, 195, 198
Constance, 181
Constantine, 203
Constantinople, 136, 154, 160, 210
Copman of Norwich, 73
Corbie, 34, 142, 156
Cornwall, 134, 137
Cosmas and Damian, SS., 118
Courcy, 151
Courville, 153
Coutances, 153
Crispin, Miles, family of, 164
Crowland, 131
Cumberland, 64
Cuthbert, St, 10, 12, 56–66, 68, 77, 79, 81,
    93, 105, 106, 107, 133, 137, 166, 168,
    201
Cyprus, 123

D

Dalmace, archbishop of Compostela, 113
Danes, 56, 61, 158
Daniel, prophet, 173
Daniel, Russian abbot, 122–4
Daniel, Walter, *Life of St Aelred,* 167, 171,
    173, 174, 177
David, King, 173
De Broc, family of, 97
Demetrius, St, 203

Denis, St, 127
Denis the Chamberlain, 72
Denmark, 77, 158
Desert Fathers, 197
Desiderius, abbot, 26, 43–5, 168
   Dialogus Miraculorum, 26, 44, 51
Diana, 10
Die, 48
Dominic of Evesham, *Miracles of the Virgin,*
   149, 155, 163, 164, 208
Dorchester, 87
Dover, 139, 140
Dulcidius, bishop, 36
Dunstable, 202
Dunstan, St, 12, 169, 171
Durham, 57, 61–5, 77, 78, 80, 81, 106,
   107, 137, 200, 201

E

Eadbert, St, 63
Eadmer, 60, 61, 138, 159, 171, 172, 177,
   188, 209
   Historia Novorum in Anglia, 171
   Life of St Anselm, 167, 171–3, 188
   Tractatus de Conceptione Sanctae Mariae, 159
East Anglia, 206, 207
Eastry, Henry, prior of Christ Church,
   Canterbury, 103
Eaves, 155
Eberhard, bishop of Salzburg, 34
Eborard, bishop, 69
Ebrand, 73
Ecajeul, 151
Edessa, 123
Edith of Oxford, 85
Edmund, St, 32, 64, 105, 106, 200
Edmund, monk of Norwich, 70
Edmund the Younger, cured in Norwich, 72
Edric, priest of Ramsholt, 213
Edward the Confessor, St, 34, 205, 208, 210
Egypt, 209
Eisulf, knight of Pontefract, 91
Eleazar the Jew, 68, 69
Elias, prior of Norwich, 69, 72
Elijah, prophet, 9, 20, 168
Elisha, prophet, 20, 168, 169, 177
Elizabeth, St, 196
Ella, 61
Elphege, 188
Elsin, abbot of Ramsey, 158–60
Emelina of Headington, 86
Emma, woman of Bayeux, 152
Emma, woman cured by St Frideswide, 87
Emma, wife of a Sussex knight, 100

Endor, witch of, 9
England, 39, 62–4, 71, 87, 89, 95, 97, 98,
   104–7, 109, 116, 132, 137–9, 149, 154,
   155, 158, 159, 167, 188, 189, 203, 205,
   218
Ephesus, Seven Sleepers of, 203
Eppo the Thief, 39, 156
Erasmus, 103
Ermengotus, count, 112
Ernold of Bonnevaux, 183, 184
Ernold the Goldsmith, 101
Esindene, 107
Etampes, 183
Etheldreda, St, 64, 106
Ethelred, king, 83
Ethelwold, St, 63
Eudes d'Etoile, 130, 131, 206
Eugenius III, Pope, 150, 182
Eusebius, 202
Eustace, monk of Canterbury, 209
Eustace, moneyer of Norwich, 72
Eve, 5
Evesham, 62, 155
Evreux, bishop of, 98
Evroul, 138
Evroul, St, 203
Exeter, 87, 137, 139, 140
Eynsham, 87

F

Faith, St, 22, 36–44, 46, 47, 51, 56, 63, 67,
   68, 75, 82, 84, 93, 133, 147, 156, 166,
   208, 212
Farne, island of, 65, 77
Farsit, Hugh, 142–4
Felician, St, 36
Ferdinand II, king of Aragon, 112
Finchale, 63, 77–81, 107, 108
Fitzasketil, 32
Fitzdavid, Robert, 218
Fitzeisulf, Sir Jordan, 91, 93
Fitzralph, William, 103
Fitzwalter, Robert, 39, 75
Fitzwimmond of Fécamp, 164
Flambard, Ranulf, bishop of Durham, 77
Flanders, 77
Fleury, 42, 43, 45–51, 56, 69, 106–9, 113,
   139, 209, 210
Foliot, Gilbert, 97, 116, 150
Fontis Calacres, count, 112
Ford, Cistercian abbey of, 200
France, 39, 46, 51, 95, 98, 103, 113, 132,
   133, 135, 137, 155, 175, 188
Franco, 180, 181

Frankfurt, 181, 183
Frederick Barbarossa, 98
Frideswide, St, 68, 75, 80, 82–7, 101, 107, 108, 123, 139, 166, 209
Miracles of, 83
Frisians, 117
Fromund, bishop of Veroli, 190
Frowin, abbot of Salmansweiler, 181
Fulbert, bishop of Chartres, 29, 39, 136, 157, 164
Fulda, abbot of, 20

G
Galdricus, 119
Garnier, 101
Gaudfrid, 105
Gaudry, 179
Gembloux, 183
Genevieve, St, 118
Geoffrey of Auxerre, 176, 178, 181–3, 189
Geoffrey of Durham, *Life of Bartholomew of Farne*, 65, 78
Geoffrey, bishop of Ely, 83
George, St, 203
Gerald of Aurillac, St, 41
Gerald, monk of Conques, 39
Gerald of Wales, 191, 206, 207
Topographia Hibernica, 7, 8
Gerard, 180
Gerard, abbot of Clairvaux, 189, 190
Gerard, monk of Cluny, 193
Gerard, abbot of Heisterbach, 28, 196
Gerard of Lausanne, 122
Gerard of Liège, 98
Gerard, brother of St Bernard, 179
Gerard the Sacristan, 147
Gerard, archbishop of York, 12
Gerbert, Pope Sylvester II, 12, 206
Germanus, prior of Durham, 78
Germany, 180, 182
Gervase of Canterbury, 93
Gilbert de la Porée, 6
Gilbert of Sempringham, St, 186, 190, 199
Giles, St, 156
Gimon, 38, 47
Gimp, 92
Giulfus, monk of Norwich, 70
Gloucester, 87, 100
earl of, 116
Glutinus, 140
Goda of Norwich, 73
Godfrey, bishop of Chartres, 157
Godfrey, monk of Clairvaux, 181
Godfrey of Kelso, 80

Godfrid the Baker, 102
Godric of Finchale, St, 63, 68, 76–82, 105–8, 123, 166, 199, 200, 205
Life and Miracles of, 77
Godric, money-changer of Norwich, 73
Godstow, 130
Grandmontines, 199
Greece, 202
Gregory the Great, St, 24, 42–4, 46, 47, 51, 52–4, 118, 168, 175, 185, 186, 192–4, 205, 216, 217
Dialogues, 52–4
Gregory VII, St, 120, 131, 194
Gregory IX, Pope, 122, 186
Gregory of Tours, 7, 210
Grim, Edward, 99
Gaudricus, 180
Gualterus of Cluny, 157
Guibert of Nogent, 27, 28, 122, 127, 128, 134, 136, 137, 140, 141, 209
Guimond, prior of St Frideswide's, 83
Guitmond, bishop of Avranches, 17
Gunhilda of Norwich, 73
Gunrada, 144, 145, 210
Guy, 179

H
Haimo, monk of St Pierre-sur-Dives, 150–2
Halfdune, 61
Halley's Comet, 206
Harbledown, 96, 100
Harding, St Stephen, 195, 198
Harpin of Thornley, 64
Hartwic, bishop of Salzburg, 34
Hathwisa, 107
Hatto, bishop of Freising, 118
Helen of Ludgershall, 86
Helena, empress, 123
Helinand, bishop of Laon, 137, 138
Henry I, 39, 115, 116, 137, 139
Henry II, 83, 93, 97, 115, 116, 130, 150, 201
Henry III, 88
Henry V, emperor, 115
Henry VI, emperor, 128
Henry of Blois, 116
Henry, abbot of Clairvaux, 195
Henry, earl of Huntingdon, 64
Henry of Huntingdon, 203
Henry, brother of Louis VII, 181
Henry of Rheims, 189
Herbert of Bosham, 102
Herbert of Clairvaux, 179, 195, 196, 198
De Miraculis, 192, 193, 195

Herbert, canon of Laon, 135
Herbert of Losinga, 30, 69
Hereford, 87, 207
Herman, bishop of Constance, 181–3
Herman, canon of Laon, 134, 135, 139–42, 156
Hermeus, 73
Hervin, provost of Steinfeld, 181
Hildebrand, 72
Hildefonsus, bishop, 141
Hildegard of Bingen, St, 11
Holy Sepulchre, 84, 89, 120–3, 125, 137, 209
Holy Trinity Abbey, London, 191
Honorius III, Pope, 187, 190, 191
Honorius of Autun, 160
Horsham St Faith, 39, 75
Hosanna, 50
Hospital of St John, Jerusalem, 77
Hoyland, 100
Huelina, 100
Huet, 103
Hugelina, 87
Hugellinus, 137
Hugh the Chaplain, 191
Hugh, abbot of Cluny, St, 50, 113, 114, 118, 162, 170, 199, 209
  Life of, 118
Hugh, bishop of Lincoln, St, 16, 17, 129, 130, 173–5, 187, 190, 191
  Life of, 167, 171
Hugh of St Mary, 50, 51, 55
Hugh of St Victor, 14, 15
Humphrey of Norwich, 73
Huntingdon, prior of, 191

I
Iachelia, 87
Ida of Norwich, 72
Igny, Cistercian abbey of, 93
Innocent III, Pope, 186, 191
Ireland, 8, 23, 176, 206
Ireneus, St, 35
Isabella, queen of Aragon, 35
Isabella of Beckhampton, 108
Isidore of Seville, St, 11, 23
Italy, 17, 46, 51, 64, 111, 112
Ithemar, St, 88

J
James, St, 33, 110–17, 123, 125, 166
  Codex Calixtinus, 110–14
James of Vitry, 23

Jean de Marchant, 153, 157
Jerome, St, 21, 77, 202
Jerusalem, 77, 103, 115, 120–5, 167
Jews, 5, 21, 68, 76, 120, 129, 161, 167
Jocelyn of Brakelond, 200
John the Baptist, St, 44, 79, 80, 169, 198
John of Beneventum, St, 45
John the Evangelist, St, 123, 138
John XV, Pope, 185
John, King, 190
John de Cheyney, sheriff, 68, 69
John, prior of Christ Church, Canterbury, 218
John, constable of Chester, 87
John of Coutances, 145
John, archdeacon of Durham, 78
John, abbot of Fountains, 190
John the Italian, monk of Cluny, 193
John, from Laon, 137
John, murdered at Northampton, 129
John, bishop of Norwich, 83
John of Norwich, bishop's chaplain, 73
John Piot, from Laon, 135
John of St Andrew's, master, 83
John, cured at tomb of St Benedict, 45
John of Salisbury, 98, 100, 171, 188
John, fisherman of Seaford, 116
John, son of Thomas, 218
John, priest, 161
John of Worcester, 207
Josbert de la Ferté, 178, 179
Joseph, patriarch, 173
Joseph, St, 123, 169, 173
Joshua, 173
Judoc, St, 203
Julian the Apostate, 29
Juliana, 95
Julius Firmicius, 12
Jupiter, 40

K
Karbuqa, 204
Kevin, St, 8

L
La Charité-sur-Loire, 196
Lambert, 135
Lanfranc of Bec, 16, 17, 62
Langton, Stephen, 190
Laon, 134–8, 141, 142, 147, 150, 153, 155, 156
Las Navas de Tolosa, 112
Lascelles, 81
Lawrence, St, 63

Lazarus, 15, 20, 21, 23
Le Mans, 46, 210
Leicester, 87
Leo IX, St, 45, 120
Leo, uncle of Smaragdus, 45
Leviva, wife of Godwin, 71
Leviva, cured in Oxford, 87
Lewin, 74
Lexceline, 151
Liberi, 171
Liège, 181, 183
Lincoln, 181, 190, 191
Lincolnshire, 77
Lindisfarne, 56–61, 77
Lixtune, 64
Lombard, Peter, 22, 23
Lombards, 46, 117
London, 85, 87, 100
Longbeard, William, 130, 131
Lorraine, prince of, 147
Lot, 173
Louis VII, St, 97, 181
Louis VII, king of France, 94
Lourdes, 125
Lyonnais, 113

M

Maastricht, 181
Mabilia, 87
Mabel of Bec, Lady, 71, 72, 74
Mabel, noble lady at Canterbury, 96
Magdeburg, archbishop of, 217
Malachy, St, bishop of Armagh, 176, 177
Malcolm IV of Scotland, 64, 201
Map, Walter, *De Nugis Curialium*, 206
March, earls of, 139
Marcigny, 193
Margaret, noble matron, 108
Margaret of Burford, 108
Margaret, granddaughter of Ralph of Stretona, 86
Margaret, cured at shrine of St Frideswide, 87
Marozia, 161
Mars, 40
Martin of Tours, St, 10, 25, 48, 63, 74, 101, 168, 169, 171, 173–6
Martin, fisherman of Norwich, 73
Martin of Oxford, 85
Mary, Blessed Virgin, 2, 5, 16, 27–9, 38, 40, 46, 48, 74, 76, 79, 96, 99, 111, 114, 115, 166, 182, 196, 197, 199, 210–12, 217, 218; *feasts of:* Annunciation, 158; Assumption, 158–62; Conception, 158,

160, 162; Nativity, 136, 137, 146, 158–60; Purification, 153, 160; *relics of,* 123, 125, 133–43, 147, 150, 152, 154, 209; *shrines of:* Chartres, 133–6, 145, 150, 153–5, 157, 208, 210; Laon, 133–42, 156; Rocamadour, 123, 133, 134, 145–9, 156, 159, 208; Soissons, 133, 142–5, 156, 210; St Pierre-sur-Dives, 134, 150–2
Mary of Egypt, St, 123, 144, 150
Mary Magdalene, St, 79, 151, 196
Mathilda, empress, 202
Mathilda, abbess, 143
Mathilda, cure attested at Berwick, 191
Mathilda of Cologne, 98
Matthew of Albano, 192, 194
Maule, 138
Maur, St, 45, 168
Maurilius of Rouen, 151
Maurius, St, 41
Maurius of Rouen, 151
Maximian, bishop of Syracuse, 43
Mercury, St, 203
Michael, St, 48
Milan, 183
Mommold, abbot of Fleury, 46
Monreale, 105
Montanus, St, 138
Monte Cassino, 26, 42, 43, 45, 46, 50, 51, 118
Monte Gargano, 48
Moricotti, Henry, cardinal, 189
Mortimer, Ralph, 139
Moslems, 120
Moses, 9, 20, 168, 169, 171, 173
Muriel, of Fécamp, 164

N

Nantua, 115
Nazareth, 123
Nesle, 138
Newbury, 87
Newman, John Henry, 1
Nicholas, St, 63, 156, 206
Noah, 173
Norfolk, 39, 73, 75, 76
Normandy, 17, 81
Normans, 48, 154, 158, 205, 208
Northumberland, 77
Northumbria, 10
Norway, 64, 98
Norwich, 30, 68, 70, 72–4, 83, 86, 101, 105, 128
Notre Dame de Ripoli, abbot of, 110

O

Odin, 60
Odilo, St, abbot of Cluny, 199
Odo, abbot of Battle, 93
Odo, St, abbot of Cluny, 50, 171, 199, 210, 211
Odo, canon of Laon, 135
Odo, layman from Laon, 135
Oliver, clerk of Nantes, 93, 98
Onalafbald, 60, 61
Orderic Vitalis, 202–4, 206
   Ecclesiastical History, 202
Orleans, 98
Osbert, 61
Osbert of Clare, 159, 208
Otto, clerk, 181
Otto, emperor, 118
Ouen, 137
Oxford, 59, 82–4, 86–8, 108, 109, 123, 139

P

Pachomius, St, 199
Palermo, 98
Palladia, 24
Pandulf of Capua, 44
Paris, 118, 196
Paschasius Radbertus, 15
Paul, St, 48, 120, 171, 173
Paul, monk of Norwich, 72
Paulus, 24
Pavia, 210
Périgord, 206
Pershore, 73, 74
Peter, St, 23, 48, 63, 110, 115, 117–20, 123–5, 147, 151, 168, 170, 171
Peter the Chanter, 19
Peter Damian, St, 26, 28, 45, 50, 157, 161, 198
Peter, bishop of St David's, 83
Peter the Deacon, 45
Peter the Deacon (in *Dialogues* of St Gregory), 43
Peter, monk of Poitiers, 98
Peter of Tarantaise, 189
Peter the Venerable, 28, 50, 162, 192–5, 199
   De Miraculis, 192, 193
Peterborough, 92
Peverall, Peter, monk of Norwich, 70
Pharoah, 9, 21, 186
Philip, archdeacon of Liège, 181–3
Philip, knight of Lorraine, 73
Philip, prior of St Frideswide's, 83, 84, 86, 87, 108, 209
   Miracles of St Frideswide, 77

Pisa, 183, 210
Pithiviers, 153
Platonists, 5, 6
Poitiers, 115
   bishop of, 188
Pons, abbot of Clairvaux, 27
Pons, abbot of Cluny, 193
Ponthieu, 31, 151
Pontigny, 98
Posen, St, 48
Prime, martyr, 36
Prosper of Aquitaine, 202
Puintel, Robert, 95
Puy, bishop of, 204

R

Rabanus Maurus, 20
Ragusa, archbishop of, 190
Raithmildis, 107
Ralph of Caen, 204
Ralph of Diceto, 131, 150, 202, 203
Ralph Godric, child, 80
Ralph of Laon, 137
Ralph, moneyer of Norwich, 73, 75
Ralph of Nottingham, 93
Ralph of Stretona, 86
Ramsey, 158
Ratramnus, 15
Raymond d'Aguilers, 203
Raymond, count of Millau, 212
Raynald, monk, *Life of St Hugh of Cluny,* 118
Reading, 33, 34, 110, 115, 116, 166
Red Sea, 5, 21
Reginald of Durham, 30, 57, 62–5, 77–81, 104–8, 205
   Life of St Cuthbert, 63
   Life of St Godric, 77
Reginald, cowherd of Norwich, 73
Reginald, priest of Wretham, 104
Reimbert, seneschal of Battle abbey, 73
Reimund, archdeacon of Leicester, 191
Renaldus, monk of Clairvaux, 196
Rheims, archbishop of, 131
Richard I, 116
Richard, archbishop of Canterbury, 83
Richard, farmer in Essex, 213
Richard de Ferraris, monk of Norwich, 210
Richard, prior of Fleury, 210
Richard, from Laon, 135
Richard of Lynn, 71
Richard, abbot of Monte Cassino, 46
Richard, cured at Norwich, 72
Richard, monk at Norwich, 69, 70
Richard, abbot of St Alban's, 62

Richard, abbot of Vannes, 120, 124
Richard, abbot of Walton, 191
Richard, bishop of Winchester, 83
Richarde, 212
Richelda, Queen, 210
Rievaulx, 173, 174
Robert of Cricklade, prior of St Frideswide's, 107, 108
Robert the Englishman, from Laon, 137
Robert, canon of Laon, 135, 137
Robert of Melun, 23
Robert, monk of Norwich, 72
Robert, son of Hermeus of Norwich, 73
Robert, cured of paralysis by St Hugh of Cluny, 118
Robert, relation of Philip, prior of St Frideswide's, 85
Robert, relation of St Bernard, 179, 193, 194
Robert, canon of St Frideswide's, 108
Robert of Torigny, 202
Rocamadour, 117, 142, 145–50, 152, 153, 155, 156, 209
Rochester, 88
Rodez, 41
Roger of Hoveden, 99, 131, 207, 208
Roland, 110
Romans, 118
Romanus, monk of Subiaco, 51
Rome, 77, 89, 97, 114, 117–20, 124, 125, 128, 160, 161, 184, 186–8, 191, 202, 206
Romuald, St, 199
Rouen, 137
Rouergue, 36, 38, 41
Rudby, 106
Rupert of Deutz, 21

S
St Alban's, 158
St Andrew's, 77
St Benoît-sur-Loire, abbey of, 52
St Clemente, 151
St Germain, 141
St Gilles, count of, 112, 203
St Michael, monastery at Chiusa, 155
St Omer, 138
St Peter ad Vincula, 118
St Pierre-sur-Dives, 134, 150–3, 155, 210
Salerna of Ifield, 95
Salisbury, 87, 137, 139, 140
Salzburg, 34
Samaria, 169
Samson, abbot of Bury, 32, 200
Samuel, 178
Santiago, 110, 112

Saracens, 112, 113
Sarah, 22
Satan, 10, 186
Saul, 9
Sawtrey, abbot of, 191
Scandinavia, 34
Scholastica, St, 44–6, 56, 209, 210
Scotland, 64, 65, 190, 210
Sebastian, St, 118
Segitis, 218
Sergius, Pope, 160
Serlo, master, 196
Sicily, 34, 108
Sieldeware of Belaugh, 74
Simancas, 112
Simon Magus, 120
Simon of Tournai, 15, 23
Siwate of Norwich, 73
Smaragdus, monk of Monte Cassino, 45
Soissons, 142–5, 147, 150, 153, 155, 156, 210
Sourday, 154
Spain, 39, 48, 110, 112, 115, 161
Speyer, 181
Stabilis, 49
Staffordshire, 150
Stephan, bishop of Clermont, 40
Stephen, St, 3, 12, 24, 29, 167
Stephen of Aberdeen, 218
Stephen of Autun, 15
Stephen of Muret, 199
Stephen of York, 86
Stubbs, William, bishop, 1
Sturt, Godwin, 71, 74
Subiaco, 51
Suffolk, 73
Sully-sur-Loire, 168, 173
Sulpicius Severus, 168, 173
Surrey, 100
Sussex, 100
Sweden, king of, 186
Sybilla, 39, 75
Symeon of Durham, 56, 62
    Historia S Cuthberti, 52
Symeon of Trier, 199, 200

T
Theobald, 191
Theodore, abbot of Camp, 181
Theoderic, 135
Theodwin, legate, 104, 189
Theophilus, 29
Theophilus the Deacon (in Desiderius' Dialogus Miraculorum), 44

Thierry of Chartres, 5, 6
Thomas of Etton, 93
Thomas of Monmouth, 30, 68–76, 83, 85, 105
   Life of St William of Norwich, 68–76
Thomas, monk of Norwich, 72
Thomas, cripple of York, 75
Thor, 60
Thorpe Wood, 70
Thurben of Holywell, 87, 123
Toke, 72
Tortaire, Ralph, monk of Fleury, 49, 51, 147
   Miracles of St Benedict, 49
Totilla the Hun, 53
Totnes, 139, 140
Toul, 183
Toulouse, 41
Tours, 69, 187, 189
Transfiguration, 123
Trier, 183
Tromund of Chiaravalle, 190
Turbe, William, bishop, 30, 70, 72
Turgot, prior of Durham, 64
Tutbury, 150
Tydi, priest, 57

U

Ulrich of Augsburg, 161, 185
Urban II, Pope, 121, 122

V

Vatican, 117
Verdun, abbot of, 122
Veronica, St, 147
Vespasian, 12
Vézelay, abbot of, 113
Victor, St, 25
Vienne, 113, 172
Viennois, 113
Villeneuve, 115
Virgilius, bishop of Salzburg, 34
Volkmar, chaplain to Herman, Bishop of Constance, 181–3

W

Walarius, St, 138
Walberg, 196
Wallingford, 87
Walter, Hubert, archbishop of Canterbury, 130, 186
Walter, abbot of Evesham, 62
Walter of Norwich, 73
Walter of Wales, 85, 87

Waltheof, earl, 131
Warwick, 87
Waverley, 202
Wendover, 87
Werberga of Chester, St, 205
Werric of Lobbes, 128, 129
Westminster, 34, 106
Weston, Elfred, sacrist of Durham, 63
Widelein, 16
Whitchurch, 103
William, St, 203
William I, 61, 137, 139, 151, 201
William II, 139
William of Auvergne, 212
William, priest of Bishopsbourne, 103
William, monk of Canterbury, *Miracles of St Thomas,* 30–2, 89–93, 95, 96, 98, 101, 104, 109, 127, 169, 189
William of Conques, 6, 7, 23
William, son of Sir Jordan Fitzeisulf, 93
William of Malmesbury, 12, 57, 62, 66, 82, 131, 136, 155, 157, 161, 163, 164, 202, 203, 205, 206
   Gesta Pontificum, 203
   Gesta Regum, 205, 206
William de Montibus, 175
William of Newburgh, 82, 129, 130
   Historia, 205–7
William of Norwich, St, 34, 67–76, 80, 83, 84, 97, 101, 104, 105, 128, 129, 139, 166, 186
William, dean of Norwich, 73
William, monk of Norwich, 72
William of Poitiers, bishop, 131
William, sacrist of Norwich, 70, 72
William of Shrivenham, 108
William of St Carilef, 61
William of St Thierry, 7, 178, 179
William, priest, cured by St Thomas, 102
William, monk, denied that Thomas Becket was a saint, 93
William, count of Toulouse, 212
William de Tracy, 84
William of Wales, 123
William of York, St, 174
Willibald, bishop, 57
Wilsnak, 217, 218
Wilton, 139
Winchester, 84, 87, 139, 158
Winneva of Estrose, 84
Wissant, 138, 172
Witbert, 41, 42, 208
Wittenberg, 217
Worcester, 158, 205
Worcestershire, 73, 75

Wulfric of Haselbury, hermit, 78, 107, 199,
    200, 211
Wulfstan of Worcester, St, 205

Y
York, 73, 97
Ysembela, 116

Z
Zacharius, Pope, 46

Designed and typeset in
Mergenthaler Garamond
by Wilsted and Taylor.
Printed by Maple-Vail on
60 lb. Old Style Wove paper.

THE MIDDLE AGES

Edward Peters, General Editor

Christian Society and the Crusades, 1198–1229. Sources in Translation, including The Capture of Damietta by Oliver of Paderborn. Edited by Edward Peters

The First Crusade: The Chronicle of Fulcher of Chartres and Other Source Materials. Edited by Edward Peters

Love in Twelfth-Century France. John C. Moore

The Burgundian Code: The Book of Constitutions or Law of Gundobad and Additional Enactments. Translated by Katherine Fischer Drew

The Lombard Laws. Translated, with an Introduction, by Katherine Fischer Drew

From St. Francis to Dante: Translations from the Chronicle of the Franciscan Salimbene (1221–1228). G. G. Coulton

The Duel and the Oath. Parts I and II of Superstition and Force. Henry Charles Lea. Introduction by Edward Peters

The Ordeal. Part III of Superstition and Force. Henry Charles Lea

Torture. Part IV of Superstition and Force. Henry Charles Lea

Witchcraft in Europe, 1110–1700: A Documentary History. Edited by Alan C. Kors and Edward Peters

The Scientific Achievement of the Middle Ages. Richard C. Dales

History of the Lombards. Paul the Deacon. Translated by William Dudley Foulke

Monks, Bishops, and Pagans: Christian Culture in Gaul and Italy, 500–700. Edited, with an Introduction, by Edward Peters

The World of Piers Plowman. Edited and translated by Jeanne Krochalis and Edward Peters

Felony and Misdemeanor: A Study in the History of Criminal Law. Julius Goebel, Jr.

Women in Medieval Society. Edited by Susan Mosher Stuard

The Expansion of Europe: The First Phase. Edited by James Muldoon

Laws of the Alamans and Bavarians. Translated, with an Introduction, by Theodore John Rivers

Law, Church, and Society: Essays in Honor of Stephen Kuttner. Edited by Robert Somerville and Kenneth Pennington

The Fourth Crusade: The Conquest of Constantinople, 1201–1204. Donald E. Queller

The Magician, the Witch, and the Law. Edward Peters

Daily Life in the World of Charlemagne. Pierre Riché. Translated, with an Introduction, by Jo Ann McNamara

Repression of Heresy in Medieval Germany. Richard Kieckhefer

The Royal Forests of Medieval England. Charles R. Young

Popes, Lawyers, and Infidels: The Church and the Non-Christian World, 1250–1550. James Muldoon

Heresy and Authority in Medieval Europe. Edited, with an Introduction, by Edward Peters

Women in Frankish Society: Marriage and the Cloister, 500 to 900. Suzanne Fonay Wemple

The English Parliament. Edited by R. G. Davies and J. H. Denton

Rhinoceros Bound: Cluny in the Tenth Century. Barbara H. Rosenwein

On the Threshold of Exact Science: Selected Writings of Anneliese Maier on Late Medieval Natural Philosophy. Edited and translated by Steven D. Sargent

Miracles and the Medieval Mind: Theory, Record and Event, 1000–1215. Benedicta Ward